# BERTRAND BARERE

*A Reluctant Terrorist*

# BERTRAND BARERE

## A Reluctant Terrorist

BY

## LEO GERSHOY

PRINCETON, NEW JERSEY
PRINCETON UNIVERSITY PRESS
1962

Publication of this book
has been aided by the Ford Foundation program
to support publication, through university presses,
of works in the humanities and social sciences
and by a grant from the American Council of
Learned Societies as a result of a contribution from
the United States Steel Foundation

Printed in the United States of America
by Princeton University Press, Princeton, New Jersey

*To*

*Gertrude and Garrett Mattingly*

# Preface

I HAVE tried in this study of a once famous terrorist, Bertrand Barère, to place his revolutionary career in the larger context of a long life and to see him as it were whole, in evolution and in the interaction of personality, thinking, and action. Accordingly, I have not only systematically re-examined the record from 1789 to 1795 when his role as revolutionist was played out, but have looked closely at what he did before and after the upheaval into which he was drawn. For he had a brilliantly successful career before the Revolution and a sorry, Kafkaesque epilogue of almost half a century after, during which he expiated the sin of having been more supple than strong during the storm. My inquiry, intermittently pursued over many years, led me to draw conclusions about the man which do not always accord with conventional judgments. In fact, I regard many of those estimations as components and illustrations of something resembling a dark legend.

As I see him, Barère was a mild and amiable man with a rare capacity for suspending judgment and seeing the merits of opposing points of view. Sucked into the Revolution which he could no more control than any other participant, after winning golden opinions, he ultimately received his share, and more, of the bitter, partisan abuse which is the common reward of would-be mediators and tempered adherents. The Revolution also brought out his defects, and those weaknesses of character became pronounced in adversity. While he did few things that were in themselves evil, many of his actions were born of expediency when considerations of personal security fused with convictions honestly held. But he acted in good faith even when it was to his advantage. He was not an evil man, nor willingly cruel. When his role as mediator was ended and he turned terrorist, he became a terrorist in spite of himself. Under less demanding circumstances than those between 1789 and 1795 he might well have lived out his life as

*vii*

the good-hearted, sympathetic, and conciliatory man that he was by nature.

This view of Barère bears little resemblance to many hostile portrayals of the man himself or to traditional explanations of what he did. It has little resemblance, for example, to the verdict of Thomas Babbington Macaulay which that pundit of Whig liberalism pronounced in the pages of the *Edinburgh Review* in the April 1844 issue. The last of the four volumes of Barère's posthumously published memoirs had appeared and Macaulay reviewed them in one of the lengthy essays which he was then contributing to that influential journal of opinion. Pleading his desire to do justice to their author, Macaulay divested himself of a summary judgment which I quote in full:

"Our opinion then is this, that Barère approached nearer than any person mentioned in history or fiction, whether man or devil, to the idea of consummate and universal depravity. In him the qualities which are the proper objects of hatred and the qualities which are the proper objects of contempt, preserve an exquisite and absolute harmony. In almost every sort of wickedness he has had rivals. His sensuality was immoderate; this was a failing common to him with many great and amiable men. There had been as many men as cowardly as he, some as cruel, some as mean, a few as impudent. There may also have been as great liars, though we never met with them or read of them. But when we put everything together, sensuality, barbarity, poltroonery, baseness, effrontery, the result is something to which, we venture to say, no parallel can be found in history."

Macaulay's judgment of Barère was the classic example of its kind, certainly the one that the English-speaking public knows best, perhaps the only one. If like Gibbons' Christian chroniclers, the English historian scorned "the profane virtues of moderation and sobriety," he was in that respect not unique. Many French accounts during the nineteenth century were almost as intemperate; indeed, in 1929, almost a century later, Robert Launay, in the only biography of Barère that has been published, *Barère de Vieuzac (l'Anacréon de la Guillotine)*, endorsed that appreciation, charitably softening it to exclude the charge of "barbarity" as groundless. Slight wonder that toward the end of the last century a careful student of the Revolution, H. Morse Stephens, in his Introduction to *The Principal Speeches of the Statesmen and Orators of the French Revolution*, wrote that "no prominent statesman, except perhaps Marat, has been so persistently vilified and deliberately misunderstood as Barère."

That reproach is now seventy years old and Barère's reputation has considerably improved in the interval, thanks to the many admirable special studies that have illuminated periods and aspects of the Revolution in which he played a role. But if vilification, save by way of exception, is of the past, a critical account based upon manuscript and printed evidence has not yet replaced it. I can only hope that my attempt to do so has not led me into special pleading and insidiously transformed sympathy into apology. That temptation is inherent in an avowedly revisionist study and I trust that I have not unwittingly yielded to it.

In order to acquaint the reader with the works on which my opinion of Barère is based, I have appended a bibliography. In the first large section I give both manuscript and printed sources which are relevant directly to Barère, the chief printed sources for the Revolution, and the writings of modern authorities. Since for the most part the provenience of quotations and controversial statements is readily identifiable from the text itself, I do not give footnote references; but a second section, the Notes which accompany each chapter or group of related chapters, does give the source of important quotations that the text does not identify. I list there, too, contemporary writings as well as articles, special studies, and more general works relating to the subject or the period treated. The final chapter is an Epilogue which deals with accounts that fashioned opinion about Barère after his death. Accordingly, in the separate Notes which accompany it, I give the most important of those works—memoirs, newspapers, periodicals, biographical dictionaries and encyclopedias, monographs, and general histories.

As it was no part of my intention at any time to attempt to rewrite the history of the Revolution from the manuscript sources, I have neither consulted them, except where they involved Barère, nor listed them in the Bibliography.

My indebtedness is great to many individuals who have aided me in my research and to the Social Science Research Council and the Fulbright Commission, each of which granted me a fellowship that freed me of teaching obligations. A grant from the Research Fund of the Graduate School of Arts and Science of New York University helped defray the costs of photostating some material. The American Council of Learned Societies made a generous grant toward publication.

Old friends to whom I owe much have now died. I am particularly indebted to Georges Lefebvre who always found time to set aside his own work to discuss Barère with me. Georges Bourgin and Pierre Caron were sympathetic guides in my early ventures in the Archives Nationales. And far more than I appreciated at the time, Carl Becker, in whose seminar at Cornell University I first came upon Barère, insinuated the thought that all was not right with prevailing interpretations of that volatile Gascon.

I would like to acknowledge the courtesies extended to me by the librarians and archivists in Paris as well as by Messrs. Mangin and Espalieu of the Departmental Archives of the Hautes-Pyrénées in Tarbes, and M. Gernet, Director of the Municipal Library. In the Tarbes area too I received aid from Dr. J. Labougle, Colonel Druène, and *Maîtres* Theil and Blanc; and from the late Léon Ducasse and Madame Mayonnade de Naïs. Among research assistants who took notes on published works and made fair copies of foul manuscripts, Mademoiselle

## Preface

Yvonne Dusser and Mademoiselle Yvonne Grand deserve my special thanks. Friends and fellow workers in the field of the French Revolution have generously given advice or material or both: Among them are Dr. Marc Bouloiseau, Signor A. Galante-Garrone, and Professors Crane Brinton, Alfred Cobban, Jacques Godechot, Louis Gottschalk, and Eugen Weber. My thanks go to Professor Robert R. Palmer for his critical reading of many early chapters, and to Professor Garrett Mattingly who read a large part of the manuscript and made valuable suggestions for which I am grateful.

As always, the help of my wife meant most to me; not least in this instance for suffering with charitable fortitude the shadow of a ghostly guest who lingered in our home for many years.

# Contents

# Illustrations

Oil portrait sketch of Barère, 1790, by David. Versailles Museum, Photo Bulloz

Barère in the Tribune delivering his "Speech on the Judgment of Louis Capet" on January 4, 1793, painting by David. Collection Baron Lambert

Heroism of the crew of the vessel, "Le Vengeur," lithograph by Mouilleron after the painting by Leullier, 1841. Cabinet des Estampes of the Bibliothèque Nationale

Barère delivering one of his carmagnoles, engraving by Denon after painting by Isabey. Cabinet des Estampes of the Bibliothèque Nationale

The Tennis Court Oath, detail, Barère in the foreground taking notes, after the painting by David. Cabinet des Estampes of the Bibliothèque Nationale

Facsimile of Barère's newspaper, *Le Point du Jour*. This issue reports the proceedings of the "Famous Night" of August 4, 1789

Louis-Philippe, Duke of Orléans, called Philippe Egalité, anonymous sketch. Cabinet des Estampes of the Bibliothèque Nationale

Louis XVI at the Bar of the National Convention, December 11, 1792, anonymous engraving. Cabinet des Estampes of the Bibliothèque Nationale

The execution of Robespierre and his accomplices, contemporary engraving. Cabinet des Estampes of the Bibliothèque Nationale

Barère, Collot, and Billaud leaving Paris to be deported, engraving by Berthault after Girardet. Cabinet des Estampes of the Bibliothèque Nationale

Bust of the Comtesse de Guibert, engraving by Danzel de Valchant. Cabinet des Estampes of the Bibliothèque Nationale

Marc Guillaume Alexis Vadier, colleague and friend of Barère, contemporary engraving. Cabinet des Estampes of the Bibliothèque Nationale

Bonaparte, First Consul, sheathing his sword after the general peace, contemporary engraving by Chataignier. Cabinet des Estampes of the Bibliothèque Nationale

Joseph Fouché, Duke of Otranto, engraving by J. Eymar. Cabinet des Estampes of the Bibliothèque Nationale

Facsimile of the first folio of the manuscript of Barère's *Mémoires*. Bibliothèque de l'Arsénal, Photo Bulloz

Barère's grave in the cemetery of St. Jean, Tarbes. Photo J. Lacaze. Bust of Barère by Ceracchi, 1800. Carnavalet Museum, Photo Bulloz

# BERTRAND BARERE

*A Reluctant Terrorist*

# ✄ I ✄

## *The Early Years*

OLD AGE did not bestow consolation upon Bertrand Barère. When he died in 1841 in his eighty-sixth year, he had long before fallen out with his brother and sisters; nephews and nieces harassed him with lawsuits; Marguerite Lefauconnier, who had shared the last twenty-five miserable years with him, was dead; and fellow townsmen of his native Tarbes esteemed him not at all. A heavy pall of ill-repute enshrouded him, and the name and sight of the old revolutionist and regicide, which in their elders aroused contempt, in children awakened fear. For them he was a bogeyman.

"I remember," wrote a remote collateral descendant, "hearing my mother say that when she was a little girl, she often went to play in the house where Barère lived. That house, which I know very well, had several stories, each with a terrace on which the rooms opened. My mother's little friends lived on the first floor and Barère on the second. Drawn by the sinister reputation of the ex-Conventional, these little girls made believe that they were on the wrong floor and ran up to the balcony of the second floor, almost to the open door of Barère's bedroom where they saw a tall old man seated in an armchair with his legs wrapped in a blanket. When he saw them he straightened up and said in a grave voice: 'What do these children want?' The terrified little girls fled as fast as they could, 'as if they had seen the devil.' Those were my mother's very words." And an old man of ninety-seven, spanning two centuries, who had seen the aged Barère when he was himself a small boy, told the writer that after all those years he could still remember how his nurse would threaten him: "Barère will get you if you don't behave!"

It had not always been so. Barère had once been admired, his company sought. Love and affection enveloped him in his childhood and youth; in his early manhood he had enjoyed security and easy circumstances. But in his last years, when debts and the infirmities of time plagued him, he was busy with the monomaniacal intensity of the very old in preparing for the posthumous publication of his memoirs so that from posterity he could obtain the rehabilitation which life had denied him. Drawing on fading memory, the tottering octogenarian looked back nostalgically upon that happy past.

"I was born in the Pyrenees," his *Mémoires* begin, "that is to say in the country of liberty." The house on the rue Bourg Vieux (now rue Brauhauban) in Tarbes where Barère was born still stands, a blurred plaque commemorating the forgotten distinction to indifferent passers-by. Long in the possession of his father's family, it was situated almost directly opposite the parish church of Saint-Jean where he was baptized. The transcript of the baptismal register, couched in the archaic terms of the day, reads as follows:

"Bertrand Barère, legitimate son of Jean Barère, Procurator to the Seneschal of Bigorre, and Demoiselle Catherine Marrast, was born in the parish of Saint-Jean of this city on September 10, 1755 and baptized by us, the archpriest whose signature [appears] below, on the following day. The godfather was Master Bertrand Barère, priest, doctor of theology, and vicar of Ouzous of the present diocese and the godmother, Demoiselle Marie Daure de Carles, granduncle and grandmother respectively of the baptized. The noble godfather signs with us, not the godmother, not being able."

SIGNED: Barère, curé
Dagno, archpriest

On his father's side he came from substantial middle-class stock which could be traced back for many generations through a double line of lawyers and ecclesiastics. Bertrand's father, Jean (1722-1788), like his father before him, was a lawyer, each having served as solicitor in the Seneschal's Court of Bigorre.

In his capacity as First Consul of Tarbes and ex-officio president of the Third Estate of the provincial estates of Bigorre, Jean had discovered certain irregularities in the treasurer's report. A man of character, he traced them and found that they derived from various fiscal favors granted to the local nobility. Since he made a point of not keeping the information to himself, the nobles for their part made representations to the royal military commandant of the province and also to the bishop of the diocese, who succeeded without undue difficulty in obtaining a royal *lettre de cachet*, which temporarily disbarred Jean from exercising any administrative office in Tarbes. The disqualification was later revoked, but Bertrand's first political impressions were formed, as he later recalled, in an atmosphere of conflict between "the liberties of his province and the arbitrary power of the monarchy."

A commoner on the paternal side, Barère could lay claim to noble birth through his mother. His mother, the charming Jeanne-Catherine Marrast, popularly called Cataline like her own mother, was a de Naïs (or de Neys), a family of old noble stock but neither rich nor poor. As dowry the young bride—she was only fifteen years old when she married Jean in 1753—brought to her future husband some real property in the Landes in southwestern France which she had inherited from her father. Her rights to other real property in that area that her mother might later leave her were also recognized in the marriage contract, but they were subsequently lost in litigation between her own children and the children of her mother by the latter's second marriage. From the terms of the settlement, though the matter is not clear, it would appear that her *dot* also reverted to the other children. At any rate nothing more was heard of it in connection with the holdings of the Barère family.

Barère's mother was also related to an older nobility, having as second cousin a wealthy landed proprietor named Jacques Hector d'Anti, who was partial to her and her sister Françoise.

5

When Bertrand was fourteen years old, "good d'Anti," as the villagers called him, began to dispose of his worldly goods to his favorite young relatives. In 1769 he turned over to Barère's mother provisional title to a valuable farm situated at Anclades a few kilometers east of Lourdes, and a few years later the title became permanent. In 1771 he started to parcel out the property that he owned in the beautiful Argelès plain immediately to the south of Lourdes, property that the young Bertrand knew and loved. While he gave the larger part of the real property, land and buildings of the fief that he owned at Vieuzac (Biéouzac in the Basque version) to Bertrand's aunt Françoise and her second husband, the fief itself, consisting almost entirely of feudal dues, he sold on easy terms to Jean Barère, husband of his other great favorite, Cataline. By that first purchase in 1774 Jean acquired for 4,000 livres the lay abbey of Vieuzac, the property consisting of the title to the abbey, patronage of the parish church, and the honorific rights. Two years later, in 1776, d'Anti also sold the feudal rights, obtaining 10,500 livres for them. And two years after that, in 1778 when he died, his will bequeathed to Jean some smaller parcels to the north of Vieuzac and the right of formal entry to the estates of Bigorre. Jean could not exercise this right because he lacked the legally requisite number of quarterings of nobility; nevertheless, the title of Seigneur de Vieuzac was his, and it passed on his death to his son Bertrand.

In 1795, when Bertrand was finding it expedient to deny that he was wealthy, which he then was not, and a noble, which he had earlier claimed to be, he wrote in the *Défense de Bertrand Barère*: "I am not of the noble caste; I pride myself that I was born of the class of the people. . . . I did not buy a barony of Vieuzac. . . . I found in my father's legacy a small fief worth 20 to 24,000 francs, without buildings, without domain land, and consisting of simple feudal dues." The records bear him out: to his aunt's family, which had installed itself in Vieuzac, had gone the chateau, the mill, the barn, the orchards, the cultivated fields, woodlands, and gardens. Nevertheless the disclaimer was not altogether honest. He was no longer rich in 1795, for the feudal dues had been abolished and the *dot* of his mother lost in litigation, but in his youth he had not been poor. He had been amply provided for against material want. Property, family prestige, social standing, all these were his birthright.

In addition to Bertrand, four other children were born of the marriage of Cataline and Jean Barère. Very little is known about them, possibly because of the fire which destroyed the departmental archives early in the nineteenth century. His younger brother Jean-Pierre, who was born in 1758, became an ordained priest, abjuring early in the Revolution to take up the other great professional career of the Barères, the practice of the law. While he was never intimate with Jean-Pierre after his childhood, Bertrand was bound to him then by ties of friendship as well as by brotherly love, and their relations remained exceedingly cordial up to the last decade of his life. On the other hand, his relations with his three sisters, Cécile, Françoise, and Jeanne-Marie, were never close during his boyhood and youth, and he saw almost nothing of them for the better part of forty years until he returned to Tarbes in 1832. All three made comfortable marriages with local notables and had numerous progeny whose inheritance rights the mothers defended with a tenacity that Balzac's avaricious characters would not have been slow to appreciate.

In addition to nephews and nieces Bertrand had many cousins, for six sons and two daughters were born of the marriage of his uncle Bertrand, the lawyer, with a Demoiselle Dembarrère, also of the local gentry. Though their paths did not directly cross, with the exception of his cousin Hector's, through the cousins who lived out their lives in Tarbes as well as through the children born of the marriages of his sisters, Bertrand was to have numerous and devoted relatives during his years of adversity, a veritable "tribe of Barères," as a government report of 1815 sputtered. Thus social relations and ties of blood assured him valuable contacts everywhere in the Tarbes region. In Toulouse, too, when the young man began his legal career he found his path smoothed for him by the numerous friendly connections that uncle Bertrand had established with colleagues who like himself pleaded at the bar of the parlement of that great provincial center.

Bertrand's boyhood was bounded by security and affection. The summer months, when there were no classes to attend in Tarbes, he spent in the Argelès valley of the *pays* of Lavedan, a spot of rugged beauty nestling in the foothills of the Pyrenees. He divided his time between the home of d'Anti and that of his indulgent grandmother, who doted upon him. In his own home there was the father whom he admired for his uprightness and independence and who, in turn, it is certain, proudly noted the progress of his eldest born. A bond of affection linked Bertrand to his gay young mother, and when they strolled arm-in-arm, so tradition reported, strangers took them for sister and brother. With Jean-Pierre, his junior by three years, he played happily. The boy grew up free from care, untouched by doubts or anxiety.

Of his early education almost nothing is known except that he attended a parish school in Tarbes, where his conduct was deemed "exemplary." Much more is known of his secondary education. Sometime after his tenth birthday he left Tarbes, his parents sending him to the then famous Collège at Sorèze, a small town off the main road between Toulouse and Castres, a short day's drive from the capital of Languedoc. Recently reopened in 1758, the Collège bore just renown among the progressive schools of the Age of the Enlightenment. Though Barère's personal file has not been preserved, the general outline of his school years and the curriculum is clear. In the director's pointed words, the purpose of the school under its revised and expanded program was "to form subjects for society, to rear gentlemen, soldiers, sailors, magistrates, and administrators rather than monks." And a contemporary critic commented perhaps more ironically than admiringly, that the students were taught singing, dancing, drawing, composition, horseback riding, swimming, gymnastics, music, modern languages, and, he added maliciously, even French. Indeed, breaking away from the traditional emphasis upon classical languages and the past, Sorèze employed French for all courses. The curriculum also gave history a place of honor, and it was no doubt at Sorèze that Barère first fell under the influence of Montesquieu, whose great seminal writings on historical developments he intensively studied.

Discipline was exact but not severe, and frequent rest and recreation periods punctuated formal instruction. Classes were small, no more than seven or eight students in each, and the pupils received sufficient individual attention to bring out their capacity and their interests. Nevertheless, the training was as solid as it was broad. Bertrand received sound grounding in the classical languages and ancient history, in modern history and French language, in geography, mathematics, physics, and astronomy. All this was to give him a long head-start in his future career and stand him in excellent stead throughout his life.

As intellectual horizons widened for the lad from the parish school of Tarbes, old standards and values were eroded. He did well in his studies and won a prize for distinction in eloquence and history. Sorèze initiated him into knowledge and schooled him in tolerance and the ways of polite society. Among the pupils were boys from the different provinces of southern France, lads too from Spain, the Italian states, and French colonies overseas. Overwhelmingly Catholic, the school also contained Huguenots. When he came to Sorèze, Bertrand had not known many sons of the aristocracy. Of more than 200 pupils of his graduating class in 1770 only one in five stemmed like himself from the well-to-do bourgeoisie. The great majority were *gentilshommes*, scions of the minor nobility.

Bertrand arrived at school a bright, promising rustic. He left it a well-spoken and well-groomed youth, at ease in company, unabashed in the presence of social superiors.

Whether, as he maintains, he went directly from Sorèze to the famous law school of the University of Toulouse at the age of fifteen—due to special dispensation—or enrolled a year later in 1771, as is more likely, is not important. He arrived there to begin his law studies when a great crisis beset the sovereign court of appeals for the vast region of southwest France, the powerful, old provincial parlement of Toulouse. Nominally only tribunals and courts of final appeal within their respective jurisdictions, the twelve provincial parlements and the parlement of Paris had long possessed great political influence. By virtue of the right to register royal edicts and of the ancient tradition, which had practically become a right, of exercising a sort of judicial review before the laws were registered, they had arrogated much political and legislative authority to themselves. From the early years of the century when the parlement of Paris had broken the will of Louis XIV, they engaged in a long, tenacious struggle with the crown. On several occasions Louis XV had countered opposition by formally and unceremoniously commanding them by fiat to register royal edicts. However, even when "exiled" to other cities, the disgraced magistrates could suspend all court activity, and for practical purposes make the royal edicts unenforceable. They were particularly obstructionist with respect to edicts concerning fiscal matters. Those lofty magistrates, it must be remembered, owned their offices and almost without exception came from the nobility. That their stand represented a kind of constitutionalism is of course true; that they were *privilégiés* with prerogatives and tax exemptions to defend is not less relevant.

The parlement of Toulouse, dating back to the fifteenth century and the second oldest of the parlements, dominated public life in the capital of Languedoc. It enjoyed the prestige of age; over and above prestige and political influence, it wielded great economic power by virtue of the employment that its work afforded to scores of lower courts and hundreds and thousands of lesser officials—solicitors, barristers, bailiffs, clerks, notaries, scribes, recorders, sergeants at arms. As the final court of appeals for hundreds of cases, it enjoyed also the almost unanimous support of public opinion. For a whole generation, and especially in this decade, the Toulouse magistrates, like their colleagues in the other sovereign courts, represented themselves as the natural defenders of the rights of the people against the arbitrary rule of kings and ministers. They were the custodians of "the fundamental laws" of the realm, hence the only constitutional authorities in the absence of the Estates General empowered to vote taxes.

In 1771, when Bertrand was beginning his first year as a law student, an edict formulated by His Majesty's chancellor, fierce old Maupeou, struck a crushing blow against the enemies of royal absolutism. It suspended the magistrates from office, "exiled" them to other cities, abolished the purchase and sale of judicial offices and, in several jurisdictions, established new sovereign courts. Where the old parlements with new personnel still functioned, they had been deprived, so declared Barère, recalling his youthful impressions, of "the last vestiges of public liberty." By that he meant their claim to make remonstrances as well as their right to register fiscal measures. Little wonder, since the edict had forbidden collective resistance, that Toulouse was, again to quote Barère, "in mourning" when he first came there.

Thus Bertrand's adolescent years, and his most impressionable, were spent, as he recalled, "in the thick of a concert of hatred against the despotism of ministers and admiration for the courage of the magistrates, defenders of the rights of the people." For the next several years he was one of the 300 or 400 students who sat at the feet of the distinguished professors of the law faculty. Distinguished they were and of resounding reputation. The professor of French jurisprudence was appointed by the king from a panel of three submitted by the *procureur* of the parlement; all others received their appointment on a competitive basis. The courses, except the one in French law, were conducted in Latin, and each course met daily for one and a half hours. The first half-hour was given over to dictation of the text of the law, the second to the *explication*, and the last half-hour to questions and recitations.

While the faculty was outstanding, the lackadaisical instruction left something to be desired. The courses in French law were normally given in the students' third year, but many students, the university register discloses, did not attend them, taking advantage of exemptions afforded them by royal writ. Complaints were frequent about disorder in and about the classrooms. Examinations, contemporary records are agreed, were formalities which did not overtax the minds of the students. There are intimations too that the students' ability to pay the degree fees, which were slightly more than 22 *louis* (528 livres) for a bachelor's degree and 70 (1680 livres) for a master's, was not ignored in the granting of those degrees.

We have Barère's word for it that he applied himself seriously to the two subjects he studied, Roman jurisprudence and French law. The formal record indicates that his mentors approved of him. He was not yet nineteen when, by the unanimous vote of his examiners, agreement was reached that "Master Bertrand Barrère [sic], native of Tarbes, had sustained his theses for the degree of Bachelor of Law." This was on July 11, 1774; almost exactly a year later on July 10, 1775, he took his master's degree (*licence*). Again, a panel of examiners agreed unanimously that he had successfully defended his theses, while a second panel voted that same day that he had satisfactorily acquitted himself in a public examination on French jurisprudence. He was now qualified to practice the law.

At Sorèze he had studied the periods of Cicero and Demosthenes; at Toulouse he read in the great modern jurists, Chancellors d'Aguesseau and Cochin. While pursuing his law studies, he also faithfully attended the audiences of the substitute Maupeou parlement, listening attentively to the pleas of the great legal celebrities. He pored over the pleas and briefs of his distinguished elders, and his soul was "in a transport of delight," since he too aspired to nothing loftier than the glory of defending the wretched and the innocent of the earth. While he steeped himself in the stilted eloquence of the Toulouse barristers, he closely followed the mounting chorus of demands, taking note of tumultuous demonstrations everywhere in France for the recall of the old parlements. In the course of four years, protests against the crown spread from the closed ranks of the parlementaires into the wider circles of the upper bourgeoisie and men of letters. So when the bewildered and inexperienced Louis XVI ascended the throne in 1774, the "Patriots"—as the followers of the magistrates styled themselves—were too numerous and too strong for the king to continue the war of attrition against them. New tactics commended themselves, and he was advised by his mentors to dismiss Maupeou, a move, they assured him, which would simultaneously break up the solid ranks of the opposition and gain great personal popularity for himself. As might have been expected, the disgrace of the defeated minister gave the signal for an outburst of joyous popular demonstrations. Before the year ended, the young ruler recalled the parlement of Paris and in the course of the next several months he also reinstated, one by one, the suspended provincial parlements.

The veteran advisers of Louis XVI had confidently expected their calculated maneuver to win the good will of the parlementaires. However, appeasement at that juncture proved a blunder. Not less, but greater, resistance followed the victory of the magistrates over royal absolutism. The triumph was celebrated deliriously in Toulouse, where noisy crowds milled about for days, dancing in the narrow, winding streets and drinking heartily, we may be sure, of the free wine that a municipality flushed with success generously distributed to the poor. The university, too, where feelings in support of the parlement ran exceptionally high, organized victory celebrations. Students presented a civic crown to the senior magistrate, and the university authorities voted to establish a permanent mass to commemorate the happy outcome of the struggle. Barère took his lawyer's oath when the excitement was reaching a crest. "All the young lawyers of that epoch," he recalled "accepted hatred of despotism and the feeling that it was then necessary to find means of arresting the arbitrary acts and the [royal] ministers as though these were a sacred tradition."

For the moment he was confident that the triumphant parlements would continue to protect the rights of Frenchmen against arbitrary rule. He held high hopes that under the guidance of his new, "enlightened" ministers—men like Turgot, Malesherbes, and Vergennes—the well-intentioned young monarch would usher in a happy day for France and all humanity. Like all other idealistic and eager young men, Bertrand burned with a desire to serve humanity. Those were years when the self-conscious new generation of literate Frenchmen were taking stock of their heritage. No institution, no practice, no ancient relationship escaped their scrutiny. Wherever these young people gathered, the seminal ideas of the great *philosophes* were discussed and debated: the law of nature and of nature's God, the natural rights of man, the social compact, the rights of the citizen and the patriot, the interests of the nation, of liberty, justice, humanity. Men of feeling, they could not rest indifferent to mankind's ills. They would suffer "no one to moan"; to the needy they would stretch out a helping hand and gain "sweet satisfaction in making people happy." So wrote one of them, speaking for them all. *Bienfaisance*, doing good to one's unfortunate fellows because they were all brothers, this humanitarian lay charity was their secular faith; and the Abbé Raynal's many-sided diatribe against intolerance, *Histoire philosophique et politique des établissements et du commerce européen dans les deux Indes,* was their bible.

There were many books they could buy or borrow from the new public libraries and the private circulating libraries which elaborated in detail upon the evils that had to be rooted out. In all the larger towns and not infrequently in the smaller, they could attend courses which propounded solutions of practical problems bedeviling an obstinately irrational society. In hundreds of forums throughout the country, reading clubs, discussion societies, and masonic lodges, idealistic youth found opportunities to exchange views and heighten their exultation, if not invariably to clarify their ideas. The old provincial academies too swelled the mood, setting prizes for essays on outstanding benefactors of humanity and notable developments which speeded humanity along the path of enlightenment and progress.

Politically, Bertrand remained safe. Not for another decade and a half would he renounce his traditional outlook on government and administration. Life humanized him in a more subtle way, liberating him from inherited values, eating away at the accepted and uncriticized conceptions in which he had been reared. Little by little as he settled down to practicing law in Toulouse, he underwent a silent transformation.

Undoubtedly the profound and sincere concern with social welfare which throughout his later life characterized his behavior, would never have burgeoned had Barère returned to Tarbes after his graduation, as his father wished him to do. While he was still pursuing his studies, his father had bought him a magistracy in Tarbes, the office of Royal Councillor at the Seneschal's Court of Bigorre. For it he had paid a high price, 8,000 livres, and to safeguard the investment, he prevailed upon the parlement of Toulouse in 1776 to grant his son permission to fill the office at the age of twenty-one instead of the statutory age of twenty-seven. In the following year, June 1777, the register of parlement recorded the reception of "Bertrand Barère de Vieuzac" in the office. Strictly speaking, Bertrand had no right to use the noble particle "de Vieuzac," which was his father's; but since the father obviously did not object to a bit of snobbery on the part of his brilliant son and heir, the parlement stretched a point. In any case, Bertrand accepted the office and the income from it, though for almost a decade he did not even attempt to fulfill the obligations. The records show that he was not formally installed until November 16, 1785. He explains later that he had "a natural aversion for the function of judge . . . and preferred the long and painful hours of the lawyer, because those functions are free, noble, courageous and serve to attack despotism and injustice." The explanation reads well. Of course he wanted to serve humanity, but when he wrote the explanation years after the fact, he had probably forgotten that he had preferred to be second, even third or fourth in Toulouse, than first in Tarbes.

Time had fixed upon Tarbes a hierarchical social structure. The administrative center of the *pays* of Bigorre, within its confines lived many noblemen and ecclesiastics, for Tarbes was a cathedral town. The bulk of the population, however, belonged to the Third Estate, and was divided into the upper ranks of the liberal professions, trade, and manufacture, and the lower ranks of journeymen, apprentices, and small shopkeepers. In Tarbes, as elsewhere in France, tensions were mounting in the last years of the Old Regime between the poor commoners of the Third Estate, of whom there were many, and the favored few of the lay and ecclesiastical aristocracy. Complaints were numerous, long-standing, and bitter about the privileges of the first two estates, their evasion of public charges, their monopoly of positions in the administration, and their possession of the best and most fertile rural property.

Within the smaller universe of the bourgeois notables, however, a coherent and traditional culture prevailed, marked by respect for the dignity of the individual, who lived according to his station in life, and civility toward one's neighbors. To the well-born and to social superiors, one was outwardly deferential even if frequently gnawed by bitterness; toward inferiors, charitable and just. To God, one discharged his obligations by faithful performance of religious duties and unquestioning acceptance of Catholic doctrine. Respect for parental authority and a deep concern for family unity was challenged by almost no one. To the king, obedience was due, though not without a robust and tenacious defense of the historic "liberties" of Bigorre and vigorous complaints against the royal fisc.

That slow-paced routine was not for Barère. Tarbes, busy by day and gay in the reflected light of the Pyrenees over its pastel-colored houses, was still at night, its quiet unbroken save for the hum of the voices of a few crones gathered before the cafés on the Place Maubourget. For artisans and nearby farmers, Tarbes with its 8,000 inhabitants may have been exciting; to an ambitious young man like himself, eager to serve humanity and advance his own career, and moreover accustomed to the ways of Toulouse, it was dreary and dull. Where, he must have asked himself, could he find opportunity to roll out the grand phrases he had been learning about the evils of society while distinguished advocates nodded their heads approvingly and cultivated burghers listened sagely to his views? There were few salons if any for a young man of feeling to make a name for himself, no emancipated patrons of the arts and sciences to take note of what he did. What could that center of traditionalism offer that was not provided by the ancient university city of Toulouse with its opulent merchants and their proud baroque mansions, its famed academicians and illustrious men of law, its museums, theatres, good company and cheer, the *douceur de vivre* in an old cultured city? Decidedly, Tarbes was not for him.

For the next ten years, from 1777 to 1787, Barère practiced law in Toulouse, drawing upon his learning and his talent and expending his youthful energy and idealism in ministering to the needy and unfortunate. From the three-volume set of his most important pleas and briefs, fortunately available in the municipal library of Tarbes, one can readily trace the evolution of his activities and his views. With justifiable pride, and the resources to gratify that human vanity, he had handsomely bound in calf the published documents, many of them annotated in his own hand. Already, in his first brief he employed the conventional turgid rhetoric from which he never recovered. Assigned the defense of an aged carpenter accused of being the father of a child born to a public prostitute, Barère drew upon the tears of presiding magistrates: "Is it believable that an artisan, worn by toil . . . and speedily approaching old age, ripened by reason and experience, should address himself to a prostitute whose gallantries were already notorious? Convinced by his innocence and counting on the justice of his judges, the petitioner awaits from them, with a confidence equalling his respect, a verdict which, while avenging morals, will assure the tranquillity of citizens."

During the four years after that sentimental and successful debut, he handled a wide variety of routine civil cases involving pension rights, damages, and family relations. Not until 1781 did he plead a criminal case before the bar of the parlement, and then he was called to support the appeal of a young girl from the death penalty for infanticide which had been imposed upon her by a lower court. He scored his first spectacular triumph when he invoked the testimony of a surgeon to prove beyond doubt that the presumably murdered child had been stillborn. The panic-stricken mother, he argued, had hidden the dead body. The court acquitted his client, and Barère could find "sweet satisfaction" in having served the noble cause of succoring the helpless and the weak. It may be assumed that his vanity too was satisfied; he annotated the published decision: "This brief was inserted in the collection of celebrated cases for the year 1781."

This case, like a score of others in which he was involved, portrays him as a typical, conventional *coeur sensible* of the period, one of the countless young men who took the obligation to befriend the victims of injustice with the utmost seriousness and solemnity. It is understandable that he should play an important part in the move to set up a panel of lawyers, old and young, who offered their services gratis to indigent but deserving clients. It is characteristic, too, that among the cases which he himself pleaded was one that restituted the confiscated estate of a Huguenot.

Other cases that he prepared, recorded also in the bound collection of his briefs, indicate that meantime he was slowly putting a new cutting edge of social criticism to the surface of his broad and somewhat naïve benevolence. In 1782, while covering his words with careful reservations to shield his position as a respectable member of society, he intimated that he looked with less than favor upon the existing system of guild controls. That institution, he maintained, "seemed an infringement of the freedom necessary for the progress of the arts, a barrier to talents, a crushing tax upon the least rich classes of society." The briefs which followed in the next several years had a bolder ring. In them he underscored the arguments against administrative and feudal controls over free enterprise. He ridiculed the plea advanced by a plaintiff to keep a contested field in pasture: "While the government ensures rewards to the hard-working citizen who clears the land, wealthy landowners get together to prevent the clearings which should supply food to several needy families. Sovereign justice will not be deceived: here we have a struggle unhappily as common in the courts as it is in society, of the well-to-do against the poor, of the strong against the weak. . . . Thus in a century of humanity and political economy the lower courts have preferred a system which stocks the land with cattle to one which sustains men." If he was saying nothing that the humanitarian critics of large-scale agrarian developments in England had not already said and more forcefully, it should be remembered that Old Regime France was not free England and Barère himself was of the rich. Twice in that decade he took up the cause of attorneys who wished to free themselves from guild restraints. On two other occasions he drew up briefs on behalf of a master apothecary, a member of the Toulouse guild, who had been denied the right to practice his profession in the county of Bigorre without formal accreditation by a local guild. The first time he spoke guardedly, but on the second occasion he indignantly protested what he called the persecution of an experienced practitioner, himself the son of an apothecary and old enough to be the father of his jealous rivals.

One case in particular, a case on appeal before the criminal court of the parlement of Toulouse in 1786, strikingly illustrates Barère's heightened social awareness. The issue at stake was whether a certain de Reys, a Knight of the Order of Malta, who had first seduced and then eloped with an impressionable maiden whom he had swept off her feet with his burning love letters, would be legally upheld in his effort to break the marriage. The technical grounds adduced by the Knight's attorneys were that neither his parents' consent nor that of the bride's parents had been obtained. Since the facts were generally known, no one in Toulouse had to be told that the real reason lay elsewhere: the Knight's uncle, a wealthy Commander of the Order of Malta, had refused to make the nephew his heir unless the marriage to a mere commoner, however beautiful, was annulled.

The case could not fail to attract wide attention, and Toulouse society divided sharply over a titillating affair of such romantic allure. Barère had strong feelings about the social issue involved. The tacit assumption that a nobleman could contemptuously discard a bride of a legally inferior rank outraged him, naturally. But he was sufficiently canny not to wear his heart on his sleeve. Indignation, he knew, did not win cases in court. So he based his case on two arguments, first, that the young man was wanting in honor, not to the abandoned bride, but to the noble caste to which he belonged; and second, that the interests of the social order took precedence over the rights of parents. The court did order the marriage dissolved. To hold otherwise was impossible, since legally there was no invalidating the argument of the Knight's counsel. Their triumph, nonetheless, was a hollow one; and it was Barère who turned out to be the real victor. The court ordered the husband to pay damages and costs to his ex-wife and brought him to trial on the charge of abduction.

If, in later years, the exultant barrister gilded the lily in characterizing the case as "the cause of the nobility against the commoners, of the aristocracy against the Third Estate," the exaggeration may be pardoned him. The trial in itself was trivial, but the broader issue it raised lifted it well above the substantive matter of the legal question. Barère, a successful lawyer already distinguished in his profession, had taken a stand on the larger question of the rights of man; and when we turn to the other activities which had been occupying his time in these same years, that stand will not appear surprising. A circumspect social and political critic was slowly being fashioned alongside the successful practicing lawyer.

# The Social Critic,
# 1782-1788

BARÈRE could not participate directly in politics as could a contemporary small-town lawyer in England or the thirteen colonies. But there was no separating the practice of the law from the study of politics and administration or discussion of the issues of the day, and in his *Mémoires* he relates how during half of each week he closely studied the writings of Tacitus, Montesquieu, Machiavelli, and Beccaria. He might have added Raynal and Rousseau, Adam Smith and Turgot, and above all the physiocrats.

From his professional activities a small but assured income came to him. If there were no regular remittances from his family, there were occasional gifts from his father, such as the 100 gold *louis* (the not inconsiderable sum of 2,400 livres) which went a long way to build up his personal library. Hence financial stringency was at no time a problem, and we can imagine him if we choose, assiduously cultivating his intellectual garden at home. The voracious reader made lengthy excerpts from the authors whose books he mentions, taking copious notes on works dealing with the problems of beggary and vagrancy, poor relief, prison reform, and improvement of that harsh criminal code which shocked the conscience of a tenderhearted generation. The earnest student of the seventies and the eighties already foreshadowed the mature revolutionist of 1793-1794 who was to play so important a role in furthering projects of social welfare.

As knowledge increased and understanding deepened, the impulse came to formulate his ideas in writing. Circumstances favored him. Like such future associates in the revolutionary movement as Robespierre, Bailly, and Brissot, Barère found opportunity to clarify his thinking in the prize contests currently conducted under the auspices of various provincial academies. Setting annual essay competitions on fixed subjects was no new enterprise; what was then novel and strikingly characteristic of provincial France was the manner in which the young competitors expressed themselves. Most of them were understandably guarded in tone, since winning a prize rather than earning a prison sentence from the watchful authorities was their intent. Models instructed the aspirants in the art of covering themselves against possible accusations, while insinuating between the lines suggestions which no attentive reader could mistake or ignore.

If Barère wished least to prejudice his standing, he was not indifferent to the promptings of his social conscience; and most probably he assured himself that what others had done and were doing, he too could do. In any case no harm would befall him if friends and clients learned that the able barrister was also a successful author. His reputation would not suffer were he fortunate enough to win a prize and have his essay printed in the proceedings of the academy.

His debut in the career of letters was less than spectacular. When the jury of the famous old Académie des Jeux Floraux of Toulouse announced the winners of the prize contest that it had set for a eulogy of Louis XII, Barère's name was not among them. All, happily, was not failure: the official proceedings of the Académie for 1782 printed his contribution. This recognition did more than console him; it encouraged him to have the essay *Eloge de Louis XII, surnommé le Père du Peuple* published independently. Thus it appeared with an explanatory subtitle, *Discours présenté à l'Académie des Jeux Floraux en 1782, par M. Barère de Vieuzac, Avocat au Parlement de Toulouse.*

As an example of belles lettres his essay has no claim upon posterity. Whether its defects arose from his inexperienced and undisciplined pen or from an exuberant Gascon temperament is a delicate question. A man of feeling, the product of an age of sensibility, he experienced no difficulty in assuming bombast for emphasis and exaggeration for eloquence. Nor did the *Eloge* have intellectual distinction to commend it. Unoriginality of thought matched platitudinous style. Yet for the biographer and the historian, it has both interest and value. Read for what it conveys by indirection as well as for what it openly states, it is a revealing expression of the political and social views that Barère then held.

In religion and politics he was a conventional, conservative traditionalist who could in full sincerity write that "Religion was the greatest and most necessary gift that Divinity makes to states." Posterity should raise monuments to good princes because "Good Kings inspire a sort of idolatry"; and the greatest glory of Louis XII was "to have been the Father of the People." If the accents of those trite tributes ring true, that is only half the story. The other half concerns Barère's studied effort to hold the mirror of Louis XII up to Louis XVI. By placing himself on record as the admirer of a monarch who deserved the appellation, "Father of the People," Barère could direct attention to what the reigning ruler thus far had failed to do to merit a similar tribute. By extolling the past, he opened the door to criticism of the present.

This interpretation of boring from within, so to speak, seems substantiated when one finds that he followed up praise of kings with an explicit reminder that nevertheless limits did exist to royal absolutism: "France then did not have in all its provinces these august senates [i.e. parlements] which watch over . . . the laws and give sovereign justice to the people. May this famous edict ever be engraved in all courts in which he [Louis XII] exhorts his parlements ALWAYS TO JUDGE IN ACCORDANCE WITH THE FUNDAMENTAL LAWS OF THE REALM, IN SPITE OF CONTRARY ORDERS . . . AND COMMANDS THEM TO SHOW HIM THIS EDICT IF EVER HE DARED TO DEPART FROM IT."

The cautious disciple of the philosophes further reveals himself in his comment on Louis XII's tolerant religious policy: "Happy the men, happy France, if there would always be princes as wise." On the score of civil and criminal justice, while Barère found that Louis XII had much in his favor, it was not the accomplishment which he chose to emphasize: it was the lessons that Louis XVI (unnamed of course) could draw from what his predecessors had left unaccomplished. "Louis XI went to his grave in the midst of despotism and superstition [and] we began to know the rights of civil liberty" only when Louis XII ascended the throne. Under Louis XII, "justice replaced superstitions and barbaric procedures [and] was established on an enlightened basis." But this king too did not live long enough to complete the great reformation: "As is the case today [legislation] was a bizarre mixture of Roman law, ordinances of our kings, and barbaric and different customs. . . . The administration of justice was retarded and vitiated by long drawn-out procedures and cumbersome forms." The administration of criminal law Barère found worse still: "We doubtless shudder [over] the apparatus of torture and secret procedures, but our philosophy and enlightenment have not yet succeeded in destroying these two monuments of barbarism. . . . Almost four centuries have elapsed and we still have not advanced toward more perfect criminal laws."

Barère was on safe ground in voicing reservations about the legal system and he risked little in speaking out. On the subject of royal censorship and the prosecution of writers, however, his approach was oblique and he prudently limited himself to the suggestion that kings should encourage notable writers of their age as well as watch over them: "When we . . . emerge from darkness, when the language is being formed, when . . . printing opens sources of instruction, then, in that happy ferment of the mind, nations need watchful chiefs to enlighten them; learning needs encouragement and rewards, and scholars benefit and honors. It is then that princes are truly worthy of the homage and gratitude of enlightened posterity . . . it is then that they make their epoch an honorable one in the age of nations."

Similarly, though his references to the economic policy of Louis XII were brief, the intent of his words was clear. He thanked Louis XII in the name of humanity for directing "almost all his attention to agriculture, this art which nourishes men and states, this nerve of trade, this base of public prosperity." Since encouraging agricultural production required that the cultivator gain relief from the heavy taxes which he was forced to pay, Barère conveyed his appreciation of the king's policy through a reference to edicts "in which we are specially glad to note that limits were set to *corvées, aides,* and *tailles....*" Encouraging agricultural production also meant establishing free internal grain trade, but this, Barère wrote more sadly than indignantly, Louis XII had failed to do. For his failure the king was not to be blamed: "Nowhere did people have any idea that freedom brought happy results. On this branch of the administration Louis XII had only the ideas of his century."

Thus, while the *Eloge de Louis XII* may have been only a veiled statement of Barère's credo and a transparent piece of propaganda, a propagandist plea it assuredly was. In it he went only as far as his fear of censorship allowed and his desire to win the prize carried him, only as far also as he then was carried by his notions of government.

Along with many of his liberal contemporaries he admired Britain as a palladium of civil liberty, religious toleration, and political equality. Yet even then he was a pronounced Anglophobe and a staunch French nationalist. No one during the revolutionary and Napoleonic era was to be more associated in the public mind with fervent nationalism and denigration of England; it would be an error, however, to assume that those sentiments waited upon 1789 and war with Great Britain. The Revolution did not give birth to them; it accentuated what already existed. In 1782 Barère did not hold to the view which was to be his in 1789 that the king was the mandatory of the legislature, which alone could speak for Frenchmen. And he did not then maintain that laws, following the pattern of the natural and essential order of the universe, should be formulated through parliamentary processes. In 1782 his position was roughly this: for England, her parliament; for France, her parlements and her king. Royal authority—how could one contest this—was to remain absolute, with all friends of humanity earnestly hoping that if the king could not himself be a philosopher, at least he would surround himself with enlightened ministers. In the meantime, pending that happy outcome, the parlements would stand on guard, eternally vigilant against arbitrary rule and ministerial despotism and courageously discharging their sacred obligations to defend these "fundamental laws" which were the priceless legacy of the past to the present.

A deep sense of the historical past of his country, pride in its cultural and intellectual ascendancy, tenacious adherence to old ways—those were the strands of the political traditionalism which somehow crossed in his thinking with an equally natural and traditionalist predisposition to dislike England and fear her as the national enemy. England's great achievements could not be denied. Nevertheless there still lingered in Barère's mind memory of many battles in centuries long past. That very year, 1782, provided the stimulus of yet another war between the two great powers to remind him, in case memory lapsed, where his heart should lie.

Thus it was not difficult for him to take over from the physiocrats and their followers not only their strong conviction that England was France's great rival, but also the gratifying belief that the days of her glory were numbered. Like them he believed that in the modern Carthage the interests of English landowners were being sacrificed to the development of commerce and industry. It required no coercion to conclude that in the conflict with the American colonies, which was disrupting her trade, inflicting great harm upon her manufacturers, and spreading wide distress among her people, there was *prima facie* evidence of the decline which could lead only to ultimate ruin. After commenting upon the wars between France and Venice, Barère added a veiled reference to England as the Venice of the present: "Do we not see another Louis, also cherished by his people, also a champion of justice, also jealous of the honor of his Crown, protector of liberty and trade, another Metropolis as haughty, as selfish in its colonies, as tyrannical on the seas?"

This cast of thought was reflected in the essay which he submitted in 1783 on another topic proposed by the Académie des Jeux Floraux, "Whether Navigation Had Proven Useful or Injurious to Men." His brief contribution—it was not more than sixteen folios—failed to receive formal mention in the official proceedings of the academy, and Barère did not have it published, fortunately for his reputation. The manuscript is exaggerated almost to the point of hysteria. Yet it retains a certain interest as an expression of his Anglophobia. He argued without qualification that foreign trade, that is navigation, had caused more harm than good to mankind: "I leave . . . for history to trace in letters of blood the horrors of this discovery [of America]. Let us not forget that our cruelties brought the inhabitants of that country, happy until then . . . to take [a] vow not to reproduce their kind as soon as they knew us." Foreign trade also injured the commercial nations, excepting only traders themselves: "Premature fortune hastens decadence [and] there is even a more poignant evil. It is the inevitable establishment of colonies . . . a dangerous luxury to the mother country. . . . I adduce as proof of this political truth the break-up of Great Britain . . . the most important revolution which we have seen since the discovery of the New World."

It would be interesting to speculate on the reasons which determined him not to publish this essay, to speculate too on his decision not to take part in the prize contest on the American Revolution which the academy set for its topic in 1784. Surely, since gloating over the humbled rival and exulting, somewhat prematurely, over the disintegration of the British colonial empire were not politically dangerous, he would be taking no chances. However there was some danger in publicly praising republicans who had successfully rebelled against a king, even when to that king clung an odor of despotism with which happily Louis XVI himself was not tainted. Possibly Barère had other good reasons for not publishing the essay on navigation and not participating in the 1784 contest, but it might not be too far off the mark to believe that prudence was holding conviction in leash.

In the same year, 1783, he published a forty-page speech which he had delivered at the closing session of the Conference of Charity, the organization of practicing lawyers which he had helped found in Toulouse. Addressing a professional audience, he chose a subject that would naturally possess interest for his colleagues. His address in its published form was entitled *Eloge de Jean-Baptiste Furgole, Avocat au Parlement de Toulouse.* Furgole (1690-1761) was a famous barrister, one of the most distinguished and learned students of the law in France. A voluminous writer on many different legal aspects, he had also compiled a valuable text of civil and canon law on which the still more renowned Chancellor d'Aguesseau relied for his own far-reaching decisions.

The *Eloge* was not only appropriate to the occasion but it also afforded Barère opportunity to commend himself to the attention of his scholarly associates. He was discharging, he said, "a sacred duty toward his colleagues," in speaking of this "savant who served society by his works." He paid respect to Furgole's learning and legal eminence and praised him for upholding "the humane principles of Roman legislation." Then he obliquely called attention to evils that still existed. In an aside, he commented on Furgole's opinion of "the tyrannical maxims of feudal anarchy" and on the jurist's scorn for "the hateful origins" of pluralism in ecclesiastical offices. Then more pointedly still, he played upon the egalitarian sentiments of his listeners: "I leave to slaves of vanity . . . the task of speaking to you of the origins of Furgole. What is nobility, what are the commoners? What are hollow distinctions between man and man, when it is a matter of learning or virtue? Merit has no need of ancestors. . . . " The approval Barère hoped for was won, at least to the extent of having the conference vote to publish the address and in 1786 place a bust of Furgole in the municipal hall housing the other distinguished sons of Toulouse.

In the following year, 1784, when Barère refrained from writing on the American Revolution, he took part in a prize contest of the Académie de Belles Lettres of Montauban. This society, founded by an outstanding enemy of the philosophes, Lefranc de Pompignan, set as subject of its prize competition an eulogy of Pierre Séguier (1588-1672), chancellor of France in the ministries of Richelieu and Mazarin. Séguier was a man of great learning and a patron of literature, having in fact succeeded Richelieu as "chief protector" of the French Academy. Nevertheless, his career was a difficult one for a supporter of the parlements like Barère to praise without some embarrassment. Up to the time of Séguier's appointment as chancellor under Richelieu in 1633, he himself had been a high court president (*président à mortier*) of the parlement of Paris and shown himself independent of royal authority. After the appointment he proceeded forthwith to humiliate and bully the court. How then would Barère treat this delicate problem?

His *Eloge* shows him carrying water on both shoulders. In form his essay was swollen and turgid; at the same time it was deft and delicate in substance. It neither gave offense to the supporters of parlement nor unduly distorted Barère's own views. Respectful to the highest degree of royal authority, the author explicitly condemned Richelieu as a dread example of "hated ministerial despotism." He defended the parlements as vigilant sentinels and curbs upon royal authority, but carefully abstained from attacking Séguier himself as a turncoat who had humbled the rebellious *frondeurs* and foes of Mazarin. With good conscience and accuracy the essayist lauded Séguier in his professional capacity as a compiler of royal ordinances which were still in use, as a patron of learning, and as a man dedicated to "the happiness of the people." But unobtrusively Barère reiterated views expressed earlier, on the horrors of war, the indignity of religious persecution, the need to encourage agriculture as the basis of the national economy, to inculcate respect for parental authority and love for one's country. Of this contribution he could be proud. The academy bestowed the prize upon him and gave him the honor of election as member of that center of orthodoxy.

In 1785 the Montauban Academy proposed as a subject the eulogy of Georges d'Amboise, cardinal and minister of Louis XII, whom Barère had already mentioned favorably in the *Eloge de Louis XII*. Amboise's record was a good one, and Barère's *Eloge de Georges d'Amboise, Cardinal Archevèque de Rouen et Ministre de Louis XII* did justice to it. He conceded that the cardinal's warlike proclivities were deplorable, as was his sale of judicial offices; but how much did the chancellor resemble Richelieu in promoting agriculture and internal trade! Amboise kept taxes down and restored order to the finances; moreover, "he served religion and the state [and] he loved France as much as did his young monarch. . . . The papal legate is tolerant not only through following the feelings of humanity, but also the principles of enlightened religion."

It may not be farfetched to surmise that once again Barère was writing a tract for the times. Setting store by Amboise's religious policy and his sound economics implied criticism of contemporary realities; discovering merit in his sound fiscal policy obliquely condemned a contemporary royal official, Calonne, for whose policy of deficit spending Barère had scant regard. To the specious glamor of Calonne he pointedly opposed the sobriety of Amboise: "May the example of his economy, his beneficence, and his justice destroy in statesmen that prodigious facility which ruins states, that hollow and arrogant magnificence which corrupts them, that offensive indifference which permits abuses to accumulate, and that absolute authority which alienates all hearts." His essay failed to win a prize. Perhaps he had mixed more condemnation with praise than the good taste or the courage of the jury could bear. His *Eloge* remained unpublished for two decades before it appeared as part of the *Eloges académiques* in 1806.

Meantime the years were slipping by and the eligible young bachelor was approaching thirty. Amiable and gracious, refined in manner and taste, by his charm and facile conversation Barère had made himself an adornment of the Toulouse salons and a welcome guest at the homes of the parlementaires. Already financially self-supporting, he could look forward to inheriting the major portion of his father's estate, including the title of Seigneur de Vieuzac. He was a good catch and he knew it. So, it is obvious, did the impoverished noble family of de Monde at Vic-en-Bigorre, a hamlet some twenty kilometers to the north of Tarbes, who had an eligible young daughter, very young indeed, not yet thirteen years of age, to marry off. Under the tactful direction of uncle Bertrand the necessary preliminary arrangements for a marriage alliance were successfully concluded. A brilliant galaxy of relatives and friends gathered in Vic on May 13, 1785, to witness the signing of the marriage contract between Bertrand and the child, Catarine Elisabeth de Monde. Elisabeth, as she was popularly called, was barely past her twelfth birthday, younger even by three years than Barère's own mother when she was given in marriage. On the following day the guests assembled again in the little church of Saint-Martin at midnight to attend the wedding ceremony of the handsome charmer and the bewildered child. Dressed in white, clasping in her arms a yellow, satin-clad doll that Bertrand had given her—so runs the tradition—she marched timidly to the altar, looking more like a maiden making her first communion than a woman celebrating a binding sacrament.

Perhaps the doll, if doll there was, filled her eye, but certainly she could not fail to note how handsome her husband was. He was tall with delicate features and dark wavy hair. His brown eyes were soft and languorous, his voice caressing. His ways were reserved and courtly. "Those gentle and tender inclinations," recalled Madame de Genlis some years after her first meeting with him in Paris, "joined to a sort of piquant wit gave his character and his person something interesting and truly original." He was the only man, noted the *belle amie* of the Duke of Orléans, whose opinion on such matters is not to be taken lightly, whom she had ever seen coming straight from the provinces with an air and manner that qualified him perfectly for high society in the court of Versailles. This portrait did not come from the pen of an admirer: Madame de Genlis, when she jotted down those recollections of the young blade, had already characterized him as "execrable."

Barère's younger brother, Jean-Pierre, conducted the wedding service and the entire immediate family was represented. His friends too were there, among them distinguished colleagues from the bar of the Toulouse parlement. Nor were they the only ones. It required more than a solid page of the printed record of the ceremony to list the friends and relatives of the groom. If the de Monde contingent was somewhat less numerous, it redressed the balance by its loftier social standing. The grandfather, Ecuyer de Briquet, was there, surrounded by a cluster of noble old maids and dowagers, resplendent in glittering costume. Two Chevaliers de Saint-Louis, "distantly related," graced the occasion; and, loftiest pinnacle of all, there were "the most high and illustrious Prince Rohan-Rochefort, Lieutenant-General of the Kingdom, and the most high and illustrious Dame d'Orléans de Rothelin, Princess Rohan-Rochefort."

Socially, Barère did well in contracting a family alliance with authentic nobility. On the other hand, if not the new "Madame de Vieuzac" herself, certainly the calculating mother could find consolation in the provisions of the marriage contract linking her family with a commoner. The newlyweds were handsomely provided for. Bertrand's parents contracted to turn over their

worldly goods to him, reserving only the usufruct for themselves
during their lifetime in addition to 10,000 livres for each of their
other children and 6,000 livres for themselves. They agreed to
lodge and feed the young people, the family, and their servants
in their own home, "at their own pot and fire." In the event
that Barère continued to exercise his profession at Toulouse,
the document went on, and the young couple would not live
with them, "the said father and mother engage themselves to
pay him an annual pension of 1,500 livres." Should they choose
not to live with the young couple, they would give Bertrand
the usufruct of the seigniory and the lay abbey of Biéouzac.
Finally, Bertrand's brother, "to whom this marriage is agreeable," promised to give the groom 7,000 livres, payable after
the death of his parents.

The de Mondes did well by the transaction, even better than
the legal arrangements reveal. That Elisabeth's *dot* was not
great is more than probable. The contract merely stated that
her parents made "a pure and simple donation of all their goods
. . . saving the usufruct and the enjoyment of half [for them-
selves] during their lifetime, the usufruct of the other half already being given to her." How little or how great those "goods"
were, we do not know. What the document also could not be
expected to state was that the de Mondes were riddled with
debts and that Bertrand had agreed to assume them. But a letter
written by Jean-Pierre many years later, on August 2, 1821,
which for more than a century lay buried in the pile of Barère
papers, supplies that information:

"I had spoken to you before [it reads] of the two letters which
I had [written?] to your spouse in which I informed her of your
sorry state abroad and that the moment had come when she
should reimburse you for the sums that you had advanced her
family [*sa maison*] in payment of their debts at the time of your
marriage. She gave a cold, dry reply in six lines, telling me that
she believed that her parents had left her her inheritance [*biens*]
free and clear. My second remained unanswered, although I

told her that she could take cognizance of the receipts of the sums that you had paid to free them. But no further reply [came] from her."

The marriage was a complete failure. In 1797, long after it had foundered, when his political career was broken and he was in hiding from the police, Barère wrote in that section of his *Mémoires* which he entitled "Melancholy Pages" that he had foreseen marital disaster at the time of the marriage itself. A leaden feeling weighed him down when he was pronouncing the solemn "yes." Tears flowed down "his bloodless cheeks" which only his observant mother could see. "Ah, Nature had given me a sort of aversion or contempt for riches. Her secret hint was ignored and my marriage was most unhappy." These words are pathetic nonsense: his pride would not permit him to acknowledge that he had been a fool.

In all probability it could not have been otherwise. More than twice his bride's age, the sophisticated groom had nothing in common with her. If she bored him, his emancipated outlook must in equal measure have affronted her inherited conservatism, even more, that of her mother. Bertrand tried to accommodate himself to the new life in his parents' home in Tarbes, and he allowed himself, reluctantly he wrote, to be installed in the office of councillor which his father had bought ten years earlier. But his heart was not in it; and a year later, in 1786, we find him busy again in Toulouse with his legal work and his writing. Details are lacking, but the evidence, such as it is, indicates that Elisabeth stayed on with her parents at Vic, where her mother—according to tradition—obtained solace for stooping to conquer by unabashed observations about would-be gentlemen.

Again the practicing attorney took up the pen, if anything more circumspectly than before. Why so circumspectly is not clear, possibly because he was cautiously feeling his way and did not wish to cut himself off entirely from his new social relations. In 1786 and again in 1787 he submitted his *Eloge de*

*Jean-Jacques Lefranc de Pompignan* to the Académie de Belles Lettres of Montauban. Pompignan, the First President of the Cour des Aides of Montauban at the time of his death in 1784, was a lawyer, administrator, and man of letters. He was also, as we have noted, a pompous, devout, and outspoken foe of the Enlightenment. Two decades earlier, in his reception speech before the French Academy, the antiphilosophe Pompignan had paid his respects in no uncertain terms to the tenets of the philosophes. They had picked up the gauntlet and the ensuing exchange between him and Voltaire was extraordinarily rancorous. So in becoming a competitor for a prize, Barère was again confronted with the delicate problem that he found with Séguier, to single out for praise facets of the subject's personality and career which would give to his essay the attributes of a eulogy without denaturing or denying his own liberal point of view.

Intellectual and ethical tightrope walking of this order called for skill and deftness, and Barère was now no tyro at the game. Besides, in fairness to him, there was much in Pompignan's life of which he could approve without unduly coercing his conscience. He could pay tribute to the savant and the learned admirer of classical antiquity and pen encomiums of the man of feeling, the friend and benefactor of the wretched and helpless. *Bienfaisance* and scholarship, did not Barère truly admire them! When he came to the famous quarrel between Pompignan and the philosophes, however, Barère rather gave the impression of writing with one eye fixed upon the Catholic judges of the contest: "While fame was publishing the glory of Pompignan, envy was poisoning his days; a false philosophy . . . withers his laurels. . . . He discovers the antique monuments of religion in a century when a haughty philosophy was rising upon the ruins of the faith of our fathers." How much was Barère nostalgically affirming the credo in which he had been reared and how much was he trimming his literary sails to prize winds? It is difficult to say. Only the results of his venture are known; the jurors gave him a large measure of approval, if not all he wished. He won the second prize.

From the aristocratic, conservative antiphilosophe Pompignan to Rousseau, the democratic-minded plebeian antiphilosophe, the distance was not so great that Barère could not cover it in a year's time; in fact in considerably less than a year's time. The first version of the essay which he composed about "the most sage of philosophers, the best of citizens," was also originally written in 1787. Since the Academy of Floral Games of Toulouse found no entry worthy of a prize that year, not even of honorable mention, the enterprising competitor had time to revise his composition and submit it again in 1788. This time his *Eloge de Jean-Jacques Rousseau, Citoyen de Genève,* fared better. The third prize went to him and with it the great honor, the greatest he had won thus far, of election to the academy itself. He was already a member of the Academy of Science, Inscriptions, and Belles Lettres. This new honor amply demonstrated that the learned world of Toulouse appreciated his talents. He could not complain of being slighted in his adopted city.

Some sixty octavo pages long in the edition published in 1806, the *Rousseau* was the most elaborate and the most ambitious of his literary efforts, also the most prolix. Verbosity notwithstanding, it was not lacking in appreciation of the historical significance of "the most eloquent writer, the most sublime orator of the eighteenth century." Barère based this evaluation upon his reading of works of Rousseau which disclosed the moralist and the man of letters. He did not concern himself in this essay with the great political writings. Perhaps he did not know *The Social Contract* too well (few readers before the Revolution did) or the *Considerations on the Government of Poland.* Possibly, he was playing safe. In any case, there was much in his own temperament to make him sympathetic to Rousseau's sensibility. He was himself a man of feeling with a strong strain of religiosity that in later life he mawkishly flaunted. He was ever an *âme sensible,* "responsive to the promptings of the heart." Many years later one of his contemporaries, in recalling the Barère he had known before the Revolution, wrote that "He made devout pilgrimages to the tomb of Jean-Jacques Rousseau in the Island of Poplars. ... He liked to distribute alms directly to passers-by, and when he had finished conversing with a poor wretch or perhaps a shrewd tramp, his eyes were still bathed in tears."

Allowing then for its conventional exaggeration, Barère's appreciation of Rousseau's tirades against the rationalist philosophers was sound as well as perceptive. He wrote with good sense as he commemorated Rousseau's feud with the rationalists of the day: "A cloud had arisen to hide from our eyes this invisible chain which links the human mind to the wisdom of all the ages. One instant had sufficed to spread a morality of calculation and personal interest. ... Imposing declarations had substituted a philosophy of reasoning for natural philosophy, desiccating the soul, dulling sensibility. ... They [the declarations] sought to enslave all minds under the pretext of generalizing our ideas. They disguise morality under a system of metaphysics and pretend to inspire love of virtue by the most abstract reasoning. A memorable day for letters: Rousseau appears to give full scope to true philosophy. He would embellish morality with imagination, he would think through feeling and depict instead of analyzing."

There was sympathetic insight too in Barère's comment on the revolution that Rousseau had effected in belles lettres. The novels of "that beneficent and sensitive being" were not penned, he wrote, "to flatter the vices of his century or to further the corruption of morals and manners, but to draw from the useful lessons of the passions the most commanding one of the human heart. ... To paint the duties of men, to give lessons to fathers, children, husbands and wives, friends, to the rich, even to Christians, such is the progress that the novel owes to the genius of Rousseau." And in this vein the essay went on, with page after page of rhetoric, until Barère came to his concluding apostrophe: "Unhappy shade . . . console yourself. . . . See you not Childhood crowning your image with respect and mothers raising to you . . . a monument as lasting as your writings. O! Jean-Jacques, every virtuous and sensitive being will recognize you as his master and model. The most eloquent painter of nature and truth cannot be the enemy of mankind."

In formal acknowledgment of his election as member (*mainteneur*) of the Academy of Floral Games, Barère gave his reception speech a month later, on March 2, 1788. The text itself unfortunately is not to be had, but its title, "On the Benefits of Philosophy," suggests that the essayist who had criticized *la philosophie* in conservative Montauban deemed it proper, perhaps only opportune, to extol its virtues in liberal Toulouse. There is no record of what his other auditors thought of it, but the First President of the Academy of Floral Games is reported as saying: "This young lawyer will go far. What a pity he has already sucked the impure milk of modern philosophy. Mark my words, this lawyer is a dangerous man."

The "dangerous man" went on that very year, in a prize competition set by the Academy of Bordeaux, to laud Rousseau's great contemporary, Montesquieu. To laud first Pompignan and then Rousseau and then, after praising the commoner Rousseau, extol the noble-born magistrate Montesquieu, patron saint of the conservative parlementaires, this was political eclecticism at its most flexible. Barère contrived in his *Eloge de Charles de Secondat, Baron de Montesquieu* to reiterate his own views. "Do not expect me," he wrote in a phrase reminiscent of what he had written in the *Furgole,* "to praise him for his noble origins. The man of genius receives his distinction from himself alone." He would set Montesquieu alongside the best of Athenian and Roman legislators and philosophers. Was he not an illustrious judge, an historian, and a scholar in whose person inventiveness was joined to method, profundity of learning to elevation of spirit, the graces of ancient poetry to the forcefulness of Roman eloquence! Like Solon, Montesquieu was a discerning traveler; like Pythagoras, he meditated deeply; he conversed like Plato; and he wrote like Tacitus. The *Esprit des lois,* in brief, was "a sublime work, the source of the ideas of Raynal, Robertson, Delolme, and Adam Smith, the inspiration for the reforms of Frederick II and Catherine of Russia." The author was "a profound philosopher, [who] sees in all the governments of the universe a single machine whose innumerable springs receive from the supreme legislator of the world a simple and uniform movement."

Barère continued in that vein with only a dissenting aside on Montesquieu's admiration for England: "England, that eternal rival of France, which has good reason to be proud of some of its constitutional laws, but which the atrocious and ambitious policy of its government will one day make execrable to the entire universe." That reservation apart, Barère discerned no flaws in Montesquieu's genius, and he concluded as he had begun: "You are no more, but your genius presides over the thinking of France. It is to your immortal works that we owe this modern disclosure of the workings of the public administration, this destruction of humiliating *corvées,* this abolition of inquisitorial salt taxes, and the restoration of this unbounded freedom which is the cry of trade." With the *Montesquieu* Barère's career as essayist came to a close.

That winter of 1787-1788 was a busy one for Barère. In addition to carrying on his regular law work, writing two *Eloges* and the reception speech, he found time to enroll as member of the newly founded Encyclopédique lodge of the Masonic Grand Orient at Toulouse. In that city, as elsewhere in France, the freemasons came from the ranks of the respectable and substantial citizens. Not only burghers, rich in worldly goods and intelligence, but liberal noblemen and ecclesiastics, and the most highly placed, joined lodges. Had anyone warned those fervid friends of mankind, those middle-of-the-road liberals, that they were contributing unwittingly to a violent revolution, they would have shuddered at the thought. Masonic relations with the authorities of the Old Regime were so little strained that one could almost say they were cordial. In most instances the regulations and bylaws expressly forbade discussion of controversial subjects, such as government and religion, and as a matter of fact, during the later, more radical, stages of the Revolution, the lodges fell under a cloud, not for their radicalism, but for their moderation.

In Toulouse, prospective members had a round dozen of chapters to pick from in 1788. The one that Barère joined, the Encyclopédique, drew its inspiration, as the name connotes, from the great *Encyclopédie* of Diderot, and it admitted as members only those who were "equipped with profound knowledge of the arts, sciences, and the crafts which they pursued." If we cannot repress a smile over this stilted statement of prerequisites for membership, we must remember the deep earnestness which imbued these well-wishers of the human race and tactfully ignore the gap between what they wished to have done and what they actually accomplished. At its most effective, Barère's group functioned somewhat after the manner of a modern lobby, putting concerted pressure upon the local authorities. More often, it was a well-intentioned discussion circle, assigning its members to fact-finding and investigating committees, each according to his special interests or aptitudes. While Barère was to find the contacts useful to him later in Paris, he could hardly have been called an active member. He was certainly not one of the petitioners who in 1787 asked leave to have the new chapter established. Nor was he one of its charter members. His name appears on the list of one committee which looked hopefully into the possibilities of setting up a bureau to do away with beggary. It was also on the list of a commission which conducted inquiries into so radical a question as that of improving the city water supply and setting up public drinking fountains. In any case, time did not permit him to do much in those fields of social welfare in which he had so long been interested. He was away from Toulouse for most of 1788 and made only a brief stopover there on his way back from Paris to Tarbes in January 1789.

He did not then know it, but an era ended when Barère left Toulouse to make his first trip to Paris. He knew, however, that he could look back with satisfaction upon the last thirteen years and with pride on the record of success which had attended his double career since his student days at the law school. The qualities which brought him social advancement and success in the legal profession also stood him in good stead in his literary avocation. Within the frame of deviousness which was particularly his, the prize essays neither concealed nor denatured his convictions. Their expression was frequently oblique. Still, in what he prudently underemphasized or refrained from saying, the *Eloges* disclose his political and social views accurately enough to give the intellectual measure of the man. He was a royalist and a true believer, that is clear; clear too is that alongside the traditionalist, from the start there was a reforming conservative who counted upon the parlements to hold absolutism, central and regional alike, in check. Little by little this attitude was tinctured by a kind of liberalism à la mode. In the essays he had not hesitated to condemn many hereditary privileges, openly denouncing abuses in the administration of the church and pleading for religious toleration. An enemy of the trading monopolies and guilds, he echoed the tenets of physiocracy, holding private property sacred and defending free economic enterprise, particularly in the grain trade. In all the *Eloges* he championed freedom of thought and expression. He was deeply concerned over the unsolved problems of social welfare, sincerely shocked by the spectacle of widespread poverty and human want. The humanitarian in him condemned the barbarity of criminal law and procedure; the philanthropist, the horrors of war.

Born and reared among the notables of the Robe and the Cloth, and advanced through his own successes to the rim of a higher order, Barère aspired to win what he could from the advantages of position, employing birth and brains to entrench himself solidly in the universe of the bourgeois progressives and utilizing his urbane grace and financial assets to penetrate into the ranks of the nobility. He was making the best of two worlds, looking forward to a regenerated France where demeaning distinctions would be done away with and careers would be open to talent, but also casting a yearning glance at the past, to consolidate his position among the privileged whose pretensions he upbraided. He was a discreet social critic and a practicing social climber.

A touch of unreality clung to all those prize contests. While in Toulouse Barère heard echoes of the crucial struggle even then raging in Versailles and Paris between the crown and its right-wing foes, they were little more than echoes. Devoid of personal and practical experience of the problems he had been discussing, he was shadowboxing with life. His political outlook derived largely from books. Not until he had the opportunity to observe directly what was happening could he submit his views to the test of reality and find out where he truly stood. That opportunity and that challenge came to him in 1788 when he went to the capital.

# A Revolutionist in the Making,
# 1788-1789

A LAWSUIT involving his father's feudal rights in Vieuzac took Barère to Paris in the spring of 1788. The suit was quickly settled following his father's death soon after he arrived. The visit proved a first great turning point in his life. He arrived early in May 1788, a reforming conservative and champion of the aristocratic parlements; he left Paris in January 1789, a convert to the ideal of government resting upon the consent of the governed. Up to this time all that he had written on politics had an academic ring. In Paris, where the century-long struggle between the sovereign courts and the crown was reaching its climax when he arrived, for the first time he was faced with reality.

Of the many problems besetting the government, the fiscal and political difficulties loomed most ominously. The roots lay buried in the past; immediately, the troubles stemmed from the revolutionary program of reform that Calonne, controller general of finance since 1783, had submitted to Louis XVI in a secret memorandum in November 1786. Having, for three years, tried palliatives, Calonne now understood that only sweeping, structural reforms could save France from the disaster of bankruptcy and worse. It was too late for halfway measures.

In the memorandum, he proposed a complete and thorough overhauling of the system of direct taxation. The existing direct taxes would be replaced by a new land tax, graduated and proportional to income, and payable by all landed proprietors irrespective of "order." To provide a more solid foundation for receipts, Calonne advised a large measure of internal free trade, including, when necessary, the shipment of grain from province to province; and to aid the petty peasant propietors he planned to lower the burden of indirect taxes. If these recommendations were startling, his plans for the reorganization of the governmental system were not less so. To break the influence of the *privilégiés* in the local administration he would have the crown establish, by decree, new provincial assemblies in the old central provinces. While still only consultative in character, they were to be elected by all landowners whatever their legal order might be.

These proposals were more than startling; they were revolutionary. With full awareness of what he was doing, Calonne was meeting the question of privilege head on and assigning to the monarchy the initiative and leadership of a popular movement against the aristocracy. If the land tax proposal were accepted and integrated with expanding agricultural production, the government would be assured of a steady and regular annual income for current needs and its dependence upon the parlements would be ended. Once the proposed provincial assemblies were set up and then gradually extended over the entire kingdom, the vast political influence of a privileged aristocracy, civil and military, secular and ecclesiastical, would be significantly curtailed and eventually completely destroyed.

Calonne's proposals faced certain rejection if they were submitted for registration, as normal procedure required, to the parlement of Paris. With the assent of Louis XVI, the minister therefore fell back upon the ingenious method that earlier kings had employed to bypass that sovereign court. An Assembly of Notables, comprising 144 grandees of the realm, all carefully screened for their loyalty to the crown, was called in February 1787 to endorse his proposals. If in the light of what subsequently happened, Calonne's procedure stands convicted of naïveté, it should be noted that he deliberately avoided an open conflict with the powerful magistrates of parlement, uncertain of the support he would get from the monarch and his colleagues in the ministry.

The recourse to the Notables proved a blunder of epic dimensions. From the outset the dignitaries had misgivings about the role set for them, and the irreverent mockery that the Parisian wags heaped upon the plan did not diminish their doubts. The combination of their own reservations, skeptical public opinion, and lack of court support for Calonne, not to speak of conspicuous non-cooperation on the part of his ministerial colleagues, undid the audacious reformer. He was unceremoniously dropped and disgraced, succeeded by his foremost critic in the Assembly, Loménie de Brienne, the archbishop of Toulouse. While clever and opportunistic, Brienne fared no better than his hapless predecessor, whose retirement he had not delayed. Common sense compelled him to revive some of Calonne's proposals, but after six weeks of bickering, further discussion became pointless, and the king dissolved the Assembly of Notables in May 1787.

With the government's plan blocked, Brienne had no alternative but to turn to the parlement of Paris. The popularity of all the parlements was at its zenith, most politically minded Frenchmen accepting at face value the magistrates' claims to be the true intermediaries between the king and his people and the legitimate defenders of the latter's contractual rights. Brienne's able colleague, Lamoignon, the keeper of the seals, strongly counselled strong-arm tactics to break the parlementaires, but Brienne, like Calonne before him, shrank from an open rupture. Persuasion and conciliation seemed the better course. Discretion that promised something seemed preferable to valor that ensured defeat.

Nevertheless, his conciliatory tactics only encouraged opposition instead of lessening it. The break came despite vast concessions. The land tax proposal was dropped, a concession verging upon surrender. Though the provincial assemblies came into being, they did so in an emasculated form far from Calonne's original intention. Encouraged by this evidence of government weakness, the parlement of Paris balked at registering a new loan. Only a *lit de justice* forced its hand. That act and other measures did not keep the parlementaires, from the fall of 1787 to the spring of 1788, from showering the country with protests against "ministerial despotism." One proposal they made in the course of the worsening controversy rooted itself in popular consciousness. It was a clever tactical move, the suggestion they insinuated, for the Estates General to be summoned within five years to examine and solve the entire problem of taxation and financial administration. "Estates General" had an electrifying ring, and well it might, considering that there had been no meeting of the Estates General since 1614. Liberals and progressives rejoiced, believing that the magistrates were committing themselves to a program of representative government. How wrong they were, they were quickly to discover; meantime the lines of battle for a final struggle between the courts and the crown were being drawn.

The call for battle came on May 8, 1788, when Lamoignon hurled a thunderbolt against the parlementaires, a stroke in the manner of Chancellor Maupeou. By the terms of his edicts the parlements were suspended from office and forty-seven new courts were set up to replace them. A new plenary court, its members nominated by Louis XVI, was established to register royal edicts. At the same time the crown, seeking popular approval, abolished some procedural abuses that had long been condemned.

Exactly at the moment when Lamoignon was secretly drafting his edicts, Barère arrived in Paris. He was already there when the parlement of Paris, getting wind of Lamoignon's measure, issued a "Proclamation of the Fundamental Laws of the Kingdom." The parlementaires proclaimed their loyalty to the monarch, but emphatically reiterated that the voting of all new taxes belonged to the Estates General. Further, they took a solemn oath to uphold the right of the superior courts not to register royal edicts unless the latter conformed to existing customs and rights. With this declaration the parlementaires threw down the gauntlet to the king. The smoldering revolt of the nobility broke into flame.

Where would Barère take his stand? Would he remain what he was, the partisan—and the dupe—of parlementaires in their disingenuous advocacy of popular rights; or would he, abjuring old loyalties, rally to the reforming ministers who would end abuses by arbitrary means? It was a difficult decision for an inexperienced provincial to make. He was bewildered, all but overwhelmed: "I found myself in this famous capital, galvanized by the rapid . . . and incessant movement of men and things. A thousand confused and contradictory ideas passed through my astonished head." "I decided," he wrote, "to introduce some order in my feelings and observations by writing down each night everything that had engaged me in action or struck me during the day. It is a diary that I wrote for myself alone and to keep track of the use of [my] time. . . ." This manuscript existed as late as 1838; it has since disappeared, and that part which is published has been retouched. Barère originally sent it to one of the two co-editors of his *Mémoires*, asking him to insert it at the appropriate place in the narrative. Shortly after, he wrote to the second of his literary executors giving him editorial carte blanche: "I beg of you to go over this manuscript and to suppress, amend, and abridge all that your excellent mind judges proper."

The permission was only too well followed. Much that one would like to see has been deleted and passages are transposed with cavalier disregard of chronology. Still, the lengthy excerpts from "Le dernier jour de Paris sous l'Ancien Régime," which are included in the published text of his *Mémoires*, recreate the mood in which Barère lived during those tumultuous months and make it possible to trace the main lines along which his views evolved.

Writing for himself alone, he was free from the fixed requirements of literary competitions and self-imposed reserve. Where the *Eloges* are contrived, the diary is spontaneous. The writing is fresh, vivid, exciting, and, above all, frank. He could wear his heart on his sleeve: no prize would be lost if it showed. The provincial proved a tireless tourist, stimulated by the glories of *la ville lumière* into paying it the tribute of time and energy that it expects and usually wins. But love, Paris did not win from him. Neither then, nor during the quarter of a century that he lived there, from 1789 on, nor again during his brief sojourn in the capital after his return from exile in 1830, did Barère write about it with anything resembling affection. Rousseauist indignation against urban luxury, the provincial's sense of insecurity, and the rustic's nostalgia for the open country mark the "Last Days." Penning trite reflections on the corruption and injustices of modern society did not keep him from taking in the town. He visited the monuments and palaces, the galleries and museums, listened to concerts, attended the ballet, and went often to the theatre. Most of all, he followed the great debate on politics.

This is to anticipate. In the first entries of the journal he showed himself, as might be expected, the fervid defender of the magistrates. There was a comment concerning the troops which had broken into the Palace of Justice and arrested two parlementaires who had written the defiant declaration against Lamoignon: "People will speak of it as a measure which disgraced the reign of Louis XVI." Then came indignant observations on the enforced registration of the Lamoignon edict. While he conceded that the changes in criminal procedure had much to commend them, he saw nothing but an arbitrary denial of the law in the creation of a court itself. "A coup d'état," he called it, adding that "despotism could not have taken a longer step . . . in two centuries. . . . The members are named for life and they are permitted only to make remonstrances. . . . 'The will of the king alone is the law,' [and] these words need no commentary; this is the style of oriental despots."

In that state of mind Barère paid a visit to Versailles, where he had his first view of the royal family. The palace itself he found overpowering, even frightening, and he left it in haste to visit the royal gardens. "The sight of verdure and playing waters refreshed my senses and quieted my indignation. . . ." While he was slowly regaining his equanimity the royal family and its entourage passed in review. Barère followed the cortege from palace to church, taking rapid notes for the character sketches that he later expanded and inserted in his diary. No one escaped unscathed, not even His Majesty: "The king was about five feet five inches tall. . . . His eyes were blue without the slightest expression, and he had a coarse laugh which sounded imbecilic. . . . His bearing was completely awkward and he had all the external appearance of a big fat boy who had been badly brought up. . . . He was very greedy and liked wine; he even drank so much of it that he almost never left the table without being a little drunk, and then his prattling became embarrassing and boring for whomever it pleased him to entertain. . . . [Still] his judgment was sound, he wished for the good, and he would always have done it, if his natural inclination had been seconded by a really patriotic minister."

While Barère recorded his impressions, the organized revolt of the aristocracy was paralyzing public life. Petitions and protests against the Lamoignon edicts flowed in from almost every corner of the realm. The provincial parlements which were requested to register them formed correspondence committees, established communications from town to town, circulated scathing critiques of the crown, and stirred up the masses as well as the lesser figures of the law whose living depended upon them. The local aristocracy made common cause with the Robe, ostensibly defending their immunities and historic liberties, in reality aspiring to get control of the several provincial assemblies which had been established some months earlier. The court nobility, irritated by the reduction of their pensions, had already entered the fray, and in June the Cloth joined with the Robe and Sword in defying the ministry. The assembly of the clergy voted down a large "gift" requested by Brienne and endorsed the demand of the magistrates for the speedy convocation of the Estates General.

Stirring up the populace was easiest in those centers of separatism where provincial estates still existed. Rioting broke out in provincial capitals, in Bordeaux, Toulouse, Dijon, and Pau, where the traditions of regionalism were deeply rooted. In Béarn the mountaineers descended into Pau and compelled the intendant to restore the local parlement. There was worse rioting in Brittany, and at Grenoble in Dauphiné the parlement, with the support of the nobility, organized a revolt against the intendant and took over control of the city.

With sedition and rebellion rocking France and the government seemingly paralyzed, Barère was caught in a great quandary. On the one hand, he was incapable of understanding that the monarchy was employing wrong means of doing good and he still considered its policy one of "despotism." Too intelligent and too honest, on the other hand, to condone the stand of the parlements' supporters, he scolded the court aristocracy for its refusal to agree to a reduction of pensions. "The people live in the mire. . . . The rich alone enjoy life. . . . The grandees form a nation apart. . . . They speak often of the public good and they never contribute to it. . . . " When he learned that a clerical assembly had moved to reduce the "free gift" of the clergy to the monarchy by 75 per cent, meantime insisting that at the coming Estates General the deputies of the clergy sit as a separate order, he made an angry entry: "Their master had said . . . 'My kingdom is not of this world' and our modern apostles claim that it is for them to rule the world. . . . Why should not this order of the clergy be merged with the order from which it comes? Why should it cast a separate vote which sure to be added . . . to the voice of the nobility, only stills the feeble voice and overrules the single vote of the Third Estate?"

By July, Brienne was nearing the end of his resources. Still hoping to placate the opposition, he announced that the Estates General would soon be assembled. At the same time, to get a lien on the good will of the liberals, he addressed a general appeal to the nation for information and guidance concerning the impending meeting. First a trickle, then a torrent of pamphlets answered his appeal. The liberals were contented; not so the parlements and their supporters, and Brienne gave ground to them. In August he set the date of May 1, 1789, for the meeting of the Estates General and suspended the application of the Lamoignon edicts. These concessions gained the monarchy nothing; on August 16 Brienne was forced to suspend treasury payments. The move was tantamount to a declaration of bankruptcy and, consequently, his already precarious position became completely untenable. He was forced to resign on the 25th, whereupon the king very reluctantly summoned Jacques Necker.

Necker was a Protestant, a foreigner, a commoner, and a liberal, but there was no escaping the appointment of a man universally regarded as a financial wizard. For a month there was a lull in the storm while everyone waited to see what the Genevese banker would do to solve the crisis. From the moneyed interests which had immense confidence in his competence the director general of finance obtained a short-term loan which sufficed to tide over the government. To quiet the aristocratic party he reinstated the suspended parlements and agreed to have Lamoignon dropped. There matters stood up to the last week of September, when almost overnight the conflict took a dramatic new turn.

By that date Barère's thinking had also taken a new direction. The diary, though tantalizingly fragmentary, suggests that under the pressures of political excitement and the influence of new liberal acquaintances and friends he jettisoned his old views. From the "Nationals" or the "Patriots," as the liberal critics called themselves, the ambitious provincial caught the vision of a regenerated France, reconstituted on the foundations of popular sovereignty. While those exciting changes were transforming the political atmosphere, he was busily attending courses and sitting in on lectures at the scientific and literary society called the Lycée, "the veritable moral and political [center] of opposition to the court and ministerial power." On his free evenings he settled down to read in the public reading room of the Lycée or followed the heated discussions on current affairs in another hall. "It was there that I often heard the most interesting literary or political discussions," among them a vigorous dispute on the merits of the old monarchy versus "the recent example of the United States [with] their fine federal constitution and their declaration of rights."

At the hotel where he lodged, he made the acquaintance of an old friend of Jefferson and Lafayette, Philip Mazzei. Mazzei, sometime neighbor of Jefferson in Virginia, was then serving as an unofficial intelligence officer of the king of Poland to whom he was dispatching periodic bulletins on political developments. "I had occasion," wrote Barère, "to speak with this learned diplomat on the state of public opinion and the ferment of ideas so stirred up by contemporary developments." More than likely, he heard *viva voce* what Mazzei wrote in his dispatch of July 28 to his royal sponsor: "Aristocratic tyranny is struggling against despotism and monarchy. The pretext is the good of the people, to which, however, the aristocracy here, as everywhere else, and always, is far more opposed than is the monarch."

If not directly from Mazzei, with whom he often spoke of "civil liberty [which was] entirely unknown in France, but . . . respected in the United States," he picked up other new notions from circles to which Mazzei introduced him. He was taken to the salon of the mother of the Duke of La Rochefoucauld. "There you will see," Mazzei told him, "people who are most distinguished for their philosophy and enlightenment." The Italian diplomat did not exaggerate. Among others, Barère met and conversed with Condorcet, Jefferson, and Lafayette. Here too the conversation turned on civil liberty, but most of all, he reported on "the Americans and the constitution they had drawn up."

The Patriots had many salons at their disposal in Paris, not the least of which was Lafayette's home, where the "Americans" gathered, those liberal aristocrats who had fought side by side with the American colonists against Great Britain. Political clubs were mushrooming in Paris and step by step the Patriots were moving toward a break in their loose working agreement with the aristocracy. They were on the verge of establishing themselves as an independent force and making articulate the aspirations of the France that was turning away from the past to look forward to a new future and the example of America. Barère was not a member of any of the clubs, and he had no entry into the most influential one of all, the recently established and somewhat mysterious Society of Thirty. But he was becoming one in spirit with these "friends of liberty." In the ranks of the Patriots were the notables of the progressive bourgeoisie, writers, scientists, jurists, and men of affairs, like Volney, Lacretelle, Brissot, Target, and Laborde.

Recruits from the liberal aristocracy also joined their ranks, men like Condorcet, the Marquis Lafayette, the Counts Alexandre Lameth and Ségur, the Dukes of Aiguillon and La Rochefoucauld, and Viscount Noailles. There were liberal magistrates in their midst, like Adrien Duport at whose home the Thirty were meeting, and forward-looking ecclesiastics, Champion de Cicé, Archbishop of Bordeaux, Boisgelin, Archbishop of Aix, and the young and gracious Abbé de Périgord, to be better known as Talleyrand. The Abbé Siéyès, about to win immense fame as a pamphleteer, cooperated with the liberal critics, as did the already famous Huguenot pastor, Rabaut de Saint-Etienne, and the still more famous publicist, Count Mirabeau.

Barère took stock in those summer months and drew up a balance sheet of his views on the key figures in the struggle between the monarchy and the law courts. He gave guarded approval to Maurepas, because the old courtier had defended the parlements against despotism, but he unreservedly sang the praises of Turgot, whom Maurepas's intrigues had undermined. On Necker his verdict was severe: "crafty," "charlatan," and "agent of despotism." On Brienne his judgment was mixed. After characterizing that enemy of the courts as "cruel and cunning," Barère added, perhaps as an afterthought: "It is he, people will one day say, who sowed the seeds of tax equality, freedom of expression among the people . . . elevated the Third Estate by making it understand its rights which had been usurped by nobles, magistrates, and priests. . . . Never was so much written in favor of the people and liberty as during his ministry."

If Barère was still loyal to the parlements, as this passage shows, he was nevertheless moving away from them. Sometime in midsummer, shortly after July 21, he broke away completely. On that day the opposition in Dauphiné revoked the old provincial estates which had not met for many years, and reconstituted them as a single body in which the commoners had as many representatives as the two other orders combined. Barère's diary recorded the news jubilantly: "Soon the parlements will be no more," it read, "the Third Estate has intervened in the struggle. It owes the Estates General to parlement, but it must strip that dangerous company of its excessive power." Then came a phrase which his earlier views would never have permitted him to write: "The spring of the parlements is worn out in the political machine. Present needs call for new intermediary bodies."

When his diary picks up the story again in November, the demand for a representative assembly was irresistible. On September 23 the parlement of Paris had returned in triumph, but only two days later, as it registered the declaration for the meeting of the Estates General, its members made a fateful decision. Convinced more than ever by the rejoicing of the Paris populace that their strength was at its peak, the magistrates proposed that the Estates General should be constituted as they had been the last time they met in 1614. The Patriots suddenly saw clearly what was happening, for the statement of the parlementaires meant that the three orders would meet separately, that each would have an equal number of representatives, and that when they assembled the voting would be not by head but by order. Thus it was all but certain that the Third Estate would be and remain in a minority of one to two. The declaration of the parlementaires implied that by "nation" they meant themselves and themselves alone. The character of the political struggle immediately changed, and the exultation of the Patriots over the calling of the Estates General turned into indignation against their associates. Their own future, and the future of France as they envisaged it, now lay in their own hands.

It lay, so far as government action was concerned, largely in Necker's hands. He himself was in favor of doubling the number of deputies from the Third Estate as well as voting in common. Caught between fear that his colleagues in the royal council would not support him in open conflict with parlement and reluctance to estrange the Patriots, Necker fell back upon Calonne's expedient. He recalled the Notables to consider the question and make recommendations, which he hoped would accord with his views.

The liberal opposition brought pressure upon the grandees, and no group was more active at this critical juncture than the Society of Thirty. The tone of the pamphlets reflected the altered situation. Pamphlets had been appearing since midsummer when Brienne made his call for information. In October and November, however, they rained down upon the country, as many as twenty-five new ones a week. In all of them the resolution of the Patriots to speak in the name of the French nation was patent. They called for a declaration of rights which would recognize the claims of all citizens to equality and liberty. They demanded that the nation be sovereign, and by nation they meant essentially people like themselves, the educated and cultivated middle class. In all the pamphlets, too, emphasis fell heavily upon drafting a written constitution.

Barère's diary was resumed in November when the second Assembly of Notables was in session and it mirrored the striking change in atmosphere. He explored in his thoughts the possible outcome of attempting to have Patriots and Notables work jointly and follow the sweeping course set by the thirteen American colonies, but he was not hopeful over the second assembly. Like Condorcet he decided that it would be wiser to set limited objectives for the Patriots. "If we allowed liberty, equality, and reason to prevail we would be doing too much at one time. Prudence counsels us to use this assembly first to obtain a little improvement for the people; for experience teaches us to do not all that should be done, but what one can and the little that is possible. . . . It [America] had no ambitious and hypocritical clergy . . . no nobility . . . no privileged orders exempt from part of the taxes; no absurd system of criminal laws and contradictory and inadequate civil laws. . . . It had not stifled industry, agriculture, trade under a mass of prohibitive laws. . . . Are we up to the Americans. . . ? Here, all circumstances are absolutely different and call for different action. The former had as leaders Jefferson, Franklin, Washington. . . . We have only a d'Esprémenil, Bergasse, and Praslin. Does that inspire the same confidence?"

Barère's decision to follow the counsel of prudence was characteristic and his words were striking. Even more striking is that the words he set down in the pages of his diary were not his own but those that Condorcet had written in a letter to Mazzei. How that letter came to Barère is a question on which neither he nor Mazzei nor Condorcet throw light: did Mazzei give it to him or did Condorcet; did one of them allow him to make a copy; why did he fail to acknowledge his source? All that is certain is that the words were not his and he sincerely adhered to the opinion that they expressed: the American example was ruled out and Barère agreed that France would have to settle for less. But he would have the less more than the Notables were preparing, more than "an aristocratic assembly in fact and in its composition, [more than] ambitious power in the hands of a perpetual corps. . . . What we need is a constitution founded on equality, a constitution that may readily be improved."

As he followed developments in Paris and out, Barère placed his hopes more and more on the monarchy. He noted that from all sides "There is a general cry for 'the doubling of the Third.' If the Notables do not wish to hear it, it will have to reach the ears of the sovereign." Five months earlier he had stormed over the "oriental despotism" of the monarchy; now he explained: "What could we not expect from a government which has destroyed the *corvées*, freed the serfs of the Jura and Saint-Cloud, restored civil status to Protestants, from a government which followed bad principles in all these acts only from fear of shocking the defenders of the aristocracy! . . . What then is the so-called difficulty in destroying abuses? . . . Does anyone believe that we would have to send troops to force citizens to elect deputies without distinction of order? All that would be easy, if one truly wished it. . . . All we need is a firm prince of genius or character with true love for his people."

Increased trust in the government of Louis XVI and more vigorous attacks upon the privileged classes now came together from his pen: "We must fear the aristocracy above all others. . . . We can bring it to terms only by force. . . . The judicial power . . . is an obstacle to all reforms. . . . If we allow parlement to regain enough authority to cease fearing the court and feel certain of being circumspectly treated by it, then we will still see long intervals elapse between the different convocations of national assemblies. The assembly which is being prepared would prove only a scarecrow skillfully used by parlement to show the court how much it had to fear. This is equally true for the nobility and the clergy."

Toward the end of November he commented approvingly on the reprimand that the king had administered to the Notables when they presumed to call his attention to the spate of pamphlets; and when two weeks later parlement, changing its tactics, disavowed its September 25 declaration, Barère jeered at its hypocrisy and rejoiced over a fresh royal reprimand: "Never have finer words come from the French throne, so full of sense and justice. . . . At long last the parlements are put in their place. . . . The nation can and should limit them henceforth to serving the public order instead of disturbing it."

After the king dismissed the Notables, Necker turned from them and parlement alike to the royal council to gain approval of his plan to double the Third Estate. Despite strong opposition within the council, he prevailed; and on December 27 the royal council announced its decision: the Third Estate would have the same number of representatives as the clergy and the nobility combined. The *Résultat*, as the decision was called, was announced to the nation at the end of the year and widely hailed as "Necker's New Year's Gift" to France. The monarchy had finally asserted its authority after a long series of retreats; the liberal wing of the opposition had won a great victory. At least it appeared so for the moment.

At this point Barère's diary comes to a close. It is not surprising that he was elated over the triumph of "the virtuous minister," as he now called the same Necker whom only a few months back he had reviled as "an agent of despotism." He was less enthusiastic than might have been expected about the future, foreseeing trouble over the failure of the council to decide whether the voting would be by head or order: "The king should at least have made a provisional ruling. . . . In fact, if the two privileged orders persist in clinging to the old practices, the Third Estate will be sacrificed; since the Third Estate cannot shut its eyes at this point, we may expect protest, and complete inactivity will result." Fearing "innumerable difficulties," he ended his diary with a plea for prudence: "I ask only that the assembly of the nation be moderate in the demands that it will make. It is up to the strongest not to win support by violence; it is up to him who has the best cause not to degrade it by excesses. O! How well things would go in this fine assembly if pride, personal interest and prejudices did not keep it from consulting reason, justice, and nature."

When he left shivering and frozen Paris shortly after the *Résultat*, Barère's intellectual preparation had been completed. The circumspect traditionalist had become a convinced but realistic patriot, echoing the convictions and reflecting most of the hopes of liberal idealists in a revolution by persuasion. He had not yet used the specific term itself, but he was already thinking of the Estates General as a "national assembly." With his new associates he looked forward to the establishment of a community of "citizens," a "patrie," and a "nation."

Leaving Paris early in January 1789, he made his way in easy stages to Tarbes, which he reached by the end of March. He stopped off en route at Montpellier and Toulouse to talk with local dignitaries over the prospects of the Estates General, but of those talks nothing specific is known. As he traveled south, the general regulations governing the coming elections were being sent out to regional authorities for posting. The electoral provisions in those writs of instructions were extraordinarily liberal, particularly with respect to the voters of the Third Estate. All in all, five million Frenchmen went to the polls, the largest body of voters that old Europe had ever known.

Excitement was high in Tarbes when on March 18 the seneschal, Count Angos, issued an ordinance for Bigorre, calling on each of the 288 local communities of the province to assemble within a week's time to draw up its cahier and elect two delegates to a special session. At that session the preliminary cahiers would be synthesized and the four deputies to the Estates General elected, two for the Third Estate and one each for the other two orders. The return of the native son naturally did not pass unnoticed and Barère's fellow townsmen turned to him for explanation of the political mysteries in the distant capital. Technically, he might have claimed noble status, since he had inherited the fief of Vieuzac on his father's death in April of the preceding year, but he considered himself a commoner and as such he was elected fifth of the twelve delegates to whom Tarbes was entitled by its population.

Nearly all the preliminary elections were over by the last day of March and on the following day the delegates assembled in the church of Saint-Jean. Civic guards patrolled the streets to keep order, church bells were tolling, and at eight o'clock in the morning of April 1, the delegates took their seats. The clergy took their places to the right of the presiding officer, prelates resplendent in their traditional attire and poor country priests in their modest soutanes. The nobles sat to the left, arrayed in brilliant costume, swords by their side. In the center seats were the commoners, "elegantly clad," so said a contemporary record, which added that poor peasants were in their humble Sunday best and mountaineers in rough shepherds' garb. The seneschal formally opened proceedings, the mass was celebrated. Then followed time-consuming preliminaries, terminating in the decision that each of the orders would betake itself to separate halls in order to draft its cahier and elect deputies to the Estates General.

Barère was a strong candidate from the start for election as one of the two deputies from the Third Estate. But a delay of several weeks held up the vote, during which his opponents made much of the opportunity to stress the fact that he, a *soi-disant* commoner, possessed noble fiefs, one at Vieuzac, the other at Anclades. The balloting finally began on April 21 and six stormy sessions had to be held before the results were announced. Barère was elected, the first of the two deputies, even then completely overshadowing his future colleague, a respected lawyer named Pierre Dupont de Luz. The nobility named the Baron de Gonnes and the clergy Jacques Rivière, a priest of liberal views.

By the time of election the drafting of the general cahier of the Third Estate of Bigorre had also been completed. Barère

was one of the twenty-four commissioners, and without question the most influential, on whom the task devolved of blending
the 288 preliminary cahiers into a composite text. Neither the
minutes of proceedings nor the original manuscript of the cahier
are available, only a contemporary printed text, *Cahier de Doléances, Plaintes et Remontrances de l'Ordre du Tiers Etat du
Pays et Comté de Bigorre.* The authenticity of the cahier is un-
questioned, but Barère's exact role in drawing it up is difficult if
not impossible to determine. Besides serving on the editorial
commission, he also compiled an extensive collection of papers
whose contents strongly suggest that he played a leading part
in the editorial revision. That collection included a twenty-page
manuscript, each page of which was signed by the lieutenant
general of Bigorre, which points to the possibility that it is the
original manuscript copy of the cahier. It contained also an un-
dated and unsigned report of the commissioners written in
Barère's hand, as well as another ten-page manuscript, also in
his hand, entitled "Minutes of the Assembly of the Third Estate
of Bigorre." There was, lastly, a manuscript table of contents for
the entire collection, this too, like the others, in his handwriting.

Close examination of the printed cahier itself, which he signed
first, lends weight to the supposition that Barère had much to
do with drafting it. The preamble is in spirit and letter close to
his diary: "The order of the commons of the Seneschal's Court
of Bigorre, imbued with heartfelt gratitude toward a sovereign
who restores its rights . . . is happy today to proclaim his virtues,
his good intentions, and his goodness. . . . Called to deliberate
on its interests, invited to give itself a constitution, without
which there is no good government, it can fully appreciate a
revolution which is so important for its happiness. Its moderation and dignity will enable it to profit from the national and
political advantages which a virtuous and enlightened minister
has just assured it in joint action with the most popular of monarchs."

The five major sections into which the cahier was divided echo the criticism and the demands of the bourgeois pamphlets that Barère surely had read during his stay in Paris and Versailles. The first section, on constitutional reform, began by calling for abolition of the "humiliating distinctions" of 1614 in the new Estates General, where the Third Estate was to be equal in power and influence to the other orders. There should be periodic meetings of the Estates General in the future. The rights of the people, consisting of "security, personal liberty, and private property," were to be "irrevocably fixed," while infringements upon those rights, such as *lettres de cachet*, should be abolished. No tax was to be voted and no law passed without the consent of "the assembled nation"; and the Estates General were to verify the national debt and establish economies in the administration. All posts in the military, the church, and the magistracy were to be opened to the Third Estate. Taxation was to be equal for all citizens and ministers held accountable for their expenditures. For deputies, there was to be parliamentary immunity; for all citizens, a guarantee of the secrecy of the mails.

Circumspection and prudence were as characteristic of this first section as was the repetition of bourgeois demands. Articles 2 and 3 left for the future to decide whether the Estates General would meet and vote in a single chamber or in two ( one for the commons and the second for the other two orders combined ) or in three separate bodies: "The Estates General will begin by assuming the form and organization most suitable for the happiness and the stability of the state." There was no explicit demand for a declaration of rights, only an inferential reference to it. Existing taxes not voted by the nation should ultimately be suppressed, but, pending future definitive arrangements, they were to be maintained. Further, while the rights of the nation were to be safeguarded ( article 18 ), "no infringement, even implicit [should] be made of the sacred rights of the monarch and the royal prerogative is to be kept in all its plenitude and force." The separation of the executive from the legislative power was not asked for, only that those powers "should be distinguished from each other in many respects." Though the Estates General were to vote the laws (article 20), these laws would then be "refused or sanctioned by the king."

The second section, concerning the reform of the tax system, adhered closely to the staple recommendations of the physiocrats as well as to Barère's own ideas. Simple custom boundaries situated on the political frontiers would be "very useful for freedom of trade." Taxes on prime commodities, because they bore heavily upon the poor, should be done away with. The entire tax structure should be reviewed and simplified, the *capitation* abolished and the *taille* and the *vingtièmes* changed into "a single moderate land tax, applicable to all lands without distinction."

The third section, dealing with reform of the laws and administration of justice, also followed familiar middle-class recommendations. Sale and purchase of legal positions were to be abolished, and the irremovability of magistrates confirmed. Civil and criminal procedure should be simplified and regularized and all special courts suppressed. New civil and criminal codes, applicable to all citizens, should be drawn up. Due process was to be followed and, except in case of "public crimes," prisoners under arrest allowed bail. A series of articles then called for the end of pluralism in ecclesiastical offices and an upward revision of salaries for priests whose income was limited to the *portion congrue* (an income providing a bare living). Three articles in particular revealed the cautious spirit of the framers of the document. Most of the preliminary cahiers had demanded the outright abolition of the tithe, without compensation, but article 4 asked only that the tithe be revised downward. There was no demand for abolition of seigniorial rights; article 23 asked only for "the redemption . . . on such terms as the Estates General chose to set in order to reconcile the rights of liberty with those of property. . . . " Most significant of all, the second article of the cahier called for strong provincial counterweights to the authority of the central lawmaking bodies: "The laws voted by the nation and sanctioned by the king should be sent to the provincial estates for recording and observance; they should also be sent to the tribunals [parlements] to be registered and placed under the safekeeping of the courts which will not be permitted to modify them. But they [the parlements] will continue to be responsible for the execution of ordinances of the kingdom and [maintenance] of constitutional and national rights by recalling the principle, if need arose and whenever they deem that those rights are attacked or only threatened, by making remonstrances to the king and voicing their criticism to the assembled nation." Moreover, for the duration of the present Estates General, the deputies of Bigorre were to refer to a provincial commission on matters for which they had received no written guidance from the cahier itself. They were subject in short to binding instructions.

Insistence upon maintaining and strengthening provincial and municipal rights was more emphatic still in the last two sections. Far from being abolished, the existing provincial estates of Bigorre were to be reformed and reinvigorated in order to serve the interests of the inhabitants of the province. The point was underscored in an addendum that Bigorre was not to take an oath of loyalty to its seigneur until he had solemnly agreed to govern according to existing customs. The rights which the provincial estates should protect and the reforms they would make were specifically enumerated. They were to abolish militia service, execrated for its severity, and suppress harmful variations in weights and measures. It lay within their jurisdiction to assess and apportion the quota of national taxes which fell upon Bigorre, as well as to pay it directly to the royal treasury. They were to be given exclusive control over all matters affecting public utility, such as road-building, bridges, highways, and quarries. Supervision of communal requests for such local needs as repairs, food supply, and the administration of the famous thermal establishments of the province devolved upon them. To further this decentralization of administration and the democratization of local public activities, justice was to be free and equal for all. Craft guilds and trade associations were to be suppressed, subject to indemnification.

In the separate sixth section, signed by twenty-two commissioners including Barère, the cahier emphatically affirmed that it was not enough to call the attention of the monarch and the Estates General to general evils. "Too often specific evils and local abuses" were ignored. "It is in the back country that arbitrary authority makes rapid progress, petty vexations and customary abuses are kept up, ordinances disregarded, and laws unenforced." Forty-six articles of this section enumerated the many economic grievances of the anonymous poorer inhabitants of Bigorre and made recommendations for their alleviation.

Nowhere did that synthesis echo the embittered tone against the privileged classes and the well-to-do bourgeoisie which was so marked in the parish cahiers. Yet, considering the social background of the formulators, it is a forceful statement. It recognized the pressing need for limiting the right of parceling out the commons and making that legal right contingent upon the specific request of the local community and verfication by the provincial estates. It approved the request of private individuals to keep arms for protection of person and property. Special tolls on goods which burdened free trade were condemned; ecclesiastical fees for baptism, marriage, and burial were to be ended. There was to be full freedom to buy and sell articles of prime necessity at fairs and markets. Billeting of troops should henceforth become a public charge borne equally by all, and provisions against beggary were to be strictly enforced. Personal feudal rights, such as *banalités* and *corvées* and all others involving personal servitude, should be abolished as contrary to human freedom. Finally, if the intendants were to be retained in office, their powers should be regulated by a law protecting "the sacred rights of persons and property."

## Revolutionist in the Making

The internal evidence of form, the orderliness of the argument, and the legalistic precision of the language, all establish a case for Barère as chief editor of the cahier. In substance it paralleled what he believed, and it reflected his personality: the stereotyped liberalism of the pamphlets and the prudent, cautious procedure he had advocated in the diary. Much too that the parish cahiers desired, the general cahier kept: equality of taxation, free and equal justice, legal equality of the Third Estate, restoration of municipal liberties, reformation of the provincial estates, abolition of the militia. But the denunciations the final cahier toned down, omitting illustrations which highlighted the poverty and the burdens upon the poor. "Let us tell him [the king]," read the Deliberations of the Commons of Tarbes of December 1788, "that we live under arbitrary laws . . . that our resources are exhausted because they are the prey of tax-collectors . . . that the largest class, the working class, is the most wretched, the least protected, the most in want, that fathers find it hard to feed their families . . . that the wretched Third Estate is deprived of all support, that it languishes in its misery and the only things it has too much of are oppression and tears."

In the last analysis what is significant about the cahier is not whether it owed more or less to Barère, but that in it was outlined a program for action that he followed. If he was to show himself one of the most useful deputies of the Constituent Assembly, it was because he was prepared in advance to pursue the policy he did. He believed in the sacred rights of the individual, the supremacy of the general will, and the authority of the national assembly. At the same time, and within the regenerated nation, he insisted upon maintaining the historical liberties of the provincial regions. In social outlook, though he was closest to the physiocrats before the Estates General met, his bourgeois liberalism was tinctured by Rousseauist, democratic sympathy for the poor. In his thinking the great achievements of the Constituent Assembly of 1789-1791 were accomplished before they were made.

## ✠ I V ✠

# *The Cautious Revolutionist:*
# *Versailles, 1789*

THE cahier drafted and the elections completed, the Bigorre deputies left for Versailles. All four travelled together, Barère and Dupont, the two deputies of the Third Estate, François de Gonnes, representing the nobility, and the deputy of the clergy, Jacques Rivière. They arrived in Versailles on May 4 in time for the solemn procession and the mass in the church of Saint-Louis, confidently awaiting the formal opening session set for the following day. Barère's hopes travelled with him. The nation had spoken; the king would not fail to heed its appeal.

Characteristically, Louis XVI was undecided, torn between the advice of Necker to have the deputies sit and vote in common and the instruction of other counsellors who pressed him not to make further concessions. The opening session of May 5 was disappointing, dashing the hopes of "the commons," as the deputies of the Third Estate called themselves, for the king's speech in effect served notice that he intended to keep the old order of voting. But to verify their credentials separately, as the commons were ordered to do, meant only one thing, that constitutional reforms were doomed in advance. They played for time, neither yielding nor organizing themselves as a separate body, and actively negotiated with the other orders to have credentials verified together.

Negotiations broke down early in June, but the commons had kept ranks during those five weeks. Better still, time worked for them. Public opinion openly favored them; many of the lower clergy did not conceal their sympathy; and they found leaders from their own ranks in Siéyès and Mirabeau. On June 12, after a final appeal to the nobility, which was rejected, they "cut the cable," beginning the verification of credentials not as representatives of their own order but as deputies of the nation. The deadlock was broken; the Revolution was under way.

Up to this point Barère had done little more, he stated, than "listen and observe." A celebrity in Tarbes and Toulouse, in Versailles he was only one among several hundred obscure and unknown provincial deputies. He found lodgings in the apartment of a chaplain of the Count Artois, directly opposite the meeting place of the Salle des Menus Plaisirs, an arrangement which ensured him the advantages of convenient geographical location and the promise of useful social connections. As a matter of fact he did more than listen and observe. Making use of his masonic contacts, and joining the Breton Club, which was the forerunner of the Jacobin Club, he cultivated the friendship of the more influential spokesmen of the Third Estate: "Two men in particular drew my attention . . . Count Mirabeau . . . [and] M. Bailly. . . . My youth and my admiration for their talents were my only claim to their attention." He chose wisely in linking himself with the famous scientist, presiding officer of the new assembly, and the *déclassé* nobleman whose forceful personality had already impressed itself upon his associates. They were, as he phrased it later in a masterly understatement, "a precious mine for a young deputy to work." Emulating his new friends, "M. Barrère [sic] de Vieuzac" answered the roll call on the 12th and had his credentials verified as deputy for Bigorre. With their encouragement he spoke from the floor for the first time on the 15th, addressing himself to Siéyès' motion that the assembly drop the title of "Estates General" and call itself "Assembly of the Kingdom and Verified Representatives of the French Nation." The commons, he declared, were justified by "reason and equity" in their act, for their mission was "to establish and not maintain a constitution." On the 17th he voted in favor of the appellation "National Assembly" and also supported an accompanying declaration which affirmed that to the assembly and to it alone belonged the right "to interpret and present the general will of the nation." He never deviated from that stand.

These resolutions were open defiance of the king, and by adhering to them Barère had entered upon his revolutionary career. Three days later, on the 20th, in their memorable Oath of the Tennis Court, the revolutionists, Barère with them, swore "never to separate and to reassemble whenever circumstances demanded until the constitution of the kingdom was completed." David's famous commemorative and incomplete painting did indeed transmit the occasion "to posterity," as he hoped it would. In the central foreground was the lean Bailly, solemnly administering the oath, and surrounding him his excited colleagues, their arms outstretched in acceptance. In the left foreground of the painting is an eager-eyed, attentive young deputy, notebook balanced on his knees, poised to jot down all he could see and hear.

The handsome reporter was Barère. Aware of the great public interest in what was happening and mindful of the wants of his countrymen, the enterprising lawyer turned deputy had taken advantage of the relaxed censorship to become a journalist as well. The first issue of *Le Point du Jour ou Résultat de ce qui s'est passé la veille* appeared on June 19, the day before the Tennis Court Oath. The newspaper was to be published continuously until October 1, 1791.

Barère himself was the principal reporter and, with the exception of a young compatriot from Tarbes, Dominique Demerville, who prepared copy for him, the only one. His name, however, was at no time listed either as owner, editor, or reporter. The name of the chief printer, Laporte, was not given until the 27th issue, and on that occasion the subscription rate of six livres for Paris and seven livres, ten sous for the provinces was also announced. Another week elapsed before a brief statement indicated that subscriptions could be made through the bookseller Cussac at Nos. 7 and 8, Palais Royal, and that the Paris municipality had granted postal privileges to the newspaper. Cussac in all likelihood had a financial stake in the venture, and in the early issues he kept reminding the readers not to forget to renew their subscriptions. That reminder was not necessary for long. Although circulation figures are not available, two years later one of Barère's fellow deputies made a malicious observation that Barère was obviously in no hurry to have the parliamentary debates end, since his paper was bringing in 1,000 *écus* (3,000 livres) every month. The figure seems fantastically high for it is the equivalent of the wages that a laborer would earn in several years' work, but the comment at least fits in with other evidence that Barère's undertaking was hardly a financial catastrophe.

As *Le Point du Jour* established itself, the small octavo pages of each issue increased in number, rising from an initial four to six or eight, even to an occasional sixteen. Checking copy presumably also grew easier with the passage of time and never again, after the issue of June 26, did Barère have to apologize to readers for "facts contrary to the truth" which had slipped into the paper or crave their indulgence for mistakes occasioned by the scant time at the editor's disposal to set up and distribute the daily issue after the close of the assembly session. In view of opportunities for self-aggrandizement Barère was exceptionally restrained in references to himself, but his friends and the deputies whom he would have for friends, Bailly and Mirabeau, the Duke of Orléans and the Duke of Aiguillon, were frequently mentioned. From the beginning, too, he was led by his political sympathy or a grasp of what was politically significant to single out for "the purity of his intentions and his political zeal" a young, still unknown deputy from Artois, whom he referred to variously as "M. Robertpierre," "M. Roberspierre," and "M. Robespierre."

Within its self-imposed limitations *Le Point du Jour* stands close to the top of all the newspapers of the period as a source of information and critical commentary on parliamentary proceedings. Barère followed those debates closely, summarizing where he thought a brief résumé would suffice and giving *in extenso* speeches and reports of special importance. Intelligent se-

lectivity, scrupulous regard for accuracy, and a sense of conti-
nuity were the hallmarks of a newspaper whose dignified tone,
respect for the opinions of participants, and discerning interpretation won it admiration and respect. The astute Mazzei read
it faithfully before forwarding it to the king of Poland, for he
found in it, he wrote, "an exact, brief, clear, and prompt" account of what was happening in the assembly.

Valuable as it is for the light that it throws upon the debates,
the newspaper is equally valuable for what it discloses of Barère
himself in that first assembly. Its pages reflect without blur or
tarnish the idealistic middle-class nationalism which imbued
him. Consistently and forcefully, with sincerity of ends tempered by studied conciliation over means, Barère echoed the
aspirations and defended the values of the progressive property-
minded liberals who identified their own interests with the
cause of the nation. Moreover, through the issues of *Le Point
du Jour* one may trace the evolution of Barère's thinking as he
moved toward a more democratic conception of the principles
of 1789.

When Louis XVI deployed troops around the assembly hall
and in the Royal Session of June 23 ordered the deputies to
leave the chamber and meet separately by "orders" or "estates,"
Barère kept his seat. He was not intimidated, only grievously
disappointed in the king. In reporting the crisis in *Le Point du
Jour* he limited himself to the comment that the Royal Session
was "a cloud which hides the throne from the citizens," but in
a long letter which he addressed to his constituents he elaborated upon his misgivings. After relating how the clergy and the
nobility obeyed the king's instructions, he went on: "We remained in the hall. We decided to adhere to our preceding resolutions and declared that the deputies were immune from arrest. We meet tomorrow morning, ready for whatever comes.
We will show the courage and the caution befitting a great nation."

Since it was the king and not the deputies who gave way, Barère plucked up courage, and a week later *Le Point du Jour* was hopefully scanning the future. Barère rejoiced that "that fatal variety of local practices and scattered administrative units which keep this vast and great kingdom a bizarre mixture of Gothic laws, feudal tyrannies, constitutional weaknesses, and ancient abuses [will soon be ended]. . . . True statesmen will readily see the beginning of the renovation which will substitute a great nation for divided provinces . . . and replace feudal France with a free and enlightened France."

Having taken his stand that sovereignty resided in the nation and that the deputies alone embodied the general will, Barère now found it neither desirable nor possible to support the binding instructions (*mandats impératifs*) upon the deputies which he had earlier advocated in the cahier of the Third Estate of Bigorre. He voted to annul them, stating that to hold the deputies of the Constituent Assembly, as the National Assembly was now called, by instructions from electors, hampered the constitution-makers. In its needs and its sovereign will the nation, he held, was superior even to the natural rights of individuals. As early as June 19 he had invoked that principle to justify the public authorities who were searching the granaries of private individuals for concealed and sorely needed food-stores. There were times, he wrote, "when we must momentarily violate general laws in the interest of public security." A month later, on July 27, he condoned infringements of the secrecy of the mail: "At this moment, when the fatherland is in danger, there are no means which it is not obliged to use to make itself secure." Those utterances are enormously significant, particularly for the light they cast upon his later career. The year was still 1789, but the spirit of 1793 was already present.

He himself had little to do with the dramatic denouement of July 14 which brought the struggle between king and deputies to its first great climax. In *Le Point du Jour* he protested respectfully against the "frightening and dangerous" course pursued by Louis XVI in summoning troops. He was one of a delegation of deputies that made formal representations to the king on that score. Probably because of his protest he was also named to a deputation which officially announced the fall of the Bastille to Louis XVI, and, on the 15th, to still another which escorted the monarch on his painful, ceremonial trip to Paris.

The assembly survived its first test, but in Barère's heart grave misgivings remained. He was uneasy over the king's attitude. It was very well, he commented in *Le Point du Jour,* for deputies to voice their great joy when they learned that the king would appear before the assembly, but thoughtful deputies, he added, were pointing out that to applaud the king was premature, that it would be wiser to wait for His Majesty to announce what he would do. Even when Louis XVI humbled himself, Barère was unconvinced of the monarch's good faith.

Misgivings concerning the king and the "aristos" were paralleled by his fears of danger from the other flank. He was no less uneasy over the Paris crowds which had seized arms and used force against the authorities than about the authorities themselves. In his carefully guarded account of the king's arrival in Paris Barère contrived to express his conviction that the uprising of the Parisian masses, helpful as it was, constituted a threat to the existence of the assembly. He vividly described "the tumultuous movements" of the 14th, "the most masculine courage" of the "militia of passionate citizens" who had seized arms to defend themselves and had taken the Bastille by storm. He then went on to contrast that turbulence to the orderly discipline which succeeded it on the 15th. The new militia, he wrote, carried its arms "like an olive branch," respectful of the "friends of the public good" in the Hôtel de Ville. The hostile weapons had become arms to protect "the representatives of the nation" who walked peacefully between the lines of cheering Parisians showering them with blessings, encouragement, even caresses "in the most touching terms and infinitely varied forms." Those floral tributes to the Parisians were less expressions of his joy than veiled intimations of his fears. His mistrust and fear of the Paris masses never left him. In rough notes which served him as copy for *Le Point du Jour* he jotted down something quite different, which he did not choose to print. Two municipal officials, Foulon and Bertier de Sauvigny, had been beheaded and their mutilated bodies dragged through the streets of Paris. This act, his notes read, was the work of "the people in their cruel fury."

The deputies, who had emerged victorious in their trial with the king in Versailles, were almost immediately confronted with danger from the provinces. A peasant jacquerie, gathering force every day, was sweeping over the country. Thousands of peasants, fed by ignorance of what was taking place in Versailles, by fear of a "royal plot," and by wild rumors about "brigands" in the pay of "aristos," had fallen victim to panic. They rose, muskets, scythes, flails, and clubs in hand, to defend themselves and sell their lives dearly against nameless enemies. This "Great Fear" soon subsided, for there were no "brigands," at least no more than normally. As panic turned to rage, the peasants avenged themselves and their ancestors by venting age-old hatreds against the lords of the manor. They put castles and manors to the torch, burned records of their obligations, murdered hated stewards, and seized the common lands. While in Versailles the deputies were effecting a political revolution, a social insurrection gripped many stretches of rural France.

Barère, like many other deputies, was aghast over the news. His instinct was for repression; however, sober thought counselled compromise and concessions. He was not alone in that attitude, and in his *Mémoires* he lifts the veil over arrangements that were worked out at a caucus of the Breton Club to quiet the storm. "In the days preceding August 4," he wrote, "I saw many conferences and noted in them the influence of Mm. de Pgd. [Talleyrand of Périgord] . . . Ch. de No. [Charles Noailles]

. . . the Duke d'Aig [Duke of Aiguillon] . . . A.Lam . . . [Lameth].
. . . I recalled clearly that having approached those gentlemen
on the 3rd and the 4th of August, I spoke to them of the plan of
several members of the commons to propose the abolition of
feudal rights, purchasable offices, privileges, and immunities of
the two clerical and noble orders. These gentlemen dissuaded
me from the plan and the instructions I had concerning feudal
rights and purchasable offices. . . . It must be the nobles, they
said to me, who propose the destruction of the feudal rights and
the parlementaires who propose the abolition of purchasable
offices. That would be better."

"Those gentlemen" planned a salvaging operation. While
they intended to have personal manorial rights abolished outright without compensation, the abolition of real rights was to
be made subject to redemption fees. The sacrificial frenzy of the
August 4 meeting of the assembly went far beyond their intentions, however. Serfdom and personal rights were abolished
according to plan, and real rights with compensations for the
owners. The deputies then went on to vote out of existence the
entire Old Regime of privileges. The system of seigniorial justice was suppressed. Sale and purchase of judicial posts were
forbidden, with compensation for present incumbents. Justice
was made free and equal for all. Along with equality before
the judge there was to be equality before the tax collector.
Citizens became eligible for all civil and military offices. Personal honors and immunities went by the board, together with
corporate privileges of orders, provinces, and towns.

The wild, memorable night of August 4 wrote the blueprints
of a profound revolution in human relations. Allaying the
menace of a class war which could have torn France apart, the
surrender of privileges established the basis of a true social
democracy. Barère had not been prepared to go that far. Nevertheless, confronted by a *fait accompli*, he put his reservations

aside and refrained from saying what he knew of the immediate antecedent calculations. He made haste to congratulate the privileged classes for their generous sacrifices and pointedly rejoiced over the future that August 4 opened for France and humanity. "There was no haggling over any particular detail, no petty debate, no stormy discussion to profane it; by itself alone the patriotism of the French nobility dealt more terrible blows to the feudal colossus than it had received from the coercive policy of Louis XI and of Richelieu. Philosophy required a century to shake the foundation of this frightful regime; the national assembly needed but an instant to efface even the traces of this odious and tyrannical servitude."

Some days later, after the hastily voted decrees had been recast in definitive and sober terms, *Le Point du Jour* was still rhapsodizing: "The grandeur of the sacrifices, the impetuosity of the resolutions, the thoughtful editing of a solemn deliberation which the most noble patriotism alone had inspired, the rapid and undoubted stimulus which these resolutions will give to the [drafting of the] constitution, the relief and the reforms which they provide, the imposing tableau they present of what a great nation which is willing to regenerate itself can do, give to this decree an entirely new character and make it worthy in every possible respect of the attention of the universe."

He was relieved in welcoming developments which almost miraculously spared France civil war and gave his country a new birth of freedom. With sensitive grasp of correct political tactics he was quick to understand that to shower praise upon the aristocracy for sacrifices not initially planned was one way not to have them regret what did take place. Perhaps, as a letter to his own tenants of the community of Vieuzac reveals, he was also honestly carried away by the generosity of the sacrifices. While the assembly was still revising the original decrees, he conveyed the glad tidings, stipulating that the letter was to be opened and read before their general assembly.

Versailles, August 8, 1789

My dear friends [it read]:

It is a pleasure to address you thus as I transmit news which is as pleasant for me as for you yourselves.

The inhabitants of the province of Bigorre had instructed me to request the abolition of personal feudal rights and the redemption of real feudal rights. We have just obtained it from the generosity and the patriotism of the French nobility. The inhabitants of Vieusac [sic] should be the first to benefit.

Something would be lacking in the joy which this decree of the National Assembly inspires in me if I were not able to have the general desire most fully realized. Consequently, I declare to you through this letter that all entry and exit rights, law of blood, watch and guard, and other feudal inventions are abolished among you. I tell you that we shall very easily reach an agreement on the rights which are truly real and constitute legitimate property, that I shall be considerate toward the poor in the matter of redemptions. . . . And I pray you to accept as a gift the redemption of the banality of the mill and all others in the records of the seigniory. You are free from this moment to grind your grain where you will, and there will never be any dispute between us on this point. I am leaving to the justice of those who are now in litigation to come to terms with the steward, unless they wish me to settle all discussion when I return. But all law suits are terminated on this subject from this moment on. I shall be eager to see you again to carry out in a more solemn manner the justice that I am rendering to you and the duty I am fulfilling. As for the gift, it is so slight that you should not even think of it. The happiest day of my life will be the one when I shall record in your midst that your lands are free and ask only to live in your memory and that of your children.

Although I shall no longer be the feudal lord of your estate, I shall always be your friend, your patron, your defender and your supporter on all occasions when I shall be able to serve you and your families.

Accept the sincere expression of these feelings from the most affectionate of your friends and servitors.

BARÈRE, deputy of the Commons of Bigorre
to the National Assembly

Considerations of political expediency tinctured his attitude. It was not disadvantageous, by swimming with a current which in any case he could not easily have bucked, to win the good will of voters who had displayed some reluctance toward electing him deputy to the Estates General. Yet his letter was not lacking in generosity of spirit and conviction; and long before the assembly officially abolished titles of nobility, Barère voluntarily relinquished the noble particle, "de Vieuzac," and signed himself simply "Barère, deputy of the Commons."

The good will he sought apparently was gained. A year later "Messieurs, the municipal officials of Vieuzac" addressed a formal letter to the National Assembly attesting their confidence in him. Barère, for his part, acknowledged their communication and assured them again of his "attachment, gratitude and consideration" and his determination to work "with the liveliest interest [for] the happiness and well-being of the inhabitants of Vieuzac." One good flourish deserved another in Gascony, and the council general of the commune of Vieuzac swept its collective panache (September 7, 1790) in a still wider arc:

"After it had been read, we unanimously agreed that the letter of M. Barère, our *ci-devant* lord, deputy of the National Assembly, shall be inserted into the register of our deliberations in testimony of our deep gratitude, so that this great man, the benefactor of this locality [Vieuzac], shall live surrounded by the same respect among our descendants as he is with us, that our children, enjoying the sweet benefits of the Constitution, exclaim as we now do: Barère contributed to it; he had been our Lord or rather our Father, he became our legislator; although we know that the reputation of this great man is spread over the entire universe, we wish his name to be rooted in Vieuzac, so that our descendants may never forget the benefits with which this good father has overwhelmed us, and that they may follow our example in respecting a cherished family, as much for its probity as because it gave birth to the author of our happiness."

Barère may have only been getting a lien upon the support of his constituents in these epistolatory exchanges. Nonetheless, shortly after he gave up his manorial rights, he voluntarily renounced the redemption claim to the magistracy which his father had bought him many years earlier for eight thousand livres. According to the August 4 decrees, though the sale and purchase of judicial offices were abolished, compensation rights were granted to existing officeholders. Why then did Barère, to the consternation of his family and at great financial sacrifice for himself, announce publicly in the assembly (September 25) that he was giving up his councillorship outright? Most certainly out of a mixture of motives. Possibly because he sensed that in the existing desperate financial state the government could not find funds to reimburse him outright; hence he might just as well get political credit for what he would be unable to receive in cash. He may also have decided that if his gesture toward Vieuzac paid rich political dividends, a similar maneuver vis-à-vis Tarbes, where the partisans of the Old Regime were stirring up the inhabitants against him, might also yield profit. Yet it would be unfair not to recognize, even if he was moved by shrewdness, that he was also propelled by sensibility and nationalist fervor. He had long been opposed to the sale of judicial positions and perhaps he was carried away by the government's appeal for "patriotic gifts" to tide it over its crisis. The *Courrier français* paid tribute to his sacrifice, listing it under the rubric, "Acts of Patriotism and Generosity."

After the violence of August, as order was slowly restored in the countryside, the deputies resumed their discussion of the constitution, which disorder had interrupted. Neither in the debates on the Declaration of Rights of Man and Citizen nor on the first articles of the constitution did Barère initiate policy. In the debate on whether the Declaration should precede or follow the constitution, he favored the first alternative, holding that the rights of men were engraved in their hearts. As for the Declaration itself, he could object to none of its provisions, since it was a proclamation "for all climes, all centuries, all governments."

The debates on the royal veto and the number of chambers that the new legislature was to have also found him hewing to the line of Siéyès and the Constitutionalists. He spoke against the proposal to permit ministers to be selected from the ranks of the deputies and also against allowing them to participate in the debates. He was opposed to the grant of an absolute veto to the king and had his doubts about the suspensive veto which the assembly finally voted. Favoring a single-chamber legislature, he informed his readers that a bicameral assembly was not only reminiscent of the Roman Senate which had betrayed the interests of Rome, but also of "that relic of feudalism, the English upper house."

When the moderates of the assembly voted Louis XVI a suspensive veto, they had hoped in return to obtain the king's sanction of the August 4 decrees and the Declaration of Rights. Ever vacillating and indecisive, Louis XVI was induced to withhold his cooperation, his advisers encouraging him in the staggering aberration that by the use of military force he could dissolve the assembly and regain control over a situation which had passed out of his hands. The miscalculation could not have been more grievous. As the summer drew to a close, Paris again was vibrant with suspicion and defiance of his good will. The efforts of conservative deputies to strengthen the royal prerogative had politically estranged the easily excited and large working-class population. The bread shortage and rising prices embittered consumers, who blamed Versailles for both. To those grievances of artisans were added the recriminations of many skilled craftsmen whom the first emigration of well-to-do customers, following the events of July 14, had thrown into the ranks of the unemployed. During the entire month of September, journalists, pamphleteers, and local ward leaders took turns at stirring up anti-monarchical feeling. Thus the storm, which all month had gathered force, finally broke, and on October 5 a crowd of women and some men disguised as women, reluctantly followed by Lafayette and the National Guard, marched on Versailles to recall the king to his duty.

Barère, remembering July 14, viewed the preparations for a new insurrection with many misgivings. While reports were already circulating within Paris that the national cockade had deliberately been trampled under foot by royalist officers (a legend like many another), *Le Point du Jour* was still praising the king for his love of justice and his devotion to the people. Even as late as October 5 when the final letter of the monarch, in which he refused to sanction the legislation, was being read in the assembly, the issue of Barère's newspaper for that day, prepared the night before, was still blandly reporting that "the most popular, the most just, and the most adored monarch in Europe" could not be guilty of such language. Although, along with Robespierre, Barère had taken the floor that same day to point out that the Declaration of Rights required no royal acceptance, that the king could neither reject nor criticize the articles of the constitution, and that the executive authority existed only by virtue of the constitution which created it, he was as loath then, as he had been during the July crisis, to have the rights and the authority of the assembly confirmed by the help of the Paris sans-culottes. At the very moment when the Parisians were moving along the road to Versailles, he was concluding his speech with a motion that "the presiding officer, accompanied by a delegation, would go to the king, request the publication of the Declaration of the Rights of Man, and present the constitutional articles purely and simply for his acceptance and promulgation."

It was now too late for constitutional procedure; and when the presence of the Parisian women in the assembly hall made it impossible to spurn their unrequested aid, Barère bent before the pressure of the masses. He did on this occasion what he was to do under similar circumstances almost exactly four years later when, contrary to all his personal desires, he gave way to the organized sans-culottes and agreed to make terror the official policy of the government. The king too, yielding to the show of force, grudgingly accepted the decrees without qualification. Louis XVI yielded again on the following day, October 6, this time to true force; when a group of rioters broke into the royal palace, he gave in completely. He agreed, as the mob which had gathered under the balcony clamored that he do, to take up his residence in Paris. Ten days later the assembly followed him there.

Barère was a member of a delegation of deputies that accompanied the king and the royal family. If he was not happy that for the second time in three months the assembly's triumph over the king had come about through the intervention of the masses, with political caution he carefully refrained from saying so openly. He had provided the nobility with good reasons for the sacrifices of August 4; he now judged it both wiser and more expedient to flatter and woo—and warn—the Parisian stalwarts into cooperation than run the risk of estranging and losing their needed support by threats. "Who could really think," so ran *Le Point du Jour*, "that the capital would ever be separated in wishes and interest from the majority of the nation? Is it not to the courageous citizens of Paris that we owe the two great revolutions which by a single stroke destroyed aristocracy and despotism! We would ill recognize the public opinion of the first city of the world, we would be slandering it, if even for a moment we held that the theatre of French liberty has become its specter. Every one of its inhabitants is the guardian of the public law and the guarantee of the safe being of each representative of the nation."

His profession of confidence in the Parisians may or may not have been taken at its face value by his readers. It was evident, however much he affected the contrary, that he was filled with grave forebodings over those tactics of direct action which he hated and feared during all his political career. Accordingly, when the deputies made formal provision to ensure tranquillity in Paris, he raised no objections, either from the floor or in the columns of his newspaper. He accepted without demurrer the stringent decree of October 21 which authorized the municipality of the new capital to proclaim martial law and use troops to disperse gatherings, armed or not, which threatened the public order. He was to act in similar manner in July 1791 when the Constituent Assembly invoked martial law against the sans-culottes who challenged its authority.

# ⚜ V ⚜

## *Militant Liberal and Prudent Democrat, 1789-1791*

As PEACE of a sort descended upon the countryside, the deputies returned to their normal routine, secure for the immediate moment from the hostility of the crowds and shielded against the friendliness of their hosts in the new capital. Abolition of binding instructions had freed them of interference and supervision from distant constituents; and delegations of petitioners in Paris only interrupted parliamentary procedure without intimidating the lawmakers. Bills were openly debated, and with turbulence, but since the basic preparatory work was done in advance and behind the scenes by standing committees, neither heated debates nor noisy delegations counted for much in the final process. The times were propitious for peaceful change.

Political parties in the modern sense, under organized control and discipline, did not exist. In a loose way the assembly was divided into several large groups, and party lines, such as they were, were as often crossed as kept. The deputies, priding themselves on their independence, followed "the promptings of the heart," which had its reasons not less cogent than those of the mind. Barère took his seat from the first with the Constitutionalists of the left-center, as the largest group into which the prerevolutionary Patriots had split was called. There sat aloof, oracular Siéyès, "Prophet Mohammed"; there was Talleyrand, wily and realistic; there also, distinguished jurists of the Old Regime, influential and respected, Target, Tronchin, and Merlin de Douai. Mirabeau, when it suited the purposes of that political titan, voted with them, and on occasion the humanitarian Abbé Grégoire, too, zealously Christian in his apostolate for religious toleration. To the left was the "Triumvirate" of Barnave, Duport, and Charles de Lameth, and far to the extreme left, the few outspoken democrats over whom the bespectacled Maximilien Robespierre by his integrity and courage was little by little establishing ascendancy.

Barère found convenient lodgings at No. 13, rue des Filles de St. Thomas, not far from the Riding School (*Manège*) where the deputies held their meetings and nearer still to the Palais Royal, headquarters of the Duke of Orléans, to which he was even then no stranger. Linked by conviction to liberals within the assembly, he kept similar company outside. He joined the masonic lodge, "Société des Amis de la Vérité," possibly also the lodge of the "Neuf Soeurs." In *La Bouche de Fer*, the house organ of the "Amis de la Vérité," he was soon described as "Barère, a young man of high hopes who employed all his resources to achieve the triumph of the nation." He also joined the Jacobins, as the Society of the Friends of the Constitution was generally known, which for long remained a citadel of middle-class orthodoxy. Nothing in the record could lead one to believe that he was affiliated with the more radical popular societies, such as the Cordeliers, nor did he take part in grass-root politics at the ward (*section*) assembly level.

For a year and a half after the October Days of 1789 the deputies applied themselves methodically to their task of regenerating the institutions of France and giving the country the constitution that they had promised in the Tennis Court Oath. A contemporary chronicler reported of Barère that "He saves all his talents and lights for *Le Point du Jour.*" The praise, if praise it was and not a covert reproach, was unwarranted. There was much else beyond the journal, to which he did give much time, to absorb his attention and energy. In the extraordinary and rapid, too rapid, reorganization of institutions he was no principal, only a dedicated second. If initiation of policy was not his, he worked determinedly to rid France of what he had already called "the fatal variety of laws" which made France a disunited state. Taking his stand on the principle of popular sovereignty, he consistently supported the liberal program of nation-making "to replace feudal France by a free and enlightened France." Speaking more and more often from the floor, busying himself as much as time permitted with lobbying in the modern manner, discharging important committee assignments that came to him, he became the man of the assembly.

The hopes Barère had expressed in *Le Point du Jour* on July 14 that the deputies would quickly draw up a concise and provisional sketch of the constitution were not realized. The constitution was voted slowly—so at least it seemed to the more impatient among them—article by article, and the work was not completed and revised until late in 1791. On the score of suffrage Barère accepted the distinction that the majority drew between civil rights, which were guaranteed by the Declaration of Rights for all citizens, and suffrage rights, which were to be restricted to citizens who paid the equivalent in taxes of the wages for three days' labor. Though he would not deny political rights to "domestics," for he found that term too elastic, he favored excluding "wage servants" from the ranks of voting citizens (October 27) on the ground that they lacked "the free and independent will required for exercising suffrage rights." He concurred too (October 29) in the view that to allow propertyless citizens eligibility for service in the legislature and the administration would be to "turn the state over to a handful of men who were too little attached to the fatherland." Without property qualifications, in short, there could be neither good lawmakers nor lasting laws. In all this, he said and believed what good progressives said and believed. Yet there was a difference. He refused to support the motion that candidates for office, in order to become eligible, be required to pay the *marc d'argent*, a tax payment roughly equivalent to the wages of unskilled labor for fifty days' work. So he substituted a proposal that the candidate be required to pay a tax not higher than the value of thirty days' labor. That this compromise suggestion was not accepted is not particularly important in the history of the Revolution, but it illustrates Barère's thinking and his nature.

Latent democratic impulses pushed him to the left, mistrust of the masses held him back.

With other liberals of 1789 he voted for the motion to have the number of deputies for each new electoral unit determined according to population and to limit the electoral procedure itself to two stages. By the spring of 1791 he was also supporting Robespierre's proposal to have all free Negro proprietors in the West Indies colonies admitted to full citizenship, their color notwithstanding. To this he added a typical qualification, "in the future." His feelings impelled him in one direction, but the West Indies were distant while the planters' lobby in Paris was close and powerful. He did not choose to espouse a radical cause with conspicuous eagerness.

These reservations did not obtain for native white Frenchmen who had been politically disqualified on religious grounds, and in *Le Point du Jour* Barère took up their cause. The reign of Louis XVI should not be sullied, he wrote, "by the blind and bloody fanaticism" which in less happy days had pillaged and tortured the unhappy Jews. He derided the arguments against granting them their civic rights, "as if they were not our fellow-citizens and brothers, as if all men should not be equal before political and civil laws." His position concerning Protestants was equally forthright. When the Huguenot pastor, Rabaut de Saint-Etienne, was elected presiding officer of the assembly, Barère saw in that election the victory of philosophy over prejudice and an object lesson in tolerance for all Europe; and on December 9, 1790, he spoke with Rousseauist fervor and characteristic personal sententiousness on the great act of justice which restored to refugee Huguenots the estates which had been confiscated from their ancestors after the revocation of the Edict of Nantes.

Barère was not honored by criticism from the rightist press, for he was not yet important enough for attack. Nor for a long time did a democratic newspaper like the *Journal de Perlet* make more than passing references to the man whose name it first recorded either as "Bareyre de Vieuzat" or as "Bareyre de Vieuzac," for most certainly he was no outstanding democrat. But the liberal journals, three in particular, Mirabeau's *Courrier de Provence*, Gorsas' *Courrier des départemens*, and the *Courrier français* of Poncelin early began to take notice of his observations from the floor. Both Mirabeau and Gorsas commented favorably when Barère rose to defend the political rights of individuals who had fallen afoul of the Old Regime authorities for their writing. Referring to the case of Rousseau who had been condemned by the parlement of Paris, he exclaimed, "As if such an indictment were proof of a crime." In the pages of Prudhomme's weekly, *Révolutions de Paris,* there was approval of his "judicious report" recommending abolition of the rights of alienage (*droits d'aubaine*), which gave to the king the succession rights to the estates of deceased resident foreigners. His report on the overcrowding of the Paris prisons drew from Mirabeau's *Courrier* a brief reference to the "sentiment of humanity and equity" which imbued it, while Gorsas in the *Courrier des départemens,* and Camille Desmoulins in the *Révolutions de France et de Brabant,* referred at considerable length to his moving plea that a pension be granted to the widow of Jean-Jacques Rousseau. Dear to Barère's own heart too was his work as a member of the committee on *lettres de cachet,* to which he was elected in November 1789, in checking on the registers of state prisons and releasing victims of arbitrary state action.

For whatever reasons, pressure of heavy committee assignments and taxing newspaper work, he shared less than one might have expected in the sweeping judicial changes which the assembly speedily effected. In *Le Point du Jour,* it is true, he gave ample coverage to the discussions, but he himself took little part in them. He agreed that the judicial branch of the government should be separated from the legislative and provision made for full legal defense of the accused. The election of magistrates, as might have been foreseen, won his endorsement. So, too, the motion to have one criminal court for each department and a proposal, which was not carried, to establish juries in both civil and criminal cases. Otherwise, he did not participate in the important debates which established the equality of citizens before the law.

Barère's role was minor in the legislation designed to regularize the civil and religious relations of the church with the new revolutionary state. What he did was consistent with views already expressed and went beyond them. He voted for abolition of the tithe and suppression of monastic vows. In the autumn of 1789, the financial resources of the government were becoming exhausted and the thinking of many deputies was turning toward the nationalization and sale of the vast church property as a solution of its needs. Again, not surprisingly, he echoed proposals to have church lands placed in escrow on the condition that the state take over expenses of worship, salaries of the clergy, maintenance of church buildings, and poor relief; on November 2, when that decision was made, he took the floor to deny that the king had the right under the constitution to pass upon it. In the spring of 1790, after the implementing decree was voted for that fundamental change in the administration of church property, Barère communicated the news to his uncle Bertrand in Tarbes (April 16) with a barbed observation about its opponents: "The nation is taking over the administration of its estates. Officeholders [*titulaires*] will be well treated. . . . The clergy is in an uproar and plotting against us [*ils cabalent contre nous*]. But the time for fanaticism and civil wars is past."

A few weeks later, he was more optimistic, writing in his newspaper: "The most useful part of the clergy [the parish priests] was displaying feelings of purest patriotism and the most complete submission to the national laws." Actually he was in error. Relations grew worse between the government and the clergy from midsummer on after the Civil Constitution of the Clergy was voted on July 12, 1790. Parishioners, probably in the millions, followed their parish priests in protesting against its provisions. At the end of that year, in December, after conciliatory advances by the government had been rebuffed, the assembly, forcing matters, decreed that ecclesiastics like all civil officials should take an oath of obedience to the nation, the law, and the king. As the day approached for incumbents of ecclesiastical posts to take the "clerical oath," feelings mounted on both sides, and the temper of "the gentle Barère" became edged. "They wish to set France ablaze with the torches of fanaticism," he complained editorially of the nonjuring clergy (January 7, 1791). A fortnight later, in a letter to his friend Mailhe, prosecuting attorney of the department of Haute-Garonne, whom he knew well from the old days in Toulouse, his tone was sharper still: "Your indictment of the fanatics who would set the temple of liberty aflame is worthy of your gifts and your public spirit [*civisme*]. . . . The question today is to enforce the necessary consequence of these great measures and to crush superstition under our heels, now that we have killed despotism and hereditary aristocracy. . . . The Constitution is advancing majestically over the ruins of old powers and ancient tyrannies and drives before it the thick fogs of servitude, superstition, and the ignorance of tyrants." The duty of priests, he was soon to say (February 28, 1791), is "to teach love of the fatherland."

In point of time the arrangements concerning church-state relations followed the administrative reorganization of France in which Barère had a more important role, at least so far as his native province was concerned. He portrays himself in his *Mémoires* as an opponent of the finally adopted plan to divide France into some eighty departments of approximately equal size, which would then be further subdivided into districts, cantons, and communes. He wrote those pages years after the fact, after years of disillusionment over the concentration of power in Paris, and in them he ridiculed the plan and regretted how much it had denatured the federative union of old France and paved the way to despotism. But in 1789 he had caught the vision of a French nation, one and indivisible; at the time that the plan was drafted, he saw its advantages to the nation more clearly than its dangers. Moreover, within that acceptance he was deeply concerned with making the most favorable arrangements possible for his own province of Bigorre.

It was no simple task to reconcile rival interests and fix boundaries to the mutual satisfaction of all claimants in the old southwest of France where he was born. Bigorre, itself, during most of the eighteenth century except for three years from 1784-1787 when it had come under the administrative authority of Béarn, had formed part of the intendancy of Auch to the north. A number of smaller *pays* surrounding it and joined to it by historic association and economic bonds, some *pays d'états* and others *pays d'éléctions,* had also formed part of that intendancy. Such was the Quatre Vallées to the southeast. Others to the north were inclined to join that intendancy under whatever arrangement would be made for a new department. When the time came to set the new departmental boundaries, supporters of Béarn pressed their claims to make Bigorre a subdivision of a new department centered around Pau in Béarn, while at the same time spokesmen for the *pays* of Comminges to the south sought also to incorporate Bigorre. With those two proposals before the deputies, the possibility was scant that Barère's own *pays* of Bigorre would retain its separate identity. His achievement was to defeat those rival expectations almost single-handedly. He did more than preserve Bigorre and the Quatre Vallées as the geographical core of a separate department to be called the department of the Hautes-Pyrénées, he succeeded in having his native city, Tarbes, designated as its capital (*chef-lieu*).

The definitive decree of January 15, 1790, it is no exaggeration to say, was based almost entirely upon a detailed report that Barère had presented to the assembly in the preceding month. In his *Observations* he recounted the efforts that he had made before the Committee on Divisions in behalf of Bigorre and the opposition which that endeavor had aroused. He pleaded that the territorial unity of Bigorre, in view of its long experience in self-administration, should be maintained, and he argued that to do less would violate its traditional cultural and economic interests. After disposing of the claims of Béarn and Auch and pleading for the establishment of Bigorre as a separate department, he went on to press the claims of Tarbes as the *chef-lieu* of the proposed department, itemizing its geographical situation as the commercial hub of great routes, its importance as a cathedral city, its position as a center of small-scale manufacture of paper, pottery, leather, cloth, iron, and its great importance as the heart of the tourist area.

For the *Observations* most of his Tarbes compatriots were eternally grateful; almost half a century later, in 1834, when Barère had it reprinted, he was still making political capital of it. In the foreword to the reprint he called attention to what he had done in behalf of the needy and to stimulate trade. He had had "the ministry concerned with public works" allocate 300,000 francs to repair the badly damaged highways and he had taken the lead to have the assembly vote 30,000 francs for emergency relief of the indigent.

In 1789, while he was pleading the cause of his *pays,* disturbing news reached him in Paris. Not only in the rural districts was there violent opposition to him, but in Tarbes itself a crowd of demonstrators had threatened to burn down his house. Since he was neither free nor willing at that moment to leave Paris to conduct his defense in person, Barère addressed himself in writing (December 24) to his detractors, composing his lengthy *Lettre de M. Barère de Vieuzac aux Communes de Bigorre, ses Commettans.*

The suspicions concerning his work, the *Lettre* began, "pierced him to the heart." For those who were misled, he had only sorrow, for ringleaders, scorn. Nothing could be more false than the accusation that he was not attending the debates; that he was lacking in zeal for the interests of the people; that he was out of touch with his constituents; and, most unbelievable of all, that he was planning in his own interest to destroy the territorial integrity of Bigorre by incorporating it into a single department with Béarn. He reminded his readers that he, the seigneur of Vieuzac, with a widowed sister (Cécile) and her three children to support, had voted for the abolition of feudal rights; he, a magistrate, had moved to censure of the parlement of Rouen; he, whose brother and uncle had two of the richest parishes in Tarbes, had voted to abolish the tithe without compensation and place the ecclesiastical estates in escrow as security for the liquidation of the national debt. He reminded them further that only three days earlier he had proposed the formation of the department of the Hautes-Pyrénées with Bigorre as its nucleus and Tarbes as its capital. He submitted in evidence the *Observations* that he had just written.

On the score of attendance and activities, he cited the approving words of the distinguished archivist Camus, of the presiding officer and secretaries of the assembly, and of the deputies of the *pays* adjacent to old Bigorre. He invoked also the testimony of the deputies of the clergy from Béarn. "By his enlightenment," they wrote, "by the sobriety of his views, his writing, his love for the liberty and the happiness of the people, he has gained the esteem, friendship, and general confidence of the assembly. . . . He has also received most flattering applause and never any marks of disapproval; and if the contrary has been written, it can only be the work of aristocrats and enemies of the people whose principles and views he has opposed." The *Lettre* ended with Barère's appeal for the endorsement of his constituents. This endorsement he obtained—and retained— from the people of Tarbes who supported the revolutionary changes, but in 1789 and during the half-century which followed his enemies never forgave him.

Superficially, what the Béarn deputies said about his love for the liberty and the happiness of the people seemed at variance with Barère's many expressions of regard for the monarch. There is no question that his utterances abounded with manifestations of affection for Louis XVI: "the most popular of monarchs in Europe"; "the most just and the most loved"; "the best of fathers"; "the august restorer of French liberty"; "the citizen king and defender of the Constitution." Here one must be cautious. In such expressions he was saying what the great majority even of the leftist deputies were saying. If later those words were held against him to prove that he had betrayed a king whom presumably he loved, one should note that expressions of regard for Louis XVI were set within the frame of a larger loyalty. His respect for the monarch neither infringed upon nor took precedence of loyalty to *la loi* and *la nation*. There was no suggestion of putting the king above the law and the nation. In mid-1790 he was writing in the spirit of Robespierre that "the history of peoples proved that the executive power was ever usurping by its very nature"; and a half-year later he repeated that to be free "one had to be a slave of the law."

He made his position clear once more in the spring of 1791 when he denied the king and the members of the royal family the right to leave French soil without the express permission of the assembly. The king was the "highest of the public officials," nonetheless the nation had rights over him which it alone could suspend. Thus had Barère also spoken on February 28 in discussing the nomination of a regent to replace the king, should that matter come up: "How could the nation refuse it to its legislators to whom has been delegated the power of binding future generations by its laws? I maintain that everything which gives the representatives of the people more respect and dignity is necessarily linked to the great system of liberty." Still later that year, in the course of the debates on the revision of the constitution, he reiterated his misgivings about strengthening the royal prerogative and with more vigor than accuracy declared that "states have never perished except through having ministers usurp power."

That mistrust of ministers, which went back to his earliest political views, he displayed in the great debate of May 1790 when Mirabeau, already secretly advising the king in a quasi-ministerial capacity, made a tremendous oratorical effort to vest the right of declaring war in the executive. Two issues were joined in the debate, the constitutional and the immediately pragmatic. The practical issue, which went beyond constitutional forms, was the question whether the new, revolutionary France would or would not adhere to the old Family Compact, contracted between Bourbon France and Bourbon Spain, and furnish armed support to the latter in its dispute with England over Nootka Sound in the Pacific. Like most other deputies Barère was for peace; like them he appealed to the lessons of history to contrast kings, who were bellicose by nature, to freely elected assemblies which were inherently pacifistic. Those phrases were conventional liberal stereotypes. The real ground of his objection to giving Louis XVI power to declare war was fear that the king would use his constitutional right of determining foreign policy to support Spain. Such a decision could lead to war and a military government within France; and a military government would without question undo the accomplishments of the deputies. The practical issue was resolved when the assembly effectively repudiated the Family Compact by decreeing that revolutionary France renounced wars of conquest. If on the constitutional level Mirabeau's eloquence and persistence swayed the deputies into voting a second decree, which vested in the king the nominal authority to declare war, that authority was only nominal. It was made subject to the prior recommendation of the assembly and its approval or rejection. Barère did not hesitate to state exactly where he stood: "In the eyes of humanity that question has already been settled. Since the nation is sovereign, it alone has the dread right of giving the signal for battle."

Sooner or later, as the astute Mazzei had foreseen, the question of the relations between revolutionary France and monarchical Europe would arise, and the adviser of the king of Poland shared the ruler's fears that in the event of war Poland would again become the prey of its powerful neighbors. Certain that it would be the assembly rather than the ministers of Louis XVI who would decide the country's foreign policy, Mazzei approved of instructions given him to cultivate the good will of pro-peace deputies. Barère was one of them, and Mazzei's dispatches speak of a medal that he was to give to Barère in the name of the king of Poland with appropriate praise of the "wise and magnanimous conduct of the French nation." Mazzei thought as well of Barère himself as he did of the deputy's newspaper, for he wrote that "he is a young man full of zeal [and] graciousness which make him well regarded by the entire assembly."

This fervent sense of the majesty of the assembly pervaded Barère's bristling criticism of the parlements of Rouen, Metz, and Rennes. In the fall and winter of 1789-1790, all three of these old corporate bodies were openly flouting the assembly's decree which had suspended parlements from the exercise of their functions until further notice. By its stand, Barère declared of the Chambre des Vacations of the parlement of Rouen on November 10, it has "scorned the sovereign authority of the nation. . . . This is a crime of lèse-nation." Turning a week later to the parlement of Metz, the sometime supporter of the parlements minced no words: "The parlements were useful . . . in the age of despotism and their resistance at that time merited our praise; today, they could be a threat to liberty. . . . When the state is in peril, when civil dissension may be reborn and destroy our important work . . . when the national authority is outraged . . . when one even attacks the sacred character of the laws, you should muster all the strength . . . of the legislative authority and do what the nation itself would do if it could be assembled." He said again, when he attacked the stand of the parlement of Rennes (January 11, 1790), that the parlements had once been staunch supporters of liberty when despotism dishonored France, but now, he continued, "When liberty is awakened, when a great constitution is regenerating all the provinces [to speak] of the rights of the Breton nation as if there were two nations in France . . . is to oppose the general freedom and deny the true sovereignty of the state." As the debates already showed, his words were closely followed on these occasions and the three liberal newspapers which had already given him favorable mention were loud in their approbation.

In the fall of 1789 Barère was elected to the Committee on Domains. The assignment was difficult and time-consuming. The Committee kept meeting for more than a year and a half, on several occasions jointly with other committees. It was also an extremely delicate assignment. Barère was the rapporteur of the Committee and, in that capacity, he presented its decisions to the assembly for adoption, amendment, or rejection. On a formal level, the work turned on the complex technical problem of establishing a principle for disposing of the crown lands. Whatever policy decision was reached, however, it involved the members in balancing the interests and needs of the nation with the prestige due to the person of the king and his status as the head of the executive branch of the government. As spokesman for the Committee, Barère was a marked man and his circumspection was put to a high test.

In the first report (December 11, 1789), which aroused "the liveliest discussion" wrote Mercier's *Annales*, he painted a vivid picture of the devastation of the woodlands in the royal domains as well as in church lands and private estates. He indicated at that time that it would be the policy of the Committee to protect "those valuable resources of the navy, the construction industry, forges, [and] manufactures." This guiding principle was at the core of the report of midsummer 1790, made by the joint Committees on Domains, Finances, Navy, Commerce,

Agriculture, and Alienation of National Lands, and implemented by a decree of the assembly. It exempted from sale both to individuals and private companies the great mass of the now nationalized woodlands, which had hitherto formed part of the crown land, and set up a central board to administer them. If that recommendation were not followed, the report pointed out, Colbert's old and dire prediction might be fulfilled that France's naval strength would wither for lack of timber and the needs of agriculture, commerce, and industry would be starved.

An earlier report (April 10) which Barère presented for discussion and action, A Report on the Sale and Alienation of Crown Domains, had already laid down the principle that the nation was sole proprietor of those domains. Nevertheless, wishing to give Louis XVI "another mark of the nation's attachment," the Committee recommended that "Such châteaux, royal residences, and other places which it would please His Majesty to reserve for himself," should not be taken over by the nation. A delegation of deputies should be sent to ascertain the royal pleasure. Negotiations with Louis XVI turned out to be more protracted than was expected. The king's request for a Civil List of 25,000,000 livres was granted by acclamation, and the assembly also agreed to grant him the income from such parks, domains, and forests as would be reserved for his personal use. His first request, however, was followed by others, and a vexed Barère soon remarked in irritation that the king was holding up the Committee's work. According to Barère's *Mémoires,* the king was in fact putting pressure on the Committee to have extensive hunting preserves and royal residences set aside for his personal use. The work advanced slowly and on September 13, 1790, the joint Committees on Domains and Alienation recommended that he be allotted the park of Versailles for his "royal pleasure." To meet criticism, it added the provision that private individuals whose possessions were enclosed within the park be permitted to hunt there when the king himself was not indulging in the sport that he loved passionately. Several democratic journalists, Marat among them, scored off "M. Barreire de Vieusac [sic]" for this ruling, but there was no general objection.

The final report (May 26, 1791) of the Committees on Domains, Feudalism, Pensions, and Finances regarding the specific royal residences which would be reserved for Louis also endeavored to balance the prestige of "the representative of the majesty of the French nation . . . probity on the throne," with the rights of the nation. It allowed him the use of the Louvre and the Tuileries and the royal palace and grounds of Versailles and recommended that the king be given the palaces of Marly, Meudon, St. Germain-en-Laye, and St. Cloud. Considering the widespread rumors that Louis XVI was planning to flee France, the settlement did not err on the side of niggardliness. It was accepted with perfunctory discussion and no recriminations whatsoever, not even from the radical press. One reason may have been the tone of the report which conveyed the impression that the committees were hopeful of placating the king by making a generous land settlement. Another possible reason for its acceptance was the committees' stipulation that the king keep the lands allotted to him in good repair and pay taxes on them and that the galleries of the Louvre be opened to the public in recognition of the fact that the palace was "the temple of the beaux arts [and] a celebrated museum."

By 1790 the once obscure provincial deputy was well known. The *Petit dictionnaire des grands hommes de la Révolution* included his name in its pages in 1790, as did *Les contemporains de 1789 et 1790*, which passed by hundreds of his colleagues to find place for Barère. For the *Petit dictionnaire* he was "one of the most hard-working deputies." In the judgment of General Dumouriez, with whom Barère struck up a friendship, he was "gentle and amiable." Dumont, the secretary of Mirabeau, recalled him many years after as "a mild and amiable [person] in love with the Revolution." Mirabeau himself dined frequently with the young deputy and thought sufficiently highly of him—

so Barère says—to suggest that they merge their two news-papers. Mazzei, too, was greatly impressed by the respect in which Barère was held by fellow deputies. Before the first year of the Revolution had ended, Barère's competence and willing-ness to serve were recognized in his election to various commit-tees; and in January 1790 he received a signal mark of esteem by being selected over the already well-known Duke of Aiguil-lon to serve as secretary of the assembly for a fortnight.

He dined out frequently with important deputies and was a familiar figure at fashionable salons, where one of his hostesses, Madame de Chastenay, was to remember him too as a gentle and amiable man. He was most at home in the drawing room of Madame de Genlis, who then had only praise for his charming ways, his wit and graciousness and, to be sure, his good looks. He frequented her salon at Bellechasse in the fashionable Fau-bourg St. Germain. At the chic Sunday at-homes of the gov-erness of the Duke of Chartres's children, he met the cream of the new revolutionary society of Paris: the two Lameths, Ca-mille Desmoulins, Barnave, Brissot, Talleyrand, the celebrated painter David, the great Volney, the Viscount of Beauharnais and his wife (later and better known as Josephine, the wife of Napoleon Bonaparte), the Marquis of Sillery, husband of the hostess from whom he was then legally separated, and the host, the Duke of Orléans. Barère recalled nostalgically "the delicious hours" he spent in that distinguished entourage, the chats he had with the host, "a citizen, though a prince." So close was he to the family circle that when Madame de Genlis drafted an additional annuity which Orléans agreed to pay to their natural daughter, "la belle Paméla," it was Barère who signed the docu-ments as witness. For this service, an innocent one so far as can be determined, he was pilloried in later years as "Paméla's guardian." He recalled, too, his frequent contacts with the Duke's eldest son, the Duke of Chartres, both at the city man-sion of Monceaux and the country estate at Raincy; and there can be little doubt that it was to these early contacts he owed

his later friendly relations with Chartres when the latter became King Louis-Philippe.

The *ci-devant* Barère de Vieuzac was happy over the good
opinion of his contemporaries but trouble lay ahead. The liberal principles of 1789, which he was ardently defending, were
challenged by city workingmen, artisans, and small shopkeepers who voiced their grievances in meetings of their assemblies
in the democratic press. Dissatisfaction also infected the Jacobin
society, and in April 1790, most of the original members took a
dramatic and threatening step. They seceded in protest and
founded another club to keep the Revolution faithful to first
principles. Since Barère sincerely shared their misgivings, he
too enrolled in the schismatic "Société de 1789." He did not
entirely cut himself off from the old in linking himself with the
new. In the membership roster of the new organization he was
listed as "member of the Jacobin Club." Characteristic too of
his temper was the fact that he attended the meetings of a
democratic Christian-Socialist organization, "Le Cercle Social,"
which Abbé Fauchet had founded. If he had no stomach for the
radical agitation, he was still going to inform himself of what
it was that the levellers wanted.

For the sybaritic Barère it must have been pleasant to for-
gather with his fellow members in the elegant quarters that the
Society rented for its meetings at the Palais Royal, relax after a
sumptuous dinner in the well-stocked reading room, and enjoy
the comforting feeling that he was meeting with his friends "to
discuss, not to overthrow; to enlighten, not to inflame," as he
wrote later. Bailly and Mirabeau, his first political mentors,
were members of the Society of 1789. So too were Condorcet
and the philanthropic Duke of La Rochefoucauld whom
Barère had first met in 1788. In their ranks were Talleyrand
with whom he was "most closely linked" according to his own
statement, Siéyès, Dupont de Nemours, and Lafayette, whom
he knew only slightly. Leading officials of the Paris Commune
were charter members and many officers too of the National

Guard. While Lafayette, the leading spirit of the Society, offered his help to the king to restore "public tranquillity," Mirabeau was making his famous secret arrangements and accepting
a huge bribe from Louis XVI to swing opinion into strengthening the royal prerogative.

Lafayette could delude himself, as he penned an anonymous
pamphlet on the desirability of merging the Jacobin Club with
the Society of 1789, that things were going well. The soldiers
who had mutinied at Nancy were brought to heel that summer;
the incorrigible Marat was censured for his provocative writings that incited men to insurrection. It was understandable that
Barère with his fear of demagoguery and direct action should
applaud those measures of law and order. It was a tribute to his
political intelligence that it did not take him long to see that
repressive acts would not close the fissures which had opened
in the ranks of the once united revolutionaries of 1789. For the
king, the Society of 1789 was still too advanced; for the little
people of Paris, it was too conservative if not too reactionary.
Since Barère had not formally severed his ties with the Jacobins and would not join in a democratic movement for which he
had scant sympathy, he returned to the fold and once again began to attend the meetings of the middle-of-the-road liberals.
He was forgiven his defection, also his flirtation with Le Cercle
Social. "With what satisfaction," wrote the then arch-Jacobin,
Fréron, in *L'Orateur du peuple*, "have we recently seen one of
the most zealous defenders of the fatherland reappear at the
Jacobins. M. Barère de Vieuzac, finally scorning the seductions
of '89 and the mountebanks of Le Cercle Social, has come back
to the Society of Friends of the Constitution; and to the people
who hastened to congratulate him on his conversion, he declared: 'Well, gentlemen, did I have to wait until December 15
to become a patriot! Rest assured that I have been one all the
time and shall be one all my life.' "

The truth of the matter was that Barère had not waited until
December 15, 1790, to become "a patriot." His views and his

position remained the same: he was only shifting his front to meet a greater danger. In the spring and early summer of 1790 he had been saying in substance, "to the left, to the left, but no further"; by winter and early spring of 1791 he saw that the threat to the assembly program came from the right. The *mystique* of 1789 had flattened into the *politique* of 1791, the goal of the bourgeois revolutionists was blocked before it was reached. On one flank were the revolutionary masses, seething over the policy of the assembly regarding the conditions for the sale of national land and the financial terms established for the abolition of manorial dues. Urban workers were bitter over the new "feudalism" which was replacing the Old Regime and clamoring against the bourgeois-minded and directed policy of the government. In both country and city aversion was strong for the assembly's ecclesiastical policy. On the other flank were individuals and groups whose privileges the revolutionary legislation had destroyed—*ci-devants,* old officials, nonjuring clergy—all deliberately playing up the democratic movement, encouraging disobedience of revolutionary decrees, hampering completion of the constitution, some of them preparing for civil war. Although Barère did not then know it, Mirabeau was at that very time outlining, in one of the most lengthy of his confidential Notes, a program of massive propaganda to enlist mounting discontent in favor of Louis XVI. In it, he advocated that the king escape from Paris, rally his followers in a strong royalist center, and dissolve the assembly.

Barère perceived the preparations and noted the provocations. He could hear vendors, encouraged by "le côté droit," as *Le Point du Jour* contemptuously called the rightist deputies, at the door of the assembly itself, hawking a pamphlet entitled *Give Us Back Our 18 Francs* [the daily salary of the deputies] *and Clear Out.* With Robespierre emerging as the parliamentary leader of the democratic-minded deputies, Barère threw his editorial support to him. *Le Point du Jour* was lavish in praise of the defender of the constitution: "Robespierre's habitual fervor for the interests of humanity"; "this independent spirit who has always linked social laws with the eternal laws of the equality of natural rights"; "M. Robespierre, ever true to his principles." Along with this editorial support of Robespierre, he included exasperated criticism of the royal family. It was then that he denied the right of the king's elderly aunts to leave France and caustically reminded a delegation to Louis XVI that it represented the dignity of the nation.

He paid public tribute to the services and talents of Mirabeau when his friend and adviser died suddenly in April 1791. So too did Mirabeau's great opponent Robespierre and other deputies who at the time had no proof of the orator's collusion with the court. Barère's praise did not indicate approval, for he continued to oppose Mirabeau's successors, Lafayette and the Triumvirate, who also sought to revise the constitution, strengthen the royal prerogative, restrict liberty of the press, and suppress the clubs. With Robespierre he defended the rights of the citizens of Avignon to petition for incorporation of their territory with revolutionary France. His vote was against Barnave and for Robespierre on the question of granting political rights to free Negroes and mulattoes in San Domingo. When Robespierre made his famous motion to declare the deputies of the Constituent Assembly ineligible for immediate re-election, *Le Point du Jour* editorially lauded "the wise, measured, and vigorous opinion . . . of a pure, firm, and disinterested patriot. . . ." Yet Barère proposed an amendment toning down Robespierre's motion, which he feared was too extreme; and the *Journal de Perlet* approved of his proposal, which it described as an attempt "to conciliate opposing points of view."

Meantime, Barère remained suspicious of the masses. He made no protest either against the decision to exclude passive citizens from the National Guard or the decree aimed at the popular societies of the sections by forbidding collective petitions. Nor did *Le Point du Jour* criticize the Chapelier law of June 14 which prohibited workers' organizations. It reported without comment the allegation that such groups were filled with "evil geniuses [and pulled by] invisible hands."

The open break within the assembly that he fought so hard to avert did not come in those spring days of 1791. Nonetheless, within two months the solid front of the reunited Jacobins was seriously breached. During the night of June 20, the king escaped from Paris. Dismay, together with indignation, swept over the capital, and Barère's own first response was one of deep anger: "May That Day Be Stricken Out ( *Excidat illa dies* )" was the heading of *Le Point du Jour*. He voted that the king be immediately suspended and the assembly assume executive authority. As for the explanatory declaration that Louis had left behind him, Barère scornfully called it "an unholy violation of the most sacred vows," and he ridiculed the "impudence" and "falsity" of the open letter in which the royalist General Bouillé assumed responsibility for the king's flight. Soon realism and prudence, "the road of wisdom," prevailed over indignation. With other moderates he drew back from instituting judicial proceedings against the runaway ruler who had been stopped and made prisoner at Varennes, and accepted the legal fiction that the king had not fled voluntarily but had been "carried away." So anxious was he to preserve appearances that he denied that a formal deposition by the king and queen before a duly constituted court would in any way constitute a degradation of the royal dignity: "It would bring together the facts that we have to know concerning the commission of the crime, with the pursuit of the accused, and from the very mouths of those who were its victims."

Thus, the king would be exonerated or, at the least, not humiliated before France and Europe; and neither French republicans at home nor monarchs abroad would be able to find in the ruler's flight the pretext which both sought to disrupt the assembly's work. Accordingly, while Barère pressed for punitive legislation against the *émigrés* (July 9, 1791), thus deflecting popular indignation from the king, he assented to the ruling that the king should be suspended but absolved of guilt and his "abductors" be brought to trial. He knew of course that he was saving face for the king in order to safeguard the assembly; he carefully refrained then, in the course of the long debate on the fate of the king, from saying what he did say many years later in his *Mémoires*: "The assembly was obliged to make a decision that was commanded by imperious circumstances."

The decision to exonerate the king and have his temporary suspension lifted when he accepted the revised draft of the constitution ended the crisis and removed the immediate danger of war with Europe. It also obviated the danger of a regency at home and, with it, the menace of civil strife. Equally important, it ended the threat of a republic, which at that time Barère certainly did not wish to see established. He acquiesced in those decisions with feelings of relief. Having done his utmost that spring to stem the counterrevolutionary tide, he would not swim with the democratic-republican current.

Relief was short-lived. The Paris republicans refused to accept the assembly's decision, continuing in their campaign of petitions to overthrow the monarchy. At Jacobin headquarters opinion was divided, which gave Barère fresh cause for alarm. If the Jacobins, the Society of Friends of the Constitution, threw their support behind the movement for a republic, the monarchical constitution on which two years of labor had been expended was doomed. The immense toil would have been in vain. Regarding what the Jacobins did and intended to do Barère was either ill-informed or panicky or both. He jumped to the conclusion that they had gone over to the republicans and joined with the Cordeliers Club and popular fraternal societies in sponsoring the July 15 petition, which called on the assembly to defer its ruling on the king until after a referendum had been held. By that date the assembly had already exonerated the king, and the petition came too late. The Jacobins therefore did not endorse it. They did at first endorse a new petition on the 16th demanding the abdication of the king and his replacement "by all constitutional means." When the assembly reaffirmed his suspension, on Robespierre's initiative, the Jacobins prudently retracted their support of the petition in question, which in any case did not explicitly call for a republic. Robespierre, perceiving the danger of misunderstanding, had warned his fellow club members not to give a handle to the monarchists in the assembly who were looking for any pretext whatsoever to use the National Guard against the democratic left. It was also due to his insistence that the Jacobins voted, on the night of the 16th, not to act jointly with the Cordeliers in sponsoring a petition which did explicitly call for "a new executive," that is, a republic. This decision of the Jacobins was announced publicly at the Champ-de-Mars about noon on the 17th.

At the most, the Jacobins had given cause for alarm by their vacillation. Probably it was this irresolution which predisposed Barère to believe that they had definitely committed themselves to the republican cause. In the preceding year, when he had joined the Society of 1789, he had temporarily ceased attending the meetings of the Jacobins. Now, with several hundred like-minded and dismayed members, he took the dramatic step of withdrawing entirely. He joined a rival club, which met at the nearby former convent of the Feuillants and defiantly appropriated for itself the formal name of the Jacobins, Society of the Friends of the Constitution. On that same day, the 17th, good politician that he was, he wrote to the Jacobins of Tarbes to inform them on what bandwagon he was riding: "The true Friends of the Constitution are now meeting at the Feuillants."

In the *Mémoires* he alleges that "the Jacobins were stirring up the people [going so far] as to challenge the National Assembly and its decrees." Possibly he believed what he wrote. Perhaps he was suffering from a weakened memory. More likely he was suffering from a bad conscience. The passage in the *Mémoires* was more inaccurate still in stating that neither he nor his fellow deputies knew that Charles de Lameth, presiding officer of the assembly, had given instructions to Lafayette and the National Guard to disperse by force the petitioners who had announced their intention to meet at the Champ-de-Mars on the 17th. One has only to turn to the pages of *Le Point du Jour* to see that he was in error, for there he reported without comment that the Commune and the assembly had been in close touch with each other during the entire day of the 17th to provide for the use of force against illegal gatherings. He reported, too, not with approval, but certainly not disapprovingly, the tragic "massacre" of the Champ-de-Mars, when the National Guard on the order of Bailly and Lafayette fired into a crowd of petitioners and killed 12 of them, while wounding 30 to 40 more. His journal related how the assembly, after the "massacre," had given its approval to everything that Bailly and Lafayette had done against "a mob of rebels, whose only object was murder, pillage, disorder, [and] the anarchy which they call liberty." Barère had not placed himself on record against the official, unnecessary, stupid, and brutal murder of unarmed petitioners; it was not the assembly or the Commune which he condemned but the petitioners whose republicanism he feared.

His panic quickly receded and he regained his balance far more rapidly than he had in the preceding year. Soon he saw that the Feuillants were the Society of 1789 all over again: the same faces and the same conservative ends, only now more open and exigent. For a fortnight the reports in *Le Point du Jour* gave its readers the impression that the Feuillants were indeed the true Society of the Friends of the Constitution. By the 26th of July, however, it was quoting from a plea that came from the "Mother Society," which Robespierre had certainly written, entreating the deputies not to be led astray by the schism and "the slanders" about the Champ-de-Mars, where "the blood of the people had flowed." During the month of August, a month of strain and tension, when the assembly was discussing the final formulation of the constitution article by article, Barère marked time, cautiously suggesting that the split should be mended. By early September he had made up his mind, and, on the 10th, Condorcet's *Chronique de Paris* printed a long excerpt from the address that "M. Barrère de Vieuzac, that incorruptible deputy who has never deviated in his views," had given on the occasion of his election as president of the Feuillants. "Gentlemen," it read, "allow me to state how sensible I am of the honor that I am receiving, and how surprised. I have neither rendered service to the Society nor been regular in attendance. But I saw that the constitution was finished, and I said to myself: 'Now is the moment for all parties to disappear, for all hatred to be stilled, for all friends of the constitution to rally around it.' Hence I accept the post with which you honor me in the hope that within several days I shall hear the news of the reunion." The formal merger was not announced; the Feuillants simply withered away, and when the second list of its members was drawn up on October 10, Barère's name was not on it. Once again he was consistent in his policy of keeping the front of the revolutionists united, consistent, too, in his determination to land on his feet.

In those last two months of the assembly's existence, whether because he felt that he had to prove that he had "never deviated in his views" or out of a strengthened conviction that it was revolutionists turned conservative who were most to be feared, he sharply criticized the work of the new constitutional committee and its supporters. He expressed his views from the floor, but it was in his newspaper comments that he clarified them. Spicing his reporting with barbed observations about Malouet and Abbé Maury, leaders of the assembly right, he came out openly in support of Robespierre, Pétion, and Abbé Grégoire. He still held out against the proposal to grant collective petition rights to popular societies and he refrained from comment when the franchise rights which earlier had been voted to free colored colonials were revoked. But in the main he stood solidly with the democrats. He combatted a motion to curb freedom of the press and supported Talleyrand's notable report on public instruction which stressed "the need for free instruction that society owes to all citizens to destroy the sources of ignorance [and] develop the natural faculties of man. . . ." Twice in August he took the floor to fight motions to extend the powers of the royal ministers, particularly in matters of taxation, "crafty [proposals] which tended to destroy the sacred principles of the national sovereignty." Years later he was to concede that the Constitution of 1791 was unbalanced, too strongly tilted in favor of the legislature; at the time it was being drafted, he thought and argued otherwise. The *Journal de Perlet* reported his words with approval and the *Courrier français* hailed them as "a tribute to his patriotism."

At the very close of the meetings of the assembly, when *Le Point du Jour* was describing the joy of the deputies who were listening to the reading of the king's letter in which Louis accepted the constitutional document, Barère interrupted his narrative to make a final jibe against his adversaries: "From these testimonials of feelings, we must exclude the entire right wing, which seemed paralyzed in the midst of ferment in the left wing, the galleries, and the speakers. *Ci-devant* nobles and priests who so loudly vaunted their attachment to the throne and their devotion to the king did not give a sign of life during the touching reading of this letter. Did they love the throne only to exercise power and waste the revenue of the state! Did they love the king only to make him their slave and the pillar of their arrogant pretensions!"

During these final sessions, too, his notions of social and cultural democracy broadened. Sincerely but in a bombastic style foreshadowing his rhetorical efforts of 1793-1794, he seconded the petition of independent artists to be permitted to exhibit at the Louvre on terms of equality with members of the Royal Academy of Artists and Painters. Along with David he had harsh words for academic bastilles, entreating with his colleagues to end the monopoly of members of the academy: "Now that the Louvre is at the disposal of the nation and the king, it is for liberty to open the temple of the arts to all citizens who cultivate them." He stressed, as he never had before, the state's responsibility for social welfare. Reaffirming his abhorrence of alienage, he renewed his earlier efforts to end the absolute authority of the *paterfamilias* in determining the succession rights of his heir in those departments formerly subject to the provisions of Roman law. In that power, which he called "the arbitrary wishes of the dying," he saw a threat to the basic revolutionary principle of equality. And he pleaded again and again in vain that an eldest son, on reaching the age of twenty-five, be permitted to inherit the property due to him: "You have just granted political and civil rights to Jews; you have freed the serfs of the Jura; the eldest son alone . . . groans under the old laws."

When a report presented by the Committee on Beggary, on which he was an alternate, proposed public relief for the ablebodied unemployed and the aged infirm, he supported it, but moved an amendment that provision also be made for foundlings: "This class is wretched enough; it can be useful to the nation. It is worthy of your solicitude and humanity. You should consecrate the debt of society to them." In a little manuscript memorandum for his own guidance, he explored the possibility of amending the Declaration of the Rights of Man to end the scourge of beggary and vagabondage, and to it he would have added the following article: "Every poor man, if he is ablebodied, has the right to find subsistence by his labor in the society of which he is a member and obtain help if he is old and infirm."

Barère's reputation was reaching it first peak and the democratic press, especially the *Journal de Perlet*, carried long excerpts from his speeches. His own department had already elected him judge of the Court of Appeals (*Cour de Cassation*). Fresh honors came to him. He was named to a delegation of outstanding deputies to present the completed Constitution of 1791 to the king for formal acceptance. A fortnight later, he was a member of another deputation which solemnly informed the king that the assembly was now about to end its sessions. In addition to these two tokens of esteem his colleagues nominated him for the presidency of the assembly. Though he failed of election, the gesture was a striking one and a fitting one for all that he had done. The Constituent Assembly met for the last time on September 30, and for twelve months Barère withdrew from active parliamentary life.

Almost fifty years later, when he summed up his career in the *Mémoires,* he pointed with pride to "the precious legacy that the Constituent Assembly had bequeathed to the French people and in its name to Europe." In the fall of 1791, he could have pointed with pride to his own share in those achievements. All contemporaries were agreed that he had faithfully discharged his responsibilities as deputy. With experience and under the pressure of circumstances his ideas took on new dimensions and he acquired a deeper and more democratic sense of the principles of 1789; and that richer conception of liberty and equality and fraternity he took with him to the National Convention to which he was elected a year later in September 1792.

Barère did not liberate himself entirely from earlier attitudes. More and more a social democrat and increasingly inclined to broaden the scope of government action, he retained his belief in the sacred character of private property and in the virtues of free economic enterprise. His predilection for the company of cultivated men like himself did not leave him and he did not get over his suspicion of the multitude. Fearing the common people and their tactics of direct political action, he also feared the old privileged aristocracy and their influence upon the irresolute and wavering king. Such apprehensions determined his conduct when he withdrew from the Jacobins and then returned; when he condoned the massacre of the Champ-de-Mars; when he recommended a generous settlement of the domains that Louis XVI might retain; when he accepted the fiction that the ruler had not fled Paris but had been "abducted."

Fearing both counterrevolution from the right and a revolution of the masses from the left, he sought to keep the ranks of the revolutionaries of 1789 united and give the impression to Frenchmen outside Paris that all was going well in the assembly.

In part this determination not to see all he saw and not to hear all he heard stemmed from his personality. He was, in those thirty months of the Constituent Assembly, what he had been before 1789 and what he remained during the National Convention in 1793 and 1794, a good fellow who followed the line of prudence and the middle course because he wished to please others and be liked. In larger part he pursued the policy of mediating disputes out of reasoned calculation and out of a tough estimate of what was possible and what was not. He was acutely aware that millions of his fellow Frenchmen were far from accepting the extraordinary changes in habits and relations that were a thousand years old. Political instinct advised him that it would be fatal to renounce in advance the option of following more than one road to ensure the success of the revolutionary cause over its opponents. He adjusted his actions to the play of antagonistic interests and went in zigzags, backtracking in his course, retreating when he had to from positions that could not be held.

If there was nothing heroic in that empirical procedure, there was a rare quality of maturity and realism. There was realism, too, disturbing realism of another stamp, in his acceptance of measures to go beyond mediation. On the eve of 1789 he thought largely in terms of a revolution by persuasion. After 1789 he was prepared to go beyond consent if the interests of public safety demanded. The procedures of the reluctant terrorist of 1793 were present in the libertarian of 1789.

The Revolution had become Barère's faith; it was also his career. He was not guided exclusively by disinterested motives. His concern for himself was as real as it was for the principles in which he believed. Without doubts over his actions he fused the strands of impersonal loyalty to a cause with the wires of self-interest. Within the frame of his convictions he behaved as honestly and courageously as circumstances permitted. In the later assembly, where he pursued an identical course, he was assailed as a weakling, a trimmer, and an opportunist; during the Constituent Assembly his conduct won him plaudits. He was rich in the esteem of his associates when the assembly met for the last time on September 30, 1791.

## ⌘ V I ⌘

# *Interlude in Tarbes,*
# *1792*

BARÈRE remained in Paris from October 1791 to early January 1792, discharging his duties as judge of the Court of Appeals. Why he then decided to leave the capital is difficult to state. Perhaps the nature of his new responsibilities proved too much of an emotional let-down after the exciting political career that he had been pursuing. Possibly the intention of his "dear friend, the Duke of La Rochefoucauld,"—which he mentions in the *Mémoires*—to have him named minister of the interior speeded his departure. The political situation was tense in Paris, and Barère may have been reluctant to accept so embarrassing an honor. Most likely, he judged it was time for him to attend to his political fortune in Tarbes; he was aware that critics had not been silent during his absence of almost three years. Whatever the reasons, he applied for and was granted a six-month leave, and the end of January saw him back in Tarbes ostensibly to settle family affairs.

In Paris he stayed long enough to note that the new Legislative Assembly had not brought a political truce. The old friction continued between the assembly and its rivals whose strength was in the sections, the electoral board of the municipality, and the local clubs. Within the assembly, mutual recriminations pitted group against group. On the right was the numerically strong bloc of conservative deputies. Their political inspiration still came from the Triumvirate of Barnave, Duport, and Lameth, though their real power rested upon the Feuillant Club. In domestic policy the Feuillants still strongly urged the king to accept the revised constitution, believing that a reconciliation could thus be effected between him and the nation. In their foreign policy they advocated closer understanding with

Austria, all but holding to a policy of peace at any cost. By appeasing the Emperor they hoped to win him away from supporting the émigrés and in that way indirectly but effectively stem the growing antimonarchical and prorepublican movement at home. On the left sat a smaller but more vocal group of deputies then called "Brissotins" after their articulate and influential spokesman, Jean-Pierre Brissot, idealistic and enterprising editor of the powerful *Le Patriote français.* Lawyers or journalists, and merchants themselves, the Brissotins were linked with foreign political refugees who had flocked to Paris, also with important French business interests who looked with favor on the prospect of war with Austria.

The dispute with Austria, which the new assembly inherited from the old, was blowing up into the threat of war; and by no group was a war policy so adopted as by the Brissotins. High-minded and ambitious, eager for glory and secure in conscience that the right would prevail, they were confident that the pure doctrines of the Revolution would fall on fertile soil in the neighboring, backward states. While they pursued their policy of intimidating the émigrés abroad and passing repressive legislation against the refractory clergy at home, they persuaded themselves that if war came in consequence of their action, it would be a military promenade. Their provocative policy found an influential supporter, Count Louis de Narbonne, minister of war. They counted on war to unmask the king and bring power and glory to the Revolution; Narbonne thought in terms of a limited war where victories would redound to the army, which could then end the Revolution, bolster the authority of the king, and restore order by a military dictatorship. On a war course they were agreed, opposing calculations notwithstanding.

To such tensions and calculations Barère gave heed before he left Paris, and in distant Tarbes he followed developments as best he could. The settlement of his father's estate took little time, but to re-establish relations with the wife he had left behind and the mother-in-law who had ill-concealed her disapproval proved impossible. The child bride of 1785 was seven years older. The mother with whom she was living in Vic was by her side, steeling her child, reared in the traditional loyalties to crown and church, against reconciliation with a man who had shown himself a betrayer of the faith. "I respected the age of the one and virtue of the other," the betrayer blandly wrote in his *Mémoires*: "I put up with these inescapable difficulties of revolution which divide families and make the best of friends quarrel." The details of the breach remain unknown but it was not healed. The husband and wife went their separate ways, never to see each other again after Barère's brief sojourn.

About this time the *ci-devant* feudal lord, now M. Barère, began to buttress his emotional and ideological stake in the Revolution with real estate ventures. He purchased a number of parcels of nationalized property, though nothing in value like the 600,000 livres that his detractors later claimed. The record is incomplete, and on his part inaccurate, but by piecing together various fragments one can make out the large outline of these transactions. In 1791 he invested 13,500 livres in the purchase of a plot and buildings in the parish of St. Paul in the Campan valley. To pay for it he began "to break up his inheritance," meaning what he had acquired on his father's death three years earlier. This venture turned out badly, and he remained saddled with the parcel for many years, finally disposing of it in 1819 at considerably less than its purchase price.

A year later he bought a more extensive piece of property for 15,000 livres. This purchase included the church of the dissolved Benedictines, cultivated fields, gardens, and woodland, all the parcels being situated at St. Lézer in the commune of the same name of the district of Vic. The record of sale indicates that it had been bought in auction in 1791 by a certain Pierre Sabatery [Sabatier?] of Vic who had made a down payment of

6,000 livres in a total bid of 15,000. The record of sale also states that early in 1793, Sabatery, after making an additional payment of 1,200 livres, had ceded his rights to Barère, who is referred to in the document as "the grantee."

Those brief entries from the official record are supplemented by a revealing memorandum that Barère must have scribbled down for himself. At the top of a large sheet of paper he wrote in a scratchy, impatient hand, "A note on the purchase of St. Lézer, May 24, 1792." The details followed; "I bought the procuration—9,000 (this is M. Sabatery's profit). I reimbursed M. Sabatery for the 6,000 livres that he paid in December 1791, to the Nation on account of the 15,000, price of the ad-judication. I owe the Nation 15,000 livres, along with the interest [?], year by year." In other words he paid, or rather agreed to pay, 15,000 livres, the total of Sabatery's obligations, in order to buy him out. Below this notation he made a new heading, "Means of Payment," and under it he jotted down the sum of 4,000 livres that he had received from the sale of a mill, and 7,570 livres that he had raised by two loans, both payable in 1793. This still left him owing Sabatery almost 4,000 livres, which presumably he had to raise or perhaps had raised in ways he does not specify. Under the same heading, "Means of Payment," came a final sentence, "Annuities payable through savings on my income and salary."

The final paragraph, "Projects," underscores the speculative character of the purchase. He had several alternative or over-lapping ideas in mind: he could sell St. Lézer to M. de Sillery, intimate friend of Barère's friend, the former Duke of Orléans, or he could sell it to the Abbé Gauderatz [Gauderat?], the king's chaplain. Alternatively, he might sell merely the church to the commune of St. Lézer, dispose of some of the timber from the woodland to a Bordeaux merchant, or set up a cotton spinning factory, perhaps a foundry.

Possibly because of these purchases, he was actually as poor as he claimed to be when, in the *Défense* of 1795, he stated that he had been exempted from contributing to the forced loan during the Terror because his net income was less than 1,500 livres. The stringency arose, he alleged, from the fact that he was in debt to his brother and sisters for their share of his father's estate. Perhaps so; possibly it came from his real estate ventures. What is clear is that sometime late in 1793 and again in January 1794, he borrowed all told 16,000 livres from the Abbé Gauderatz and forty years later, according to the editor of the *Mémoires* he was still honorably repaying that debt. To what use that large sum was put, on what security he raised the loan, and why, no certain answer can be given. If his post-Thermidorian enemies are to be believed, it was to support his mistresses and satisfy his taste and theirs for high life. The allegation rings false; it is more likely that he fell heavily into debt because of commitments to pay off the property he had bought or because of his ruinous efforts to exploit its value. What in any case is indisputable is that from 1794 on, for the rest of his life, he was rarely free from financial embarrassment.

The St. Lézer purchase turned out to be a catastrophe. In 1794, he tried through a proxy to rent or sell it, "whichever was most advantageous," for not less than 24,000 livres. That price would have netted him a handsome profit. The sale was not effected and seventeen years later he was still trying to get rid of it, this time to the department of the Hautes-Pyrénées for conversion into a poorhouse. As his cousin Hector wrote him, however (November 28, 1811), the prefect and the departmental authorities demurred, not without cause, over the price of 30,000 livres that Bertrand put on it, and Hector advised that it be considerably lowered. If his effort failed, which he judged likely, why not, suggested Hector, a fictitious sale of the property to him? Giving him the title would take the curse off Bertrand's ownership and strengthen Hector's chances of making a resale. To recompense the good cousin for his "interest and activity" they could amicably arrange the percentage of the profit on the higher sales price between them. The suggested way out was none too promising; in any case Hector died suddenly, and the plan with him. Ten years after, when Hector's widow, Lili, was badgering Bertrand to repay what he had borrowed from her husband in order to raise a mortgage, Barère was still trying to sell the St. Lézer parcel through his brother. Money was then scarce; real estate was going begging, and the Barère name was no more of a recommendation in 1821 than it had been a decade earlier. One offer of only 2,000 francs "was so vile and niggardly," wrote Jean-Pierre, "that I turned it down." So again Barère failed. The property was no longer in his possession when he died, probably lost in litigation with his collaterals.

These financial reverses, however, were to come later. In 1792 politics engaged most of his time. The National Guard of Tarbes turned out to greet him when he arrived in the city, but all was not well. He had local complaints to satisfy and animosity from both political flanks to overcome. For monarchists and Catholics he was too extreme; in the Jacobin Club which had also split in the controversy following the Champ-de-Mars massacre, he was judged too lukewarm. Conveniently forgetting that by his own secession to the Feuillants, he had been a principal mover of that split, he appealed for unity, summoning the members "to spread patriotism, establish the religion of the law, strengthen respect for the constituted authorities, inculcate love for the Constitution, enlighten the people, watch over the other citizens and officials and summon them before the tribunal of public opinion." For a short time, dissension was ended and Barère was given the honor of being named president of the club. In the early spring, however, when he was terminating his presidency, strife broke out again and his Feuillant past was raked out of the embers. For the remainder of his life, in fact long after his death, passions ran high in Tarbes over their native son.

In the meantime, war with Austria was drawing near, and to the impending conflict Barère turned his attention. Too far away to follow the Paris political scene and the diplomatic maneuvers at first hand, he kept himself informed as best he could by correspondence, and among correspondents was his old neighbor of the Constituent Assembly days, the famous veteran soldier and diplomatist, General Dumouriez, who early in March was named minister of foreign affairs in the pro-war Brissotin cabinet. A letter dated from Tarbes, March 30, 1792, addressed to "My dear friend and distinguished patriot," hailed the general on his appointment: "What a brilliant career is opening before you! With your energy, your understanding, and your military and diplomatic knowledge, I already see you preparing either solid peace or decisive war. France will rise to the point where destiny has been summoning her for two years. . . . You have on several occasions communicated your ideas to me on the only diplomatic system which befits France. . . . I limit myself here to expressing the wish that success will soon crown your great plans."

The "great plans" looked forward to breaking the French-Austrian alliance, which Dumouriez execrated, and actively preparing for a war, which would strengthen the authority of the king. Like Narbonne, Dumouriez counted on a victorious army to break the Jacobins' hold over his country. Into the plans also entered intricate diplomatic efforts to separate Prussia from Austria and ally France with England. Barère was not the only revolutionary to be embarrassed a year later when the "dear friend" whom he had praised so fulsomely went over to the Austrians. He was still in Tarbes when the revolutionary armies advancing to conquer Belgium broke ranks and fled before the pursuing Austrians, while panicky Parisians, far behind the battle front, raised the cry of "treason." In Tarbes too, he learned about the *journée* of June 20 and how a mob, drawn from the radical sections of Paris, invaded the Tuileries Palace. He was still in Tarbes in July when the *fédérés* of the provincial National Guard which had come to Paris to strengthen the defense of the capital fraternized with Paris sectionnaires and openly prepared to overthrow the monarchy.

At this moment a royal proclamation recalled all officials to their posts to defend the country and Barère speeded back to the capital. Arriving in Paris on August 8, two days later, from the lodgings that he temporarily occupied on rue de Richelieu, he could hear the bells and alarm guns summoning the insurrectionists to attack the Tuileries. Before night fell he could see that all was over. The Tuileries had been taken by storm and its defenders mowed down; the monarchy was toppled and the king was a prisoner. The Insurrectionary Commune of August 10 controlled the municipal government.

His *Mémoires* denounced "that terrible day of August 10" and the account is not distorted. For three years he had been serving warning against the radicals of the capital, and now the Paris sans-culottes had set themselves up as rivals to the national government. Impatient of slow parliamentary procedure, controlling powerful levers of action in the police and the National Guard, they were resolved to win equality for themselves with the middle classes. Barère naturally did not make a public profession of the views he later expressed in the *Mémoires*. On the contrary, speaking for the Court of Appeals and for himself, he hastened to proclaim his loyal acceptance of the suspension and imprisonment of Louis XVI.

He then began his curious and brief association with Danton, the hero of the radical Cordeliers Club. Danton's role in organizing and carrying through the insurrection of August 10 has long been a subject of controversy. His proud boast, when he was fighting for his life before the Revolutionary Tribunal, established in the spring of 1793 to try political cases, that he had "made" August 10 must be discounted; that he was deeply involved in the overthrow of the monarchy is clear. It was precisely because of his hold over the rank and file of the insurrectionists whom presumably he had unleashed and presumably could control that the Brissotins accepted him as minister of justice in the provisional executive council which formally took over the functions of the suspended ruler. Through him they hoped to hold the sans-culottes in line.

As Danton looked about for advisers and assistants, his attention was called to a fellow lawyer, Barère, whom he then barely knew, if at all, but of whose reputation he had heard. If Barère hesitated to accept an invitation to work even in an unofficial capacity with a man whose radicalism he mistrusted, he finally accepted an assignment which gave him a foothold in the government without imposing on him responsibility for policy. His services as Danton's assistant were not for long— both were elected to the new national assembly—nevertheless contact had been established. For almost a year more these two men, so different in temperament and yet so essentially alike in operational techniques, were to pursue a common policy within that assembly of closing revolutionary ranks at home and reconciling France with the powers abroad.

Shortly after the attack upon the Tuileries, France again went to the polls to elect deputies to a National Convention which would draft a new constitution in place of the defunct royalist constitution of 1791. Meantime the Prussian armies under the Duke of Brunswick were methodically moving on Paris, and the capital was gripped by hysteria. A collective fear that hidden "aristos" were plotting to butcher the defenseless population after volunteers had left for the fighting front swept over the city. Shops were closed down and citizens ordered indoors. Armed patrols roamed the deserted streets. Watch committees interrogated citizens without credentials and arrested suspects and for days house-to-house searches sought to ferret out secret plotters. On September 2, Paris heard utterly terrifying news: Verdun, the last bastion barring the road to the Prussian juggernaut was about to fall. Pent-up fears then exploded and the "September massacres" that shocked the civilized world began. For three days they continued, while "patriots" slaughtered presumed enemies and "fifth-columnists" with and without trial. The blood-letting was odious. Horrible though those massacres were, they ran their course until the homicidal patriotic fury spent itself. They were the work of no single individual or group; they were neither systematically prepared nor methodically organized. Perhaps no one and nothing could have stopped them; and the authorities did not try, neither the municipal government nor the deputies of the assembly.

While Paris let blood, Frenchmen elsewhere were going to the polls. In Barère's own department of the Hautes-Pyrénées, 224 out of the 278 secondary electors named him deputy to the Convention. Before the news reached him, he learned that he had also been elected by the electoral board of the Seine-et-Oise, that is of the Paris area, by 456 out of 673 votes. After some thought, he accepted the mandate from his native region and on September 21, 1792, took his seat as one of the 750 new deputies.

# ⚹ V I I ⚹

# *The Man of the Center,*
# *1792-1793*

THE decree calling for elections to a National Convention was passed by the Legislative Assembly on the morrow of August 10. By its provisions, primary elections were set for August 27 and secondary ones for September 2. Though the Insurrectionary Commune which had overthrown the monarchy was committed to the establishment of a republic, the men of the Commune realized that there was strong opposition to the republic both in Paris and the country as a whole. Consequently they put into action all their resources to carry Paris. Without control of the Paris deputation, they were lost. In bringing pressure upon voters who were not already too intimidated to refrain from voting in the primaries, they were aided by the sections, which abolished the secrecy of the ballot and adopted the procedure of an open roll call. What was begun in the primary elections, held under the shadow of the massacres, was completed in the secondary. On this occasion the electors were compelled to vote in the hall of the Jacobin Club, now officially renamed "Society of the Jacobins, Friends of Equality and Liberty."

The radicals swept the capital: all twenty-four members of the Paris delegation were Jacobins, all resolute republicans. Robespierre, the Incorruptible, was first on the list and after him came Danton. They were followed by men who had gained notoriety in the insurrection of August 10 and the September massacres. Such were Legendre, the butcher; Sergent and Manuel, members of the Insurrectionary Commune; the former actor Collot d'Herbois; and his friend, Billaud-Varenne, ex-schoolmaster and lawyer by training, in character irascible and vindictive. In the Paris deputation there was the charming

Camille Desmoulins, who had made a fine art of journalism. The painter David, already celebrated, was part of it; also the former Duke of Orléans, now self-styled Philippe Egalité, and, last to be elected but not least in influence, the choleric Marat, "The Friend of the People." They sat together on the high benches of the Riding School to the left of the rostrum and the president's chair where they were joined by fifty like-minded deputies elected from the departments. Because of the high seats they occupied, they were soon known as the "Mountain" or the "Montagnards." Among those not from Paris itself were Couthon, cruelly crippled by arthritis, and the volcanic youth, Saint-Just, both to join forces with Robespierre. Carnot, the future "Organizer of Victory," sat with them too and others whose fame came later.

In the departments distant from Paris, both Girondin and Jacobin pressure and threats kept many Frenchmen away from the polls. More than four million of the eligible voters of the entire country abstained from voting, fewer than two million cast their votes. Of the 750 new deputies, a third had already served, either in the Constituent or the Legislative Assemblies. The Brissotins, now generally spoken of as the Girondins because their foremost speakers came from the department of the Gironde, mustered 120 followers who took their seats on the right. There were men of substance and culture in these elites of the law, the administration, and the liberal professions, many of whom had supported Brissot in the Legislative Assembly. Vergniaud, lethargic in temperament but capable on occasion of rousing himself to oratorical heights was one of them. Ironic Gensonné, honest and obstinate in his views, and Guadet, caustic and too prone for his own good and his associates, to abuse his great skill as debater, had also served in the preceding assembly. Newcomers included the intemperate journalist, Louvet, embarrassing to colleagues for his violent outbursts, fiery Barbaroux from Marseilles, a recklessly courageous man, and the young and handsome Buzot.

The great majority of the deputies took their places in the seats of the center. Barère sat with these well-disposed yet irresolute representatives of the "Plain," but his behavior was not theirs. Without solid party ties of their own or any clearly formulated policy, they counted on time and normal parliamentary procedure to establish harmony. Since they stemmed mainly from the lower middle classes and liberal professions, they were at first sympathetic to the views of the Girondins and turned to them for guidance. They did not conceal their fear of the sans-culottes: "I shuddered when I arrived in Paris," exclaimed the Breton lawyer Lanjuinais, and he spoke for them all. Given the opportunity, they would have dropped mutual accusations over responsibilities for the massacres and readily applied themselves to drafting the republican constitution and settling the fate of the imprisoned monarch. This opportunity the Girondins did not provide.

They threw away their resources and advantages of strength and numbers by pursuing a vendetta against the Montagnards. The responsibility for not establishing a united revolutionary front of bourgeois deputies was largely theirs. Divergent political views might have been composed, for all the deputies were revolutionaries and republicans. All secondary electors had voted for a republic; not one of the 750 deputies had stood for election as a royalist. But the Girondin spokesmen were too conscious of their worth. Believing in their superior talent, they aspired to control the government of France. Uneasy in the swarming capital, they were too jealous of the prestige of the departments to accept the necessity of according a special place to Paris in the direction of national policy. France was at war, the country was invaded by the enemy; still the Girondins were too choked by fear of a Parisian dictatorship to recognize the need for revolutionary concentration of power. Though many of their constituents were men of property and they were linked with the powerful commercial interests in the southwest, the rival groups were not so far apart in social outlook that they could not have been brought together. Both believed in private property and a system of free economic enterprise. The Montagnards charged their opponents with being enemies of the working classes and the Girondins countered by taxing them as levellers. There was little substance to those charges. What they meant was that while the former reconciled themselves to accepting minimal and temporary restrictions over the play of economic enterprise, the latter would not bring themselves to institute controls. The opportunity for united action was lost. Fundamental contradictions over policy, the clash of temperament, personal ambition, and political ineptitude pitted one group against the other.

After voting with the Montagnard deputies to establish the republic, the Girondins passed over to the offensive. For the first month, until the end of October, they fared well, better by far than they ever were to again. They took over control of the key positions, the presidency, the secretaryships, and the important committees. When Danton resigned from the council of ministers, it too came under their domination. Many of the moderate sections, regaining their balance after the turmoil of August and September, gave the Girondins vocal support. A moderate was elected mayor of Paris. The *fédérés* who flocked to Paris after the opening of the parliamentary sessions were friendly to them. Law and order were slowly being restored.

The fatal weaknesses of the Girondins now became apparent. Despite high personal distinction, they lacked true cohesion. They had no outstanding leader around whom they could rally. Indignant and terrified by the massacres, they could not comprehend what was legitimate and well-grounded in the clamor of the working class for government control of prices. As massive demands were released which they neither understood nor were able to control, they gradually lost the support of many moderate deputies who had first accepted their high profession of principles at face value.

They called for a departmental guard to protect the Convention. "I demand," cried one of them, "that the National Convention should be surrounded by so imposing a force that not only will we have nothing to fear but our departments will be assured that we have nothing to fear." They were answered in kind: "Paris," a delegation from the sections declared, "made the Revolution, Paris gave liberty to the rest of France, and Paris will maintain it." So they were charged with wishing to break national unity and "federalize" France by reducing the capital to its one-eighty-third degree of influence. All departments should be equal in power. Far from disavowing the charge of federalism, which connoted not alone the end of national unity but the sacrifice of the sans-culottes to the large business interests, the Girondins gave it credence. They accused the Commune of plotting to rule the Convention; they condemned the men whom they designated as the instigators of the September massacres and threatened to have them brought to trial. They charged the capital with electing only deputies who had actively participated in the butcheries. Consequently, in that first month when their spokesmen denounced Marat as a demagogue, Danton as chief agent of September, and Robespierre as a would-be dictator, hope for harmony waned.

Under the best of circumstances such divergent views would have delayed and impaired the smooth conduct of affairs in any legislative body. But circumstances were hardly of the best and parliamentary procedure, such as had in theory at least established itself in England, was nonexistent. There was neither a recognized majority representing the government nor a recognized opposition to challenge it and take over as the new government. The majority of the moment was in fact the government. There was no cabinet to resign if it failed to receive a vote of confidence, no provision for an appeal to the country through a new election. Each issue was taken to the floor and each debate could become the occasion for partisanship, too often for irresponsible charges and countercharges. There was heckling from delegations of petitioners from Jacobins or sections, threats from visitors in the galleries. Such became, such remained the parliamentary spectacle during the first nine months of the assembly's existence. Statesmanship and cool judgment were at a discount, the long perspective obscured by the short view of divided deputies.

In that setting Barère's talents, developed by two years of experience in the Constituent Assembly made him a valuable figure, almost a unique one. He was a close friend of many of the Girondins, sharing with them his rare moments of leisure and dining frequently with Vergniaud. Like them he was a provincial with little love for Paris and great feeling for regional liberties and ways. In social origin, education, and taste he was close to them too, sharing their views on free enterprise of the mind and purse.

Here the resemblance ended. Barère neither shared nor condoned their fatal genius for making trouble. Level-headed and calm for all his verbal fluency, he soon perceived his friends for the obstructionists they were. While they declaimed about liberty and showed themselves doctrinaire and intractable, he recognized the realities of power, possessing an intuitive feeling for what was possible and, for him, desirable. As fearful of the Paris populace as ever, more so now if possible, because of his aversion for the Insurrectionary Commune, he did all he could to prevent an open break between the capital and the Girondin deputies. For many months his tactics were to forestall a test of arms between the rival factions. The self-imposed task was not accomplished, but he persevered, placating or reprimanding as the occasion warranted, shifting the weight of votes to keep a balance, holding the back door open when the front door was closed, reiterating the gospel that sacred unity of the propertied groups alone could save the Revolution. His end was synthesis of belief; he succeeded only in effecting temporary compromises over procedure.

During the bickering of the first month Barère did nothing notable. Sometime royalist, sometime constitutionalist monarchist, he too voted for a republic. When Danton, amidst Girondin clamor, proposed that the republic be declared "one and indivisible," Barère proposed the addition of the qualifying phrase, "and the government is representative." He opposed the Girondin-Plain majority which put pressure upon Danton to remain in the ministry against his will rather than resign and take his seat as deputy. When Danton, for reasons difficult to understand, made a motion to have the assembly declare that France was out of danger, Barère spoke up against it as "a dangerous and impolitic" proposal, reading into Danton's proposal the implication that Paris alone without the departments could save the nation. The peacemaker mediated between a Montagnard attempt to remove General Montesquiou from his command on the Savoy front and a Girondin effort to have him retained, sensibly calling for an adjournment of the mischievous discussion. In those early weeks of maneuvering, he criticized a proposal to have members of the Convention excluded from politics for six years following the adoption of the constitution. If both factions saw tactical advantages in the motion, Barère saw in it a futile gesture. With memories still fresh of Robespierre's self-denying ordinance, he would not again expose the nation to the dangers of relying upon untried deputies to guide it.

By then the time had come for Roland's report on the formation of a departmental guard. The minister of the interior was earnest and hard-working; he was also officious and suspicious of the Paris masses almost to the point of paranoia. By then, too, Barère was ready to speak with authority. His colleagues had shown their confidence in him: he had been elected to the Committee on Instruction (which at that time he did not accept), to the Commission on Monuments, and, most important of all, to the key Committee on the Constitution.

The agitation was great in the assembly hall on October 29, when Louvet accused Robespierre of aspiring to establish a personal dictatorship. Robespierre succeeded in obtaining a week's time to prepare his defense, but emotion ran high at the Jacobins that night where supporters rallied around their acknowledged leader. Emotions were running high in the streets too, where newly arrived fédérés were clashing with the armed sectionnaires. In the assembly, altercation followed altercation, and Barère was kept busy.

On October 30 he rebuked Roland in one breath and the council general of the Commune in another. He spoke up again on November 4, on the eve of Robespierre's defense. The atmosphere was tense to the breaking point. Outside the assembly rival groups were jostling each other. Cries could be heard: "Robespierre, Marat, Danton to the guillotine!" "Death to Roland!" There were rival petitioners in the assembly, the fédérés charging the sectionnaires with preparing a *journée*, the sections protesting against the distribution of arms to the fédérés. In that tumult Barère took the floor.

The trouble arose, he began, from the "impolitic, even impotent" proposal for a paid departmental guard to defend the deputies against the Parisians. That was not all. There was "a monster we had to attack and strike down, the monster of anarchy which raises its head from the Commune of Paris." Let us end "all partisanship in this assembly. . . . I propose that you scorn these curious conflicts of wounded vanity and pass on to the true interests of the republic." Rejecting the idea of a departmental guard, he moved that petitions be printed and distributed to show that Paris did not fear the fédérés in its midst. "Citizens, when your brothers from the departments came and aided you in overthrowing the throne of despotism, did you repulse them? The blood of the eighty-three departments has cemented the walls of the temple of Liberty." In *Le Patriote français* Brissot was all praise: "Barrere [sic] spoke like a wise

and independent man." He had won time, but nothing was settled. Robespierre was yet to be heard from.

The galleries were packed with Jacobin sympathizers when
Robespierre came to the rostrum on November 5 to deliver his
carefully prepared defense. Certainly many of his fellow deputies shared Pétion's view that the Incorruptible was "suspicious
and distrustful, his temperament bilious and his imagination
splenetic"; the charge, however, that he planned to usurp power
and establish a dictatorship was so manifestly absurd that the
assembly quickly dismissed Louvet's accusation and passed to
the order of the day.

That was not the end. Louvet angrily opposed the motion, the
discussion began again, and Barère arose once more to pour oil
over troubled waters. He spoke at length, determined to have
"all individual passions yield to the great passion of the public
good." His prestige was higher than before: he had just been
elected secretary of the Convention. A simple dismissal of Louvet's charges, he indicated, was not sufficient: the Convention
should explicitly place itself on record as being concerned only
with the interests of France. "What signify . . . all these accusations of dictatorship, of ambition for supreme power and the
ridiculous projects of a triumvirate? Citizens, let us not attribute
importance to men whom public opinion will put in their places
better than we; let us not set up pygmies on pedestals. If you
had a Caesar or a Cromwell, or a Sulla, or a legislator of great
genius, I would ask what were his means of power. . . . But men
of a day, petty revolutionary entrepreneurs, politicians who
will never enter into the domain of history, should not take up
the time which you owe to the great work with which the people have entrusted you. To accuse a man of having aimed at
dictatorship . . . presupposes a great character, genius, boldness, and great political or military successes. If a great general
with laurels on his brow infringed upon your rights, you
should impose the severity of your laws on his head, but to
give this terrible honor to those whose civic crowns are min-

gled with cypress, that I cannot conceive. . . ." He pleaded
with the Convention to put a halt to political duels and cease
offering a sorry spectacle to all Europe. Calling on it to get on
with the tremendous task on hand, he moved that the "Convention pass to the order of the day, since it should consider
only the interests of the republic."

*Le Patriote français* naturally gave a cordial account of Barère's speech, but Robespierre was furious over the "insulting
preamble" to his exoneration, and at the Jacobins that night
Barère received rough handling. He squirmed his way out after
a fashion, explaining away his oblique and unflattering references to the men of September. What he meant was that if to
ordinary men the massacres were a crime, in the eyes of true
statesmen they were of paramount significance. They had struck
down conspirators "whom the sword of the law" had been unable to reach. His words, Barère insisted, while different from
those of his fellow club members were not less revolutionary.
"Of that day, I said, we must no longer speak, for we must not
put the Revolution on trial."

The Convention tabled Louvet's accusation without Barère's
qualifying phrase, but his subtle move had not failed. By deliberately associating the Jacobin triumvirate with the men of
September he had satisfied the vanity of the Girondins, at the
same time showing up the hollowness of their charges. By his
scathing observations about "Septemberers" he tried to give as-
surances to the departments that such butcheries would not be
tolerated again. But he aligned himself with Danton to stave off
an investigation of what had taken place two months earlier.
Above all, he had warded off a test of arms between fédérés and
sectionnaires, a clash in which the Convention and the Revolution would undoubtedly go under. And by assenting to the presence of the fédérés in Paris he kept a check on Paris agitators.

The Scottish tourist, Dr. Moore, skilled in parliamentary ways,
was sensitive in his appreciation: "I am persuaded," he wrote in
his journal, "that Barère thinks that Roland's party . . . is on the

whole the weaker of the two and that he means to attach himself to that of Danton." Five days later Barère, who had complained about the provocative plan for an armed guard but not of the presence of the fédérés, rejected a proposal to have them sent to the war front. The early election returns to replace the Insurrectionary Commune of August 10 were for the moment showing a trend for moderate candidates; for the moment fédérés and sectionnaires were fraternizing, not feuding. Since no threat to the Convention was involved by keeping the fédérés in Paris, why needlessly affront the departments by sending them off to the front? Did Paris fear their presence, he asked. Rather, it should fear the Insurrectionary Commune, the secret agitators and royalist plotters, and the refractory clergy. The trial of the king was drawing near; the republic needed all the supporters it could rally in the capital.

The Jacobins fumed over his stand, and *Le Patriote français* approved. Barère, himself, was guardedly hopeful, buoyed up by the thought that a corner had been turned in home affairs as it now had been on the field of battle. The situation on the front improved miraculously in the six weeks since General Kellermann's artillery had stopped the Prussians dead in their tracks at Valmy in the passes of the Argonnes. The Prussians had withdrawn in a retreat remarkably free from French molestation, and by the end of October the last of the enemy recrossed the French frontier. The republican troops then took the advance, biting deep into Savoy, Nice, and the Rhineland. On November 6, the great victory of Dumouriez at Jemappes put the Austrian Netherlands under French control. Propaganda war was now to begin.

In France's relations with the powers, Barère favored a negotiated settlement. Brissot could cry, "We must never rest until the whole of Europe is ablaze"; Barère thought otherwise. Loath to sever the thin thread on which peace with Britain and negotiations with Prussia hung, he made repeated pleas to his fellow deputies to proceed cautiously. On November 1 he entreated them not to compromise the future of the Republic by a "political invasion" of the Netherlands and enjoined them three days later to ponder and reflect before endorsing the demand of a hand-picked delegation from Nice for the incorporation of their state with France. He spoke in similar vein (November 21) against the annexation of Savoy.

After the attacks on Robespierre had been repulsed, Barère was momentarily hopeful that affairs within the assembly would go smoothly. On November 1 he was elected secretary, one of two, and a month later, by a striking plurality, the assembly elected him its presiding officer. The date of his election as president was significant. The formal trial of Louis XVI, which all parties had been anticipating since August 10, was about to begin. It seemed fitting, when the eyes of France and Europe were turned upon the Convention, that the deputy who had distinguished himself by upholding the authority of the assembly should preside over the trying sessions which lay ahead. Dr. Moore was not wrong when he wrote in his journal: "He has not hitherto taken a decided part with either party, but I am told he is courted by both."

To determine whether or not Louis XVI was inviolable under his constitutional rights and whether the Convention was competent to try him was no simple matter. On November 7 the Committee on Legislation ruled that the Convention, as the sovereign people in council, was above the constitution and could not be bound by constitutional limits. The nation had deposed the king; the Convention as the voice of the nation had the right to try him. While for the remainder of the month the assembly debated the complexities of the ruling, the populace, embittered by mounting bread prices and stirred up by political strife, clamored that the Convention take action against a recreant king. No doubt existed in their minds that a king guilty of treason and of mowing down innocent citizens merited the death penalty. The radical sections pressed for a trial.

If the king counted on the Girondins to save him from the sections and the Jacobins, no calculation could have been more mistaken. The Girondins did in fact oppose a trial, wishing to save the king's life if they could. But to save his life, they would not risk their own. If a trial were held, two alternatives presented themselves, neither agreeable. They could speak out in defense of the king, giving the Montagnards an opportunity to fix the deadlier charge of royalism on men they had already accused of federalism. If they voted to condemn him, they would bear the stigma of regicides and thus forfeit the support of their moderate following in the departments. Therefore Montagnard strategy called for a trial to force the Girondins into the open and commit themselves.

A small but resolute minority of Jacobins went further, taking the stand that no trial was required. Robespierre made the point tersely: "If the king is not guilty, then those who dethroned him are." Similarly, in one of his first appearances on the rostrum, Saint-Just declared: "There was nothing in the laws of Numa for judging Tarquin. . . . In such a trial formalities are mere hypocrisy." He was appealing to that classical antiquity whose lessons in civic virtue all revolutionists had dutifully studied.

Without the support of the Plain, however, there could be no majority in the assembly for a trial. While the men of the center were already inclining in that direction, the theatrical discovery of the king's secret safe (*armoire de fer*) in one of the apartments of the Tuileries made their assent inevitable. Among the mass of compromising papers found in the improvised safe deposit box were Mirabeau's confidential notes and records of Louis's secret relations with émigrés. The projects for his flight were also in the box, various efforts of his agents to bribe popular agitators on the eve of August 10, and instructions to counterrevolutionaries. To oppose a trial after the disclosure of those incriminating papers was to be an enemy of the republic. So the Girondins, bowing to circumstances, shifted their tactics and acquiesced. They still hoped, by heaping one diversion upon another, to bury the main issue under irrelevancies and then in the ensuing confusion direct public opinion against their political foes. The trial was decreed on December 3 when the king was arraigned.

Barère favored a trial. The retreat of the Prussian armies had removed the fear of war which earlier prevented the punishment of the ruler whom he held guilty of treason. Believing that Louis was guilty of intelligence with the enemy, he believed that the deputies would also find him so. The tearful account in his *Mémoires* to the contrary notwithstanding, it is likely that if he had to, he would not shrink from imposing the sentence of death. If Barbaroux's word is to be trusted, Barère initially favored banishment. But he insisted that the trial be conducted with all legal correctness and dignity. So long as he was presiding officer of the Convention, he would neither permit Jacobins to obstruct proceedings nor sectionnaires to intimidate the deputies. Well aware of existing anti-Paris feelings in the provinces, he was determined not to give the many royalist sympathizers in rural France still another occasion to turn against the capital.

He was in the president's chair on December 2 when a delegation of sectionnaires came before the deputies with a peremptory demand that the Convention "redouble its zeal" and vote without further delay on the following question: "Does Louis, *ci-devant* king, merit death; is it to the advantage of the republic to have him die on the scaffold?" Without hesitating Barère picked up the gauntlet: "The Convention will always carefully listen to petitioners, for that is its duty. But it will never allow any section to instruct it on matters of public safety. . . . It will have the courage to crush all factions that surround the cradle of the republic. . . . The National Convention need account for its work, its thoughts, and its rulings concerning Louis, the traitor, only to the entire republic."

Having upheld the dignity of the assembly, he was forced on the following day to defend his own good faith. Among the many papers found in the *armoire de fer* was a letter written to Louis XVI by the intendant of the civil list on February 19, 1791, which Roland disclosed to the deputies. In it the intendant expressed his opinion that Barère was well disposed toward the monarch and would present a friendly report on the question of the royal domain. The letter was genuine, the substance accurate. At that time, almost two years earlier, Barère had been well disposed toward Louis XVI and there was no gainsaying the fact that the report in question was friendly. If he were to be labelled a royalist sympathizer on the basis of an attitude which dated back to a period when revolutionists were still well inclined toward the king or at least not openly hostile, then others too would have to be held royalist sympathizers. The implication was dangerous: many Montagnard deputies did not wish their remote political past examined too closely. Besides, Barère was an important figure, too important and too respected, for his colleagues to allow him to be tarred in that crude fashion, particularly when Roland was charged with suppressing documents damaging to his own friends. So when Barère rose to defend his revolutionary record, he was quickly and enthusiastically cleared. Even *Le Patriote français* reported with forbearance what might have been an awkward incident, while the Jacobin *Journal de Perlet*, as could be expected, commented on "his calm air, his serene countenance, his frank brow where innocence was painted."

Barère was happy over this mark of confidence, happy and reassured. He was still presiding on December 11, when the king came before the bar to answer the counts of the indictment against him. Plainly dressed in an olive-colored silk coat, the former monarch was pale and drawn from his long confinement in prison. He had been driven from the Temple under close police escort through the streets of a city tense with excitement and patrolled by armed National Guards. "He was calm, simple, and noble," wrote Barère, adding "I could not shirk the sad duty of interrogating the king, nor even let it be suspected that this function was disagreeable to my heart." No question that it was disagreeable, but he may have then forgotten that he had publicly called Louis "a traitor" and expressed the belief, then popularly voiced, that "kings alone did not belong to the human race."

In the assembly hall the galleries were thronged with spectators quick to display hatred for the king. Barère, in his dark coat and scarlet waistcoat, lead-colored woolen breeches and white silk stockings, opened proceedings with a stern warning to the galleries that the majesty of the people was invested in the Convention. Toward the prisoner he was severe but considerate, addressing him as "Louis" and carefully avoiding the appellation "Capet," which he knew the king detested. He solicitously ordered an attendant to bring a chair for the prisoner and sharply reprimanded Santerre, one of the deputies, who had deliberately insulted the fallen monarch. For three long hours the prerevolutionary royalist relentlessly put question after question to Louis XVI. Barère's procedure was correct, but the king's lame and extemporized replies to the indictment of which he had received no copy in advance, forced the assembly to grant his request for counsel. Further formal action was put off until counsel could prepare his defense against the charges of plotting against the nation and seeking to overthrow the constitution.

The Girondins took advantage of the interrupted hearings to renew their obstructionist tactics. Two days earlier, on December 9, they had made an attempt to have the primary electoral assemblies convoked to rule on the recall of "deputies who betrayed the fatherland." The maneuver and the phraseology were clever and dangerous. By betrayal, they meant specifically the September massacres; the particular deputy they had in mind was Marat whom they all detested. If the Mountain voted against the motion, it ran the risk of tarring itself in provincial public opinion as Marat's accomplice and supporter; if the motion was carried, a precedent would be established to deprive deputies of their parliamentary immunity. The precedent could then be employed to oust those who voted against the king. Since the Girondins still commanded a majority, they forced Barère to call for the question, giving Marat's newspaper, *Le Journal de la République*, another opportunity to label him a secret royalist and Roland's tool. After calling for the question, Barère yielded the chair to take the floor himself in order to plead that the motion be referred to the Constitutional Committee. He stated that it was both premature and reckless, injurious to the assembly and provocative of disorder and division. If the precedent were followed and a referendum held on the verdict concerning the king, it could only result, he argued, in civil war. The motion was lost.

A week later the Girondins tried again, this time using the former Duke of Orléans as bait for the trap they set. They called for the banishment from French soil of all members of the royal family, the king's immediate family alone excepted. Again the Montagnards were invited to impale themselves on whichever horn of the dilemma they found most comfortable. Widely circulated rumors held that Philippe Egalité was involved in plots for a royalist restoration which would make him regent for the dauphin. Since those reports were not without foundation, the deputies of the Mountain were doubly embarrassed. It was noised about, again with justification, that Danton was hopeful of re-establishing the monarchy in favor of Egalité's son, the former Duke of Chartres. If they voted "No" on the Girondin motion, they exposed themselves to the suspicion of harboring secret royalist plotters in their midst. If, on the other hand, they voted "Yes," their vote could be taken as proof that it was the vigilant republicanism of the Girondins which had unmasked their true designs.

Discussion of the motion got out of hand almost at once, sucking up other divisive issues and controversies. From the left of the assembly Montagnards raised cries that Roland be dismissed from his ministerial post, and Girondins countered with shouts for the dismissal of Pache, the Jacobin minister of war. Pandemonium reigned when at length Barère obtained the floor in what the *Thermomètre du jour* called "the longest, most stormy, and most scandalous" of all parliamentary sessions. The Convention, Barère declared, would never defend secret royalists—a thrust at Orléans, his friend and sometime host. Nor would it tolerate in the government men whose presence endangered its stability—a jab at Roland and Pache. They had all done their duty and public opinion would be their judge, but in the circumstances they all had to go, and he moved that the Bourbons be banished and the ministry immediately reorganized. It is probable that he wished his motion to be defeated; in any case, it was. Still, his stratagem achieved its intended effect: all proposals were tabled until after the trial of the king. He had scotched a maneuver rich in divisive potential and won time for calm reflection. The trial of the king continued.

It continued, but by December 26, when the Convention rejected a gallant, futile plea of the king's counsel for exoneration, the verdict was in sight. Sensing victory, the Mountain pressed hard for the vote on the question of the king's guilt. The Girondins, equally aware that time was running out, threw their foremost orator, Pierre Vergniaud, into the breach, not to oppose the voting but to plead that the first question should be whether or not the ultimate verdict be ratified by the primary electoral assemblies. Vergniaud swept the assembly with the magic of his eloquence, and it was at this crucial point that Barère took the floor (January 4) to break the spell that Vergniaud had woven.

He was rich in confidence. His prestige was higher than ever before: that very day he had been elected to the new Committee of General Defense, forerunner of the later Committee of Public Safety. He took the floor against the friend whom he esteemed, persuaded that a referendum on the verdict would only shatter such bare unity as the assembly had won. With supreme self-assurance he stood in the rostrum and addressed his fellow deputies in the longest and most convincing of his oratorical efforts. David's great canvas commemorates the dramatic moment: The portrait shows Barère standing proudly in the rostrum, hand on hip, eyes blazing, long hair ruffled, rallying the irresolute to hold fast. Rising above rancor and speaking without exaggeration, he addressed himself to the still undecided center. He spoke with studied persuasiveness, paying tribute to the nobility and generosity of Vergniaud but calmly and methodically analyzing the recklessness of the proposal and deriding the argument that the condemnation of the king would align the powers of Europe against France. The coalition of enemies was already formed (as indeed it was in spirit); did the deputies shrink from their responsibilities? He emphasized how prudent and deliberate the Convention had been in the debates and how cowardly and superfluous it would be for the deputies to appeal to their constituents for fresh instruction. "Am I not in the midst of the National Convention which constitutes the sole hope of republican France," he concluded; "Proud and bold with Belgians, are you slaves and timid with Frenchmen? You are the envoys of the nation; it counts on you to take all the necessary measures of public safety."

On the effectiveness of his words in overcoming the scruples of the waverers historians are agreed. So too were his contemporaries. Brissot, who rejected Barère's argument, hailed "his patriotism and his eloquence." At the Jacobin Club the rafters rang with praise: "Impossible to find anything finer, more clear, more methodical, better reasoned." In a unanimous resolution it was voted to have the speech printed and circulated among all the affiliated clubs in the departments. The Jacobins could exult with good reason: Barère had shattered the spell of Vergniaud's words; he had overcome the scruples of the center; he had doomed the captive king. The motion was passed that the Convention would proceed forthwith by roll call to vote first on the question of the king's guilt and then on the penalty to be imposed if he were found guilty.

Ten days later a virtually unanimous assembly voted "Yes" on the question of the monarch's guilt. Later that night, by a vote of 424 to 286, the deputies rejected the referendum. Barère voted with the majority on both occasions. The question of the penalty was put on the 16th and voting continued for thirty-seven hours without interruption. The rowdy, the impassioned, and the cruel crowded the visitors' galleries, jeering or applauding as each deputy went in turn to the rostrum. Barère cast his vote for the death penalty: "The law tells me that between tyrants and peoples there are struggles only to the death. . . . As a classical author said, the tree of liberty grows only when it is watered by the blood of all species of tyrants. The law says death, and I am only its voice." By his vote Barère broke completely with his past. The fervent monarchist of 1789 had become the republican regicide of 1793. His heart never forgave him for what reason told him he could not escape doing. His contemporaries never forgave him his phrase that "the tree of liberty grows only when it is watered by the blood of all species of tyrants."

One last hope remained for the king and it was Barère who denied it. The Girondin leaders themselves, for all their words, had not dared to vote "No," but since many of the rank and file had joined the center in refusing to vote for death, the plurality for the death penalty without reservation or qualification was one bare vote, 361 to 360. Hoping against hope, Buzot moved for a reprieve. For the last time in this harrowing, agonized drama (January 20) Barère threw the weight of his eloquence in the scales against the king. Marat, who praised Barère with difficulty, unbent sufficiently to concede that "the speech produced a very good effect." The commendation was a classic of understatement: Barère's words were decisive. The notation in the diary of an upright Montagnard deputy named Romme is eloquent on the effect that they produced: "[Barère] showed with his close dialectic that a reprieve was as impolitic as it was immoral and cruel. He showed also that [the difficulties] lay in our divisions, our suspicions, our panicky fears, and petty intrigues. . . . He called for a roll call and the discussion ended forthwith." The reprieve was turned down by a vote of 380 to 310 and the execution set for the morrow. In the drear morning of January 21, as the drums of the soldiery beat loudly and the crowd shouted "Vive la nation!" the head of Louis XVI fell heavily into the basket. The life of the king was played out; the revolutionary career of Barère took a new turn. Royalists never forgave him.

# ⚥ V I I I ⚥

## *The Would-Be Mediator,*
## *January-June, 1793*

THE struggle for control of the National Convention and of the direction of government policy at home and of relations abroad continued for four more months. The issue in domestic affairs was still whether the right of center bourgeois Girondins with their essentially liberal ideals of 1789 would prevail, or whether the left-of-center bourgeois Montagnards, supported by the Paris radicals, would strip them of the authority they had seized after the overthrow of the monarch. In foreign relations the Girondins had committed themselves to a war of propaganda and the territorial expansion of revolutionary France to its "natural frontiers." To that policy in itself the Montagnard deputies were not opposed. Their opposition was directed, when military reverses began, against the ineffectual war effort and the blundering of the Girondin generals. As much from calculated expediency as from conviction, the Montagnards refused to have the costs of war saddled upon the working classes in the towns. They insisted that Paris, the heart of revolutionary France, direct the conduct of the war. Personal rivalries and ambition blended with those fundamental issues, exacerbated by the passions which the trial of the king had generated. The issues of controversy were indivisible.

Despite their sorry role in the trial of the king, the Girondins still enjoyed great prestige when the struggle was renewed after the monarch's death. The foreign war had placed them in a position of authority and as long as their generals were victorious, their authority remained unshaken. Victories increased the prestige of the Republic, but the triumphant advance of its armies in the fall of 1792 added to its problems. The revolutionary republic could not let down its civilian supporters in Savoy,

Nice, and the Rhineland; it could not abandon the provisional administrations that had replaced old authorities in the conquered and liberated territories.

Under the joint impress of the new crusading zeal to set Europe ablaze by pitting peoples against kings and aristocrats and the older expansionist drive to reach the "natural frontiers" of France, the Convention repudiated the 1790 decree by which France renounced wars of conquest and pledged itself not to interfere in the domestic affairs of its neighbors. By the decrees of November and December, revolutionary France proclaimed its resolution to bring "fraternal aid to all peoples who wish to recover their liberties." In practice, the new policy became one of coercion and extortion. The liberated peoples turned against their liberators. England joined the Austrians and the Prussians in the war against France, against what Burke had already characterized "this wild, nameless thing . . . in the heart of Europe." With the entry of the United Provinces and Spain in the lists, the first of the European coalitions was formed, and France was ringed by armies on land and the British fleet on the Atlantic.

Reverses began in the early spring of 1793. The Rhineland was lost, and the Austrians laid siege to Mainz. Dumouriez, repulsed in Holland, fell back to the Austrian Netherlands. Raging over the condemnation of the king and the annexationist policy, he tried to lead his troops against Paris, but failed. Foiled in his moves to crush the Jacobins and restore the monarchy, he abandoned his command and deserted to the Austrians. At home the royalist and Catholic peasantry in the Vendée, the coastal area between the mouth of the Loire and La Rochelle, took up arms against the king-killers in Paris. The Convention also fell under attack from the sans-culottes, who turned upon deputies incapable of halting inflation and soaring food prices. They found new leaders in men contemptuously dubbed "*Enragés*" by the Girondins, madmen, foaming at the mouth, who formulated a drastic program of political and social action.

Hungry Parisians sacked food shops in the last days of February; in mid-March the Cordeliers Club proclaimed itself in "insurrection" against the government.

The insurrectionary move failed, but the Convention could not resist popular pressure for emergency measures against enemies at home. It agreed to have a revolutionary tribunal in Paris and watch committees in important communes. A decree promised a revolutionary army of the interior. Representatives of the Convention were sent on missions to trouble spots; a Committee of Public Safety was formed, the first step toward a powerful wartime cabinet.

These emergency measures could not be enforced effectively, and political strife grew fiercer still in early spring as the factions dragged the roles of Dumouriez, Danton, and Marat into their disputes. By mid-April the Girondins had lost practically all control of the executive and administrative branches of the government as well as of the standing and special committees. They kept their majority in the Convention, thanks to the aid of the center, and their press was still powerful and persuasive. The spoken word, however, was more direct in its appeal, and the Montagnards, exploiting the grievances of the ill-housed, ill-fed, turbulent masses, organized the armed intervention of the sovereign people of Paris against their Girondin rivals. The Girondins rallied their supporters in the moderate or conservative sections of the capital. Their followers in provincial centers, in Lyons, Bordeaux, Marseilles, and Nantes, ousted Jacobins from the municipal administration. Those acts in the provinces did not save them in Paris, where the crescendo was reached in late May in the campaign of petitions and organized demonstrations to expel their leaders from the assembly. The tragic denouement came between May 31 and June 2.

Where did Barère stand in those fearful months of crisis? What is the key to the contradictory moves he made, now for Girondins, now for the Montagnards, moves which failed to effect a sacred union within the assembly and to rally France around the assembly? The key is his mistaken conviction that irreconcilable partisans could be brought together in order to allow a united Convention to pursue a middle course; that in foreign policy, as in domestic, peace could be gained by negotiation. For all his revolutionary nationalism, he was still the man of the center. He was aghast over the ineptitude of his Girondin friends, appalled by their blind vendetta against Paris, which only strengthened the aristocratic, clerical, royalist counterrevolutionaries. He was equally frightened by the calculated Montagnard policy of exploiting radical discontent and yielding step by step to the social program of the *Enragés*. All shifts and maneuvers fall into the pattern of his determination to restore harmony at home and attain peace with the enemy. He was a left-wing Girondin and a right-wing Montagnard, in consequence unacceptable in his role of mediator to them both. To the moderates of the Convention his intentions were clear, and he retained their support; but in the end his mediation failed. With its failure his conduct was to take a new direction.

The execution of the king widened the chasm between the revolutionary republic and monarchical Europe. Upon France it imposed a shock without parallel. The Convention itself was never so divided. All this the regicides knew. Turning first to the gravest danger, they tried to assure their fellow citizens that in sending Louis XVI to the scaffold, the Convention had saved the fatherland, to convince them that the threat to the nation's security came not from an assembly falsely accused of favoring massacre but from fanatical royalists.

This difficult assignment fell to Barère, "the impartial," as Robespierre mockingly called him to his face. For the austere Robespierre, Barère was "impartial," because in voting against the reprieve he had supported a move to banish Orléans and, on the eve of the king's execution, approved a motion to bring "the men of September" to trial. Neither proposal was carried, and it strains credulity to believe that Barère wished to have them approved. He was not appealing to the assembly; he was addressing himself to provincial France. Robespierre should have known this. He should have perceived that Barère was obliquely covering the Convention against its critics outside, seeking to prove that even as the assembly's dread act against the king attested its strength, so condemning the men of September bespoke its sense of justice.

With such intentions in mind, Barère made his Report to the French Nation (January 23). It was the first of many similar reports he was to present in the course of the following year and a half. Bitter prejudices and deep fears, he began, had pitted the deputies against each other. "Those different opinions were inspired by honorable motives. Feelings of humanity . . . fears more or less justified concerning the rights and powers of the representatives divided our minds. The time has now ceased, the motives have disappeared. Respect for the freedom of opinion should efface those stormy scenes from our memory. . . . Henceforth the National Convention and the French people will have only a single thought, a single feeling, liberty and civic brotherhood. . . . The time has ceased for disputes; we must act. We need prompt, efficacious measures. The despots of Europe can be strong only if we are divided. . . . Let us rise before an astounded Europe. . . . Let the entire nation rise again . . . in the defense of the republic. This is the cause of Frenchmen; it is the cause of all mankind."

His Report to the French Nation beat the nationalist drums, and not for the first time. "Your finest mission," he had declared in speaking against the reprieve, "is to bring the Revolution to the powers." While whipping up patriotic feeling against the foreign enemy, however, he pleaded for harmony at home, for a sacred union of republicans. The olive branch which he extended to Montagnards and Girondins came too late. The trial of the king had shattered the false truce of the fall, and in the late winter and early spring of 1793, unresolved antagonisms heightened tensions and accentuated verbal intemperance. Those antagonisms strengthened the resolution of the sectionnaires to make an end of the futile parliamentary bickering. Their program went far beyond that of the bourgeois deputies, Montagnards and Girondins alike. To halt inflation and soaring living costs, they advocated a graduated tax on the well-to-do, governmental requisition of grain for the fighting forces, and price controls of prime commodities to bring relief to civilian consumers. On the political front, they called for the establishment of a revolutionary tribunal to try and judge arrested counterrevolutionaries and suspects and the creation of a revolutionary army of the interior to second the activities of local authorities. Above all, they demanded repressive measures against the Girondins. Until those political obstructionists were disposed of, all roads to the goal that the Enragés and the followers of Hébert in the Cordeliers had in mind were blocked.

Barère could not go that far. He was still hopeful of establishing a modus vivendi within the Convention and by deft concessions to each faction to bring them both together. When the Girondins sponsored a proposal at the end of January to oust the Jacobin Pache from the war ministry, he supported the move. To keep the balance, he endorsed the Jacobin motion to set up an auxiliary committee made up of club members to collaborate with the Committee on the Constitution which the Girondins controlled. When, in February, pillagers sacked the food shops, he condemned the violation of property rights and denounced advocates of an "agrarian law," but he also dissuaded the assembly from instituting proceedings against the "good Parisians." They were led astray, he explained, by evil advisers.

When the Cordeliers Club gave the signal for an insurrection, he again played for time. Convinced that the attempt would fail—neither the Jacobins nor the majority of the sections were behind it—he called only for an investigation of the disorders. If *Le Patriote français* found that "the measures he proposed were not up to the level of his speech," those measures were deliberately soft because he feared that the formal condemnation of the would-be insurrectionists would incite the National

Guard of the departments to march on Paris. "We shall know in a few days," he said, "if there were really plots to destroy our freedom." It was not until the immediate danger, both of insurrection and departmental intervention, was over that he called for the punishment of the Paris ringleaders (March 17). Brissot's journal rewarded his good sense by berating what it called an attempt to reconcile "crime with truth."

Barère tried to curb mass reprisals when news of reverses on the fighting fronts flowed into the capital and volunteers were being summoned from every section of the city to fight in the front lines. Once again the cry was raised to leave no traitors behind and give short shrift to the enemies within. Again the sections clamored for a revolutionary tribunal to try arrested suspects. To that demand Barère assented, but remembering, as well he might, how volunteers had marched off in August, leaving the city to irresponsible popular elements, he tried to have the assembly decree that the tribunal should have jurors as well as judges. On this point he succeeded; he was not successful in his motion to have jurors named from the ranks of the deputies rather than from members enrolled in the section assemblies.

While he reiterated that the Convention was "neither on this side nor on the other, [but] in the whole gathering," the daily altercations went on, finding fresh substance in Dumouriez's desertion. His betrayal stupified France, and deputies closest to him scurried for cover to disassociate themselves from the traitor. The Girondins were vulnerable: Dumouriez was their general. To deflect indignation from themselves, they attempted to incriminate Danton. Danton too was vulnerable. His name was linked with Dumouriez's in undercover moves to seat the Duke of Chartres upon a restored throne. He had sung Dumouriez's praises and shielded the commander from investigation in March, and suspicion existed that the two men were in accord to establish a dictatorship. In his alleged racketeering in Belgium, from which he had just returned, the Girondins had a handle against him and a smoke screen for themselves.

Barère was in an exposed position. His name was associated in the public mind with Danton and the policy of propaganda and expansion to which Dumouriez's defection dealt a crushing blow. When France declared war upon Great Britain (February 1, 1793), Barère had appealed to the British people to repudiate their government, and the Francophile London Constitutional Society elected him an honorary member, holding him "one of the most judicious and enlightened friends of liberty." When Dumouriez began his invasion of Holland, Barère had summoned "the noble Batavians" to take up arms for the French liberators. Though for months he endeavored within the Committee of General Defense to delay the declaration of war on Spain, there was no intimation of those efforts in his public utterances, and when Spain entered the coalition, he had assured his fellow Frenchmen that the break with the old Bourbon partner of the Family Compact was "only an additional triumph for liberty."

A year earlier he had addressed an admiring letter to his "dear friend," whose triumphs he foresaw in his mind's eye. Though that was not known, the public could remember that on the very eve of Dumouriez's desertion, he had openly stated that "Dumouriez alone was worth an army." Besides, his name was brought up in the investigation of a ring of unsavory adventurers who had attached themselves to the general. Earlier, they had distributed secret funds to save Louis XVI; now they were charged with making huge profits from war contracts. Barère had nothing to do with their tortuous activities and at no time was he accused of complicity with the ring. Yet, it was not only the endlessly suspicious Marat who called attention to the fact that in response to a personal appeal from Dumouriez Barère defended two of its members charged with peculation on the very floor of the assembly. He too had to scurry for cover.

Both Danton and Barère successfully disentangled themselves. The former broke dramatically with the Girondins, who accused him, as they once had accused Robespierre, and with more reason, of seeking to establish a dictatorship. Barère also denounced his sometime friend, casting the odium of Dumouriez's treason upon the Girondin leaders. The two agile politicians saved themselves, and they did more. Out of the nettle of danger the master improvisers plucked the flower of safety for the hard-pressed Republic. Overcoming the misgivings of the center, they prevailed upon it to support the creation of a small, compact committee of deputies to guide the entire war effort.

Thanks in large part to their efforts—though in 1795 Barère went to great lengths to minimize his role—the Convention decreed the establishment of the first Committee of Public Safety (*comité de salut public*) on April 6. It was a small board of nine men, meeting in secret session, composed of deputies elected by their peers. Contrasted with the closely-knit and virtually self-perpetuating board of a year later, the first Committee lacked effective executive authority. By comparison with the large unwieldy Committee of General Defense, which it superseded, it was a long step forward in the direction of centralized government. The members were to hold office only for a month, re-election dependent upon the pleasure of an assembly not yet prepared to delegate its powers for a long period. The funds placed at the disposal of the Committee were limited, and a motion to permit it to use those funds without accounting to the Convention was voted down. It could not make arrests in its own name nor remove and replace existing administrative personnel. It was not yet empowered, as it was to be later, to govern by decrees nominally endorsed by the assembly as a whole. For the present it could only make recommendations and speed up legislative action. Its controls over representatives-on-mission in danger spots in the interior and on the fighting fronts were slight. Yet for all that it could not do, its creation gave hope that the paralyzing parliamentary ineffectiveness would be overcome. A strong executive was in the making. For many Montagnards, however, its power was not enough; for

Girondins, Danton's ascendancy within it was too much. The struggle went on.

No Girondin was elected to the Committee. Save for Danton and two adherents, all the deputies elected came from the moderates of the Plain. Barère was the first on the list: he received 360 votes, the total in his favor exceeding by 127 the ballots cast for Danton, who was second. He could correctly interpret the vote as endorsement of his efforts at mediation, of his determination to make the Convention and the Convention alone the repository of the general will. A letter that he had just received from the two deputies-on-mission to the troubled southwest throws a revealing light upon the esteem in which he was held. One of the writers was Jeanbon Saint-André, hard-working and perspicacious, himself to become one of the pillars of the Committee. "Barère," the letter read, "you have the confidence of a large part of the assembly . . . but it only imposes greater duties upon you. It is with tears over the fate of the country that [we] urge you to work with all your strength to fill in the gaping void beneath our feet. . . . You see only the public good. What are we to do . . . ? We await your reply impatiently. . . ."

In the Committee, Barère first served as secretary together with Robert Lindet, like himself a moderate and like himself to remain a Committee member until Thermidor. Because of his experience, he was given joint responsibility with Danton to supervise the conduct of foreign affairs within the Committee. Until the denouement of the parliamentary struggle for power in the last weeks of May, this assignment kept him fully occupied and he mediated the issues of political strife less frequently than in the past. The record of his attendance at the two daily sessions of the Committee testifies to the conscientious discharge of his responsibilities. Available evidence shows that of the 116 meetings which were held between the first session on April 6 and the proscription of the Girondin leaders on June 2, he missed the roll call only eleven times at most, possibly fewer. Obviously, he was not shirking his duty.

Jeanbon had pleaded for guidance: "What are we to do?" Barère's response was to persevere in his own policy of appeasement. Under his direction and Danton's, foreign relations took a new turn. For propaganda and annexation, the course laid down in the first flush of military victory in the preceding fall, the Committee substituted coexistence, entering upon an intricate course of secret peace negotiations with the powers. Barère was cutting losses: if the Committee could come to terms with the coalition, it would be free for the great tasks at home. Seconding Danton in this policy, as he had done before when he nominally subscribed to the expansionist program, he expounded and defended the merits of the new policy (April 18) which would establish peace on a solid basis: "You have declared with all the forcefulness of republican reason that you will never suffer any government to influence your own and interfere with the constitution that you wish to give to France; and at the same time you declared that you will never meddle with the forms of other governments."

Protests were loud against a policy of appeasement to which clung a strong odor of defeatism. It devolved upon the policymakers to answer protests, in fact to deny, that the disclosures which had leaked out to the public were true. During the month of May, while the political strife in Paris was moving toward a climax, Barère was hard at work drafting and presenting on the assembly floor a series of progress reports on the foreign situation. There were six of them in all but only a single theme: rumors of peace negotiations were without substance; rumors were the work of disruptive foreign agents.

His reports were in the nature of official government releases. He was in the government, not in the opposition, and he could not divulge what the Committee judged inopportune at that delicate moment to disclose. Negotiations were indeed going on. With England and Austria the French agents took unofficial soundings; subsidies were offered to Sweden for its continued neutrality; as reprisal against other neutrals which had bowed

down before British naval coercion, the Committee was preparing coercion of its own in the form of a stringent Navigation
Act.

The foreign policy that Barère defended was a poor one, and,
in the circumstances, impossible. Of the good faith of the ama-
teur diplomatists—no one in the council of ministers which cooperated with Danton and Barère had professional experience—
there was no question, but the validity of their assumptions was
more than dubious. To disavow propaganda and adopt coexistence, to initiate secret peace negotiations when everywhere
the enemy was advancing, when at home there was no unity of
will and command but strife and confusion, that was not treason
as critics bitterly held. It was a stupendous, staggering error of
judgment. It was putting second things first, leading from weakness, inviting the enemy to stiffen its terms. It was of a piece
with Barère's and Danton's impotent policy of conciliation at
home. Only total war, the *guerre à outrance* which Jacobins and
sections demanded, could save the threatened Republic. For
that there had to be an end of temporizing with the Girondins,
and neither Danton nor Barère yet agreed to the radical surgery
of attaining political unity by political amputation. They would
not give up the Girondins, and the Girondins would not give up
their obstructionist policy. Though the shadows were beginning
to fall, the latter continued in the path adopted from the
very start. The courage with which many of them sealed their
fate merited a better end.

They undertook to have Marat indicted for incendiary writing, an augury of what could follow for other prominent
Montagnards if the Convention sacrificed his parliamentary
immunity. The attempt failed when the Revolutionary Tribunal
(now established) exonerated him and the Mountain took
stock. Their critics were many and strong in the great provincial cities of Orléans, Lyons, Marseilles, and Bordeaux. The
Paris anti-Jacobins who fought to get control of section assemblies and ostensibly supported the Girondin point of view called

themselves moderates. Some in fact were moderates; others, however, were monarchists, adherents of the refractory clergy and the *ci-devants*. They were as little in favor of the Girondins as they were for the Mountain; they were true counterrevolutionaries. In the letter from the two deputies-on-mission Barère had read a fearful warning of how much revolutionary unity had disintegrated. "People are everywhere tired of the Revolution," they wrote. "The rich detest it, the poor lack bread. . . . All those whom once we called moderates, who after a fashion had made common cause with the patriots, who at least wished some kind of a revolution, do not want one any longer. . . . They want the counter-revolution, and they are linked in feeling, in intention, and in resolution—and soon will be in deed and action—with the aristocrats." These were prophetic words.

The Montagnards realized how great was the threat to them and the Convention. If the anti-Jacobin section movement spread from the provinces to Paris, the Girondins would prevail, sufficiently strengthened to impose their will upon the assembly. In Paris it was still touch and go. The sections in the western part of the city were openly hostile to the Montagnards. They had adherents in nearly all the other wards of the capital and in many of them opposition of the word had become opposition of the fist. A memorandum that Robespierre penned for himself, possibly for discussion with his associates, leaves no doubt that he foresaw the necessity of enlisting the aid of the democratic sections to hold the reaction in check without, however, permitting either the Enragés or the Hébertists to direct the popular movement and make political capital of it. Gauging the situation coolly, he realized that to obtain the support of the section assemblies the Mountain would have to pay a price. The first quid pro quo was price controls, for which the sans-culottes in all the towns and cities had long clamored. Since the Plain too reasoned in his fashion, on May 4 the Convention was able to vote a decree extending the existing practice of price control over the sale of grain and fodder in local communities to the entire country. By the provisions of the decree the fixed price (*maximum*) would be set by each department. Though the decree was to prove unworkable, its value as a token of the anti-Girondin working agreement was high.

From early April, then, the Montagnards in the Convention coordinated their action with the rank and file of the section assemblies, the activists in the council general of the Commune, and the Jacobins to purge the Convention of the Girondin leaders and assure themselves a majority within it. The last fortnight of May was crucial and each side prepared for a denouement. Petitioners for the Girondins threatened war if their leaders were arrested and expelled. In Paris, Mayor Pache and his colleagues of the Commune winked at the meetings of delegates from section assemblies and ward watch committees. Even before the delegates gathered at the Archbishop's palace on the Ile de la Cité on May 19 to propose that course, rumors were circulating that they planned to seize the Girondin chieftains and execute them: "to september them," was the phrase. The Girondin deputies fumed over the proceedings, but Pache defended the legality of the meeting. In a reflex of fear Guadet demanded on May 17 that the Commune should be reorganized. He demanded that the alternate deputies *(suppléants)* to the Convention be summoned to the provincial town of Bourges to take their seats in a truly representative assembly of the sovereign people if the Convention itself were to be dissolved by force in Paris. This proposal gave the measure of the Girondin panic. If from their point of view it was understandable, it was from the point of view of their own interest too late by several months. It played directly into the hands of their enemies.

Barère spoke against Guadet's motion on the following day, May 18. He called attention to the "concerted movement" of the aristocracy in Lyons, Marseilles, and other cities to destroy liberty. He cited evidence, professing not to believe it, that the sections, the department of Paris, and the Commune were plotting against the Convention.

Though he held such a plot unlikely, he agreed that it should be investigated. "If I wanted anarchy," he said of Guadet's motion to suppress the existing municipal administration, "I would support it." The proposal to convoke the supernumerary deputies, he held inadequate and dangerous: "I close by asking that a commission of twelve members be named to examine the resolutions that the Commune has passed in the last month."

Superficially, his intercession sounded naïve or disingenuous or both; and perhaps in retrospect his entire course in the month-long crisis was unrealistic. Whether it was or was not, in any case he was adhering to the line of his earlier conduct: he was employing his tactics of temporizing, censuring both sides and playing for time to let passions cool. If time were gained, he believed, the Committee of Public Safety would step in and exercise its authority. He was referring the quarrel, which the legislature itself could not end, to the new executive committee of the assembly to solve in the name of the latter. Whether wise or not, his move satisfied no one. Danton supported the establishment of the Commission of Twelve, but Marat thought the idea "scarcely better" than Guadet's proposal. Barère complained two years later of the criticism: "I was called weak . . . because I did not wish to enroll under any banner . . . , march under the bloody standard of the 'Friend of the People' or under . . . the banner of *Le Patriote français*." Criticism notwithstanding, he continued in his course, even after the section delegates formed their own committee at the Evêché on the 19th, and called on the Convention to use its legal right to requisition the armed forces for its defense, a right which took precedence over that of the Commune. This attempt to strengthen the Convention was rewarded by *Le Patriote français*, which commented on "the perfidy and cowardice . . . of the amphibious Barrere [sic]."

The Commission of Twelve made no true effort at inquiry. Packed with Girondin sympathizers, it ordered the arrest of outstanding sectionnaires, including Hébert, editor of *Le Père Duchêne* and assistant prosecutor of the Commune. Hébert may have been an irresponsible demagogue but he was the darling of the masses and the Commune vigorously protested his arrest. Passing to the offensive, it demanded that the commission members be brought before the Revolutionary Tribunal. Now the Convention became what Danton called it, "an arena of gladiators." The Girondin president of the assembly was carried away by hatred into voicing a furious threat: "If these constantly renewed insurrections should violate the integrity of the national assembly, I declare to you in the name of France that Paris will be destroyed [and] soon people will be searching the banks of the Seine to see whether Paris had ever existed."

The threat was sheer madness, but Danton and Barère did not give up. On Danton's motion, the commission was abolished, only to have the Convention reinstate it. The next move came from the left. That same night, May 29, the steering committee of the insurgents proclaimed itself the Insurrectionary Committee and made final preparations to overawe the Convention. Danton and Barère bestirred themselves as never before to forestall the new *journée* that was being planned, but the long, detailed report which they jointly composed for Barère to read in the assembly fell on angry ears. At their night session, the Jacobins scored him for his "temporizing spirit" and *Le Patriote français* attacked him fiercely: "Barère painted anarchy in muted colors and true republicanism under false colors; but he forgot to paint men who, to play a role, proclaim neutrality, and woo all parties in order to receive honors and assignments from each."

The Insurrectionary Committee proclaimed Paris "in a state of insurrection against the aristocratic and oppressive faction." It ordered the city gates closed and named the swashbuckler Hanriot commander of the National Guard. Robespierre gave those ultimate preparations his blessing, not, however, without misgiving: "I am incapable of prescribing to the people the means of saving itself." If he had long been ready to exploit the grievances of the masses, he intended insurrection to be one kept within bounds. A new September massacre was not in his calculations. Between the 30th and the 31st the Central Revolutionary Committee, as the Insurrectionary Committee now called itself, repeated the procedures of August 9-10, it merged with sympathizers from the department of Paris and the Commune and took over formal control of the municipal government.

On the 31st, delegation after delegation of petitioners invaded the assembly hall demanding the arrest of the twenty-two Girondins. The Plain held firm on that day, rejecting all petitions; and when the session ended, the deputies went out en masse from the palace of the Tuileries, where their meetings were now held, into the gardens outside, fraternizing with the crowds. The threat of the sans-culottes had evaporated, so it seemed, and after weeks of living on the brink, the peaceful outcome brought vast relief. Now the Committee of Public Safety tried to seize the initiative, as Barère had wished. In its name he moved the dismissal of the Commission of Twelve and requested again that the National Guard be placed at the disposal of the Convention. Another decree called on the Committee to report on the activities of the Girondins to the assembly within three days; meantime it would issue a proclamation to inform the nation what had taken place. The Convention survived the first test, but the outcome was still in doubt. Barère "rejected my observations with a mocking smile," wrote Marat.

Barère drafted the proclamation which he read from the rostrum of the assembly on June 1. Life and property, he pointed out, were secure. A day which awakened grave anxiety had ended peacefully. Though the tocsin had rung and the alarm gun boomed, the sectionnaires had defended the Convention and they "deserved well of the *patrie*." With his words and the turn that events had taken the deputies of the

Plain were more than content. When he read that "liberty profits by all that happened," jeers from the Girondin benches greeted his words, and at that point, Barère "the impartial," Barère of "the mocking smile," lost his temper and his poise. He turned on the hecklers. "Did you inquire on July 14, on August 10," and his words poured out in a torrent, "who were the persons who rang the tocsin; did you call for an accounting of the abuses, the excesses, the very horrors that sullied the day of July 14? . . . Let us not probe into the causes of yesterday's events, let us consider only the results." Brissot no more than Marat was mollified by Barère's version of what had taken place. "The seditious hands that sounded the tocsin would not have traced the events differently," was his comment in *Le Patriote français*.

"The results" that Barère wished the Gironde to consider were not final, for the insurrectionists were gathering their strength to strike again. June 2 fell on a Sunday and this time the sectionnaires turned out in force. Five thousand National Guards ringed the assembly with cannon and bayonets, defiant of the Convention's order to obey only its command; in the adjacent gardens a throng of 80,000 to 100,000 patriots, men and women, largely unarmed, shouted rough encouragement to the troops. Again petitioners followed petitioners, and again the deputies held out. To break the deadlock Barère suggested a solution which would maintain the semblance of legality, a proposal that the Committee had already discussed: "Let the twenty-two suspend themselves voluntarily from office" until the Committee was ready with its report.

The Girondins spurned his effort and the agony of coercion went on for hours. Levelled bayonets and muskets greeted each attempt of the representatives of the people to leave the hall. It was nearing five o'clock in the afternoon, time for the first of the two sessions to adjourn, when Barère clutched at a last straw. "Let us prove that we are free," he cried out, "let us adjourn this session; let the deputies assure themselves of [the people's] good will by joining the men under arms." Perhaps he was discounting the inevitable and anticipating the failure of his move in order to prove to the Plain that if it did not give up the Girondins peacefully, the whole Convention would succumb. Perhaps he believed that deputies and troops would fraternize as the deputies had fraternized with the civilian crowd two days earlier.

His proposal was unexpected, and Robespierre turned angrily against him, upbraiding him loudly for the "mess" (*gâchis*) that he was making. At this juncture Barère was indeed making a mess. If one guard lost his nerve, if one trigger were pulled, a massacre could ensue. Small wonder that Robespierre, resolved to use the sectionnaires without yielding the initiative to them, was furious. But nerves held, no one fired as the deputies moved about forlornly in the gardens, turning from one closed gate to another. The end had come. Broken in spirit, they returned to their seats and voted the house arrest of twenty-nine Girondins and two ministers. Mediation had failed; political unity by partition was in the making.

This dramatic finale shattered Barère's hopes. He had done all that could be done to save the Girondins short of sharing their fate and he had failed. Failure was a *fait accompli*; in a revolution, he had said again and again, one accepted results, one did not look back. He was no hero and he had decent respect for his own security. He chose to survive and serve. With eyes suffused with tears—so reported a former friend, Helen Williams—he set to work to prepare a report to the French people which would prove that the cause of liberty had prevailed on June 2. Though he still refused to sacrifice parliamentary immunity and persevered for several weeks more to have the arrested deputies reinstated, June 2 was not to be undone. Step by step he accepted the consequences, and before the summer was over he was speaking the language of terror.

## ᢂ I X ᢂ

# *The Making of the Terrorist,*
# *June-October, 1793*

THE mediators of the Committee did not avail. The Girondin leaders were expelled and the Montagnards took over direction of Convention policy. Enforcing control, however, proved as difficult as acquiring it. Though seventy-five Girondin deputies who had not been molested signed a protest and the deputies who had been arrested were soon to escape from Paris and organize the federalist rebellion against "the Republic, one and indivisible," the Committee clung to its conciliatory policy. Indeed both Danton and Barère contemplated reinstating the victims of the June 2 purge. On June 6 Barère presented the Committee report on developments between May 31 and June 2, together with recommendations for action. The Committee remained convinced, it began, that in its report of June 1 it had correctly assessed a complex situation, but since grave fears to the contrary persisted, the Convention should dispel them. It should abolish the Insurrectionary Committee: "The revolutionary committee of the republic is you. . . . It is the Convention . . . one and indivisible." The real trouble, it continued, blinking the truth, came from foreign agitators, hence the Committee proposed that they be expelled from French soil. To cement the union of all patriots the deputies should resume their great task of drafting a new constitution: "The moment has now come to establish liberty upon its true foundations." Pending its completion the fear of provincials should be allayed; accordingly, the Committee proposed that the Convention send hostages from its own ranks to guarantee the personal security of the arrested Girondins: "It was Danton who first made the suggestion [and] Couthon, who had called for the arrests, offers himself as a hostage to Bordeaux. All the members of your Committee offer themselves . . . and they have only one fear, that you will not find them worthy of the preference that they seek."

That was all that Barère proposed in the name of the Committee. It had labored and brought forth a timid mouse. In the heated two-day debate which ensued, Robespierre led the opposition to this gesture of containment. To reassure the possessing classes that there would be no knuckling under to the terrorist program, he argued, was one thing. "The people en masse," he stated with staccato brevity, "cannot govern," but to send out hostages was cowardly opportunism, tantamount to apologizing for the triumphant finale to months of struggle. He was right, and Barère beat a retreat, meekly explaining that the Committee "had to yield to circumstances." There was the trouble: in the place of leadership the Committee proposed adaptation to circumstances.

Meantime the ambiguous relations between the Montagnards in the train of Robespierre and the sectionnaires who had supported those deputies on June 2 came into the open. When the Parisian allies presented their bill, the Montagnards would not honor it. It was not within Robespierre's calculations to allow the sections to make policy for the Convention, least of all to dictate it. If the deputies would not endorse the Committee and appeasement, neither would they advance toward the stringent controls that the sections advocated. To avoid foundering on the shoals of appeasement and escape the coercive course which they neither desired nor had the power to enforce, they and the Committee convinced themselves that drafting the new republican constitution would solve their problems. A draft was rapidly elaborated by a new Montagnard subcommittee, briefly discussed, article by article, and adopted by the whole assembly on June 24. If in the light of what was to happen, the hope was fatuous that a charter would bring peace, seen in the light of the deputies' dilemma, it was understandable. The constitution could appeal to men of substance. It broadened the category of the natural rights of man by including within it freedom of economic enterprise, and it toned down the generous provisions for social democracy that Robespierre had advanced in earlier discussions. If accepted, it held forth to the moderates of the assembly the prospect that they might regain control over the new legislature at the forthcoming elections. The constitution could appeal to men of the left, for to obtain a lien on the good will of the sans-culottes the charter contained several articles providing for a future regime of political democracy.

Barère had little to do with the substance of the new constitution, less even than he had in drafting the Constitution of 1791, which was little enough. He was still one at heart with the moderates, sharing their outlook. His interest was pragmatic. He took part in the debates to support provisions for religious and economic freedom and gave his approval to an article which guaranteed the sacredness of private property rights. Anticipating a charge from the left that the Convention was not conducting the war with needed vigor, he seconded a clause which forbade peace negotiations with any enemy that occupied French territory. Uniquely concerned with having the constitution restore national unity, he placed himself squarely on record on June 18, stating: "I support the printing of the draft. In the circumstances it can have great influence throughout the entire republic."

Three weeks after his report on the revolution of June 2, he reported again to the Convention on the completed constitution. In letter, this report of June 27 conveyed the Committee's gratification over the rapid completion of a difficult assignment; in spirit, it was a revealing personal document. It made clear that while he was leaving immediate appeasement behind, he was not renouncing hopes in an ultimate reconciliation, a reconciliation which the new constitutional charter would effect. There had been disarray and confusion after June 2, he began, but how rapidly had the united Convention garnered the wisdom of the ages to guide it in its course. Did not the constitution ensure equality to all Frenchmen, also civil liberty and freedom and worship; did it not guarantee to property owners their rights and to citizens, not yet proprietors, large opportunities for economic advancement! Was it not fitting, therefore, that copies of so fundamental a charter of liberty be widely circulated and distributed "in districts and departments which have been dishonored by revolts, so that citizens could be reconciled and united by common interests!"

On his motion the Convention decreed that first, the primary electoral assemblies would hold a referendum on July 14, and second, on August 10, the anniversary of the fall of the monarchy, delegates would convene in Paris to announce the awaited and expected glad tidings that the sovereign people had ratified the new document of liberty. The motion was clever, but more clever than realistic. Moreover, it was not enough. Obviously, popular endorsement of the constitution represented only a spurious recognition of the principle of popular sovereignty. If it could be counted upon to generate enthusiasm in areas already safely republican, even if ratified by the people, it could at best only be a solution for a peaceful future. The future, however, was not peaceful in outlook; and constitutional government was no answer to the immediate crises of civil and foreign war. The constitution met none of the demands of the sectionnaires for drastic emergency measures. Providing for the future when the present was so dark was building upon sand. In the kit of constitutionalism there was no miracle drug to effect a cure.

Barère dutifully sang the praises of the proposed remedy, but the sensitive antennae of the master opportunist were sending back signals to him that in the circumstances neither appeasement nor conciliation could work. The plight of France was growing worse, not better. In the belt of departments around Paris the government could keep supporters in line, but elsewhere the outlook was black. The arrested Girondins who fled from Paris to Normandy fanned the federalist rebellion. Behind them were the men whom Jeanbon had singled out in his despairing letter to Barère—frightened property owners, outraged champions of parliamentary government, disillusioned patriots, secret royalist sympathizers, protectors of the refractory clergy. The threat from Normandy was contained, but in the Vendée, ablaze in a royalist and Catholic insurrection, the rebels held the line of the Loire, poised to cross over into republican territory. In the great cities of Lyons, Marseilles, and Toulon, counterrevolutionaries had taken over the reins of government, arresting, shooting and hanging the local Jacobins.

Reports from the military fronts were grim. The Spaniards, after crossing the Pyrenees, were advancing upon Bayonne and Perpignan. On the east and the northeast the Austrians were investing the border fortresses of Condé and Mainz, while an English task force lay siege to Valenciennes. The Atlantic waters off the coast of France were a British lake. At home, bread was selling at famine prices, the old harvest was used up, the new not yet gathered. While hoarders and black market operators prospered, the assembly which had reluctantly agreed to partial price controls made no serious effort to enforce the inadequate provisions it had voted. Pillagers were again sacking granaries and breaking into food shops in towns and cities. From all sides the cry welled forth for an end to empty words, for the long-promised revolutionary army of the interior to bring "rich egoists" to heel, for the arrest and punishment of "aristos" suspected of complicity with secret foreign agents, for severe steps to prevent the "pacifiers" (*endormeurs*) in the Convention from shielding the guilty entrenched in high places.

In his June 27 report Barère had shown that his confidence in persuasion and long-range appeasement was eroding. Without giving it up entirely, he was edging his way toward the use of force. "What matters to public liberty," he had said in a rhetorical aside, "the passing fate of a few individuals. The nation, like philosophy, sees only results." Since to the sans-culottes he was one of the "pacifiers," the intimations of his new temper notwithstanding, they attacked the Committee through him. For them he was its voice. It was he and his ilk, they spluttered, who were hampering the war effort and supporting treacherous *ci-devant* officers in command of pure republican soldiers. In that instance they were berating him because the Committee had recommended that the former nobleman, Alexandre de Beauharnais, the inept commander of the Army of the Rhine, replace the stout sans-culotte lieutenant Bouchotte as minister of war. Barère was their target because the Committee had named another "aristo," Custine, general of the Army of the North. "It is Barère," fumed one of the critics, imaginative in words but accurate in spirit, "who had Custine appointed; it is he who nominated Beauharnais, and when Chabot protested from the rostrum, Barère had cried out: 'He is my friend, he is my friend.'" And he was repeatedly taken to task for his situation reports on the fighting in the Vendée which concealed, they charged, the desperate state of affairs.

Marat who detested Barère with a contempt matched only by Barère's own distaste for the unbalanced "Friend of the People," made him the target of his ire. During the course of the protracted Girondin-Montagnard wrangling, *Le Publiciste* had already paid its respects to "the glacial Barère," "the supple Barère," "Barère, the royalist," "Barère of the mocking smile." Marat carried on in that vein. On June 21 his newspaper informed its readers that Barère was "the most dangerous of men"; and on July 14, on the eve of his assassination, Marat trumpeted a final blast: "It is he who has paralyzed all vigorous measures, lulling us all the better by his charm to massacre us. I defy him to give me the lie. . . ."

As late as July 8, five weeks after the climax of June 2, when the Committee was still undecided what action to take against the expelled deputies, the currents of anger were running sharply against "the pacifiers . . . who blow hot and cold." The end was drawing near for a Committee which could neither meet the expectations of sans-culottes and more resolute Montagnards nor cope with the opposition of moderates. Thus when the regular monthly re-election of Committee personnel came up on July 10, the war board which had shown itself unequal to responsibilities was swept away. Danton was unceremoniously dropped, rejected for sins of omission and commission. Of the nine original members elected in the preceding April, six others beside Danton also failed of re-election, like him discredited by the policy of appeasement. The two of the nine who remained, four Montagnards added to the Committee late in May, and three new Montagnards now elected, made up the new Committee of Public Safety.

Barère was one of the two to be re-elected; and, together with his friend and admirer Jeanbon, he obtained the greatest number of votes cast for any member. He had thought of not accepting office, but was prevailed upon to reconsider and serve. Despite all the savage attacks to which he had been subjected he obviously retained the confidence of his fellows. The spectacular verdict could be interpreted only as a mandate for him to continue what he had been doing: simultaneously not going so fast and sharply as to strengthen provincial resentment for the government and not so slowly as to turn the radicals in Paris against it. Basically, of course, his procedure was the realistic one that Robespierre pursued, differences of emphasis notwithstanding, the tactic of having the Convention concede piecemeal to the sectionnaires what it could not avoid of their demands without at the same time yielding initiative and control to them. If, then, the overthrow of the Danton Committee was a great divide for the Convention, it was also a watershed in Barère's revolutionary career. It marked the end of association with Danton; it signified his readiness to heed the wants of the sectionnaires; it cemented official cooperation with Robespierre, who was elected to the Committee less than three weeks later. Barère's course was now the course of Robespierre.

Six more weeks elapsed before the changes in personnel were completed in the "Great Committee" which eventually was to surmount the peril that threatened the existence of the French nation; three months elapsed before the Committee won recognition as the supreme war board of the beleaguered country. Three new and important members joined the Committee in midsummer. On July 27 the Convention elected Robespierre; early in August, largely upon Barère's initiative, it added two captains of military engineers, Lazare Carnot and Prieur de la Côte d'Or (so called to distinguish him from the other Prieur, Prieur de la Marne, who was already a member). To the enlarged wartime cabinet the Incorruptible brought more than the prestige which it still lacked. He brought to it his experience in parliamentary tactics and the program for political action which Barère accepted in its entirety: government in the name of the Convention; flexible contact and accord with the world of the sans-culottes; and effective executive authority for the Committee. Paris radicals could bay at the Committee as "a new Capet with nine heads"; Robespierre remained unshaken. If Carnot was little interested in political action, he too assented to Robespierre's tactics. Stolid and methodical, single-minded, he was unperturbed by the siege of the frontier fortresses. He was building for future action. Taking over the direction of the over-all war effort, he devoted himself to organizing and disciplining the hundreds of thousands of men who were soon at his disposal, laying plans to hurl them in overwhelming numbers against the troops of the enemy. On him devolved the tactics and strategy of victory; to Prieur, with whom he worked closely, fell the great assignment of procuring arms and material, a task for which he was superbly qualified.

Leaders were now present and a coherent policy in the making. But difficulties confronted the Committee, many trials and tests of strength. By the end of July, Belgium had been lost to the advancing Austrians. The Rhine front had collapsed and the border fortresses were falling, Condé on the 10th of July and Valenciennes on the 22nd. On the 28th, the republican troops gave up Mainz. In the south of France the federalists were in control; in the Vendée, the republican command was rent by feuds and dissension; in Paris, Charlotte Corday plunged a dagger into Marat's heart. A psychosis of rage and fear gripped France. Unless the new Committee acted and acted promptly, its days were numbered, numbered too would be the days of the Republic.

Challenge brought response and a new Barère revealed himself. The Committee was authorized by the Convention to make changes in the high command and to order arrests. On its behalf Barère called for the dismissal of the *ci-devant* General Biron from his command in the Vendée and the arrest of General Custine, who had failed to relieve Mainz. In the last days of that terrible month of July the Committee at last took action against the Girondins. It arrested those who had remained in Paris and moved their impeachment; the thirteen who had fled the capital to organize the federalist revolt, it placed outside the law. "The moment has come," this was Barère speaking, "for you to assume the proud attitude befitting national justice and strike down all conspirators without distinction." "Without distinction" was verbal bravura, for distinction there was in fact; but the decree of outlawry that he moved against old friends was cruel enough without the flourish that he added for the benefit of the sectionnaires. In the passage of the *Mémoires* where he expatiates upon the decision he is abject in tone, disingenuous in explanation; in July 1793 his accent was metallic. That he was sad at heart is certain, but he had no choice: there was no alternative for him or the Committee. The civil war was a reality; the Girondins whom the Convention outlawed on his recommendation were rebels in arms.

Proscribing the Girondins was only a first step, and on August 1 the Committee went further. The heightened mood, the shrill tone that Barère adopted, the pandering to nationalist passions that marked the report he read on the state of the republic were his personal contribution. The plots he denounced were far from baseless. He himself had received and read the letter of an émigré, frighteningly rich in details about fifth-column operations. How it came to him we do not know and he does not state. He read it and turned it over to the Committee on General Security. At the same time a secret British agent was arrested in northern France on whose person his captors found a treasury of incriminating instructions for sabotage. With evidence in hand against Pitt and the British enemy, Barère catalogued in impassioned phrases the long record of English crimes against France and mankind and moved the arrest of all Englishmen resident in the country. Then summoning the people to "vast, prompt . . . and vigorous action," he presented the new measures proposed by the Committee. They called for a sweeping reorganization of the high military command and a policy of scorched earth in the Vendée. The estates of the outlawed rebels were to be confiscated, all nondomiciled foreigners arrested. The sacred tombs and the royal remains at St. Denis would be destroyed, all the living Bourbon princes except the young minor children of the former ruler expelled from republican territory. He demanded that the imprisoned Marie-Antoinette, "that woman who has been the cause of all the woes of France," be transferred to the Conciergerie and brought to trial before the Revolutionary Tribunal.

He was proclaiming to all France that the Committee needed no instruction in coercion from the patriots of the clubs and section assemblies. But at no point in his harangue did he sacrifice the Committee's prerogative. The Committee was not relinquishing control; it was holding firm. Hence, the popular leaders were not content with what it conceded. They were not put off by the decree (August 7) which categorized Pitt as "the enemy of the human race," not satisfied with a loose recommendation that all men from the age of sixteen to sixty would be requisitioned for service.

During the fete of August 10 there was a lull in bickering, an occasion for rejoicing over the first commemoration of the overthrow of the monarchy and, too, the sweeping ratification of the constitution. Rejoicing and festivities, nevertheless, could not permanently retard the pressure for action. The clamor could not be stilled for the levy-in-mass which delegates from the electoral assemblies and their fraternal hosts in Paris were insistently demanding. Much as the Committee held back, it could not resist the torrent, and Barère no longer would. Through him the Committee did lip service to the principle of a levy, recommending on August 14 that the delegates, when they returned home, fulfill "a moral and sacred mission . . . to spread the spirit of unity and invincibility of the republic . . . and arouse the youth of France to fly to its defense." Actually, the hard-headed realists in the Committee had no intention of letting the movement get out of hand. They were aghast over the idea, dismayed by the prospect of a mass upheaval. So working *in camera*, the Committee drew up its own plan to organize the details and keep under control the revolutionary élan which it could not repress. The credit for the substance of the decree on the levy-in-mass which the Convention voted on August 23 must be given to Carnot and Prieur. To Barère belongs the credit for the spirit of the Report on the Civic Requisitioning of Young Citizens for the Defense of Our Country, which he drafted.

His report opened with renewed warning. He implored the deputies not to act hastily on so grave a matter, entreating them "to examine our needs and resources coolly," listing one by one the dangers of a mass movement which, by playing into the hands of the counterrevolutionaries, would only "produce frightful commotions, immense needs, incalculable disorder." The Committee agreed that the requisition of all resources, human and material, was required, but it insisted that the steps should be gradual and worked out with precision and care. In concluding, Barère larded the Committee's specific recommendations with his own memorable words: "Liberty has become the creditor of all citizens. Some owe it their toil, others their fortune, some their counsel, others their arms; all owe it the blood which flows in their veins. Thus all French, both sexes, all ages, are called by the nation to defend liberty. . . . Young men will fight, young men will be summoned to conquer; married men will forge arms, transport equipment and artillery, prepare supplies of food; women, who at long last should take their place and follow their true destiny in revolutions, will set aside their useless labor; their delicate hands will work on soldiers' uniforms, make tents, and bring their hospitable care to shelters where the defender of the fatherland will receive the aid that his wounds require. Children will make lint from old linen; it is for them that we are fighting; children, destined to gather all the fruits of the Revolution, will raise their pure hands toward the heavens; and old men, taking on again the obligation that they discharged in antiquity, will be borne to public squares; they will inflame the courage of the young warriors; they will stir up hatred of kings and [preach] the unity of the Republic."

The tone of this famous report was epic. There were few whom it failed to touch and the applause was thunderous when Barère took his seat. Under his emotion-laden words Barère was presenting angular, sparse recommendations. While the spellbinder played with the feelings of his listeners, his own head was cool. The decree made provision to turn public buildings into barracks and have space in the public squares utilized for munitions production. It requisitioned saddle horses for the cavalry and draft animals, other than those needed for agriculture, for the artillery and the transport of food. To store the needed grain supply, the harvest from nationalized property would also be requisitioned and all peasant proprietors would henceforth pay their taxes in kind. The emergency measures for production of arms and munitions were put under the direction of the Committee. Representatives-on-mission charged with implementing the law would work under Committee supervision and were to be invested with all the authority given to the Committee itself. While the decree in principle did requisition all French citizens for service until the enemy was driven from republican soil, it specified that for the present only non-married citizens and widowers without children, from the age of eighteen to twenty-five, would be called for military service at the fronts.

By the terms of this stupendous, awe-inspiring decree, the Committee laid the foundations for total war. Under the nominal authority of the Convention it took over leadership of the war effort, containing and directing the total force of the entire nation to ends that it had decided and defined. Not the rash, unrestrained patriotic élan of the masses but the wisdom and the cold resolution of the Committee would see France through its ordeal. Barère served his cause well on this crucial occasion, and what he did was fully recognized by his associates.

If the future promised well, immediate needs remained. Spurned by Cambon, the Convention bestirred itself to level the heavy burden of the public debt. A capital levy on the rich, a thinly disguised refunding of government paper, and a partial demonetization of the assignats issued during the monarchy brought some relief. Those measures against inflation were only palliatives, yet all summer long as food prices continued to mount the Committee tried expedient after expedient to escape decreeing the maximum which angry and hungry men and women beseeched it to institute.

Barère shared his colleagues' aversion for stringent limitations upon the free play of the natural laws of supply and demand. Like Robespierre he feared, or professed to fear, that foreign agents were whipping up the agitation for controls and hoping in that way to intensify class feelings. He had voted to rescind the existing partial regulation both of sales and prices, justifying his action by alleging that there was need for free sale and trade in grain during the interim period when the old harvest was exhausted and the new not yet gathered. Like his associates, he reluctantly gave up the tenets of physiocracy. He admitted that private purchases in a free market were leading to catastrophe. As he grudgingly retreated from defense of free trade, he rationalized his new position with the argument that the newly harvested crop now permitted the Committee to take necessary steps to reprovision towns and cities where shortages were most severe and hoarders most active. On August 9 he announced the Committee's decision to have food granaries set up in the districts that were hardest hit; and on the 25th, he moved in the name of the Committee to rescind the law which had permitted free interdepartmental grain trade. Henceforth, if they judged it necessary, the departmental authorities could requisition grain for urban centers within their jurisdiction.

Barère and the Committee had gone as far as they deemed desirable and prudent, but their halfway proposals did not arrest rising bread prices, did not still complaints. Verbal attacks went on, and Robespierre himself was not spared. Once more the sans-culottes made ready to employ the tactics of direct action that had served them on August 10 and June 2 with such striking effect; and when word leaked out on September 2 that the royalists in Toulon had surrendered that great naval port on the Mediterranean to the English, the appalling news became the catalyst of their fears. Sectionnaires, Enragés, Jacobins, the Commune, and the extremists among the Montagnards completed their preparations for a new *journée* by September 3; and on the following day, thousands of armed Parisians crowded the streets, exhorting their fellow citizens to take action.

Before they moved in strength against the Convention, they lashed out at Barère whom more than ever they regarded as the voice of the Committee. At the Jacobins that night of the 4th, he was savagely assailed for his "devious course during the Revolution." In attacking his loyal second, they were serving notice on Robespierre too. Robespierre was beyond open and direct attack at the Jacobins, but Barère was vulnerable: his words had been ambiguous, his reservations and qualifications numerous and repeated. Robespierre did not hesitate:

"As for Barère, perhaps I have more than one reason for complaint. Barère attacked me personally at a time when my enemies were pooling their efforts against me. But I would not remind myself of private insults when public security is at stake. So I declare that I have always seen a weak man in Barère but never an enemy of the public good. I shall say so again whenever necessary, if ever anyone should seek to raise charges of the same nature against him. I have seen him at work in the Committee giving himself wholeheartedly to the interests of the nation, seeking and grasping all ways and means of serving it ( *la rendre heureuse* ). And ever since Barère understood the great crimes of a faction whose full villainy he had not at first comprehended, he has found occasion to show how deeply he abhorred their principles. He has done so with vigor. He was designated as Committee spokesman to the National Convention and on every occasion that we found it useful to acquaint it with our work, he discharged his obligation with fervor and vigor truly worthy of a republican, with fervor and vigor commensurate with the dangers to which the fatherland is exposed."

Robespierre spoke eloquently with the realistic understanding that only if it closed ranks could the Committee survive. Barère was open to attack, but he was extraordinarily valuable, far too valuable to be sacrificed to the rancor of extremists. On the following day Barère gave proof that Robespierre's confidence in him was not ill-founded. On September 5, petitioners swarmed into the halls of the assembly tirelessly pressing their demands; and for hours the representatives of the people fought a delaying action, waiting for the Committee to take the lead. Twice in the course of that agonizing day the Committee sent word that it was deliberating, that presently it would announce its policy. Repeatedly its critics shrugged off the temporizing tactics, retorting through the voice of Billaud-Varenne that the Committee's intentions were immaterial, it was for the Convention to act. The Convention had in fact already acted—after its fashion. On the preceding day, the 4th, it had accepted the principle of the maximum; on the 5th, while waiting for the Committee, the Convention agreed to pay the sectionnaires the equivalent of their workday for attendance at two weekly meetings of the section assemblies; it agreed also to arrest suspects. Beyond that the deputies would not go.

Late that day when the Committee was at last ready with recommendations, Barère presented them. Again the tone of his report was intensely personal, a calculated effort to give emotional gratification to the armed petitioners and would-be insurrectionists. For the Committee he accepted "the great slogan which we owe to the Commune of Paris: 'Let us make terror the order of the day.'" He added, in a parenthesis which in the excitement may have passed unnoticed, that the Committee would have "organized and regularized" terror against all conspirators, against Brissot and Marie-Antoinette too. In the name of the Committee he paid further tribute to the Commune for its great work in provisioning the capital and he commended "the excellent Society of Jacobins which watches day and night over public safety." And then the Committee gave the petitioners what they had come principally to get: Barère recommended for ratification by the Convention the immediate formation of a revolutionary army of the interior.

Here petitioners withdrew and the troubled day ended. On the face of it, the sans-culottes had gained their ends and bent the Convention and the Committee to their will. Barère and his associates knew better. Except for the provision for the revolutionary army of the interior, the Committee had absorbed the shock of attack. Bending before the storm, it rose again unbroken. Terror was in fact the order of the day, but terror that the Committee intended to control and direct, legal terror from above, not anarchic violence from the streets. By giving ground where it chose to do so and on its own terms the Committee had met the challenge. It emerged not weakened but stronger from the test of September 5.

On that day Barère paid off a first installment of his debt to Robespierre, and from that day he no longer hesitated. The relentless pressure of the militants, the cumulative weight of danger, and fear for his own person had transformed "the gentle Barère." The humanitarian of 1789 had become the "commissar" of 1793. The inclination was long present; the willingness was latent even in 1789, to sacrifice the individual upon the altar of the nation. He flaunted his credo of state supremacy on September 6: "It was a sacred duty to use all the resources of the state to crush its enemies, to impose republicanism upon all who wished to live on French soil. . . ."

Ready now to employ terror, the Committee also employed guile to neutralize critics. It took out insurance, advising the Convention to increase the personnel of the Committee and elect, as two additional members, the Montagnard deputies who had been foremost in rebuking it for its Fabian tactics. In that way it obtained the services of Collot d'Herbois and Billaud-Varenne, both vociferous champions of the sans-culottes, both devotees of state supremacy. Both were now harnessed by election into cooperation with their colleagues. The Committee strengthened itself more directly. Having curbed Collot and Billaud by responsibility, it broke the cadres of the popular movement. It dissolved several revolutionary societies and arrested the leaders of the Enragés. As agreed upon earlier, the meetings of the section assemblies were limited to two per week. There was no dissenting voice when, on the 11th, Barère asked that the powers of the Committee be confirmed for an additional month. There was no opposition two days later when the Convention voted the Committee authority to nominate the members of all the other committees of the assembly, including those of the great rival Committee of General Security, also to assume direct supervision over the field agents sent out by the council of ministers.

As the Committee moved forward to legal dictatorship, the potential of the sans-culottes for obstruction grew weaker. Nonetheless they renewed demands which they had failed to impose on September 5. They exerted unrelieved pressure for purges in the military and civilian command, for the actual arrest of suspects, and for the trial of those already in the coils of the police. On the recommendation of the famed jurist, Merlin de Douai, a law defining categories of suspects was voted on the 17th. It was a wretchedly ill-defined law, vindictive, loose, and intemperate, but Barère sealed it with the Committee's approval: "In a revolution everything which tends to save the fatherland, to strengthen the new government, to ensure liberty, is religiously commanded...."

Political terror was now legal and "religiously commanded"; economic terror was in sight. However, before the Committee could finally institute control of prices and wages, it had to overcome recalcitrant deputies who held out against it. There were still many in the Convention who doggedly opposed the maximum—deputies jealous of the Committee and dismayed by its new power, moderates who hoped against hope that the constitution would become operative, representatives-on-mission chafing under the restrictions that the Committee would put on their initiative. This parliamentary opposition came to a head on September 25, and Robespierre met the challenge to unseat the Committee unflinchingly. Certain that he would be sustained, he called for a vote of confidence, and Barère echoed his appeal for support: "The Committee needs your strength; it needs your confidence; if it has forfeited your support, recall us to your midst." The deputies did not dare to go beyond complaints; they did not dare to act upon their convictions. They voted to support the Committee. And on the 29th the Convention finally voted the Law of the Maximum for national control of prices and wages.

With that law, the sans-culottes were for the moment satisfied. They were mollified too by the first of the punitive legal measures against the supporters of the Girondins and by the decree committing Marie-Antoinette to trial before the Revolutionary Tribunal. With relative calm outside the assembly and within it a surly opposition too cowed to act, the Committee was in the saddle. On October 10 its triumph was officially sealed. The Convention formally suspended the application of the constitution and decreed that "the provisional government of France is revolutionary until the peace."

The effort to establish an executive government had succeeded and the Committee of Public Safety had established its domination. In its ascent to power Barère had served the Committee well. He was more than the echo of its resolution to wage total war and practice total terror. He was a comaker of that policy, important and influential in formulating the doctrine, organizing the action, and forging the instruments of power. The sometime mediator made his adieux to temporizing and conciliation. He was now one of the rulers of the revolutionary republic.

# Revolutionary Terrorist,
# October-December, 1793

THE Committee was formally recognized as the provisional government when the republican constitution that Barère had lauded and the citizens endorsed was set aside on October 10. In theory "the Great Committee" was subordinate to the Convention; in practice, it was a true executive, possessing many of the means to make its collective will effective. In Paris, where the organized sans-culottes remained strong, full political control was not attained, but clubs and revolutionary committees elsewhere were being disciplined and enrolled, after a fashion, into government service. Against disunity, apathy, and hostility, the Committee was forging a coercive apparatus to curb its critics from the left and the right and marshal the resources of the nation against danger. Its members were becoming imbued with the conviction that in them was incorporated the general will, the sovereign will of the people, which no one could oppose without revealing himself an enemy of the revolutionary cause.

In this evolution there was nothing metaphysical: it was a response to circumstances. Under the pressure of multiple danger the members of the Committee became convinced that control and coercion alone could save the Revolution. That Barère responded to the challenge as he did is not surprising. As early as June 1789, he had written in *Le Point du Jour* that "when the fatherland is in danger, there are no means which it is not obliged to employ to make itself secure." In September 1793, in endorsing the Law of Suspects, he made it "the sacred duty" of the deputies to crush the enemies of the Revolution: "If we had thunder, we would use it. . . . In a revolution everything which might save the country, strengthen the revolutionary government, ensure liberty, is religiously commanded and becomes legitimate."

In 1797, after he had fallen from power and lay in hiding from the authorities, he looked back upon the revolutionary scene and wrote in a small book, *De la pensée du gouvernement républicain*, "I was a revolutionist, I am a constitutionalist. . . . Liberty is conquered by force, wisdom preserves it; energy established the republic, laws will maintain it." He looked back upon "the shocks of the Revolution . . . its excesses . . . the violent men swept by their enthusiasm for liberty . . . fanatics but honest men with false ideas of equality and a touchy love for liberty . . . men carried away by the revolutionary torrent. . . . " That revolutionary regime, he reminded his readers, however "violent, unfair, terrible [was] necessary." So in 1793 he made his farewells to conciliation. Like Robespierre, who defended him against critics, like Robespierre, whom he was supporting with all his strength, he saw the revolutionary cause embodied in the progressive middle-class republican government. Until all individuals and all groups that opposed it were crushed, the Terror had to continue. He was not operating in a void; he served an ideal, conscious of what he was doing, because he was not of the stuff of martyrs or fanatics, fusing considerations of self-interest and self-preservation with deepest concern for the interests and the good of the new community that the triumphant Republic would found.

With the means of coercion at hand, Barère supported his colleagues of the Committee in their punitive measures against the imprisoned and fallen. War was total, political terror was total. The wretched Marie-Antoinette went to the scaffold on October 16, the first notable victim of the state trials, and his comment was brutally terse: "The guillotine has severed a powerful knot of the diplomacy of the courts of Europe." He made no protest when his friend, the spent old savant, Bailly, went to his doom, and he was silent when his sometime patron, the former Duke of Orléans, met his inglorious end. When Robespierre, at the end of that month, stifled the legal defense of the impeached Girondins, Barère unctuously approved of the proceedings: "I support Robespierre's motion. It is a request which leaves the prisoners in possession of their full liberty. . . . I call for the adoption of Robespierre's motion." He gave his signature to a letter that Robespierre had drafted in the name of the Convention on October 13 for the arrest of General Kellermann, the victor of Valmy: "Perhaps you have too favorable an opinion of Kellermann. We beg you to sacrifice it to the harmony of the government and the general will. Public safety demands it. The voice of the people has been accusing Kellermann for years; the Convention thinks as the people do." To cover the Committee from a blunder of its own making he also pressed for the dismissal and the arrest of General Houchard, despite the fact that the doughty old warrior had routed the Hanoverians at Hondschoote early in September; and he acquiesced without demurrer when the honest but inept commander went to a traitor's death under charges which he knew were not true.

As the fighting turned against the foreign invaders and republican troops advanced steadily against the federalists in the south and the southwest, the military peril subsided and Barère echoed his colleagues' exhortations when the republican troops took the offensive. His language was theirs. It was Robespierre, Collot, Billaud, and Hérault who on October 23 signed an order bidding the soldiers to "march, strike [so that] the people may be revenged . . . liberty strengthened . . . tyrants and slaves disappear from the earth. . . . " It was he who reported to a wildly cheering assembly (October 12) that Lyons was recaptured: "The city of Lyons shall be destroyed. Every dwelling of the rich shall be demolished. Only the homes of the poor shall remain. . . . The name of Lyons shall disappear from the name of the cities of the Republic. . . . Lyons made war on liberty; Lyons is no more."

After political terror, economic terror. Not that Barère enthusiastically welcomed passage of the comprehensive Law of the Maximum which, a half year later when it was politically safe to relax the rates, he characterized as "a trap set for the Convention by its enemies." In September 1793, however, he knew there was no alternative. There were the new republican armies to clothe, equip, and feed. With the English blockade cutting off supplies, raw materials were despairingly scant and famine prices were ravaging the city consumers. He assented to a decision which ran counter to his fundamental views on economic enterprise and became one of the principals to make controls effective. Not choice but necessity compelled him and the Committee, as they felt their way and improvised a system of planned economy, unprecedented and unparalleled, to ensure needed supplies for the fighting forces while mitigating as best they could the conflicting interests of agrarian producers and urban consumers which that immense effort entailed.

The intent of the original provisions of the Maximum was sound, their deficiencies were glaring. No account had been taken of variations in local and regional costs and prices; seasonal changes were ignored; transportation charges had not been calculated. Within a month (October 22), Barère was presenting corrective measures for the Committee, and on his motion the Convention set up a Subsistence Commission and gave to this three-man board—which very rapidly became the key agency in the system of controlled economy—the authority to have its field representatives requisition supplies and preempt for the state all that was required for the armies and the fleet. It was empowered to draft workers for government service in the nationalized munitions factories and to invoke the death penalty against anyone who interfered with or obstructed the requisition of workers in the greater Paris area where the new factories were concentrated.

Barère again represented the Committee on November 1 (on 11 Brumaire, according to the terminology of the new revolutionary calendar that was adopted early in October) when a second revision was made. The new provisions, while keeping the prices of 1790 as a base, made allowance for transportation costs in determining how much local and regional commodity prices could be set above the national average and, to contend with the black market, allowed a 10 per cent mark-up to wholesalers and a 5 per cent profit to retailers. Much of this new approach remained on paper until the following spring, for only then did the research staff of the Subsistence Commission have the required statistical data to permit the desired new schedules for each commodity to be fixed and posted. Except in the larger cities, especially in Paris where the Commune used its authority to introduce exceptions which protected the interests of the wage earners, real wages did not keep up with real prices. The black market flourished and the complaints of consumers were loud. Hoarders, speculators, and monopolists made enforcement doubly difficult. Ineffective and unfair as they were, government control measures were nevertheless to spare France the worst in the hard winter of 1793-1794. They saved the civilian population from hunger and the full horror of runaway inflation prices; they fed and clothed and equipped the troops.

Once undertaken, economic regulation could not be arrested midway. Control of prices and wages, requisitioning labor for the nationalized industries, and enforcing the right of the government to purchase at legally fixed prices whatever was required for the conduct of the war compelled the Committee to go further and assign to the Subsistence Commission full direction over all economic activities within France and foreign trade as well. The blockade, the classification of food and prime commodities as contraband of war, and neurotic fear of British secret agents, were building up a fierce xenophobia. In the fall of the assignats, the mounting cost of living, declining domestic production, popular resentment against the merchants of the Gironde who had joined in the federalist revolt, there was material to accentuate the mood. The Convention placed an embargo on the export of all commodities, hoping to conserve for its own people the little that there was. It took steps to end the threatening flight of capital abroad, and it retaliated against neutrals carrying goods for the account of the British.

The immediate consequences of this sterile policy of reprisals were disastrous. French ports were effectively closed to imports and French foreign trade plummeted to one-fifth of the pre-revolutionary total. Compelled to do so by political considerations and public opinion, the Committee placed the blame for this appalling situation upon England and adopted the policy of directing against the island kingdom the practices that England had successfully employed against her enemies. It would break English controls and end English supremacy by refusing to buy British goods, whether finished products or raw materials. It would not use British shipping for her trade. France would go it alone—or so it seemed by the provisions of the Navigation Act of September 21.

Announcing and defending the new policy fell upon Barère, who was already busy with working out the details of the controlled domestic economy. He had been instructed by the first Committee of Public Safety to prepare a Navigation Act; and for four months he and an able young economist Ducher, once consul in the United States and now the Committee's foremost technical specialist on foreign trade relations, kept revising the preliminary drafts. On September 21, he presented the Navigation Act for adoption by the Convention. Modeled upon the English Act of 1651, Barère's bill was a declaration of total commercial warfare on England and her allies of the coalition, and by its provisions sealed France tight against all export and import trade by sea with the enemy. It forbade all overseas and coast trade not carried on French bottoms and manned by French crews. Barère enumerated the advantages that enforcement of its terms would bring to France and stressed the damage that it would inflict upon England: "the terrible blow that it will strike at its industry, its trade, its navigation, its factories, its manufactures. . . . " Pleading with his fellow citizens to remain patient until the full effects of retaliation could be felt, he appealed (October 9) to their patriotism: "Pitt has successfully nationalized the war that he is waging against you. Well, you have a way of nationalizing the war that you wage upon Great Britain: it is to strike at her manufactures. You will teach [the people] that Pitt is the author of the loss of its trade."

Before the assembly formally denied entry into France of all products manufactured in the British empire, the Committee explored one more possibility of action. "The Committee of Public Safety," read a secret *aide-mémoire* that Barère himself drafted and all committee members present signed, "charges the ministry of the navy to make all the necessary preparations in the shortest possible time for the prompt and immediate debarkation of 100,000 men on the shores of England. The ministers of war and the interior will cooperate with the minister of the navy on the speediest way of carrying out this measure." That "speediest way" haunted the thinking of the revolutionists for ten more years and in all those years it was present in Barère's mind.

Nationalizing the war on English commerce had its counterpart in the decision of the Committee to conduct total diplomatic war on the enemy. In a directive for the instruction of the ministers, the governing committee declared that the Republic would deal with no foreign agents and ministers unless they had "a positive character toward the French Republic." Until the war was brought to a successful completion, all accredited French diplomatic agents to foreign powers were to be recalled from their posts. The Republic would send no ministers plenipotentiary or ambassadors to hostile foreign powers. France would employ only secretaries of legation and chargés d'affaires who would carry neither written instructions nor letters of accreditation. Their orders would be secret, the oral instructions given to them on their departure abroad.

Though the Committee severed diplomatic relations with the enemy and declared economic war on Britain, there was more in fact to the Navigation Act than closing France to British goods and ships. The opening words leave no doubt on that score, for they explicitly stated that France would observe all its commercial obligations and treaties with the neutrals. France then would not fight alone: the neutrals would take up the slack. While all diplomatic relations would cease with the enemy, France would send duly accredited representatives to the "two free peoples," the Swiss cantons and the United States. To make sure that the new policy would be understood the order was given to translate the Navigation Act into English, German, and Italian, and obtain for it the widest possible distribution abroad. Not drying up foreign trade but reviving it through a combination of coercion, control, and encouragement of private traders within and bids for neutrals without, this was the reality that marked the Committee's policy and Barère's public support of it from the winter of 1793-1794 through the following spring. The Committee undertook to revive and control trade, coordinate it in all details, and direct it for the advantage of the all-out war effort.

Barère was an important link between the Committee and its subordinate agencies. He was also active in the policy of strengthening ties with the neutrals to obtain from them and through them the grain and raw material that England denied the revolutionists. Both spokesman for its policy and policymaker, he drafted instructions for the council of ministers to send competent agents abroad and to "take such measures as it deemed necessary to buy grain in Turkish Dalmatia, the Barbary Coast, Italy, Sweden, Denmark, and also in North America." From Ducher and their mutual friend, Tom Paine, with whom he was in contact despite the political cloud which hung over the latter, he obtained valuable information on bettering the estranged relations with the new republic overseas to which the ineptitude of Genet had amply contributed. He spoke in the Convention on November 17 to echo Robespierre when the Incorruptible refuted the distortions which made the Convention's "intentions suspect to its allies, particularly to the Swiss cantons and the United States." The treaties linking France to the United States and the Swiss cantons, he made clear, would be faithfully kept. To the enemy France would "show itself terrible, to its allies generous, to all peoples just."

Hence on December 10, when he drafted the announcement that "the Committee [authorizes] the Subsistence Commission through its agents to inform all neutrals and allied nations that they can import prime commodities and materials into France," his words confirmed an existing reality. The Committee had already permitted individual French merchants to export luxury products on the condition that, in return, they would import an equivalent value of commodities which the Subsistence Commission had placed on the urgent and necessary list. It permitted neutrals in Basel, Genoa, Hamburg, Copenhagen, and most of all in the United States, to trade on those terms. After it had also allowed French traders to pay for imports in specie if no other means of payment were available, it compelled the leading bankers of Paris to raise fifty million livres in foreign currencies. Making wide use of its preemptive authority to obtain luxury goods for the payments abroad, it dispatched agents to requisition wines and brandies, colonial goods, silks and other specified textiles, precious metals and stones, even confiscated prize goods. This policy was followed during the winter months and on March 11 (21 Ventôse) the Committee instructed Barère to announce in its name that all goods which the Subsistence Commission did not classify as primary necessities could be exported by French merchants, by the allies of France, and by neutrals complying with the conditions that were set. As it revised the list of exportable goods, the Committee instructed Barère to explain in the Convention that honest traders merited the full encouragement of the government and that it was not fitting for a nascent republic to cut itself off and renounce all commercial relations: "It is . . . good for the republican government to make contact with great and skilful traders . . . who will bring the government the fruit of their commercial experience. . . . " Thus the trade lanes were kept open, and by 1794 the revival was marked. Barère supported the new and more flexible commercial policy without reservation, accepting a controlled economy which left ample room for the workings of free trade.

While it was making headway on the economic front, the Committee did not lack for trouble in consolidating its political authority. In its struggle to maintain itself, Barère also faithfully carried out the Committee's agreed policy. The moderates of the Convention had tried in September to swing the assembly into denying the Committee a vote of confidence, and they tried three times more from October to December to undermine it. On October 12, the deputy Fabre d'Eglantine, one of Danton's less creditable friends, made a startling secret deposition before the Committee of Public Safety and the Committee of General Security. An elegant, money-hungry playwright and poet, well known for his charming light verse, and recently risen to fame as the author of the lyrical names given to the new revolutionary calendar, Fabre, along with well known Jacobins and various foreign refugees of questionable probity, had involved himself deeply in extortions upon private business men. Fearing exposure from his fellow grafters—the Law of Suspects was in full force and the state trials were in full swing—he made disclosures before he himself would be accused. He theatrically revealed to the committees the existence of a widespread "Foreign Plot," financed by English gold, to overthrow the republican regime. His disclosures were more than a smokescreen to cover himself, they were a subtle political maneuver to drive a wedge between the Committee and its leftist supporters. He did more than implicate shady foreign refugees and adventurers in the Plot; he involved their friends and abettors among the left-wing patriots who were identified in the public mind as followers of Hébert. It was the Hébertist slogan, "Make terror the order of the day," that the Committee had accepted and was enforcing. To embarrass the government further, he denounced one of the members of the Committee of Public Safety itself, the *ci-devant* Hérault de Séchelles, as the source of leaks of government secrets to the Austrians.

While there was not a Foreign Plot in the cloak and dagger style, and Hérault's guilt was problematical, the activities of the foreign adventurers with whom the rakish ex-noble consorted gave plausibility to Fabre's story. From the start the suspicious mind of Robespierre was prepared to accept the disclosures at their face value, and within a month he was convinced. For Barère too, the disclosures were plausible, perhaps all the more because he had little reason to think well of the Hébertists in whose eyes his own tactics had not found overwhelming favor.

In this wily stratagem of tarring the Committee by its close association with the radicals, the moderate deputies of the Convention found their opportunity to win back the political authority on which the Committee had encroached. The hands of some of those deputies, particularly the ones named by Fabre in his accusation, were not clean. They feared that, like the Girondins, they too might be arrested and condemned without trial. Among them were Basire and an ex-Capuchin friar, Chabot, both friendly with Danton. Other deputies, innocent of wrong-doing, were still not reconciled to the eclipse of the legislative body. Under the direction of Basire and Chabot, they pooled their forces and pushed through the Convention a decree which formally reiterated that accused members enjoyed parliamentary immunity and the right to plead their cases before their fellow deputies.

Parliamentary immunity was not the principal issue at stake in that debate of mid-November. It was a test of strength and the Committee could not give way. A strengthened Convention, Barère and Robespierre knew, might use its regained authority and prestige to refuse to extend the monthly powers of the Committee. Most probably it would do so. If the Committee were to survive, normal constitutional safeguards would have to go. Barère was troubled, but he did not fail the Committee. Again he convinced himself that he had no choice. Playing with skill upon the patriotism and the fears of the deputies, he made a powerful speech to keep them in line. It was a close call, but the

Convention rescinded the decree it had voted, and two days later, on November 14, it dutifully confirmed the Committee's powers for an additional month.

Chabot and Basire had directed the parliamentary maneuver of November. Frightened over its failure, they too now made haste to speak up and supply details about a lucrative racket of falsifying the liquidation proceedings of the India Company in which they confessed that they had participated with Fabre. While their story, which made them out as innocent dupes and Fabre as the guilty leader, did not come off, and they too were placed under arrest, it confirmed Robespierre's suspicion, Barère's too, that there was in fact a Foreign Plot with two wings, a Hébertist foreign wing seeking to discredit the Republic by practising needless terror and a Dantonist group, corrupt and tarnished, sowing political dissension in the Convention in order to end Committee controls.

What further strengthened Robespierre's belief in the reality of the Foreign Plot was that in the second fortnight of November a wave of anti-Catholic feeling reached its height in Paris. This Dechristianization movement had roots deep in the religious developments of the Revolution. Embodying a revulsion of patriotic feeling against the counterrevolutionary activities of the nonjuring clergy, the emotionalism and exaltation of many simple-minded men of the people vented themselves in grotesque ceremonies contemptuous of the old religion. The enemies of Christianity attacked the rites and liturgy of the Catholic faith. They desecrated precious relics and mutilated the statues of saints in the churches. While many of them formally abjured their faith, priests unfrocked themselves in public ceremonies. Parish churches were closed and, most sensational of all, the ex-bishop of Paris transformed the hallowed cathedral of Notre Dame into the atheistic Temple of Reason.

Initially, many deputies also gave the anti-Christian campaign their approval. But Robespierre, and Barère with him, were frightened by their stand, frightened still more that the Commune had officially endorsed it, and that its staunchest adherents were sans-culottes. Neither Robespierre nor Barère understood or chose to understand that the Dechristianization groundswell was a profound social protest as well as an outburst of patriotic fury against ecclesiastics. They would not see that through passionate anti-Catholicism the supporters of Hébert and Chaumette, both Commune leaders, were inveighing against a policy which still favored the rich against the poor and tolerated profiteers and swindlers while placing the burden of sacrifice upon workers. Both Robespierre and Barère were deists, neither desiring to revive Christianity, both eager to replace it with a revolutionary religion and find for it a new liturgy and new symbols. Both, moreover, were aware of the political dangers in the ribald acts against the church and revealed religion. Since the country was profoundly Catholic, to persecute believers would certainly add millions of citizens to the antirevolutionary ranks. Atheism, Robespierre held, was "a doctrine of the rich, alien to the poor." If the atheistic movement were unchecked, Hébert and Chaumette could reap a political harvest, perhaps enough to have the Commune and its sansculottes following grasp at the direction of revolutionary policy.

An experienced tactician, Robespierre grappled with the greater danger and dealt first with the Commune and wayward Jacobins, many of whom had joined with the anti-Christian demonstrators. His ascendancy was so great in those circles that they fell into line. Then to cope with the deputies in the Convention he did not disdain help from Danton, who had returned to Paris from semi-retirement. He understood that Danton was cooperating with the government and disavowing the religious buffooneries to get a lien upon the Committee's good will, which he could later use for his own ends. It was a calculated risk, and he took it. Barère hewed to the Committee policy. Though he had jeered about "the filth of [Christian] superstition" and ridiculed the saints as the "last émigrés of the Revolution," for tactical reasons he joined with Robespierre and pleaded for religious toleration. The combined efforts within and without the assembly brought results, and on December 5, the Convention passed a decree punishing all acts of violence against the freedom of religious worship. Thus the threat of atheism was rolled back.

Although the working entente between the Committee and the Paris militant leftists had been severely strained, the Committee was in the saddle again, thanks to the support it had received from Danton and the moderates. It took immediate steps to consolidate its victory and on December 4 ( 14 Frimaire ) obtained from the Convention a decree which recast into a single organic text the piecemeal legislation on which dictatorial control rested.

It was fitting that Barère should have moved that the decree, the "Constitution of the Terror," be printed *in extenso* in the official *Bulletin de la Convention*. He himself had drafted and presented to the assembly for ratification a score of key resolutions systematizing the administrative work procedures of the Committee. Governing in the name of the Convention, within France it had acquired jurisdiction over all constituted agents, both departmental and municipal. It had the authority to dismiss governmental personnel and issue arrest warrants. It could nominate the members of other committees, including those of the powerful police board, the Committee of General Security, control armed forces within France, and make drafts upon the millions of livres placed at its disposal. No official or unofficial body could go beyond the functions assigned to it; new local agents and old ones who had survived the purges, "national agents," they were called, were removable at the Committee's pleasure and directly accountable to it. On the Committee and the Committee alone also devolved responsibility for foreign policy. There was nothing in all Europe to match the concentrated power of the new leviathan, nothing to compare with the quick flow of command from the vital center to the outlying parts of the immense administrative bureaucracy. Unity of revolutionary purpose and will had been attained. The collective dictatorship of twelve men who had thrown in their lot with the Revolution was a reality; and to its standard rallied many practical-minded men of substance, ready or resigned to accept its realistic flexible policy of republican concentration.

Within this junta of statesmen, politicians, and administrators, Barère—"whom so many people regard as sacred," wrote a captious critic—had won for himself a high position. He buried himself for the following six months in the tasks of the Committee whose daily work routine he had done much to establish. Outside the entrance door of the Pavillon de Flore of the old Tuileries palace, sentries stood on duty, constantly on the alert, while upstairs, all was bustle and commotion. Secretaries, clerks, staff subordinates, and messengers moved in a steady stream across the corridors which were thronged from early morning with hundreds of petitioners eager and anxious to get the ear of one or the other of the Committee members delegated in turn to receive them. For the Committee, work began early and ended fifteen or sixteen hours later, often after midnight. By eight o'clock in the morning for most of them, earlier for some, the exacting grind began, each secluding himself in his private chamber to study the incoming dispatches from the field and prepare the work that he would take care of or refer for group discussion. The dispatches read, the lines of decision outlined in their minds, those who were free to do so came together in an informal meeting around ten o'clock, the first of the two meetings that they customarily held each day. The Salle de Diane in which they met, with its rich carpetry, glistening candelabra, and polished wall mirrors, was sumptuous, as befitted a palace room of the Old Regime. The work equipment, a large oval table draped with a green cloth and covered with inkwells and huge piles of official papers, was austerely republican.

No minutes were kept of the meetings, no presiding officer called the members to order. There was no fixed agenda to follow. Each member spoke as the need arose, perhaps on occasion without need. They spoke freely, according to temperament or subject matter, quietly or passionately, expounding their views with full consciousness of their status and dignity. Resolutions were adopted for later presentation to the Convention, orders penned, instructions to field agents drawn, proclamations agreed upon for later drafting. Around noon, when the main daily session of the assembly was about to open, some of them, Barère and Billaud more often than the others, crossed the Tuileries gardens to the Convention hall. Others, like Carnot, Lindet, and Prieur de la Côte d'Or, for the most part remained closeted in their offices attended by their staff members. The long day went by until the brief break for dinner, usually at neighboring restaurants. Shortly after seven o'clock they were back again at their labor, working steadily until ten o'clock. It was then that the all-important general conference took place, always behind closely guarded doors, to last sometimes well beyond midnight. As the attendance register shows, not all the members were present. Some were away on mission, others too busy, some like Robespierre and Collot, keeping contacts with the Jacobins. Carnot almost never went to the Club and Barère rarely.

He lived nearby, a short walk away on the rue St. Honoré, but on many nights he remained in his office, throwing himself exhausted on a cot to snatch a few hours of sleep and restore his strength. There is a plaintive memorandum in his handwriting in which he appealed to the maintenance staff for a more comfortable bed, like the one, he suggested hopefully, that had just been installed for Saint-Just. "I should like to see a picture of the little room in which the Committee used to meet," he wrote many years later, "those nine members working night and day. . . . Often after a few hours' sleep, I would find a huge pile of papers in my place—reports of the military operations of our armies. . . . Around our little meeting room we had organized our offices in the Salle de Diane. . . . We wanted to give a lesson in economy. Otherwise we would not have done the great deeds that still astonish the world."

The masters of revolutionary France did not suffer each other's foibles gladly, but each in his way, save for Hérault, was a dedicated man, tirelessly working for the cause. They were young, those "twelve who ruled." Only Lindet was over forty in 1789, the others in their thirties, and Saint-Just only in his twenties when the Revolution began. With the exception of the former actor, former writer, the coarse and frustrated Collot d'Herbois, all had reasonable financial security. Some, like the *ci-devant* Hérault de Séchelles and the studious Carnot, like Barère, too, were already successful and distinguished in their professions. Save for Collot they were well educated, all men of the Enlightenment. Hérault was a nobleman, the others stemmed from the middle classes. Eight of them had been trained in the law; Jeanbon Saint-André, the ex-Huguenot pastor, had been a sea captain; Carnot and Prieur de la Côte d'Or were both outstanding engineers. Though all were deeply concerned with problems of social and economic reform, not one of them had worked with his hands, not one through firsthand experience was familiar with the problems of trade or industry.

Risen to power by their competence and their services, they respected each other's special skills. Of the twelve, it was the trio of Robespierre, Saint-Just, and Couthon that came closest to forming a united working team, united less by personality traits than by the ideal that they shared of social democracy. Couthon was most tractable, mild in manner, and stoical in bearing the cruel arthritis that crippled him. If Robespierre commanded their respect, he taxed the patience of them all. Strait-laced and austere, a friend of humanity in the abstract, in personal relations he was aloof and distant, censorious, intolerant of disagreement, and suspicious, quick to take offense. Nor was close friendship, let alone intimacy, possible with the imperious youth Saint-Just. Steely in determination, passionate in his convictions, he had a head of fire, a heart of ice. Collot and Billaud, too, were not pliable, for they were terrorists in temperament as well as in views, disliked for their vindictiveness by their colleagues, and barely tolerated even by the affable Barère. The three great technical specialists, Carnot, Lindet, and Prieur de la Côte d'Or, provided little occasion for bickering and recrimination. These hardworking experts were apolitical. Immersed in their immense tasks of equipping the troops, procuring supplies, devising tactics and strategy for victory, not until the last months did they too become involved in the power rivalries which rent the Committee. Jeanbon, the Committee's naval expert, was often away on mission. The blade of the guillotine was early to fall on the pleasure-loving and unprincipled Hérault.

From the start, working together was trying and difficult, but for almost a year, from July 1793 to June 1794, they transcended divisive passions and rivalries, hammering out of the crucible of toil and common devotion the great joint decisions that led the revolutionary Republic to triumph. Barère, more than any other, kept them together on a purely human level of relations. "So different from the others," wrote Prieur in his *Révélations sur le Comité de salut public*, "Barère had a most lovable character. Sprightly and affectionate, he spiced his conversation with flashes of wit. . . . Even at the most critical moments Barère always kept his head, remaining gay and vivacious, and continuing to work with his customary promptness. . . . He sought only what was just, fine, great, and useful for his country." To Carnot's son, Prieur stated, as they later discussed the long-vanished days of the great Committee, "Often when we were hastily eating a piece of dry bread around the Committee table, by some pleasantry Barère would bring a smile to our lips." But he was more than the great emollient of the passions within the Committee. Once its powers were established, he framed many of its policies and defended them in the assembly hall against the challenges to its authority which did not end with the draft of the "Constitution of the Terror."

# ☒ X I ☒

## *Revolutionary Terrorist,*
## *January-April, 1794*

THE renewal of the attempts to dislodge the Committee after the crisis of Dechristianization came from Danton and his followers in the Convention. It was not betrayal of the Revolution that prompted Danton to moderate the Terror and return to normal constitutional procedures. He was no venal politician, no unprincipled demagogue seeking power for power's sake. An extrovert, full of vitality, he enjoyed life and good things. Though he had not hesitated to accept money for his services, like Mirabeau he might have said that he was paid to be of his own opinion. For deep convictions he had, if not good judgment. Distrusting doctrinaire idealists, sickened by acts of blood, he thought the time had come to abate the dictatorship. The Revolution, he held, had prevailed over its enemies in France and in Europe.

Both his close associates and the steps he took injured his cause. Among "the Dantonists" there were notoriously corrupt deputies, men deeply enmeshed in various financial swindles that were coming to light. By his tactics he raised grave doubts about his intentions. He might easily have been elected to the Committee, but he chose to oppose it from without rather than employ his prestige and vast popularity to modify its policy from within. Though sincere in fighting against the Dechristianization movement, when he gave Robespierre his support he was playing for tactical advantage to save his friends and relax economic controls.

He lent indirect support to the campaign for peace negotiations at a time when war weariness was turning many Frenchmen against the sacrifices that the war effort imposed upon them. Precisely how he conducted those operations one cannot say. While police observers in Paris informed their superiors that his name figured in all rumors of a coming peace, from their listening posts abroad the agents of the Committee also sent back reports that he was negotiating with the enemy. He was lending his great talents and renown to a policy that obstructed and hampered the work of the Committee. So it seemed to Robespierre, so Barère judged it. Soon the Committee could believe that his stand was treason.

The Committee had accepted Danton's aid against the Commune and the democratic section assemblies in the crisis of Dechristianization. Robespierre also tacitly approved of the journalistic venture which Danton had induced his friend and Robespierre's, the debonair and witty Camille Desmoulins, to launch. The Incorruptible welcomed the first issue of *Le Vieux Cordelier* on December 5. The newspaper aided the Committee in checking men like Ronsin and Vincent, who were upbraiding it for harboring ex-nobles in the military high command and who provocatively called themselves the "New Cordeliers." Camille's gifts were precious in satirizing the "Ultras," as the extremists were to be dubbed. Robespierre had seen the first two numbers of the journal in advance of publication; he did not see the third issue until it appeared in mid-December. Its contents sowed consternation in government ranks for in it Camille showed his hand. Purporting to be a translation of Tacitus's famous denunciation of the tyranny of Caligula and Nero, the famous third number painted a harrowing picture of a society gripped by terror and honeycombed with spies and delators. Under the cover of unmistakable and scathing references to the Law of Suspects and all the petty officials who used and abused it to satisfy personal vengeance, Camille was initiating a great public campaign to end the regime of Terror. Petitioners flocked to the assembly hall, echoing his cry for pity and clamoring for the release of the arrested: "Let a regime of love replace the regime of Terror." The Convention, swayed by his appeal, decreed that a "Clemency Committee" should be set up in behalf of the falsely accused. Robespierre himself voted for it, for he knew there had been flagrant acts of injustice.

That number of the newspaper appeared several days after the Dantonist deputies, encouraged by the success of the first two issues, had tried for the third consecutive month to prevent the Convention from renewing the Committee. The Committee survived, but the margin of victory was slight and it had to move warily. To hold the support of the moderate deputies the Committee assented to the arrest of Vincent and Ronsin. But the intention to give up the government policy was farthest from Robespierre's mind, and he had made the Committee's position clear in his memorable Christmas Day address "On the Principles of Revolutionary Government." The moralist and the statesman were one in this manifesto in which Robespierre served warning that he came to bring not peace but a sword: "We must crush both the internal and foreign enemies of the Republic or perish with it. And in this situation, the first maxim of your policy should be to guide the people by reason and repress the enemies of the people by terror. If the mainspring of the government of the people during peace is virtue, the mainspring of popular government during a rebellion is at once virtue and terror—virtue without which terror is disastrous, and terror without which virtue is powerless. . . . Terror is merely justice, prompt, severe and inflexible."

Barère spoke on the following day to defend the Law of Suspects in particular and government policy in general. Toward Camille he was gracious and urbane: "I am far from attacking the intentions of one of my colleagues whose patriotism and talents I know." The tribute paid, then came the threat. Agreeing that the Law of Suspects had been abused, he attacked the folly of wishing to rescind "a terrible but necessary institution, an institution . . . which has saved France." He went further: "I shall say with more reason than the pamphleteers, who without knowing it and without wishing it perhaps, are reviving the counter-revolutionaries and rekindling the ashes of aristocracy, I shall say: 'the noble, suspect; the priest, the courtier, suspect; the foreign banker, the open speculator, the citizen concealing his foreign loyalties, suspect; the man who complains about everything that is done in the Revolution, suspect; the man dismayed by reverses, suspect.' "

Barère's words were double-edged: he was hitting out against both Ultras and Citras, the men who blew hot and the appeasers who blew cold. There was open guilt and there was guilt by association: let those who criticized desist and cut themselves clean from true counterrevolutionaries. His warning was clear, and Camille chose not to heed it. In the fifth number he met Barère's covert threat with a barrage of irony. Raking out of the revolutionary past Barère's own record of conciliation, he apostrophized his old friend with studied scorn: "You, my dear Barère, you the happy guardian of Paméla, you the president of the Feuillants, you who on June 2 had the Committee deliberate on the question of arresting Danton, you whose many other faults I could itemize if I wished to dip into the old sack [punning sardonically on "Vieuzac"]—that you should suddenly become a figurehead for Robespierre (*passe-Robespierre*) and that I should be so sharply berated by you . . . !"

Barère withheld his rejoinder for later use. He could afford to wait. Robespierre had turned on the old and dear friend of his schooldays, appealing to the Jacobins to stand behind him against the self-styled "old Cordelier," and hopeful that if they did so, Camille would retract. By way of persuasion he cast in Camille's face the ominous declaration that "we must be severe. . . . I call for the burning of his issues in the Society [of Jacobins]." To this Camille retorted with the mordant quip that burning was no answer. He was mistaken. For the moment burning was an answer. His supporters in the assembly were stilled, and for the time being the propaganda for clemency was aborted.

As rumors persisted that the government would negotiate with the foreign enemy, the task of scotching them was assigned to Barère. There had been a time, before he renounced mediation at home, when he, like Danton, favored a negotiated peace to save what he could from the ruins of the Girondin-inspired war plans. Since his conversion to the policy of total war at home and abroad, he spoke another language. And he spoke at a most favorable moment. The republican troops had reinvaded the Rhineland and were sweeping on to reconquer Alsace. After announcing the news of great victory on January 22 (3 Pluviôse), he thundered against the peace advocates: "Who then dares to speak of peace? Aristocrats, the rich, the descendants of the *ci-devants*, the friends of conspirators, the faint of heart, bad citizens, false patriots. . . . What we need today is redoubled boldness against conspirators, redoubled sternness in our reports, redoubled force in our measures, redoubled scrutiny of men who call themselves patriots, redoubled discipline and means to keep up the great and victorious armies of the Republic, redoubled production of weapons, gunpowder and cannon. . . . Yes, neither peace nor truce nor armistice with the coalition of tyrants."

The applause which greeted his exhortation was resounding, and the Committee called on him again on February 1 (13 Pluviôse) to sustain the patriotic élan. Reporting ostensibly on the prodigious effort that the Committee was making to speed up war production, Barère utilized the occasion again to warn the gullible against the voices of cowardice and defeatism. He satirized the rumor-mongers who belittled the record of war production and pleaded with the deputies to hold fast, promising that volunteers would soon return to their homes and peasants to their land. "Generous friends of peace," he continued, "watch out. The aristocracy applauds you and the coalition of kings is listening to you. . . . You wish peace; the Committee of Public Safety, the National Convention, and the French people also wish peace. The Committee of Public Safety has made preparations for a terrible war to win a solid peace. The Convention can sign only a frank and lasting peace. The French people can wish only for a peace that it will dictate to Machiavellian governments." Then his peroration: "Let us not stop forming our battalions, producing arms, building ships, forging cannon, gathering saltpeter, manufacturing gunpowder. It is from our arsenals, it is from our gunpowder factories that the main articles of the peace treaty will come."

His exhortations and threats silenced the rightist critics in the capital and a flood of approving letters flowed in from the departments. Camille did not lack courage and prepared a biting riposte to Barère in a projected seventh number of *Le Vieux Cordelier,* but it was not to be published while he was still alive. The Committee had won more than a round. After many tests of strength, it had at last broken the Dantonist potential. The final reckoning was deferred for two months, until the Committee settled scores with the Ultras. With them too it was locked in struggle.

On February 5 (17 Pluviôse), Robespierre gave before the Convention the great address which was at once a justification of what the Committee had done and a definition of its ultimate aims:

"We desire an order of things in which all base and cruel feelings are suppressed by the laws, and all beneficent and generous feelings evoked; in which ambition means the desire to merit glory and to serve one's country; in which distinctions arise only from equality itself; in which the citizen should submit to the magistrate, the magistrate to the people, the people to justice; in which the country assures the welfare of each individual, and each individual enjoys with pride the prosperity and glory of his country. . . .

"We desire to substitute in our country, morality for egoism, honesty for mere honor, principle for habit, duty for decorum, the empire of reason for the tyranny of fashion, contempt of vice for scorn of misfortune, pride for insolence, large-mindedness for vanity, the love of glory for the love of money, good men for 'good company,' merit for intrigue, genius for wit, truth for show, the charm of happiness for the dullness of pleasure, the grandeur of man for pettiness of the so-called great, a people stouthearted, powerful and happy for a people easygoing, frivolous and discontented—that is to say, all the virtues and the amazing achievements of the Republic for all the vices and puerilities of the monarchy."

Robespierre's moving words made explicit ideals to which Barère subscribed. The program of the ideal community, however, where each individual out of personal disinterestedness made sacrifices for the good of all carried no appeal to practical men who moved on the plane of unexalted reality. The future goal also seemed a present mockery to wage earners in Paris whose thinking was framed by the terrible urgency of surviving the hard winter that lay ahead. Yet the Committee could not relax the effort that was translating the theoretical provisions of the levy-in-mass into workable reality. The government had called 600,000 men to the front for military service. To serve the needs of that immense fighting force it had drafted all resources, all skills. From the peasants came their grain and fodder, wool, flax, and hemp; from the city workers their brawn and their technical skill. From them all the revolutionary government demanded raw material for war production: metals, paper, rope, saltpeter and potash for ashes. Many scattered and small-scale enterprises had been placed under state control or supervision. New state-owned establishments had been set up, mills and foundries, arms and ammunition works, for which the Committee preempted the products of mines and quarries, forests, forges, and tanneries.

So immense an effort could be coordinated and directed only from the top, under the supervision of specialists whose managerial skills the Committee employed without much regard for the political outlook of those subordinates. No one in the Committee, and Barère was no exception, thought of this nationalization of economic enterprise as lasting. They did not look upon their controls as first installments leading to a profound social reorganization of their country and the establishment of a socialist commonwealth. The basic concern of the bourgeois leaders of the Revolution was with supplying, equipping, and feeding the troops and keeping counterrevolutionaries under control. As much as possible they tried to protect the consumers and the wage earners from inflation and shortages, but from the very nature of the existing economy of the country and its social structure they were obliged to court the good will of peasant owners who could produce what was needed and of urban shop-keepers, merchants, and producers who could manufacture and sell what there was to be sold.

Hence the decision of the Committee placed the burden of sacrifice upon the urban consumers and wage earners, and the cadres of the Paris rank and file remained intact. They had only given ground when the Dechristianization movement was crushed; they had not yielded to the government. They remained intrenched in the popular societies, section assemblies and committees, and the Cordeliers Club. If the Committee were not to be overthrown by organized popular action, it would either have to win over the disgruntled or crush the leadership and the organization of the sans-culottes. Preferring the former alternative, nevertheless it chose the latter. It was compelled by considerations of national security to pursue an economic and social policy that resulted in still further alienating the most militant at the very moment that the material distress of the rank and file was greatest.

Barère's mentality was that of the Committee. With unfailing discernment he grasped the essential. Winning the war came first, even if to defeat the foreign enemy the government had to use its coercive power against city workers. The army was the sword of the Republic, the symbol of its unity and strength, and winning the war meant enlisting the support of men who produced and sold what was needed and binding them to the war

Oil portrait sketch of Barère, 1790, by David

Barère in the Tribune delivering his "Speech on the Judgment of Louis Capet" on January 4, 1793, painting by David

Heroism of the crew of the vessel, "Le Vengeur," lithograph by Mouilleron
after painting by Leullier, 1841

Barère delivering one of his carmagnoles, engraving by Denon after painting by Isabey

The Tennis Court Oath, detail, Barère in the foreground taking notes, after painting by David

Facsimile of Barère's newspaper, *Le Point du Jour*. This issue reports the proceedings of the "Famous Night" of August 4, 1789

LE POINT DU JOUR,

O U

*RÉSULTAT de ce qui s'est passé la veille à l'Assemblée Nationale.*

N°. XLV.

*Du Vendredi 7 Août 1789.*

Continuation de la Séance de la nuit du 4 Août.

« S'IL y avoit dans le monde, dit l'auteur de l'esprit des loix, une nation qui eût une humeur sociale, une ouverture de cœur, une joie dans la vie, un goût, une facilité à communiquer ses pensées, qui fût vive, agréable, enjouée, quelquefois imprudente, souvent indiscrète, & qui eût avec cela du courage, de la générosité, de la franchise, un certain point d'honneur, il ne faudroit point chercher à gêner, par des loix, ses manières pour ne point gêner ses vertus. »

Jamais les François n'ont mieux suivi cet esprit de leur nation, que dans cette fameuse nuit où *les provinces & les ordres* sont venus, tour à tour, abattre leurs priviléges devant l'espérance d'une constitution nationale. Au milieu de ces sacrifices politiques, plusieurs curés ne pouvant offrir l'abandon des novales que des loix modernes leur ont injustement ravies, ont renoncé à leurs droits, connus

E

Louis Philippe, Duke of Orléans, called Philippe Egalité,
anonymous sketch

Louis XVI at the Bar of the National Convention, December 11, 1792,
anonymous engraving

Vive la Convention Nationale, qui par Son energie et Surveillance
a delivré la Republique de Ses Tyrans.

The execution of Robespierre and his accomplices, contemporary engraving

Barère, Collot, and Billaud leaving Paris to be deported, engraving by
Berthault after Girardet

Bust of the Comtesse de Guibert,
engraving by Danzel de Valchant

Marc Guillaume Alexis Vadie
colleague and friend of Barèr
contemporary engraving

Bonaparte, First Consul, sheathing
his sword after the general peace,
contemporary engraving by
Chataignier

Joseph Fouché, Duke of Otranto, er
graving by J. Eymar

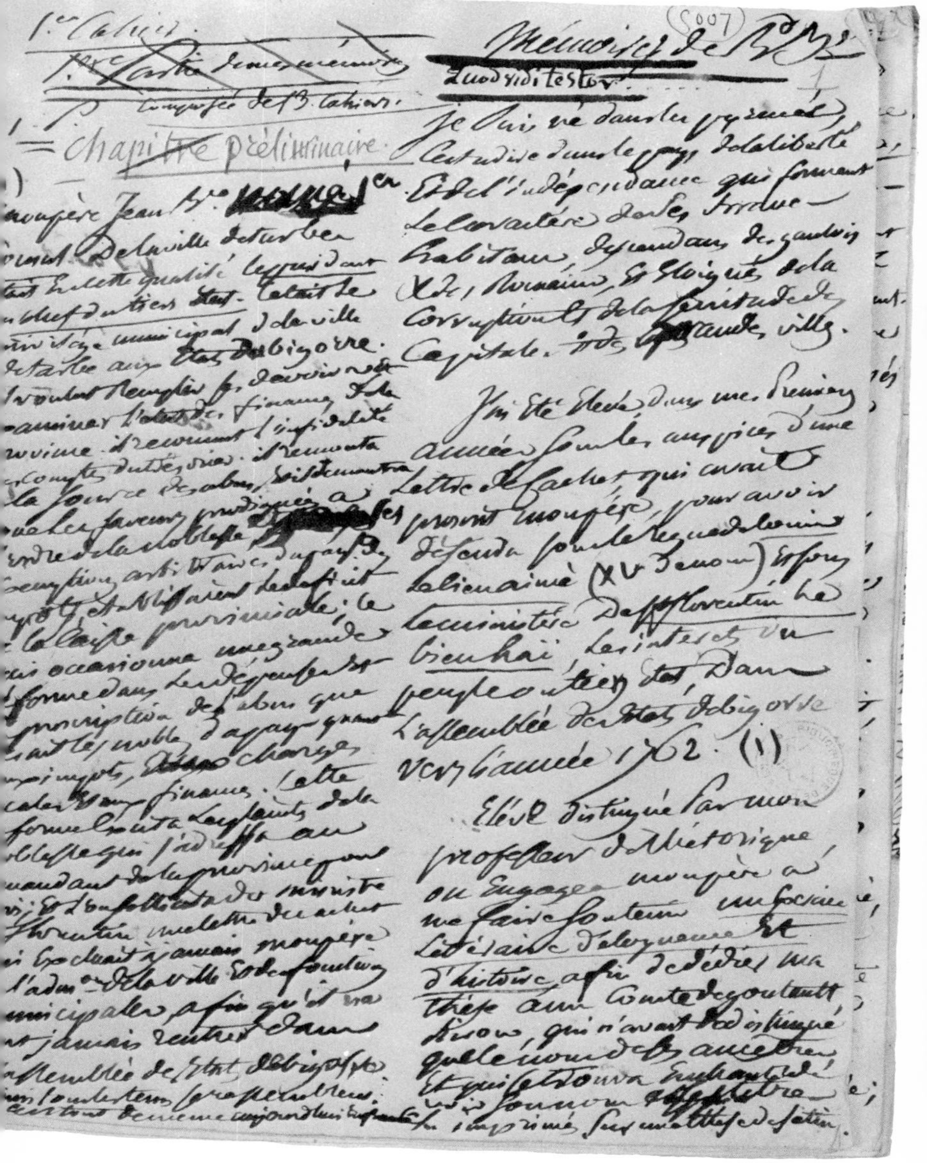

The first folio of the manuscript of Barère's *Mémoires*

Barère's grave in the cemetery of
St. Jean, Tarbes. The bust of Barère
is by Ceracchi, 1800

effort by paying them higher prices for their goods than the schedules fixed by the Maximum permitted. The sans-culottes of 1794 were not true proletarians who thought and acted under the consciousness of a permanent class struggle. If the great majority were wage earners, there were also many shopkeepers in their ranks, petty employers, and modest artisans. Their ranks could be split and the strategically significant segment won over. The Committee hoped that such would be the case, and partly in that hope it called upon Barère to present for the Convention's approval the revised schedule of prices on which the Subsistence Commission had been working since early fall.

The Maximum, his report of February 21 (3 Ventôse) began, was "a present from London," a trap which the enemies of the Convention had set for it. It had imposed hardships, constraint, and coercion upon all classes. The new tables of prices that he was now presenting would rescue the country from its plight. "[They] will stimulate industry, bring manufactures, traders, and hardworking citizens together. No longer will the consumer have to buy goods that have passed through . . . greedy hands. . . . It is not enough to conquer the armies of kings, destroy tyranny, crush the aristocracy, divide wealth, break up great fortunes: we must pass laws for the people, improve the lot of each citizen, increase agricultural production, revive industry, honor labor . . . and, rejecting intemperate, violent ways and wasteful practices, favor the useful day laborer, amply satisfy modest needs."

His words were studied, combining patriotic appeal with veiled menace. What he said in substance to the sans-culottes was that they should not listen to false spokesmen and violent leaders, they should leave all to the wisdom and justice of the government and support it. If, however, they chose "intemperate, violent ways," the Committee would not stand idly by waiting for the blow to fall.

While the Committee raised fixed commodity prices for the benefit of peasant producers and counted upon the modified rates to relieve the urban consumers by ending the black market, it also played for the good will of the great mass of landless peasants. On February 26 and March 3, Saint-Just recommended and the Convention voted two epochal decrees. The measures provided that the real property of persons "recognized as enemies of the Republic," convicted political suspects in other words, be transferred without sale or payment to "indigent patriots." Of Saint-Just's sincere desire to effect that massive transfer of real property there can be no question. He had already voiced that intention: "If you give land to the wretched, if you take it from scoundrels, I recognize that you have made a revolution."

The hope animating his proposal was large and generous; but his recommendation was also tinctured by political expediency. Together with Robespierre and Couthon, he saw the advantages of deflecting immediate discontent from government policy by focusing patriotic resentment against visible and recognized political enemies. Expediency notwithstanding, those decrees as first voted, smacked of communism. They recalled the dread "agrarian law" of the Gracchi that Barère had vigorously denounced almost a year earlier on the assembly floor. Opposition within the Convention, within the Committee itself, proved too strong, and the deputies amended what they had voted. As they were finally passed on March 6 (16 Ventôse), the decrees denatured the original intent of their sponsor. They provided not for free transfer but for supplementary sales of nationalized property. As a concession they also promised future government aid to the needy, the aged, and the infirm in towns and country. Promises were not sufficient, as the Committee speedily learned.

While Saint-Just's proposals were being whittled down, the Committee aggravated popular grievances by its measures to broaden opportunities for private trade. "What we wish to do," Barère informed the assembly on March 4 (14 Ventôse), "is to cure trade which is injurious, monarchical and counterrevolutionary; but to do that, we must bleed it, not kill it." Six days later he repeated his words: "There are goods and products which are so superfluous that proprietors would be ruined if we did not allow them to be exported. . . . It does not behoove a powerful republic to isolate itself and renounce all commercial relations." These pronouncements, which he subsequently repeated, also did not rouse the enthusiasm of urban consumers.

As Barère was making the position of the government clear, the "New Cordeliers" tried to force the hand of the Committee and spoke loosely of "sacred insurrection" and of "great measures" to get relief. If what their leaders, Hébert and Chaumette —and Ronsin and Vincent, too, who had been released from prison—actually had in mind was a new *journée* their miserably organized venture was doomed in advance to failure. The Jacobins withheld their support, the liaison between the Cordeliers and the sections was wretched, and the Committee of March 1794 was no longer the weak body that had yielded to threats from the street in September 1793.

Fearing that the opposition would act together, on March 6 (16 Ventôse) Barère served a final warning to both wings: "Let conspirators of all sorts tremble. . . . We must crush the ambitious or turbulent leanings of the leaders. We must watch over the factions of the Indulgents and the Appeasers as much as that of would-be insurrectionists. We must concentrate the authority and the influence of the Convention." After the warning came action, first against the radicals. The Committee allocated 2,000,000 livres of its available funds to provision the capital, obviously intending, by replenishing food stocks, to create the impression that the Hébertist chieftains had been responsible for shortages. Barère worded a resolution for the executive government which called on the mayor of Paris to take all needed security measures. Saint-Just read the Committee's report on the crimes of the extremists. It was Barère who drafted the Committee order to have 200,000 copies of Saint-Just's report printed and distributed. With all preventive measures completed against possible street action, the two governing committees placed the extremist leaders under arrest.

The arrest of the sans-culottes leaders on the night of March 13 (23 Ventôse) was not the courageous reply of a government menaced by insurrection. It was a demonstration of government strength. The charges against the prisoners, when they came to trial before the Revolutionary Tribunal, could not have been sustained before a regular law court. It could not be proved that the men on trial for their lives had plotted to starve Paris, massacre prisoners, and organize an insurrection to seize power. The trial was a mockery of justice. The accused had no chance to defend themselves, and neither Barère nor his associates intended that they should. To tar them in public opinion the Committee lumped together with them a number of notorious foreign agitators, the better in that way to show that the popular movement was in reality counterrevolutionary and one of the two facets of the Foreign Plot. For the Committee, Barère drew up an order which authorized the public prosecutor to employ as many "observers" as circumstances called for to obtain conviction. Perhaps "spies" would better convey the sense of the word *surveillants*.

The sans-culottes were shocked by the arrest of their leaders, but the populace did not stir. Dismay was no weapon against overwhelming force. The Revolutionary Tribunal gave the verdict of death, and before it pronounced sentence Barère was ready on March 22 (2 Germinal) with the Committee's report to the French people. In it he called for the punishment of "the plotters, assassins, tyrants, agents of England," who had slandered and corrupted the representatives of the people and plotted new September massacres: "Let us promptly answer terror with death, death to the enemies of the Republic. . . . Thus the National Convention showed itself when it . . . punished the Federalists and the Tyrant." He was at hand again, two days later, when the guillotine fell, to draw up the order to print and distribute 100,000 copies of the Convention's proclamation on the conspiracy that had been crushed.

The Ultras were crushed, and the reckoning with the Appeasers soon followed. Though Robespierre, on the day that the Hébertists went on trial, gave warning of what impended, he still hesitated to order the arrest of Danton. Not for long, however; once he overcame his scruples, he did not falter. The swindlers who surrounded Danton were indicted; he could not exempt their leader. In the last days of March the two committees ordered the arrest of Danton, Camille Desmoulins, and other leading Dantonists. Robespierre unburdened himself: "I too was the friend of Pétion; as soon as he unmasked himself, I gave him up. I was associated with Roland; he betrayed and I denounced him. Danton would take their place, and in my eyes from now on he is only an enemy of the country." Only two members of the joint committees had the courage not to sign the arrest warrants. Barère was not one of them. Perhaps he wrestled with his conscience, it is likely that he did, but in public he did not hesitate.

Barère did not hesitate either to invoke technical rules of order to prevent Danton from addressing his accusers on the floor of the assembly: "The jury [the Convention] has only to know the facts; it has no need to hear the accused." The "facts" were available for all to consult: Robespierre had written "Notes" on the conspiracy and Saint-Just had elaborated upon them. Without a dissenting voice, the muted Convention turned the prisoners over to the Revolutionary Tribunal. What the representatives of the people endorsed without debate had to be communicated to their constituents, and the Committee gave the order to have 200,000 copies of Saint-Just's report on "the corrupt idol" printed. The minute of the order carried two signatures. Barère's was one of them. His signature was also on the arrest warrant of Hérault.

The trial of the Dantonists was brief, and on April 5 (16 Germinal), they went to the guillotine. The masses remained silent, perhaps indifferent to Danton's death, more likely too cowed. All open opposition to the Committee was now crushed and for a hundred days the triumvirate of the Robespierrists within the Committee dominated the government of revolutionary France.

When Barère looked back many years later on this crisis of the Revolution, he made a sorrowful entry in his journal: "During the pomp of power I was pensive and melancholy. Every day I saw my friends, colleagues, fellow men, go to their political death. Love of the fatherland alone sustained me and gave me strength. But I did not believe that human sacrifices were necessary in Paris at the feet of the statue of liberty as they had been before in Carthage at the temple of Neptune." Believe in the necessity of those sacrifices he did not; publicly, he justified them. The one-time mediator was now a pillar, albeit a reluctant pillar, of orthodoxy. He was the organization man par excellence, coercing and terrorizing the lukewarm, the indifferent, and the hostile into patriotic compliance. His services were immense for the good they did in galvanizing the energies of his fellow citizens and mobilizing the resources of the country, for the evil, too, that he would not condemn.

The strain of softness in his character which had made him so useful in the Constituent Assembly and had led him to mediate the struggle between Girondins and Montagnards now made him equally useful as the apologist of the Committee. Earlier, out of necessity he had consciously addressed himself to several audiences at once; now, he spoke only to one. Before, he feared that a victory achieved by violence would split the Convention and incite the departments against Paris; now, he declaimed that peace without total victory would be in vain. For him the Revolution had gone beyond the fate of individuals: it was more important to achieve total victory than preserve the lives of old colleagues, than to distinguish between error and political sin. In that behavior there was new conviction; in it, too, the old fear for his security. It was understandable, perhaps even unavoidable, that he should have spoken the language of totalitarian revolutionary patriotism. It was pitiful that he was so ready to speak it.

# ⚜ XII ⚜

## Minister of Culture and Propaganda, April-July, 1794

AFTER its double victory over the factions, the Committee wiped out the remaining few islands of opposition. Barère did what was expected of him and what had to be done. He supported the move to disband the revolutionary army of the interior, which under the duress of the Hébertists he had voted to establish in the preceding autumn. From him came endorsement of the purges in the revolutionary committees of the radical sections and approval of new requisitions which gave jurisdiction over political cases to the Committee. The abolition of the provisional council of ministers, whose existence still hampered the Committee, found favor in his eyes. When the Paris workers, especially in the new nationalized war industries agitated for better work conditions and wages higher than those officially fixed by the Maximum, he threatened them with arrest and the Revolutionary Tribunal. He drew up and signed the Committee order to draft recalcitrant workers for the shipyards, laborers in field and factory, woodcutters, men engaged in handling, transporting, buying and selling food supplies. In all those measures to obtain virtually forced labor for the war effort, he was the loyal and conscientious echo of the collective will.

He made a special place for himself in the public mind as the bard of victory. All France knew him from his carmagnoles, those flowery bulletins of military victories which he addressed to the civilian population. From the early fall of 1793 to the summer of 1794 he gave almost 200 reports on the triumphs of the troops. "Each evening," he wrote later, "Carnot would turn a portfolio of dispatches from the generals to me; and sometimes I extracted from them enough to draw up a general report on the state of the armies and military operations; sometimes I made a special report when it involved the recapture of one of our fortresses or a particularly resounding victory in some key position."

For once his own words do not do him justice. With his love of the theatrical, his knowledge of the facts, with his striking physical presence and his magnificent oratory, he was perfectly qualified for an assignment which almost from the start he monopolized. The Gascon in him found full expression as he ascended the forum, free to laud the heroic lads on the battle field, taunt the enemy, swell the bosoms of his compatriots with pride. He had no peer in satisfying the psychological wants of his countrymen behind the lines of fighting by assuring them that the valor of the soldiers and their own sacrifices for the armies were not in vain. There had never been such military bulletins before, so many and so inaccurate, so swollen with rhetoric, so studded with clichés, so dripping with sensibility, so banal, and so cheered to the echo.

"The visitors to the Convention"—said the younger Carnot recalling conversations with his father—"and the Convention itself were so accustomed to see in the rapporteur of the Committee of Public Safety a messenger of good news that his appearance was greeted with acclamations. From all sides the cry was raised: '*Barère à la tribune!*' Everything had to cease until Barère read his report. . . . When they were read in the camps, the soldiers went wild with joy. 'My children,' shouted a colonel as he led the assault of a fortress, 'we must send Barère to the rostrum today,' and the redoubt is captured. The story is repeated in all the armies and the soldiers charged, crying: 'Barère to the rostrum!' "

To read one of the carmagnoles is to read them all, looking at a master script that merely changed names of the battles and dates. "Yesterday," he reported on July 1 (13 Messidor), "You listened to the letter [of the] representative of the people on the flight of the brigands of the coalition. Today we come to present to you the thirty-eight flags of despotism which we captured in seizing Ypres. . . . In the action which preceded the capture of Ypres, this soldier [standing beside him] is threatened by the Austrian, sabre in hand, who calls on him to surrender. 'A republican does not surrender,' he replies, and he dodges the sabre that the Austrian thrust at his head. But he succumbs to superior numbers; he is taken prisoner and led away by the Austrians. Soon he sees nearby the battalion to which he belongs. The battle is joined between this battalion and the Austrians. While the fighting is going on, this brave soldier advances on the Austrian flagbearer, and at the very moment that the troops are engaged in hand-to-hand combat, he throws himself upon the standard-bearer, seizes the symbol of slaves, and rejoins his battalion. Thus this citizen, all alone but led on by his courage, hurled himself into the midst of the ferocious foes. . . . Here he stands before the deputies of the people, this good tiller of the soil, who has only just left his ancestral hearth to defend national liberty."

The most celebrated of the carmagnoles was the one entitled "On the Heroism of the Republicans Who Manned the Vessel, *Le Vengeur*," which Barère gave on July 9 (21 Messidor) before an audience wild with patriotic ecstasy. The facts which Barère embellished into the epic story of French heroism that was to edify several generations of school children were lean. A French fleet under the command of Admiral Villaret-Joyeuse had moved out from Brest to protect a convoy of more than one hundred ships which was bringing to France an immense cargo of grain purchased by government agents in the United States and the West Indies. Though Villaret's instructions were to avoid battle so as to keep the fleet in reserve for the invasion of England, on June 1 he engaged his forces with the English patrol squadron under Lord Howe's command. On the level of national needs the engagement was a heartwarming triumph: the "life-giving argosy," 116 ships laden with grain made port. On the level of naval operations it was a disaster. The untried French captains were no match for the veteran and experienced

English commanders. With his fleet out of line and all in confusion, Villaret gave orders to have his dismasted ships taken in
tow. His orders were not obeyed, and he abandoned the ships.
One of the disabled ships, the *Vengeur du Peuple*, went down
as the British, hoping to save the crew, approached it. More than
half of the men were picked up and rescued; 206 sank to their
death with the stricken ship, crying "Vive la République!"

The first reports that reached the Committee came from
London newspapers, which published accounts that the *Vengeur* had refused to surrender and sank, fighting to the end.
Fuller details came from the report of the captain, who had
survived. With the captain's report and the English papers
before him Barère responded to instructions given him to inform
the deputies how French sailors died but did not surrender,
jealous to the death of their honor.

"The Committee has instructed me to inform the Convention
of the sublime deeds of which neither it nor the French people
should be ignorant. Since the sea became a field of carnage and
the waves were made bloody by war, the annals of Europe
had not recorded a combat so stubborn, valor so sustained,
action so terrible, so murderous as that of the 13 Prairial [June
1] when our squadron saved the American convoy. . . . The fleets
of the French Republic and the English monarchy had been
confronting each other for a long time and the most terrible
battle had just been engaged on the 13 Prairial. The most concentrated fire, the most legitimate fury of Frenchmen were aug-
menting the horrors and the perils of that day. Three English
vessels were sinking; several French vessels were disabled; the
English cannonade had made a great gap in one of those vessels
and joined together the double horror of certain shipwreck with
a struggle to the death. But this vessel was manned by men who
were filled with intrepidity of soul which braves danger and
that love of the fatherland which makes them scorn death. A
kind of warlike philosophy had taken hold of the entire crew.
The vessels of the English tyrant surround this vessel of the

Republic and desire the crew to surrender. A host of artillery pieces thunders on *Le Vengeur;* broken masts, torn sails, the spars of the vessel cover the sea. So much courage, so many superhuman efforts, are they then to be in vain? Miserable slaves of Pitt and George, do you think that republican Frenchmen give themselves up to perfidious hands and make terms with enemies as vile as you? No, do not wish to have it so. The Republic is watching them, they will know how to conquer or die for it. Several hours of struggle have not exhausted their courage; they fight on. . . . Imagine the vessel, *Le Vengeur,* riddled with cannon shot, leaking from all sides, sealed off by English tigers and leopards, a crew composed of the wounded and the dying, struggling against waves and cannon. The third battery is about to touch the waves, but it still vomits death to the perfidious islanders before being swallowed up. All at once, the tumult of the struggle, the fear of danger, the wounded men's cries of grief are stilled: all of them mount the deck or are borne there. All flags, all oriflammes are hoisted. The principal flag is nailed down. Cries of 'Vive la République! Vive la Liberté et la France!' are heard on all sides: it is the touching, living spectacle of a civic fete, not the terrible moment of a shipwreck. For one instant they must have deliberated on their fate. But no, citizens, they deliberate no longer, they see the Englishman and the Fatherland, they prefer to be swallowed up than dishonor it by surrender, they hesitate no more. Their last wishes are for the Republic and Liberty. They disappear. . . . "

In those bulletins Barère carried his listeners away from sober realities to a world of fantasy where republican courage prevailed over enemies as despicable in character as they were overwhelming in numbers. And by his encouragement of the efforts to enlist specialized skills for the fighting he made victories possible. What he contributed to the victories of which he sang redeemed the bombast of his words. In the spring of 1793, when the twenty-year war broke out against the coalition, France was dismally unprepared for it. Of republican ardor there was no dearth but military competence was in default. The republicans lacked trained soldiery and experienced officers. Denied access to indispensable materiel for war production by the blockade, they were appallingly short of arms and materiel, gunpowder, saltpeter, cannons. They lacked most of all the skills required for military and naval production. The close contact and smooth working arrangements of the Old Regime between government on the one hand and scientists and technicians on the other had broken down.

There was no escaping that disruption. The war against the coalition came in 1793 when France and Frenchmen had not yet adjusted themselves to the destructive shocks which the preceding four years had inflicted upon old political and administrative structures. Millennial social relations, traditional religious ways, legal forms and practices, were all disrupted. The organization of scientific research also broke down in that trauma of rapid destruction and slow rebuilding. If the revolutionists had not wilfully repudiated the great tradition of French scientific thought and research, in destroying the royal and aristocratic structure of French culture they had severed themselves from the men of learning. Many of them they tracked down from crudely partisan political passions. They were, nevertheless, conscious and proud of the heritage, and when they could and when they had to, they renewed their contact with the tradition, preserving as best they belatedly could what remained, rebuilding from available old resources, seeking also to draw upon talents never before exploited in the Old Regime.

What the revolutionists accomplished in the last year of the Convention's existence, from September 1794 to September 1795 was a signal triumph of their resolution to give to the Republic victorious in battle a similar primacy in the world of the spirit. They founded the Polytechnical School and the Conservatory of Arts and Crafts. The metric system was elaborated, the Bureau of Longitude set up, and the Academy of Science budded off from the Institute. The achievements were great, but that remarkable flowering of French scientific genius came from soil that had been generously worked in advance: the preliminary preparations to strengthen the foundations of research and enlist the services of the scientific and technological élites were taken at the height of the Terror.

In their first stages those preparations were starkly utilitarian, grandiosely fumbling improvisations to overcome the military crisis. It was then life or death for the Republic and the nationalist in Barère knew it well. He had been elected to the first Committee of Public Safety in the spring of 1793 because his fellow deputies saw in him a pillar of political sagacity. He also proved himself farsighted in technical military and naval policy. He supported the initial efforts of the great chemist, Guyton de Morveau, his colleague in the first Committee, to begin recruiting scientists and technicians. Probably on Barère's recommendation, after Guyton failed of re-election to the great Committee in July, he was named associate director of the arms factories that were established in Paris. After consulting with Guyton, Barère saw to it that the required steps would be taken to elect the two outstanding military engineers, Carnot and Prieur, to the second Committee early in August 1793; and a fortnight later, when his report on the levy-in-mass announced that henceforth all human and material resources of France were on call for the war, he revealed how profoundly aware he was of the task before the government.

Prieur and Carnot had good reason to praise the cooperation of their associate in whom they had a tireless second for their draft of scientists and their systematic reorganization of research. In their company he went on inspection tours of the laboratories at nearby Meudon to obtain firsthand information about the basic experiments in physics, chemistry, and mechanics that such distinguished scientists as Fourcroy, Guyton, Monge, and Berthollet were conducting. With Prieur and Carnot he braved the wrath of sans-culottes and saved the eminent mathematician Lagrange and the remarkable naturalist

Lamarck from political proscription, mobilizing their talents for the work of the Committee. He subscribed without reservation to the plea of the chemist Fourcroy that "the first republic in the world" should press into its employment not only civil and military engineers, ship captains and artillerists but also physicists and chemists, botanists and zoologists, doctors and surgeons.

On February 1, when he rallied the deputies against conducting premature peace negotiations with the enemy, Barère entreated citizens not to relax their efforts. It was on the following day that the Committee made the decision to establish a training school for war production and on the 18th of the same month that the projected course became a reality. Some eight hundred carefully screened students drawn from all quarters of the country were assembled in Paris to start on a schedule of intensive instruction under the guidance of an extraordinary galaxy of scientific talent. This course lasted only one month, from February 19 to March 19, and when it ended the hastily trained fledglings returned to their workshops in the provinces, to serve in their turn as qualified instructors for the workers under their charge for the production of gunpowder and the extraction of saltpeter.

The course was only a small step in the right direction, and if the hastily improvised training program brought some improvement in the provinces, it was not enough nor rapid enough to meet the imperative needs that Carnot and Prieur, more than any of their colleagues, could appreciate. Paris, alone, still produced as much as all the other workshops of the entire country. The curve of production in the capital registered striking gains: the production of saltpeter rose from one million to seventeen million pounds; smelting foundries increased from four to thirty; six hundred muskets were being turned out every day. It was magnificent and it was not sufficient. If it barely met immediate needs, it did not come close to meeting the needs of the future. The team of Carnot and Prieur did not relax, and under their pressure the Committee drew up more extensive plans, which Barère presented in the Convention on June 1 (13 Prairial) in the Report on Revolutionary, Republican and Military Education.

The report could not have been more frank. What other deputies for months or years had been saying, Barère now also said, that nothing had been done to establish a system of national education from the primary schools to advanced instruction: "A void threatens the Republic . . . which will be strongly felt in a few years." To cope with the danger the Committee referred to the deputies for their approval a comprehensive plan "to form republican defenders of the fatherland, revolutionize the youth as we have revolutionized the armies [and] accelerate the public military instruction" of young men too old for elementary instruction and too young for military service. The Committee moved and the Convention voted to establish the School of Mars where 3,000 selected and qualified lads, chosen from the families of deserving sans-culottes of modest means, would be educated at government expense. They would be dressed, outfitted, fed, and supported by public funds. At the school they would get training in handling arms, in infantry, cavalry, and gunnery maneuvers, in the principles of the art of war and military administration. There too they would be fashioned in fraternity, frugality, good morals, love of the fatherland, and hatred of kings.

"Do not think," Barère said, "that our project is limited only to making soldiers. . . . It has the equally precious advantage of forming young citizens in all the republican virtues and developing talents that nature has strewn in thatched roof cottages as well as in cities." The disclaimer was not insincere, the Committee was looking far ahead. Nevertheless the heart of his motion lay in his avowal that the primary objective of the proposal was to train soldiers and officers, engineers, cavalry commanders, artillerists, and military commissars.

In its broader aspects Barère's report was the profession of faith that inspired all the idealists, the noble and the terrifying

Rousseauist vision of the good community, which it was their duty to establish. Since the beneficent revolutionary state was "to the human mind what the sun of Africa is to vegetation," no bounds could be set to its jurisdiction. The premise of his thinking was categorically stark: "Children belong to the general family, to the Republic, before belonging to private families. Without this principle there can be no republican education." The present was still dark and painful, but in the welter of the confusion that had ripped apart the traditional pattern of unity, the revolutionists were looking far ahead. In the new springtime of hope, they were drafting the blueprints of the heavenly city on earth where a new spiritual cement would hold the faithful together. Like all revolutionists before and after, they were embarking on the long journey to utopia, confident that the dreams of the age of reason and of faith would now be realized. Life in that better new world would reward the patriots for their sufferings and sacrifices. If not they, then their children and their children's children after them, would enjoy the new blessings. The future belonged to the young—if the revolutionists did their duty. With what touching faith Barère announced, with what sadness one now reads, that the redemption of mankind was at hand. "The Committee is busy," he reported on March 30 (10 Germinal), "with a vast plan of regeneration, the result of which would banish from the Republic both immorality and prejudice, superstition and atheism. . . . We must found the Republic on principles and morality. If you lend it your support, it will dedicate itself to the great design."

The Committee would found an ideal union based on virtue. Having saved the infant Republic, it would make republicans of infants and the youth. It would establish lasting republican institutions, such as Saint-Just was then drafting for the guidance of his associates, such as Robespierre had fashioned in thought, such as Barère envisaged in his mind's eye. It would make the Republic one and indivisible, manifest and real to the senses.

Nevertheless, before it undertook to lay the spiritual foundations of the true republican community, it had to provide for material security. In truth much had already been done to improve the lot of the poor in town and country. The abolition of the manorial dues and immemorial work obligations were great boons, the expunging of the execrated tithe a blessing. Military service absorbed thousands upon thousands of marginal peasants, while mills and factories provided work opportunities to many farmhands and poor peasants, to croppers and small proprietors alike. Much had been done, much to accomplish still remained. The sales of nationalized land did not requite the secular dream of the landless. Their land hunger still tore at them; vagrancy was still endemic; beggary remained the great rural scourge. Out of political considerations alone it was necessary that the Committee act quickly and succor the needy.

It endeavored to act, as has been seen, in the last days of February (the early days of Ventôse), when Saint-Just raised before the eyes of the landless poor the prospect of a vast transfer of landed property. "The wretched are the powers of the earth," he cried out, "they have the right to speak as masters to governments which neglect them." In his sense of tactics he was realistic, for he appreciated the political worth of his proposal, yet he was fundamentally sincere and compassionate in his intention to have the confiscated estate of suspects placed in escrow so that the estates of the enemies of the Republic could be drawn upon "to indemnify the unfortunate." But the free distribution of land that he and Robespierre originally had in mind was not included in the definitive decrees of March 6 (16 Ventôse). The opponents of the initial recommendation, Barère presumably one of them, dashed the hopes it had aroused among the landless. Though the decrees instructed national agents to draw up lists of the propertyless peasantry eligible for the confiscated land, they did not violate the sacredness of private property, not even that of arrested suspects. The spectre of free distribution of land was laid to rest. It was to be sold like the other property of the church and of the émigrés that the state had taken over.

Since the radicalism of an agrarian law that evoked memories of Gaius Gracchus was too much for the property-minded deputies, the palliative of relief measures had to suffice, and on May 11 (22 Floréal) the Committee had the remedy in hand. Barère presented its report on the means of uprooting beggary in the countryside and on the aid which the Republic should give to needy citizens. The report reaffirmed the principles of the Ventôse decrees: the ownership of land would "attach all citizens to property and the fatherland." The provisions of the decrees were also restated: the land would be made available "in the form of national sales." The Committee did not stop with reiterating what the Convention had voted. Directing attention to the defects of existing legislation which neglected the interests of "the true indigents," Barère reported that he and his colleagues proposed to remedy the defects by providing for a large-scale, national plan of social assistance and welfare.

"The Committee would do away with the ravages of beggary which is making terrifying advances in . . . the Republic. [It would] fix its eyes on the humble thatched roof cottage. It is on the poor, hardworking inhabitants of the country who only find new toil after their toil is ended, disdain for their infirmities, and oblivion in old age, that the republican dew should fall. . . . It is for the Convention to repair the injustice of the laws of the monarchy, end the great inequalities of fortune, to efface the name of the poor from the annals of the Republic and banish beggary by benevolence. . . . " Soon, too, the Committee would provide welfare measures for the relief of the city poor: "We can never forget the artisans. . . . We are aware . . . with what barbarous indifference the rich employ the workers, [aware] that the hardworking poor are exploited [that] their youth and their health are the prey . . . of the rich." At this moment, however, the Committee "fixes its consoling eyes" upon farmers, shepherds, and rural workers, on the aged, the infirm, whose rights it would safeguard. "Yes . . . their rights, because in a democracy . . . everything should tend to raise each citizen above his primary needs, by work if he is able-bodied, by education if he is a child, by aid if he is disabled or aged." The decree which the Committee then voted created in each district a national register of the indigent aged, disabled cultivators, shepherds and workers, widows and mothers of numerous children who would be entitled to government relief. It laid down procedures for bringing home relief to such worthy citizens and to those requiring them, free medical aid, free medical supplies, and financial assistance.

Barère had doubts about many Committee orders that he publicly endorsed; about this proposal he had none. From his early days as essayist and practicing lawyer he had pressed for such legislation; and in 1797 he was still writing that if the citizen could not live from his labor, his property, or his savings, the government should intervene in his behalf: "Nothing can honor the Republic so much as the abolition of beggary." The honor did not fall upon the Republic, for time ran out on the Committee. This specific plan was not carried out. Barère's many subsequent proposals on behalf of the rural poor and the most financially constrained unemployed workers in Paris were unavailing. Certainly, the measure was not extravagant in what it provided. It was hardly adequate at best, yet the intention was a generous one. The decree was a step and the first significant step in the direction of having the government meet its social obligations. If it fell short by far of what Saint-Just would have wished according to his fragment, *Republican Institutions*, it went well beyond anything that had yet been done. The proposal was in keeping with what liberal progressives in the Committee and the Convention desired and in it was embodied the humanitarian, the philanthropic, and the physiocratic credo of their age.

With provision made for material security, republicanism of the mind and the heart could now become real. Here, too, however, the government had to sweep away the debris of the past before it could build afresh. Illiteracy and ignorance were rampant, folkways were entrenched. Probably four out of every five Frenchmen did not use the French language in their daily intercourse. They spoke their provincial patois or made use of non-French dialects. To the self-conscious nationalists in the Committee, to Barère himself, that adherence to the past invited political and military danger. Adults were not the stuff of the future, nor were they to injure the present. Loyalty to non-French languages could strengthen disloyalty to the Republic and offer aid and assistance to the internal enemy.

Barère had such thoughts in mind when he gave the Committee report on foreign dialects and the teaching of the French language on January 27, 1794 (8 Pluviôse). Though the tyrants of the coalition were taking advantage of ignorance to breed fanatics and counterrevolutionaries, it read, the Committee had fathomed "this plot of ignorance and despotism." Enlightenment would prevail over darkness. "I come today," Barère declared, "to call your attention to the finest language of Europe which first frankly consecrated the rights of man and the citizen [and] assumed the obligation to transmit the most sublime thoughts of liberty and the loftiest speculations of politics to the world." There were four danger spots that troubled the Committee: the northwest, where Breton was spoken; the Rhine area, where German prevailed; the region of the west Pyrenees, where one heard Basque; and the department of Corsica, where the Italian tongue was spoken; four regions which "have perpetuated the reign of fanaticism and superstition, assured the domination of priests and nobles . . . kept the Revolution from spreading. . . . " Too little had been done to make the inhabitants of those regions citizens, but "to be a citizen one had to obey the laws and to obey them, one had to know them. . . . We must popularize the language. . . . We have revolutionized the government, the laws, the ways, the manners and morals, the dress, the trade, and thought itself. Let us revolutionize the language. . . . "

Barère elaborated on a series of ironic contrasts between the universal and republican French language and its rivals. Italian was a fitting medium for soft corrupt poetry, German was the language of a feudal and military government, Spanish was the tongue of the Inquisition. Having thus paid his revolutionary respects to European culture, he moved the specific decree and the Convention voted to send linguistic legionnaires, qualified by their patriotism, to each rural commune of the departments that he had named in his report: "The instructors will be required to teach the French language and the Declaration of the Rights of Man and the Citizen on alternate days to all young citizens of both sexes. . . . On *décadi* days [every tenth day of the new revolutionary month, corresponding to the old sabbath] they will read to the people and translate orally the laws of the Republic, preferably those relating to agriculture and the rights of citizens."

Along with this oral indoctrination of citizens whose illiteracy made it impossible for them to read the sublime thoughts of liberty, went supplementary measures to ensure that those who were literate would not be exposed to printed words which could lead them astray. A working journalist himself, in theory Barère was an exponent of the fullest freedom of the press. But in practice, he subordinated the principle to "the evident and irresistible law of public security." He wrote that phrase in 1797; in the years immediately before, he had already pursued the philosophy that it embodied. In 1790 when he voted to censure Marat for abusing journalistic liberty, he invoked the right of the revolutionary state to supervise the contents of newspapers. He went much further three years later, and on December 4, 1793, he drew up a resolution specifically attributing to the government alone the right to judge what journalists could freely express in their pages. "The Committee of Public Safety," it read, "considering that it is its duty and interest to be informed

on the state of opinion and its progress, as well as on the agents
who contribute to it, has resolved that each journalist will be
invited every day to forward to it a copy of his newspaper." And
in the following spring, when the armies of the Republic were
once again liberating the peoples of the Rhineland, he drafted
decrees to establish a translators' bureau in one of the sections
of the Committee, to give instruction in foreign languages to
the Republic's agents abroad, and purchase foreign type, so that
the emancipated people would not lose any of the advantages
available at home to Frenchmen.

The vast plan of regeneration also appealed to the other
senses. It involved the cooperative efforts of creative artists to
sway the masses and inculcate in their hearts a dedicated loyalty to the republican nation. By the spring of 1794, control of
prices and wages had after a fashion stabilized the domestic
economic front and revolutionists qualified in scientific and
technical skills were supplying the armies with indispensable
war materiel. Then the Committee could call upon sculptors,
architects, poets, dramatists, painters, choreographers, and musicians to awaken the emotions of the multitude and direct them
into paths of loyalty. In that fresh springtime Barère took on the
last of his assignments. The apologist of the political Terror, the
advocate of controlled economy, the minnesinger of military
victory, became the spokesman of artistic propaganda. From
April to July of that year, more than half of all the orders and
resolutions which the Committee presented to the deputies for
action were either drafted by Barère or else signed alone by
him. Qualified by the breadth of his interests, by his rich appreciation of the heritage and tradition of his country, he became
in fact if not in title the minister of cultural propaganda.

The idea was not new in 1794 to use the fine arts to mold public opinion in favor of the government. There was nothing in
the historic practices of the Old Regime to discourage that
thought. The philosophes had not frowned upon it, and in
Rousseau's deeply emotional writing on the regeneration of

Poland there was a rich treasury of suggestions which the revolutionists in France could draw upon to arouse and deepen nationalist fervor. Where scientists in the main did not have to be
coerced to impart their skills, artists, too, gladly lent their talents
to the cause of mankind.

Barère himself required no persuasion to accept the assignment. The Rousseauist in him did not question the moral right
of the state to mold its citizens. He had stated many times that
what the Revolution commanded had to be religiously obeyed.
In the first years, when he raised his voice against the artistic
bastilles, he had been as much concerned with applying the
talents of thwarted artists for the needs of the state as with af-
fording free opportunities for creative self-expression. As he became more and more linked in personal friendship and community of views with David, he also came to share fully with the
great painter the belief that patriotic art should be made an
essential feature of democratic public instruction. Like the
Saint-Just of the *Republican Institutions,* he had in his mind a
single vision of cultural and artistic indoctrination in which all
the creative arts would work as one in inspiring in the breasts
of Frenchmen a burning and lofty love of the Republic. The
heart would not be exempt from the despotism of virtue: along
with total coercion of the flesh, total uplift of the spirit.

Within that undertaking, painters of course would take
their place. As early as 1791, Barère had urged the assembly to
grant David a financial subsidy to complete the celebrated un-
finished canvas of the Tennis Court Oath. In 1794 he pressed
again for governmental aid so that engravings of the master's
painting, which commemorated a lad, Barra, who had fallen in
the Vendée and whose heroism was now a symbol, could be
placed in every primary school of the nation. Borrowing directly
from Rousseau, he advocated that painters should participate
in prize competitions to depict "the most glorious epochs of the
French Revolution," and that government commissions be given
to the prize winners. While the painters worked on their can-

vases, sculptors too would make their contributions in bronze and marble. From his pen came a memorandum advising the Committee of Public Instruction to give David its support for a bronze monument which would represent "the French people striking down Fanaticism, Royalism, and Federalism," and on his motion a decree was voted to set up a statue of philosophy holding in its arms the Declaration of the Rights of Man in the Convention hall.

After the sculptors, the architects; and there were many orders which appealed to architects to draft blueprints of public monuments, such as law courts, national theatres, public baths, and fountains, and political halls where "the sovereignty of the people will be exercised [and] games held on the *décadi* festivals." Musicians, too, were to serve the public good. On the same day, May 17 (28 Floréal), that Barère appealed to architects, he also addressed himself to them. "The Committee of Public Safety calls on all musicians and teachers of music to compete . . . in civic songs, compositions for national festivals, theatrical representations, martial music, and all that is most appropriate in their art to recall to republicans the dearest feelings and memories of the Revolution." Poets, too, were summoned to celebrate the principal events of the Revolution, compose patriotic hymns and poems and republican plays to transmit to the public "the heroic deeds of the soldiers of liberty, the acts of courage and devotion of republicans, and the victories won by the French armies." Pleading with historians to link yet another muse to the great endeavor, he asked them to "transmit to posterity the most striking acts and the great epochs of the regeneration of Frenchmen, to give to history the severe and resolute character which befits the annals of a great people attacked by all the tyrants of Europe [and] to compose classical works and infuse with republican morality writings designed for public instruction."

Thus, all artistic media were to be correlated, and most of all in the stirring pageantry of the fetes. There were many of them for the masses to attend, not as passive spectators but as active participants, and in them they were given the opportunity to identify their personal interests with the larger needs of the triumphant Republic. On May 7 (18 Floréal), Robespierre had outlined the fundamental principles of the new political faith which would replace the tenets of Christianity by a religion of equality, liberty, and humanity. In that report on the relationship between religion and moral ideas with republican principles he proposed a system of national fetes to link citizens together and infuse in their hearts the ideals of republican fraternity. There were to be solemn fetes common to the entire Republic, specifically the celebrations commemorating January 21, when "the tyrant" was beheaded; May 31, when the Girondins were expelled from the Convention; August 10, when the monarchy was overthrown and, greatest of all, July 14, when the Bastille was stormed. There would be lesser fetes, to be celebrated on *décadi* days, festivals in honor of liberty, equality, the human race, truth, justice, friendship, love. All would awaken—of this Robespierre was confident—generous fraternal feeling, love of the fatherland, respect for the laws.

First and foremost of them all was the fete which David organized with pomp appropriate to the occasion, the festival in honor of the Supreme Being under whose auspices the Revolution pursued its majestic course and whose worship was the first duty of all Frenchmen. Barère's views did not run counter to the ideals of the patriotic, deistic religion of national patriotism that Robespierre had formulated. There is no reason to doubt the sincerity of his feelings when he signed a decree for the printing and distribution of 200,000 copies of the report. Five weeks later, however, by the time that David was completing the extravagant preparations for the fete itself, June 8 (20 Prairial), the sincerity of his public approbation may be questioned. He was to write derisively in his *Mémoires* of Robespierre's arrogance in wishing to be recognized publicly as the first of the deputies who were all equal. It is probable that he too was one of the representatives of the assembly who sneered at Robespierre as "the republican pope." If privately he saw in the great celebration an opportunity to tax Robespierre with aspiring toward a dictatorship, he refrained in public from voicing his suspicions. He busied himself within the Committee preparing official costumes for the participants, and there is an order in his handwriting on the night before for printers to work through the night if needed, to complete their part in having the official program ready for the next day.

Until early June at the least, and in all probability for several weeks more, Barère was still joined with Robespierre in practicing patriotic coercion until the reign of liberty became real and love of the Republic was enshrined in the hearts of citizens. Relations, however, were strained, and the break which Barère wished to avoid was finally to sever their long entente.

# ☆XIII☆

## *The Denouement,*
## *June-July, 1794*

BARÈRE was a master in persuasion, but in the last analysis making republicans and founding republican institutions rested on force. His private doubts were great, but he chose not to air them. At no time during the last months of the dictatorship did he give public indication by word or deed that the time for coercion had come to an end. He did not oppose the passage of the comprehensive police bill which Saint-Just introduced on April 15 (26 Germinal), ten days after Danton was guillotined. The decree ordered that nobles and foreigners were to be banished from the greater Paris area, while Frenchmen guilty of counterrevolutionary speech were to be deported from their country. To implement the Ventôse decrees, six popular commissions were to be set up—actually only two were at first—to make a preliminary sifting of cases involving arrested suspects, so that those innocent of charges against them could be liberated by the responsible regional commission while only those presumed guilty at the first hearing would be sent to Paris to have final action taken by the Revolutionary Tribunal.

There was more to the regularization and the reorganization of revolutionary justice than providing for the enforcement of the Ventôse decrees. The decree extended the enormous powers already in the hands of the Committee of Public Safety by endowing it with the authority formerly possessed by the Committee of General Security alone, to investigate and prosecute suspected conspirators. To it was given exclusive jurisdiction over cases involving government personnel. The intent of this provision was clear: in police as in policy, the Committee of Public Safety would assert its governing authority.

However, in order to save the time and energy of men heavily burdened with policy making, the decree stipulated that a Police Bureau would be established within the Committee to prepare police matters primarily concerning government officials for consideration by the Committee as a whole. In examining the evidence the Bureau could or could not, as the deputy in charge saw fit, request further information from the Committee of General Security or even turn cases over to it. After that review, if evidence warranted, the charges and the charged would be referred to the Revolutionary Tribunal for final disposition.

In form, the fact-finding Police Bureau was not different from other clerical staffs of the Committee. It had a director, two assistants, and ten clerks. But from the start it was supervised by the Robespierre bloc. The member of the Committee designated to direct its investigations and evaluate the data was without exception one of the triumvirate. Saint-Just was in charge for several days and then again, jointly, with Couthon, at the end. For five weeks, during the months of May and June, it was Robespierre who handled its affairs. Even after he ceased attending the plenary sessions of the Committee at the end of June and Saint-Just had replaced him in supervising the Bureau, the latter still consulted him on the papers that he brought to Robespierre's home.

On what actually took place within the Bureau, little is known, and the little that can be said comes largely from the hostile testimony of men who, when they gave it, were less concerned with the truth about the Bureau than in denying that they had been associated with it. The Bureau lent itself to the suspicion, they alleged after Thermidor; it was a little stronghold within the larger Committee, a decisive lever that the Robespierrists intended from the outset to use "for the benefit of their ambitions," as Barère put it.

Although the available evidence does not substantiate the charge that Robespierre and his two closest associates succeeded in having the Bureau take over the administration of political police from the Committee of General Security and place it in their own hands, undoubtedly, Robespierre wished to do so. As the struggle deepened between the triumvirate and their opponents, the latter readily convinced themselves that such was the case. The Bureau did encroach upon the original police committee, but the Committee of General Security still remained the principal organ and handled about four times as many political cases as did the Bureau. As for the plea that the anti-Robespierrists did not participate in the operations of the Bureau, it is utterly false. When they tried to exonerate themselves during the reaction which followed Robespierre's overthrow, they were fighting desperately to save their own lives by saddling the odium for the Terror upon the fallen alone. The examination of the extant recorded minutes of the Bureau, roughly one-quarter of the total number of its transactions, tells a different story. Far from disassociating themselves from what the Bureau did, they concurred largely in its recommendations. Slightly more than half of the available arrest orders that it recommended were drawn up by the triumvirate; the others were either written in the hand of other members of the Committee or countersigned by them.

Barère himself, his denials notwithstanding, was as responsible or as guilty as any or all of his colleagues. Of the extant arrest orders which the Bureau recommended to the whole Committee he signed or drafted eight and possibly two more. If the same proportion exists for the total number of recommendations, his share would presumably rise to thirty at the least. A calculation of this nature is of course conjectural, in itself proving nothing definite. What is not conjectural is that he endorsed two of the most odious of the arrest warrants. One of them sent a "batch" of prisoners to the Tribunal for their presumed participation in a prison break. The second lumped together a wretched motley of forty prisoners of diverse political opinions and dispatched "the parricides" in a block to the supreme revolutionary court as guilty of plotting to assassinate

Robespierre. Barère's later protestations of innocence were falsehoods.

When he ratified those measures, he had reason to believe that the plots to assassinate Committee members were real. The danger of massive prison breaks and the attempts at assassination were not pure or impure figments of the imagination. Collot was wounded by a certain Admirat who had originally set out to shoot Robespierre. Several days later, the simple-minded girl, Cécile Renault, armed with the lethal weapon of a pen-knife, tried to enter Robespierre's lodgings. When she was interrogated after her arrest, she did not deny that she was a royalist and considered Robespierre a tyrant. These incidents were minor in themselves, but they were symptomatic of the temper of the opposition. The fears of the deputies were real.

Barère elaborated upon the incidents to tell what the Committee already believed, what he himself largely believed, and what it served the Committee's purpose to have all France hear and read. In his first report of May 23 (4 Prairial) he denounced "the tyrants of Europe and their vile supporters in France." The tyrants were first and foremost the English; their supporters in France were "the noble and priestly aristocracy," and with those enemies of the Old Regime he coupled "the parricidal shades of the Dantons, the Héberts [and] the Brissots." Three days later, on May 26 (7 Prairial), he elaborated in detail about the English in one of the longest and most popular of all his anti-British harangues, Report on the Crimes of England against the French People and its Plots against the Liberty of Nations. Picking up the press campaign in London against Robespierre, he pinned responsibility upon "perfidious Pitt" for the accusations that Robespierre was seeking to establish a dictatorship. After itemizing the many crimes of England against mankind, he catalogued its specific crimes against the French people and concluded that the time had come to give up a futile distinction between a vile government and its deluded subjects. Hitherto the French had followed the code of humanity in their treatment of enemy soldiers; now, in the spirit of Carnot's words that the French soldiers were "turning soft [and] taking pity on the hypocritical and blood-thirsty enemies of our liberties," he beseeched them not to allow enemy troops to return to their country. The Convention should decree, he moved, that "French soldiers would take no English or Hanoverian prisoners [for] only the dead did not return."

There was delirious applause in the Convention for this counsel of blood, at the Jacobins, too, where he repeated his speech. But tension was building up between him and the Robespierre bloc. He had already fallen into Robespierre's bad books by his covert attack on the new religious policy. It is clear that he shared the misgivings of the men who openly sneered at the "republican pope" during the fete of the Supreme Being. He had joined with Vadier and other freethinkers of the Committee of General Security in an insidious campaign to ridicule and discredit the Incorruptible by linking him with a demented visionary, the "Mother of the Savior," she had called herself, who had been cajoled into writing a letter which proclaimed Robespierre her prophet. Though the intrigue was scotched, Robespierre did not forget that Barère had been in it.

Two days after the religious ceremony, on June 10 (22 Prairial), Couthon introduced a bill against the evildoers who still opposed the foundation of the republic of virtue. The courts, he maintained, were wedded to ideas which obstructed revolutionary justice and failed to serve the interests of society. The existing legal forms were a travesty of justice and a mockery of morality. Justice and morality were one, and morality was identical with political orthodoxy. The definition that Couthon's bill made of crimes against the state added nothing specific to categories already established by the Law of Suspects. But by making still more vague and general the already long list of the "enemies of the people [who] compromised the liberty, unity, and safety of the Republic," the new Law of 22 Prairial gave the government a free hand to strike out against whomever it willed. Article ten was new and terrifying, for it conspicuously omitted a guarantee of immunity to deputies from the provisions of the law. Their nominal immunities had already been whittled down in practice. It seemed now as though they were being surrendered for good. Most frightening of all were the provisions which denied the arrested the services of counsel and stripped them of all legal guarantees of defense. The preliminary interrogation of the accused by local authorities was eliminated. When the case came before the Revolutionary Tribunal, it was left to the discretion of that supreme court to call witnesses for the defense. Witnesses, Couthon had explained, could be in error. The Revolutionary Tribunal itself was divided into two sections to speed up procedure, and the only verdicts it could give from now on were acquittal or death.

Couthon's proposal was judicial terror at its starkest, and Barère was revolted by its provisions. He knew of course that the Committee itself was divided and that Collot and Billaud were outraged that in its final form the bill had been discussed not by the full Committee but only by the Robespierre bloc. He knew, too, that the Committee of General Security had not been consulted at all over legislation which cut down its already diminished jurisdiction over police operations, that it had summoned Billaud to meet with it in protest, and that a majority of the two committees meeting jointly cast the charge of dictatorship at Robespierre. All that he knew, yet he hesitated to come out in the open. Airing inner differences on the floor of the Convention would certainly destroy the unity of the government; if he openly opposed the bill, his own security was threatened. So he played for time, waiting to see what course the debate would take, hoping by delaying tactics to arrange for satisfactory modifications. "I called in vain for postponement," he later alleged, and after a fashion he told the truth, if not all of it. When the motion was made for postponement, he had hedged: "Certainly the postponement that is called for is not an indefinite one." And when he was assured that it was not, he put himself squarely in both camps: "When a law is proposed wholly in favor of patriots . . . the lawmakers can have only one desire. I call for an adjournment of three days at the longest." This maneuver Robespierre also did not forget.

On the first day of the debate the deputies gave ground before Robespierre's eloquence and veiled threats and voted the measures as Couthon had introduced them. On the second day, 23 Prairial, they regained their courage and passed a preamble specifically guaranteeing their own parliamentary immunity. How Barère voted on that day is not known; what he did on the third day of debate, is known. Again Robespierre overawed the opposition and intimidated the Convention into rescinding the preamble it had voted. Barère leaped courageously into the ranks of the stronger and aligned himself with Robespierre. To vote for the preamble, he explained, was tantamount to accusing the Committee of wishing to violate constitutional laws. Of that intention Couthon was innocent, "but such," he continued, "was not the case of some of the sponsors of the insidious protests and maneuvers against the Committee." He covered himself by this surrender; but Robespierre again did not forget that Barère had joined him when there was no alternative.

The new judicial system that Robespierre had defended became the instrument of the monstrous "Great Terror." In the seven weeks between its enactment and the fall of the Robespierrists, the guillotine claimed more victims than it had in the preceding fourteen months, and as "heads fell like slates from the roofs," the appalling surmise made headway that it was in fact the design of the triumvirate to exterminate their opponents. The Law of 22 Prairial was the catalyst of fears, old and new, in the Convention. The belief gained ground that the parliamentary immunity of the deputies had ended. Actually, the purge of the factions and the subsequent reprisals against their followers had not established peace in the assembly. Cowed Dantonists and Hébertists seethed with bitterness. Among them were men resentful about the fate of friends whom they had not been able to save, frustrated and shamed over their own lost initiative. To these old enemies Robespierre added new. Outraged in his exalted morality, he had the Committee recall a number of deputies-on-mission whose vindictive cruelty in punishing rebels was notorious. They took their seats again in the Convention, Fouché, Tallien, Fréron, Barras and the others, publicly humbled and reproved. All of them conducted intrigues, knowing that if Robespierre prevailed, they would be given their deserts.

It was not only within the Convention that Robespierre's enemies nursed grievances against the fanatic-idealist for whom there was only one road to political virtue. The old animosities between the movers and the principals in enforcing the police measures and their rivals in the Committee of General Security could no longer be checked. Hatreds had come out into the open. Worst of all, the collectiveness of the Committee of Public Safety itself had been ripped to shreds. It had never been more than a coalition government, and now it had finally lost the unity of will and purpose which somehow had transcended the incompatibilities of its members.

Differences of social outlook were too irreconcilable to be composed, personal antipathies too sharp. Strained to the point of exhaustion by the herculean demands placed upon them, overcome by fatigue, their nerves raw and tempers out of control, they split into opposing coteries. The feud between Carnot and Saint-Just for direction of the war effort and control of the armies was a matter of public notoriety. Prieur de la Côte d'Or sided with the "Organizer of Victory." Lindet was suspected of secret sympathies for the Dantonists. Collot and Billaud, Robespierre loathed for the coarseness of their religious views, which ridiculed his deism. He feared them for their ties with Hébertists and the recalled terrorists-on-mission. Fouché and Collot were intimates. When the former was expelled from the

Jacobins, Collot feared he would be next. Robespierre appreciated the great services that Carnot had rendered, but he was obsessed by fears that his colleague harbored deep-seated plans to overthrow the rule of the civilians and with the victorious field commanders set up a military dictatorship. By the beginning of the month of June the rifts in the government had become a chasm, and by the end of the month the London press was speculating openly on the chances of Robespierre's opponents.

Barère had contained the animosities for a year. As late as the spring of 1794 his relations remained cordial with Robespierre. According to Carnot's son, Robespierre still held Barère "an honest man who loves his country." There had been disagreements between them in the past but never lasting rancor. It was different by early summer. Barère did not desire a break with the old associate for whom his admiration was great, his respect sincere. By his recommendations for the France of the future Barère had given proof that he was in large agreement with Robespierre's lofty idealism. Never intimate with either Collot or Billaud, he had deep repugnance for their friends among the disreputable deputies-on-mission. He had not been opposed when Robespierre had them recalled from the assignment that they were discharging with sanguinary excess. But he was more and more troubled by Robespierre's apocalyptic sense of mission. The adulation that Robespierre so openly savored at the fete of the Supreme Being aroused misgivings which he had not been able to conceal. He could not share the latter's fears of a military dictatorship. So by his transparent hesitancy and his covert demurrers he fell under suspicion in the eyes of a colleague who demanded unreserved endorsement. The inflexibility and intransigence of the one, the opportunism of the other in serving a purpose common to them both, brought about the break which neither of them desired. The provocation came largely from the querulous Incorruptible; to the very end, by placating him, Barère tried to keep the unity of the government unbroken.

He trod warily after 22 Prairial. On June 27 (9 Messidor), when Robespierre exploded wrathfully against slanders in the press, Barère repeated the warning and the threat against "the tormentors of public opinion." On the following day, June 28 (10 Messidor), when Collot and Billaud openly accused Robespierre in the Committee of seeking to make himself dictator, Barère studiously did not support them. A day later still, as altercations continued, Robespierre stalked out of the Committee and threatened to resign in order to bring his struggle against conspirators directly to the Convention. "In London," Robespierre had protested, "they are denouncing me . . . as a dictator. The same slanders are repeated in Paris. You would shudder if I told you where." Barère chose to ignore the reference clearly addressed to him; instead he preferred, five days later on July 4 (16 Messidor), to repeat Robespierre's charges against "the cunning friends of peace" and the advocates of "premature clemency" at home.

Although his standing remained high in Robespierre's own citadel of the Jacobins, who cheered his appeal on July 9 (21 Messidor) for unrelaxed vigilance and elected him their presiding officer for a *décade*, Robespierre himself was not appeased. To Collot, who called for a new William Tell to shoot down a new Gessler, he gave the retort direct that such were the words of a suspect. For Barère, he reserved an indirect token of his displeasure: "When we hear platitudes against Pitt and the enemies of mankind, when we see the same men secretly attack the revolutionary government, now moderate and now beyond all restraint, ever declaiming and ever opposing the useful means that are proposed, it is time to be on guard against plots." Again Barère turned a deaf ear to the innuendoes and kept his composure. He still hewed to the line in mid-July, joining with Robespierre in suppressing proposals for "patriotic banquets" to commemorate the storming of the Bastille and the great military victory of Fleurus in the Netherlands, the news of which had just come to the capital. He, too, was quick to see that under the cover of those public celebrations men and women who were sick at heart over the Terror could insinuate doubts over the necessity of having it continue when all was going well.

He could bare his teeth too, and on July 18 (30 Messidor) he chose not to ignore an overt thrust at himself as the bard of victory, the reporter of the carmagnoles. "No citizens," was his riposte before the assembly, "the republican orator is not a hollow declaimer. . . . He is the Committee of Public Safety instructed by you yourselves to take political profit from the victory of the troops." He went further still in retaliation on July 20 (2 Thermidor): "We must see to it that citizens clad with necessary but terrible authority do not influence the sections of the people with their prepared speeches. The people must stand on guard against them."

Barère's nerves were holding in these verbal exchanges; none-theless the situation was moving swiftly to a close. Well-grounded rumors were bruited that proscription lists were being drawn up, the triumvirate and their henchmen on one and on others, in different combinations, leading anti-Robespierrists. A frightful disaster threatened if there was no end to drift, a disaster that would destroy all unity among revolutionists. If the feuds came to open war, whoever the victors, Barère himself was in jeopardy: he had not given unreserved support to any coterie. For him, as well as for the government, safety lay in a truce. The hour was late for mediation, but he returned to his old role and made a final attempt to avert the break.

Almost entirely upon his initiative the two committees met in joint session on July 22 (4 Thermidor) to patch up differences and reach agreement for future action. It was agreed that four additional popular commissions would be set up to speed the lagging enforcement of the Ventôse decrees. In return for this concession to the social-economic policy that he had sponsored, Saint-Just agreed for himself and his two associates that in future they would no longer isolate themselves but would work together with all their colleagues in repressing the remaining conspirators, the "Hébertists and foreigners." Cases within the jurisdiction of the Police Bureau would be referred to the two committees before final disposal. It was hoped that this accord would induce Robespierre to end his virtual boycott of the Committee whose meetings he had not attended for a month.

Robespierre had not attended the fete of reconciliation, but he met with the committees on the following day. At first he rejected the proffered overtures. There was long wrangling, and bitter words were exchanged when he attacked two of the members of the Committee of General Security and Collot and Billaud of his own. In the end his reluctant assent to the agreement was obtained. Barère could be jubilant: he had preserved unity and safeguarded himself. The Terror would continue under joint auspices and not against him. Collot was commissioned to inform the Jacobins that all was serene again, Saint-Just instructed to report to the Convention that harmony reigned.

Seeking safety in unity, Barère had made those advances in good faith. The good faith of others was lacking in the arrangements. For the men in the two committees whom Robespierre had repeatedly denounced, the agreement settled none of the issues over which they were so fiercely divided. It won them a respite, time to attack later. Nor did the agreement provide safety to the recalled deputies-on-mission. There was ample room for them within the category of "Hébertists" whom the peacemakers had agreed to punish. They too gave only lip service to the understanding.

Robespierre had been prevailed on over his better judgment to accept the truce, but his assent was only for the moment. He returned to his conviction that he was being isolated and that the plots against him would go on. Certain in advance that the Paris forces would stand by him, he secluded himself after the meeting and prepared his supreme appeal to the Convention, which had always supported him in all previous tests.

While he gathered his strength to strike, Barère made his last protestations of loyalty. On the same 5 Thermidor, he threatened

# The Denouement

government action against Parisian workers who were preparing to go out on strike in protest against a newly posted scale of fixed wages: "Hébert is no more, but his spirit lives. His followers are in hiding, but their tenets still circulate." He was reminding Robespierre that he could be counted on. Two days later, on July 25 (7 Thermidor), he enumerated the categories of enemies with whom the Republic would presently settle accounts —deluded citizens, secret intriguers, profiteers, spies, aristocrats. Despite those threatening words he ridiculed rumors of a new May 31 against the Convention itself. A great republican stood on watch, strong in the "patriotic reputation that he merited by five years of toil and his unshakeable principles. . . ." And Robespierre did not stand alone, for the two committees stood by him, determined to save the country "through the better police measures on which they are working, through speeding up the trials of the arrested and the prompt punishment of counter-revolutionaries."

Barère claimed, months later when he had to answer the charge that he had remained true to Robespierre almost to the end, that necessity, not conviction, lay behind his words on 7 Thermidor: "I had to speak in that way; we would not have been able to batter down that enormous popularity which he still enjoyed. . . . Yes, we followed the line of prudence." The disclaimer was not honest, and the falsehood is obvious. Until Robespierre turned against him too, he remained loyal and he defended the Terror. But while Barère talked, Robespierre worked alone in his small suite of rooms, preparing a long and detailed exposé of the pass to which the Revolution had come and making ready to strike before his enemies did. He addressed the Convention on July 26 (8 Thermidor), the last time that he was ever to speak freely to fellow deputies. His words were eloquent, and courageous. They were a bombshell to Barère, who thought he had purchased immunity.

Robespierre derided the charges against him. Defying his listeners to prove that he was seeking to establish his personal

249

dictatorship, he denied too that he was drawing up a proscription list. After a cool and impersonal analysis of the weaknesses
of the Republic and the dangers that lay ahead, he turned contemptuously on the would-be mediator: "You have been told
that all is well in the Republic. I deny it. Why do they who predicted such frightful storms [now] see only light clouds? Why
do those who recently were saying: 'I declare to you that we
are marching on volcanoes,' believe today that they are tread-
ing on roses . . . ? They say much to you of your victories with
an academic frivolity which would lead you to believe that they
cost our heroes neither blood nor toil. . . . What have they done
to make our military successes serve our principles, to forestall
the dangers that lie in victory, or to assure us of its fruits?" He
did not stop with this onslaught on Barère; he went on to reject
the offer of peace. Yes, he agreed that there was a conspiracy,
but it was a conspiracy directed against him, a conspiracy
against freedom. It was not only deputies in the assembly who
were guilty of plotting in order to discredit the Revolution. They
had accomplices in the government itself, in the Committee of
General Security, and even among his own colleagues in the
Committee of Public Safety. Assuredly, the situation was critical, and in the crisis only one way out remained if liberty and
the Republic were to be saved: "to punish traitors, change the
subordinate personnel of the police committee," purge it of its
betrayers and place it under the control of the Committee of
Public Safety. The major Committee too had to be cleansed of
its false members and then, only then, could he "establish the
unity of the government under the supreme authority of the
Convention."

His courage was superb as he appealed from his associates
in the government to his colleagues among the deputies; perhaps a little of the cunning which he did not possess would have
served him better. He had chosen the worst of tactics in rejecting the mediation that, to be sure, he had good reason not to
accept. He overestimated the strength of his position; and by

shutting his eyes to the immense peril of a simultaneous attack on all fronts he made himself responsible for his ultimate defeat. But the first stunned reaction to his challenge gave him false hope, for only one deputy, Bourdon de l'Oise, who had opposed the Law of 22 Prairial and whose life was forfeit anyhow if Robespierre prevailed, dared to brave his wrath and move the deputies not to print the address.

Robespierre's words and Bourdon's motion put Barère in the greatest predicament of his revolutionary career. He had to think fast now, improvise faster still, if he were to emerge unscathed. Keeping his wits, evaluating alternatives of action, he did what instinct and training impelled him to do, he waited for the Convention to act before committing himself. He could not give the accolade to the man who had mercilessly flayed him; least of all would he stand up to Robespierre alone. If the Convention made common cause with Robespierre, Barère too would stand shoulder to shoulder with the deputies; if they turned against him, Barère too would have time to shift. He repeated the tactics he had made use of when the fate of the Girondins was still in doubt a year earlier on June 2, 1793, the tactics he had followed when the preamble to the Law of 22 Prairial was debated. He took his stand in dead center. "Speaking here as an individual," was his tentative approach, "and not as a member of the Committee of Public Safety, I insist that the speech be printed, because in a free country no truth should be hidden . . . and there is no assertion which cannot be attacked and examined. . . . "

After a brief debate the Convention voted to have the speech officially printed by the government printer, and Barère could breathe easily if only with a sense of cowardly relief. The respite from danger, however, was a short one, only a lull in the fierce discussion which broke out again. Had Robespierre agreed at that point to give the names of the deputies whom he charged with plotting against him, there would have been no renewal of the struggle. By designating some selected victims, he would have reassured the great majority and swung the relieved moderates of the assembly to his side. Though they pleaded with him to speak out, he kept an obstinate and ominous silence. With the courage born of stark dismay, the deputies rescinded their vote and referred the decision of printing the speech to the two committees. The action of the Convention ended Barère's hesitancy. In the company of the many and the stronger he could now be bold. He could now speak openly, and he took the floor: "It is time," he advised the Convention, "to end this discussion which can only benefit Pitt and the Duke of York. . . . If Robespierre had followed the work of the Committee for the past four *décades*, he would have suppressed his speech. . . . We will answer this declamation with the victories of the armies, with the measures we take against conspirators, with those we will take in favor of patriots. . . . "

Barère was sniffing the wind and trimming his sails to it. If he did nothing noble on this occasion and if his words were not noble when he read his old companion out of the ranks of the patriots and lumped him with conspirators, the death duel was not of his making. If deaths there were to be, he would fight for his own life. Robespierre was still confident of victory, assured that he would be upheld in the debate which was to reopen on the following day. In the meantime, to rally his supporters he took himself to the loyal Jacobins where he reread the entire speech. His last will and testament, he called it, promising, if his followers failed him, to drink the hemlock. The Jacobins did not fail him that night. In a meeting which bordered on hysteria they rapturously hailed his words. He tasted the pleasure of victory at that meeting, and he retired sanguine of the outcome. Too sanguine, for while he slept the plotters wrested the initiative from him.

Barère was with them on the night of 8 Thermidor at the joint meeting of the two committees. It was the hour of decision for him and for them all, for Collot and Billaud who had been hooted out of the Jacobins, for Fréron and Tallien, for Fouché and Barras. Robespierre could count on the Jacobins and the Commune and rely upon Hanriot, who commanded the National Guard of the capital. They had only themselves to count on—and the moderate deputies of the Convention, if they could keep those wavering ranks intact. They thought, that night, that they could also count on Saint-Just, who was present at the meeting. Since he had not yet drawn up the report he had agreed to draft three days earlier, they attacked him with their united anger. Barère railed against the triumvirate: "Who are you, then, insolent pygmies, that you want to divide what was left of our country among a cripple, a child, and a scoundrel?" That is what he claimed he said. Most likely he did use those words, or something very like them. Under fire, Saint-Just yielded. He agreed to draft the report, agreeing too to submit his text to them before he presented it in the assembly on the following day.

A wedge in the ranks of the united trio promised well, but negative action would not be enough against the forces that Robespierre could command. The meeting went on to the early morning hours and, before it broke up, the plotters had worked out their plans for the following day. While Tallien, Fouché, and Barras spread panic fear among all the deputies whom they could find that night, Carnot, Billaud, Collot, and Barère stayed on. Whoever furnished the initiative, it was Barère who drafted the texts which they prepared in advance. He drafted a decree to relieve Hanriot of command of the National Guard and have supreme authority assigned in rotation to each of six subordinate legion commanders. To divest the mayor of Paris and the executive council of the Commune of their jurisdiction over the political security of the Convention, the decree provided that responsibility would henceforth devolve upon a new board in which the legion commander of the moment would have a voice. Since the authorization of the Convention would be required for the decree, Barère prepared the text of the accompanying report that he would read at the appropriate moment. Leaving nothing to chance, on their instructions he also prepared a proclamation in the name of the Convention summoning the French people to stand behind their representatives.

Their preparations were complete. Their legislation would checkmate the Commune and the National Guard. Through Fréron, Tallien, and Fouché, they would hold the deputies of the center in line. With Collot in the chair as presiding officer, they would deny Robespierre the floor. And Saint-Just, they thought, they had in line. But at the last moment he turned against them. From the stormy meeting where he had been bludgeoned into agreement, he had gone directly to Robespierre, and Robespierre won him back. He would not show the draft of his report to the schemers. A terse note that came to the committee members as they made ready around noon of 9 Thermidor to take their seats in the assembly conveyed his decision: "Injustice has closed my heart; I intend to open it to the Convention." With open heart he would announce to the deputies that it was not only Collot and Billaud who were plotters, but Carnot and Barère too.

He was in ceremonial garb when he strode to the rostrum, in a chamois-colored coat and white waistcoat, high stock, and pearl-grey knee breeches. Robespierre, too, was dressed as though for a reception, in knee breeches and white stockings, his wig powdered, his famous coat of blue over his shoulders. But Saint-Just could not get beyond his opening words, for Tallien denied him the right to speak for the committees. Nor could Robespierre get the floor. With both Robespierre and Saint-Just silenced, Billaud was free to denounce the Robespierrists as the true conspirators. The assembly hall rang with cries of "Down with the tyrant!" and again the deputies shouted down Robespierre as he tried to speak. The arrangements were holding, holding when Tallien moved the decree to arrest Hanriot and when the deputies shouted for Barère to take the floor: "Barère to the rostrum!"

This was his cue and he took it, first to read the prepared re-

port and then the decree. Without referring to Robespierre by
name, he explained that it was for the Convention to save the
unity of the government and take action on "several individuals
who are discharging important duties." Free people and the rule
of individuals were self-contradictory; men who were free and
equal could not long live in common with men of swollen repu-
tations; the country had to be served for itself and not for the
sake of individuals. His report was accepted, the decree voted.
It stripped Hanriot of his command; orders were now to be
given by the legion commanders. As had been prearranged too,
political responsibility for the capital was vested in a three-man
board consisting of the mayor, the national agent for the Paris
area, and the commanding legion chief. Finally, Barère read the
proclamation to the citizenry. Inveighing against the royalist
and aristocratic conspiracy, it pleaded with the Parisians not to
hesitate, not to lose in one day the gains of six years. It called on
them to stand firm behind the Convention which was watching
over liberty. Where the military gave orders to the civilian authorities, he declared, liberty was dead.

With the enabling decree voted, the order was given to post
the proclamation. Things were moving fast, only an hour had
elapsed and victory was in sight. Though Robespierre fought
back and for almost an hour more tried again and again to make
himself heard in the fierce din, he was stilled for the last time. It
was not yet two o'clock when he was placed under arrest, and
with him Saint-Just and Couthon. Robespierre's younger brother, Augustin, and the young deputy Lebas who would not desert the triumvirate were also arrested. The crowded visitors'
galleries were emptying now, as the gendarmes led off their
prisoners, the spectators speeding home to spread the tidings
that the tyrant had fallen.

Their jubilation came too soon. The arrest warrant against
Hanriot was not enforced and for all practical purposes the arrested Robespierrists were still free. From the headquarters of
the Committee of General Security, where the gendarmes had

taken Robespierre, he was first moved to the Luxembourg prison. The jailer would not receive the prisoners, and for several
hours more he was safe in the section *mairie* of the Ile de la Cité,
harbored by the friendly district police. Late that night he, like
the other prisoners, was escorted to the Hôtel de Ville. There
they were safe also, for the Commune had declared open rebellion against the Convention. The mayor and the national
agent were now heads of an insurrectionary committee and the
National Guard remained under the command of Hanriot. So
the chances of the Robespierrists were not slight when evening
fell. They counted upon the military strength of the section units
of the National Guard, and they had faith in the political loyalty of the clubs and the general assemblies of the sections.

From Robespierre himself, however, there was no word, no
order or command. His followers implored him to act, but all
entreaties to take up arms failed to move him. While he lay inactive, resolved not to give substance, by taking command of
the insurrection, to the charge that he aspired to a dictatorship,
the Committee took vigorous steps to crush the rebels. It instructed Barère to draft a new order categorically forbidding
all section battalion commanders of the National Guard to obey
Hanriot's orders and directed all the revolutionary committees
of the forty-eight sections to remain in session and report developments every hour to the Committee.

If the outcome was still in doubt when the Convention assembled again at seven o'clock, the insurrectionist strength was
on the wane. Of the six legion commanders, four refused to
take orders from Hanriot. The revolutionary committees of the
sections also wavered. Twelve or more of them hesitated over
the course they would take, uncertain where their duty and
loyalty lay. Eighteen failed the insurrectionary committee of
the Commune and made the decision to obey the Convention
and the legal authorities. Of them all, only ten went over to the
insurrectionists. As for the section assemblies, they were almost
all lost to the insurgents, for of the thirty-nine that were in per-

manent session, thirty-five declared without reservation for the Convention and the remaining four were won over in the course of the night. The revolutionary ardor of 1793 was dulled among the sans-culottes. In some of the section assemblies the coercive terror of the Committee had destroyed all initiative, in many others the new wage scale and the suppression of the "fraternal banquets" had embittered the members. They refused to sell their lives so cheaply for the Robespierre-dominated government which had given them so little. The strength of the insurrectionists was ebbing, but until late that night, they might still have turned the tide. They had a decisive superiority in cannon, for the gunners in the artillery units of the Guard were more loyal to the rebels than the infantry units of the section battalions. If fighting took place, in the narrow streets of Paris, artillery strength could have brought victory. But they had no commander; they had only Hanriot, an incompetent drunkard. From Robespierre there was silence.

Nonetheless disaster threatened the Convention early in the night when Hanriot's gunners without opposition took possession of the headquarters of the Committee of General Security. Hanriot did not press his advantage and invade the assembly hall. For reasons that will never be known, he ordered his troops to fall back from the Tuileries gardens. No second opportunity came to him, and when the fearful deputies regained their balance they knew what had to be done. Their first move was against Hanriot himself whom they placed outside the pale of the law. Hanriot outlawed, they named one of theirs, Paul Barras, commander-in-chief of the entire National Guard. With this step they put the Convention itself at the head of the military defense. Now only the outlawry of the political rebels had still to be effected. If in spirit the deputies had already done so, the memory of Robespierre's great record lay between them and the letter of proscription. Yet there was no alternative; unanimously and without debate they adopted the Committee report outlawing their colleagues. Barère drafted and read it. Even at this last moment his report did not name them by name; it required an amendment to designate "Robespierre, Couthon, Saint-Just, Lebas and their accomplices" as the leaders of "the plot against the national representation."

The resolution of the deputies did much to make the ultimate outcome certain, but the confusion of command and the divisions in the rank and file of the rebels contributed heavily to their defeat. A number of the units of the National Guard followed the orders of the section assemblies and retired from the square in front of the Hôtel de Ville to their section centers; others broke ranks without orders, worn with fatigue after the long day, confused by long inactivity. Detached squads of Barras' National Guard patrolled the streets, by the light of torches reading out the proclamation bidding all citizens to support the Convention and the decree that outlawed Robespierre. As the hours went by, the streets were becoming deserted, and by one o'clock in the morning only three artillery companies remained before the Hôtel de Ville. Robespierre was still there, in a small room adjacent to the one where the council general of the Commune sat, but no word came from him; and within a half-hour the last of the fighting forces of the Commune melted away. Not a man, not a cannon, was left, as Robespierre could see for himself through the open windows of the Hôtel de Ville. It was then, as he heard the pronouncements of the Convention read, that the terrible truth came to him that all was lost. Two shots then rang out in the stillness, and to the council general the incredible news was brought that the Incorruptible had made his last protest. That he had attempted to commit suicide is very doubtful: "The elder Robespierre wounded himself," those were Barère's words a day later in his report on the end of the conspiracy. Systematic vilification had begun.

A bare quarter of an hour later the first detachment of Barras' troops swept unresisted into the Hôtel de Ville. As they poured in, the wretched paralytic Couthon tried to flee but fell helpless to the ground. The younger Robespierre jumped out of a window, while Saint-Just, haughty to the end, stood by impassively awaiting arrest. Lebas had shot himself to death; Robespierre had tried and failed. He was already out of the fight when the bullet of a guardsman shattered his jaw. They removed him on a stretcher from the Hôtel de Ville, and for hours he lay on a table in the antechamber of the Committee, barely conscious, until his wounds were dressed.

In the twilight of July 28 (10 Thermidor) the tumbril rattled once more to the Place de la Révolution. Robespierre's agonized cry pierced the square when they tore off his bandage, but the drums rolled, and the guillotine claimed its victim. The Robespierrists had fallen without defending themselves. The republic of virtue passed into history.

Barère lived on for many years, but the drama and the tragedy of Thermidor marked the end of his days of glory. Under fear for his life he had joined the plot against Robespierre, allying himself with men unworthy of his cooperation. In him there was no inkling that the overthrow of Robespierre would be the prelude to the end of the revolutionary government whose unity he had wished to keep. Barère could not know that in relinquishing the colleague with whom he had worked for years to regenerate France, he also killed the hope which sustained him, himself. He lived long enough to regret bitterly what he had done, but in those days of Thermidor, the brooding, vindictive, almost psychopathic, idealist gave him no choice.

# ≭ X I V ≭

## Under Fire,
## 1794-1795

THE working agreement of the deputies who pooled their strength to overthrow Robespierre did not survive the victory of 9 Thermidor. His open intention to crush all who thwarted or denatured his program had united them, but they had nothing in common except fears and hatreds. After his downfall they were to fall out, each group reading the future with its own eyes, looking to its own interests, seeking to exploit victory for itself. Different groups fought to control the Convention, among them Girondins, who had silently nursed their grievances during the Committee's domination, and hard-core Dantonists. Hébertists still rankled over the reprisals of the preceding months and there were dissident Jacobins who out of personal antipathy or opposition to Robespierre's religious policy had let him down. One new group came into being, the Thermidorians, who took their lead from Tallien and his friends.

Immediately, however, the victors remained united to rejoice over the fall of "the tyrant" and to exploit success. Thermidor had opened the sluicegates of emotions. Everywhere, in the unchained press, in the streets, in the assembly itself, feeling exploded in the jubilant cry, "Down with the Terrorists!" Sentiments long pent up broke into the open. Into them entered the bitterness of thousands of consumers upon whom the major sacrifices of the Committee's controlled economy had fallen and hatred for the agents of the government. There were fathers and sons, victims of the Terror, to avenge, and yearning for simple pleasures that a puritanical program of austerity had denied. And there was the resolution of browbeaten deputies to restore the parliamentary regime of free discussion that the dictatorship had suppressed. The mood of France turned ugly and vindictive as those tides of feeling lashed against the hated dictators.

Once under way the reaction could not be contained, and the Thermidorians put themselves in charge of it. They were quick to sense the new mood, quicker by far than Barère to ride the crest of feeling, and make capital of the role that devolved upon them of heroes who had saved France. In that course lay their own security, for the records of many of them were written in blood. Tallien had been recalled from his mission in Bordeaux for his terrorism, accused of hoarding and speculation, and ignominiously expelled from the Jacobins. Thermidor saved him from the fate that Robespierre had reserved for him, but his mistress, the famed beauty Theresa Cabarrus, still lay in prison, arrested on orders of the Committee, on orders, he knew, that Barère had signed. Fréron, too, had to act fast. Roué and sadist, a terrorist tarnished by the regime of rapine and blood that he instituted in his mission to Marseilles, he, too, had been recalled on Robespierre's initiative. He, too, had been hooted out of the Jacobins.

The records of the men who had rallied behind them in order to denounce before they themselves were denounced could not bear examination. So they saddled undeniable horrors of the past upon "the Robespierre-lovers," "the tail of Robespierre," as the notorious supporters of the Incorruptible were contemptuously tagged. "Citizens," Tallien declaimed from the Convention floor on the very night of Robespierre's execution, "all the plotters have not yet been struck down; there are men today who only a few days ago were his warmest supporters."

Did Tallien already have Barère in mind? Perhaps, but if so, in those first days Barère could not come under direct attack. His prestige was great; he enjoyed the immunity due to his stature and his services; he had in fact joined in the final maneuvers against Robespierre. It was too soon to bestow upon him the honor of the guillotine. Still, the instincts of the renegade revolutionists were sound. Barère was not one of them.

He had broken with the Robespierre bloc, but reluctantly, and only at the last moment. He remained confident of the strength of the Committee and assured, in the first days, that the elimination of his doctrinaire colleagues would restore pristine harmony and win new support for its policies. True, the moderates of the center had dared lift their heads, but the Committee knew how to deal with rebellion. Barère intended the concentration of power to remain. There would be no return to the parliamentary bickering and floundering from which the Committee had rescued the Revolution. Though the allies of 9 Thermidor had inspired in him neither respect nor good will, he could work together with men of their stripe. The Revolution was not fastidious. It had employed the services of *ci-devants*; it would not cavil over men whose morality was dubious.

For once, however, Barère failed to feel the public pulse. He, whose political antennae were so delicate, did not sense the new mood. Misgauging the intensity of feeling, he overestimated his capacity and the Committee's to ride the wave of revulsion. So, hopeful in his expectations, he addressed the Convention on 10 Thermidor (July 28) reading in behalf of the two committees, his Report on the Conspiracy of Robespierre, Couthon, Saint-Just, and Their Accomplices. He hailed the victory of national justice over "the dangers to which the arrogance, the spirit of domination, and the poison of despotism had exposed liberty." On "the worthy citizens of Paris," who had never been more great, and the loyal sections of the capital, he bestowed high praise for their defense of the Convention against the disloyal Commune and a misguided club. Automatically he paid lip service to the old fiction that he had mouthed so many times: the powers of the Committee derived from the assembly and the Convention alone was the rallying point of France. But he served notice that the Terror would go on: "Indulgence! There is none save for involuntary error, but [since] the maneuvers of the aristocrats are felonies, their errors are crimes." As he had done after the guillotining of Louis XVI and after the arrest

of the Girondins, he concluded his report with a Proclamation
to the French People and the Troops: "On May 31, the people
made their Revolution and on 9 Thermidor, the National Convention made its own. Liberty applauds both equally." There
was no debate and both the report and the proclamation were
unanimously adopted. Revolutionary business would continue
as usual during the necessary alterations in personnel. So at least
it seemed, and so he thought.

He could not have been more mistaken, and the great debate
that began on July 29th (11 Thermidor) opened his eyes. When
a motion to abolish the Revolutionary Tribunal had been rejected, he took the floor to expound the position of the government. The two committees, he stated, were agreed to reorganize
the Tribunal, but they held firm against abolishing "this salu-
tary institution which destroys the enemies of the Republic. . . ."
The 9 Thermidor, he went on, was "a disturbance which leaves
the government unaffected with respect to its political, administrative, revolutionary operations both at home and abroad." He
then proposed the names of three new temporary members until
the regular monthly election for the Committee of Public Safety
could be held, little expecting any discussion of his motion, let
alone the rejection of his nominees.

Things were now different and the ensuing debates revealed
how ready the moderates were to assert the claims of the parliamentary regime. Barère's report gave them their opportunity.
Tallien at once made his own position clear: "We have struck
down the triumvirs; we have no wish to replace them with the
decemvirs." Dismissing Tallien's open threat, for he was certain
that the assembly would back him, Barère put to the test a
countermotion to have the Committee personnel renewed by
one-quarter every month by an open roll call. Here came his
first great shock, for after two days of heated discussion, his
proposal was turned down and the countermotion carried.
While only one of the candidates whom he proposed was included among the six new members, Tallien was one of the five

to be selected. This was not the only rebuff that Barère experienced. While his nominees for replacements to the Committee of General Security were also voted down, Legendre was voted in. Legendre had once supported Danton; from fear of Robespierre, he had grovelled and denied his friend. It was now his turn. The first long step toward the restoration of parliamentary rule had been taken: the Terror government was beginning to break up.

For another month the crucial debates over the structure and function of the government continued, and Barère stood firm, fighting hard not to yield ground. He demurred against a motion to have each of the twelve executive commissions, hitherto subordinate to the Committee, made responsible to one of the twelve elected committees of the assembly and have their personnel nominated by the assembly as a whole. Acceptance of that motion, he declared, meant that there would be "twelve governments, twelve legislative commissions, and moral federalism instead of republican unity." For a moment, as the deputies wavered, torn between fear of completely destroying executive authority and dread of again falling under Committee domination, Barère pursued his advantage: "We were saved by the revolutionary government. Only rascals and intriguers fear the revolutionary government. We must refer everything to this single face, to this . . . guardian of victory." His words were unavailing. Fears prevailed, not unaccompanied by threats, and on August 11 (24 Thermidor) the motion was carried.

When next the major agencies of repression and coercion came under attack, Barère still pursued his course. He conceded that the reorganization of the Revolutionary Tribunal was in order, but as he had done on the earlier occasion when Camille Desmoulins had mobilized sentiment against the Law of Suspects, Barère agreed to mitigate the Tribunal's severity "by conciliating morality with politics and enforcing revolutionary laws with justice." Abolishing the Tribunal, however, and rescinding the Law of Suspects was recklessly dangerous: "One does not overthrow a new tyrant to smooth the path back to the old tyranny. . . . It is not revolutionary institutions which are wrong or vindictive or culpable, it is individuals. Good patriots speak with enlightened wisdom against abuses of power, but aristocrats speak with intemperate heat against institutions. Grant the aristocracy the destruction of one republican institution today, tomorrow they will call for the suppression of the word 'republican.' " If his words were prophetic, his warning carried no weight. The Law of 22 Prairial was then repealed and the authority of the Tribunal blunted. Old cases still pending were referred back for re-examination, the execution of convicted suspects suspended. Meantime the prison gates of Paris were opened. In the first week of August almost 500 suspects were released; in the last three, 3,000 regained their freedom.

By the end of August the unity of the revolutionary government was shattered, and Barère's rearguard action had failed to save the institutions of Year II. The dismantling of the Terror government was only the beginning. The attack was now directed against the men of the government and he, the bard of victory, was no longer entrusted with reporting the triumphs of the troops. "The people could not conceal their astonishment," was the police report.

The day of mudslingers and muckrakers had come. Among the many journalists and pamphleteers who vied with one another in sensational disclosures, a certain Jean Claude Méhée (he added the noble particle de la Touche), a sometime police observer during the Old Regime and left-wing agitator in 1792, was the first to make his mark. Writing under the pseudonym of Felhémési (Méhée *fils*), he scored a spectacular success with a series of shocking charges against the Jacobins. From his most successful pamphlet, *La queue de Robespierre*, which appeared in the last week of August, emerged a harrowing picture of the degradation of France under Robespierre. Tallien and Fréron echoed him in the Convention hall and the manhunt of the leading terrorists began.

An obscure deputy, Laurent Lecointre, on August 29 (12 Fructidor) drew up a long itemized arraignment of seven of them. He was experienced in heightening the emotional atmosphere; in October 1789, by adding enough colorful details of his own to the facts of the banquet of the Flanders regiment in Versailles, he had whipped up the passions of the Parisians. He now singled out Barère, Billaud-Varenne, and Collot d'Herbois of the Committee of Public Safety, and Vadier, Amar, Voulland, and David of the Committee of General Security as the most culpable. This move to have them indicted was the first of several; and the twenty-six items of his accusation were repeated frequently during the next half year. What he said in substance was that the accused were responsible for the terror which had gripped France; they were instrumental in organizing the loathed dictatorship of the governing committees; they had coerced the Convention and filled the prisons of France; they had shielded notorious counterrevolutionaries, while aiding and abetting the Robespierrist triumvirate in their felonies. Justice demanded that they pay for their crimes against humanity.

As much as any man of the Terror government, Barère was open to such charges. For what the Committee did and for what he did within it his responsibility is total—for its achievements and its failures, for its exaltation and its stupendous mistakes, for its coercion and its excesses. But there was no justice in the attempt to distinguish between the "pure" and the "impure" Committee members, only a maneuver for political gain. Lecointre cited their signature of terroristic measures, but the fact of signature of a given decree was meaningless. Men working at high speed could not be expected to read all the orders that were put before them for signature; they had to take for granted that the orders corresponded with decisions made in preliminary discussion. That they carefully read the most crucial orders is certain; how many they did not read of the thousands that were signed is impossible even to guess at. As for the criterion of first signature of a specified order, it raises more problems than it solves. Proving responsibility by establishing the fact that a given member drafted the original minute of an order is more realistic without however yielding certain proof. Successive orders on a specified subject were drafted by different hands; frequently copies of the original minute were not signed by the member who had drawn it up; many manuscript minutes have disappeared. For good and for bad, responsibility was collective.

As crowds gathered in the public squares to air their opinions, the deputies debated the charges with fervor and fury. The tone of the debates demonstrated that Lecointre had spoken too soon, that it was not yet time for sweeping terrorism in reverse, that the reaction had not progressed so far that, in the persons of picked scapegoats, the entire revolutionary rule could be disavowed. One of the pamphleteers described "the faded complexion of the accused, their hollow bloodshot eyes, their sinister faces, their haughty, contemptuous bearing." He then added, sorrowfully, "By one of those weaknesses which do not honor the human heart, their colleagues vied with each other for the honor of talking to them, for the privilege of shaking their hands. They were dethroned kings in whose behalf it was an honor to plead." The Convention tabled the accusations, characterizing them as "slanderous."

Lecointre had gone too far and too rapidly. He made amends to Barère six years later: "I recognized too late my mistakes and my injustice." Some of the deputies, "the repentent Thermidorians," drew back from the reaction they had unleashed, but Tallien and Fréron, "Thermidorians of the Right," could not retreat. They had committed themselves. The one, publicly branded a thief and a débauché, was forced to resign from the Committee of Public Safety; both were again hooted out of the Jacobin Club, this time Lecointre with them. Rebuffed in the assembly, they appealed to forces outside. They fixed the responsibility for the mysterious explosion of an arsenal upon the

Jacobins. They made the Club guilty of a so-called attempt to assassinate Tallien. They called on Méhée again and upon lesser pamphleteers, and they marshalled the *Jeunesse dorée.*

The "Gilded Youth," whom Fréron recruited in cafés and dives, were an unsavory lot. Among them were dissatisfied salesclerks, shopboys, assistants of law offices, domestics whose fun and idleness the demanding Revolution had ended. Requisitioned for military duty, many were slackers, others had deserted the front after Thermidor. Liberated suspects joined them. It was these suspects who made the tonsorial style *à la victime* fashionable, hair cut short in back, worn very long in front, and falling over their eyes. They and their lady friends gave gay parties, inviting as guests only those who could boast of guillotined relatives. They aped the manners and exaggerated the speech of the *ci-devant* petit marquis, drawing out the words and slurring over the letters. Armed with leaded canes, they were thugs on the loose, in the name of humanity and justice terrorizing and beating up Jacobins and other well-known patriots.

Up to now Barère was still a member of the Committee, but the luck of the draw turned against him and he too, like Prieur and Jeanbon, was forced by lot to resign. Counting on Jacobin resistance outside the assembly and the support of left-wing deputies within, he took the floor as a simple deputy on September 7 (21 Fructidor) to mobilize republican strength against the reaction, renouncing the manifestly doomed attempt to maintain a centralized government. He took a new tack: good citizens should know that the real enemies of the Revolution were the men who endeavored to prolong "the convulsions," meaning the attacks on himself and the old Committee members. Insisting that the time had come to reap the harvest of the Revolution, he moved the appointment of a commission which would be instructed to draw up a plan of republican institutions. Without those permanent bases, he argued, the Republic could not endure. While to reassure the moderates he stated explicitly that his project was not that of "one of those petty tyrants," meaning Saint-Just, "who had carried the principles of democracy to excess," nonetheless, he intended that the democracy without excess which he would now establish should protect the rights of the urban unemployed and the rural landless. Again to win support, he reaffirmed his belief in private property, but he denounced the abuse of the principle, castigating war contractors, moneyed men, and speculators. He summoned the Convention to set limits on the amount of nationalized property that could be purchased and called on it to make provisions for the division of the property of émigrés into small plots for the benefit of "good sans-culottes and unfortunate citizens."

His proposal to consolidate the Revolution came too late. The deputies of the left were too few to maintain the ideals of the Terror government; and the center, for all its eagerness to call a halt to the reaction, was too weak. His motion was lost and the vendetta ran its course. On October 3 (12 Vendémiaire), Legendre in his turn moved the indictment of the leaders. Again they hit back, Barère denying that he had supported the Law of 22 Prairial. Pleading circumstances, he also defended the role he had played on the eve of Thermidor. "I had to speak as I did. . . . We followed the line of prudence . . . and we said to ourselves: 'If we attack him [Robespierre] we will go to the scaffold like vile conspirators and the tyrant will continue to oppress Paris and the Republic.'"

Legendre had restricted his charges to Barère, Billaud, and Collot, ostentatiously exempting Carnot, Lindet, and Prieur from his charges on the ground that those great technical specialists were "always relegated to their offices." Seeing his chance, Barère counterattacked and called upon Carnot and Prieur—Lindet, who had already defended the Committee was not present—to corroborate his contention that the Committee had acted as one. They responded to his plea. They had not been relegated to their bureaux, they testified; on the contrary, as Barère maintained, the Committee had functioned as one. All matters had been discussed in common, many decrees signed without being read. Their task had been so time-consuming, their confidence in one another so great, that it was only after many months that they discovered that Robespierre was conspiring against the Revolution. With him, with Couthon and Saint-Just, rested the blame for atrocious police measures. The Committee had saved France.

The words of a Carnot and a Prieur still carried weight and for the second time the deputies thrust back the attempt to indict the Revolution. They tabled a motion to form an investigating committee and passed to the order of the day. After this second test, deputies of good will would certainly have amnestied their accused colleagues if they could or at the very least deferred their trial to a later date. But mob passions were too strong and they were powerless against the jubilation that greeted each fresh disclosure of Jacobin infamy. Carrier, "the butcher of Nantes," he was called, was indicted most likely, as the evidence now discloses, for crimes not of his doing. The Gilded Youth beat up Jacobins, the doors of the Club were shut, and Barère could do nothing to turn back the tidal wave. In the Palais Royal one of the young hooligans punched him in the face for his audacity in crying, "Long live the Republic!" In the Convention he was now all but silent, and when again, on November 14, he pleaded for a slow and orderly transition from the revolutionary government to a parliamentary regime, fellow deputies hooted him down. He who had swayed the Convention with his eloquence and thundered against its critics was now reduced to pleading.

Systematic vilification began in earnest with the October 5 issue of Fréron's *L'Orateur du peuple*, two days after Legendre's attack. In that issue Fréron attacked viciously Barère's entire revolutionary past. A royalist in the early days, Barère had gone over to the Lameth triumvirate and Lafayette, then turned Feuillant; he had hedged on the fate of Louis XVI, then abandoned his king; for eighteen months he had been the most ferocious of the terrorists. Now, as rumors circulated that he was about to flee to London with his mistress, Fréron sneered at the sanguinary revolutionist whom with baffling inconsistency he also accused of being "the soul of the cabinet of St. James." "Go and gather the millions that you sent off abroad," was his satiric advice.

On October 22, Tallien's *L'Ami des citoyens* with Felhémési as chief editorial writer first appeared, supplementing the tirades of Fréron. And early in November the most notorious of all the pamphlets was published, Vilate's *Causes secrètes de la Révolution du neuf au dix Thermidor.* Former juror of the Revolutionary Tribunal, sometime secret agent of the Committee, Vilate had just been released from prison and had good reason to attack Barère. Such a procedure would save him from investigation, he was reported saying. The success of the *Causes secrètes* was spectacular, and in it Vilate spared Barère nothing. Barère was a trimmer, utterly devoid of principles, driven by fear into cruelty. He had betrayed everyone in turn, the king, the Girondins, and Robespierre; a ruthless cynic, after his morning audiences with petitioners, he would throw their appeals into the fire, remarking: "Here we are; I have finished my correspondence." He, the sworn enemy of all men of substance, was himself a profiteer. He was a sadist who mused over the thought of burning Paris to the ground: "Do you know, Dupin, Nero's idea when he set Rome on fire for the pleasure of rebuilding it, was a truly revolutionary idea!" He was a libertine who had kept a notorious courtesan, La Demahi, in style in Paris, and with the companions of his erotic pleasures he had disported himself in a fashionable hideaway in the suburb of Clichy, where he held orgies that even Vilate's pen forebore to describe. Other pens were less reticent, and the *Journal de Perlet* lifted the veil on similar episodes in the private lives of Robespierre and Couthon. Those presumably austere men, the public now learned, also maintained pleasure haunts in the suburbs of Paris.

Other pamphleteers embellished upon Vilate's chronicle of scandals and drew upon imagination to add titillating charges of their own. "From the depths of [the prison of] La Force"— thus Fréron—"a prisoner has just disclosed to the public a work which throws new light upon the conspiracy. . . . My pen trembles under my fingers, my heart leaps with rage and fury; vengeance, vengeance!" Two weeks later, on November 17, *L'Ami des citoyens* informed readers that "Barère dances, laughs, proscribes, murders, guillotines as he wills; he is at the service of whoever wishes to employ him."

The air was thick with hate. Catholics, long persecuted, were boldly attending services in the reopened churches; appeasement of the Chouans and Vendée rebels was giving heart to royalists; Girondin deputies were taking their seats in the assembly. In this setting Lecointre once more took the floor on December 5 (15 Frimaire) to repeat the old charges. He designated by name the three that Legendre had named, adding to them that of Vadier of the Committee of General Security. This time he took the precaution of documenting his case, and the printed text of his charges had wide circulation in and out of the assembly. While in the streets the people were speculating on how long it would be before the trial of the four began, the Convention gave its first answer and decreed that three committees would take up consideration of the charges preferred by Lecointre.

On December 27 the committees presented their report, ruling that a case had been established against the four. On their recommendation the assembly appointed a Commission of Twenty-One, which was instructed either to exonerate the men named or draw up an indictment, whichever action it deemed appropriate. The report was not unexpected, but if in retrospect the indictment that the Commission subsequently made seems inevitable, such was not the case at the time. The accused still had their supporters, not many, but influential, and sufficient to force the Convention to decree that the replies which Barère was preparing should be published officially by the government printer.

Two lengthy rebuttals appeared in January, *Réponse des membres des deux anciens Comités . . .* and *Second mémoire des membres de l'ancien Comité de salut publique.* Fréron and Tallien sneered at the refutations, the first of which was almost entirely written by Barère, and called attention to "the diabolical plot" to save "the four monsters." But the Commission of Twenty-One took formal cognizance of the *Réponse* and the *Mémoire* and gave Barère a hearing. If his later word is to be accepted, it would have voted nineteen to two to absolve him, but Siéyès prevailed upon it to rule that all four should be tried together. Yet January and February of 1795 went by without a decision from the investigating board, and as late as February 20 Barère was writing confidently to his brother in Tarbes and reproaching Jean-Pierre for fears over the outcome.

Perhaps the Commission delayed because of disagreement in its ranks; perhaps the persistence of the deputies in defending the accused held it back. It may be that it was biding its time, waiting for public opinion to harden to the point where no deputy would dare to speak up against impeachment. If such were the case, Fréron was not remiss in alerting the public on its duty. In mid-January he exhorted the Gilded Youth "to awake from their lethargic slumber and avenge the deaths of old men, women, and children by exterminating the cutthroats"; and presently he gave thanks to that "republican youth for its courage and its patriotism." That youth fared well without his blessing or encouragement. They thronged the streets, fighting pitched battles with armed sans-culottes, smashing plaster statues of Marat and breaking the heads of living Jacobins with equal gusto. On the anniversary of the guillotining of Louis XVI, on January 21, the royalists took up the refrain. The streets resounded to a new song, *Le Réveil du peuple,* which incited good citizens to rise in their wrath and exact vengeance. "What is this barbarous slowness," thus the second stanza. "Haste, O sovereign people . . . make war on all the agents of crime, pursue them to the death"; and in the fifth stanza, "Ah, let them perish, those wretches and devouring cutthroats whose souls are filled with crime and love of tyranny."

Scores of pamphlets echoed the appeal, regaling the public with instance after instance of Barère's infamy. Among them there was *Cry of Humanity, Death the Order of the Day, The Barère Family Unmasked, The First Session of Jacobins in Hell,* and *Their Heads Are Reeling.* And early in March the press was spreading a rumor, professing with mock horror not to believe it, that in the last odious days of the Terror, Barère had established a tannery of human skins and had worn the clothing of his victims. The allegation was not new. Robespierre had already been thus honored.

With public opinion fashioned, on March 2, the Commission gave its report. As its spokesman, Saladin, one of the returned Girondins, took the floor to present it, the presiding officer called for quiet. But the deputies loudly cheered the reporter and hooted Barère, Collot, and Billaud. Vadier was in hiding. Cynical to the core, he had taken flight, casting a parting jibe that even if he were accused of stealing the two towers of Notre Dame he would still run away. His opinion of the proceedings may not have been wrong. Though the Commission's report reviewed the evidence in detail, the reporter might have saved his breath. His listeners were prepared to vote the impeachment that he called for. For Legendre, impeachment was not enough. He called for one additional precaution, moving the arrest of the indicted deputies pending trial, and his motion was carried.

Barère accepted the ruling; there was nothing else to do, and he requested only that he be given full freedom of word and pen to conduct his defense. He remained in the assembly hall until nine o'clock that evening, waiting for the arrest order to be executed. Then, in the falling snow, alone, he walked the short distance to his apartment on the rue St. Honoré. He might have taken refuge with friends. He went home, and an hour after he had retired the gendarmes arrived.

In the three weeks before the trial opened, he was under closely guarded house arrest. While two gendarmes installed themselves in the anteroom of his small apartment, police observers, stationed nearby, drew up detailed reports on who came and went. The precautions, it is clear, were unnecessary. Barère fell into a rage which no one believed him capable of when friends offered him a passport and funds to escape abroad: "Life is not worth living at the price of such cowardice," he is reported as saying. It was less courage than hope which sustained him. He prepared for publication the response he wrote to Saladin's report and rapidly wrote another rejoinder, *Les Alors,* quoting back in it to his accusers their own terrorist utterances. He arranged for the distribution of the *Défense de Barère. Appel à la Convention nationale,* which had just been published, in which he reviewed his career before and during the Revolution. In it he took up in turn and ridiculed the specific charges against him, that he had been a trimmer, that he had enriched himself during the Revolution and bought vast estates of nationalized property, that he had been a terrorist who coerced the assembly and supported the dictatorship. It was moving and eloquent, and it convinced no one.

Except for the denial that he had been a terrorist, which was patently false, he told the truth after a fashion about La Demahi and the "orgies" at Clichy. Not enough, however, to puncture Vilate's tissue of innuendo and falsehood which enjoyed a long life. He explained that he went to Clichy "to enjoy a frugal meal three or four times in the course of the summer in the company of a few deputies and their wives and with several lady citizens who were known for their uprightness and their patriotism." The *Défense* added, probably untruthfully, that Robespierre had denounced those meetings because he had learned from agents that the conversation took a turn sharply critical of his tyranny. What Barère did not say either in the

*Défense* or his *Mémoires* was that among the lady citizens whom he had the pleasure of escorting to a salon that was set aside in the Clichy retreat for the use of his fellow deputy and friend, Dupin de l'Aisne, was the "Demahi" on whose ill repute Vilate provided such scabrous details.

A Madame de Mailly, an attractive young woman, with whom Barère most certainly was friendly, did in fact exist. From the records of her arrest we know that Pierrette Jeanne Charpentier—this was her maiden name—was the divorced wife of a well known printer named Mailly. For five or six years she had been living with a certain Travanet, also divorced, also a friend of both Dupin and Barère. In the Old Regime Travanet—actually his name was Jean-Joseph Guy Bourguet—had been the director of a gambling establishment patronized by Marie-Antoinette. During the Revolution, while establishing a commendable reputation for himself as a loyal patriot who conscientiously discharged all his civic responsibilities, he found time to make a good deal of money, buy great quantities of nationalized property, and set up a spinning and weaving mill in one of them, the former abbey of Royaumont. In Brumaire, Year II, however, he fell afoul of the authorities, or at least of a spiteful member of the Committee of General Security, and was placed under arrest. In the arrest warrant, his patriotism was challenged; he was called a speculator and accused in a vague way of working to bring about a general bankruptcy in France. His *belle amie* vigorously protested what to her seemed like a police frame-up, and for her pains Madame de Mailly was also arrested a few days later. When the watch committee of the section in which she and her lover Travanet were living investigated the arrest, both of them received the highest character references as exemplary republicans. Thanks directly to Dupin and indirectly to Barère, who interceded in her behalf, Madame de Mailly was released from prison two months later. Travanet, on the other hand, remained in prison for six months more until after the overthrow of Robespierre. Either Barère's memory played tricks upon him when he wrote that Robespierre was responsible for their arrest and that he had sheltered Travanet between the latter's release and Thermidor or else he lied deliberately.

When Travanet was questioned in his turn, the accusation of speculating was not repeated. He was asked whether he had corresponded with émigrés, sent money abroad to enemy governments, or concealed gold and silver specie in his apartment. To all these questions he answered in the negative. Whether he was as guiltless as the friends in the Committee of General Security who interrogated him professed to believe need not concern us. Whatever Travanet was up to himself, Barère was not linked to any charges against him, indeed not even mentioned in connection with them.

Though he was at some pains not to admit it, Barère was in fact a friend of Madame de Mailly and moved in her circle of artists, painters, sculptors, musicians, and publishers. He was also on friendly terms with Travanet and at home in the latter's world of financiers, large-scale real estate operators and speculators on the stock market, and out of friendship he had interceded for them. It may be, that as Vilate charged, Madame de Mailly bestowed her favors on him as well as upon Travanet. If she did, she appears to have been the soul of discretion and she was certainly no notorious courtesan as Vilate ungallantly alleged. It is possible too that Barère was not only friendly with her and Travanet but also frequented the gambling den that they were still running in Travanet's apartment in Paris, an activity which came to light in the course of the interrogation. The company that Barère kept could have been improved upon, but the facts at Vilate's disposal were lean. His imagination, guided by spleen, larded them, and in the prevailing atmosphere his account passed for the truth.

Even if Barère had demolished Vilate's accusations, his refutation would probably not have been believed by his fellow deputies. They were not eager to share the fate that seemed in store for him. Still, if adherents among deputies were relatively few, well-wishers outside the Convention, especially in the working-class quarters, were many. Despair had seized the poor. The paper assignats had plummeted to eight, the lowest point yet reached in their calamitous fall; removing food and price controls brought untold deprivation. In that bitter winter of 1794-1795, food sold at famine prices. Even when available it could not be shipped, for the transport barges froze in the rivers. The bread ration had fallen to two ounces a day and Parisians were literally dying of hunger. Embittered by such unparalleled suffering and outraged by heartless profiteering, disillusioned sans-culottes looked back yearningly upon the regime of Year II that so many of them had eagerly repudiated on 9 Thermidor. As the day neared for the trial of the four there were daily clashes between armed sans-culottes and the Gilded Youth and stormy demonstrations against the government.

The trial opened on March 22 (2 Germinal). Outside, detachments of the National Guard patrolled the building, while within, the Gilded Youth packed the visitors' galleries, swamping Barère's few sympathizers. From their seats behind the presiding officer where they faced their peers, the three prisoners could hear a handful of adherents chanting the *Marseillaise;* it was easier to hear the strains of *Réveil du peuple.* Lindet spoke at length in behalf of the accused, and Carnot again took the floor to defend his former colleagues. Each went beyond the immediate charges, each once more invoked the solidarity of the accused with the committees and that of the committees with the Convention. They derided the accusation of political crimes and contrasted the achievements of the "Great Committee" as a whole to the limited police activities of the Robespierre triumvirate. Since it had been agreed that the prisoners would also be heard, Barère went to the rostrum, defending himself effectively, so effectively according to his own version, that the Thermidorians were thrown off balance: "Have I ever feared to present at the rostrum the opinions of the majority of the Committee, sometimes even against my own judgments? Did I not have both the wisdom and the modesty, should I not have had them, to place the general view above my personal opinions?" The trial went on for more than a week, incident after incident was raked up, old charges rehashed, and arguments turned in circles. Public opinion continued skeptical over the outcome and police observers reported conversations on the street corners that a deal was being arranged. Perhaps it was. Barère later wrote that he had been sounded out and promised full exoneration if he turned state's evidence against Collot and Billaud. The disclosure is more than probable.

While the Thermidorians were running into this unexpected opposition inside the Convention, the turbulence of the populace reached its height. Since the despairing sans-culottes had lost all confidence in the deputies, each day heard new complaints about the food shortages and fresh demands for the Constitution of 1793. They wanted the Convention dissolved and new elections held at once, not deferred for a year. They called for a truce to prosecution and persecution. And the old Committee members meanwhile were swaying the assembly, for after Lindet, Carnot, and Prieur had finished testifying, the motion was made to have the trial postponed until the next assembly. The crucial moment had come. With their courage stiffened the deputies were damming the flood waters of the reaction. Would the dam hold?

For a brief period Barère's confidence had wavered, but at this point he regained it, so he affirmed. "The two of us," he wrote in the *Mémoires*, "were planning that spring to go and live in a little rustic house near Meudon. [Then] the lightning struck me almost in the arms of a consoling friend." Who the consoling friend was, we can only speculate. A gentleman of the Old Regime, Barère refrained from involving a lady love in his disgrace. The address he gave suggests that she may have been Madame de Mailly who possessed a country home in Meudon and with whom his relations remained of the friendliest for years. The address notwithstanding, the "friend" may have been Madame de Guibert, widow of the great artillerist of the Old Regime, who gave him the consolations of her love in the following years, or she may even have been his cousin Sophie for whom, as he wrote to Demerville, "his heart was pining."

If he did make such plans, he was most naïve; he should have known that his enemies would not give up their prey. In their press the Thermidorians were brandishing the scarecrow of a popular insurrection to rescue the indicted deputies and calling for strong repressive measures. On the day before the trial opened, the Convention passed a sweeping law prescribing penalties of deportation or death against sedition and armed attacks upon the national assembly. The demonstrations continued nonetheless in the last fortnight of March. Clashes did not end between sectionnaires and the Gilded Youth, between the sans-culottes and government troops. On March 31 (11 Germinal) angry crowds milled outside the Convention hall; within it, petitioners again pressed their demands for bread and the Constitution of 1793. In the concluding words of one of the petitioners the frightened deputies thought they heard the signal for the insurrection that they dreaded: "We have risen to maintain the Republic and liberty." From those words and from the many meetings in the general assemblies of the workingmen's sections the Thermidorians convinced themselves that the insurrection was planned for the following day.

The "insurrection" took place on April 1 (12 Germinal). For four hours, from 2 to 6 P.M., hundreds of women and unarmed sans-culottes piled into the hall, denouncing profiteers and hoarders, shouting demands again for bread and the Constitution of 1793. A throng, estimated at 10,000 men and women, filled the gardens of the Tuileries outside. But there is no evidence that petitioners within and agitators outside the Convention wished to try to break up due parliamentary procedure. At no moment in the long afternoon of commotion and fiery speeches did the deputies suffer physical violence. At no time did they lose control of proceedings and by evening enough battalions of the National Guard had shown up to dispel the last threat of danger. The crowd outside the Convention melted away, while at the sight of National Guardsmen, bayonets drawn, in the lobbies, the petitioners silently withdrew. The "insurrection" was over. There had been no plan of action; nothing had been prearranged to obtain specific measures or remedies. The petitioners had wasted four hours in noise and empty words.

The intimidated deputies then acted, and their first move was to order the arrest of the leading Montagnards who had defended the indicted four. Boissy d'Anglas, the presiding officer, then addressed his colleagues, denouncing the demonstration as an attempt to keep the Convention from passing judgment on the "brigands who have flooded the Republic with blood," and moving their deportation that very night. It took rare courage to stand up at that juncture and speak up, but fifty-two deputies called for an open vote on his motion. Prieur was one of them, not Carnot or Lindet. The protest was in vain: the decree of deportation against Barère, Collot, Billaud, and Vadier was carried by acclamation. Fearing further trouble on the next day, the deputies voted a decree placing Paris under a state of siege and gave command of the armed forces of the capital to General Pichegru, victorious conqueror of Holland but dubious democrat. When the session was adjourned at six o'clock in the morning, the Convention was safe. The Thermidorians were free to ignore the demands of the sans-culottes. They had stilled the protests of their fellow deputies. The curtain had fallen on Barère's days of glory.

# ⚥ X V ⚥

## *In Hiding,*
## *1795-1799*

BARÈRE did not attend the fateful session of the Convention on April 1. He had worked in his room preparing a speech for the next day, and then went to bed confident of exoneration. In the middle of the night his door suddenly banged open and a justice of the peace, accompanied by two gendarmes, stormed in. While the soldiers were sealing Barère's papers and his private effects, the judge read out the Convention's decree for his deportation. He reeled in astonishment, but apparently recovered sufficiently to sleep calmly through the night, no doubt sustained, as he maintained, by his sense of innocence.

Getting the deportees out of Paris the next day proved difficult and Barère's suspicions were aroused by the preparations of the authorities. The large gilded and mirrored carriage sent to his door around noon to transport him to the Tuileries and the long delay in starting convinced him that attention was deliberately being directed to his departure in order to provoke disturbances in which he could providentially be killed. Since in the capital there were many who thirsted for his blood and, according to the police observers as well as Barère, so many sans-culottes who were outraged by the deportation, that he may not have been too wide of the mark in his supposition. However he reached the Tuileries—the several accounts do not agree—it is reasonably certain that a hooting crowd did stop the carriage at the church of Saint-Roch and clambered over it to get at him. The coachman somehow cleared a path and deposited his cargo in the offices of the Committee of General Security. Later in the day he was joined there by Billaud, who had had a similar adventure. Collot had already been moved out of Paris.

## In Hiding

Meantime, in the adjacent hall of the Convention, Tallien was urging his fellow deputies to condemn the three prisoners and execute them forthwith. Only by such summary justice, he argued, could the fury of the patriots who had vowed not to let them get out of Paris alive be assuaged. "But Providence," explained Barère, "was watching over me." At about 6:30 P.M. the two carriages which were to take him and Billaud out of Paris left from the offices of the Committee of General Security. But they were stopped by men under arms in the Place de la Révolution. The horses were unhitched and the two prisoners were led back to the Committee headquarters. Shortly after midnight he started out again, this time on foot under heavy military escort, Billaud with him. In the dead of night they made their way through the closely patrolled streets of the capital, trudging wearily toward the road leading to Orléans. Two ordinary carriages were waiting for them at the city limits. Billaud took his place in one and Barère, along with two officers, got into the other. Ever gracious, Barère thanked his escorts for the protection they had accorded him, not failing to protest his innocence. They acknowledged his words with "stony silence."

With Paris behind them, the two carriages rolled their way southward toward the Atlantic. On the first day out they caught up with Collot and they were now three, joined less by mutual good will than by fear and hopelessness over the future. Their coming was everywhere heralded in advance—by a mysterious rider, Barère alleges, but it was not likely that the rider's services were needed to spread the word. Though Barère's carriage got by Orléans safely, the crowd that had gathered there pulled Collot and Billaud out of their carriages and, had it not been for the National Guard, would have beaten them to death. It was only hours later that they succeeded in whipping their way out of "the living hell."

They counted on the darkness when they reached Tours, but the postmistress at the relay station where they changed horses had given the alarm and again the dismal procession could bare-

ly get away in time from the expectant crowd. The worst, for
they were now approaching the Vendée, still lay ahead. In the
Vendée little love was lost on the men of the Committee of
Public Safety. But they skirted around Poitiers and Niort, thus
escaping their pursuers, and finally reached the coast at La
Rochelle. There at least they were safe from the crowds, and
there they learned that their immediate destination was the
island of Oléron, some twenty miles at sea, and that at Oléron
they were to await transportation to the dread penal colony of
Guiana.

It took eight hours for two sailors to row them over from the
mainland—why so long it is difficult to say—and Barère, to save
himself from despair, kept reading a translation of Young's
*Night Thoughts*. So, at least, he later recalled. After they landed
on the island, it took them three more hours of plodding through
sand dunes and marshes before they reached the chateau,
drenched, hungry, and exhausted. They were locked up in separate cells of the citadel, a sentry posted at each door.

The instructions to the guards were obviously not to pamper
their prisoners. Barère was forbidden to communicate either
with the garrison or the townspeople. For a short time he had
the consolation of walks along the ramparts from which he
could look at the ocean and see the ships as they passed by. Then
that relief was denied him and he had to content himself as best
he could with solitary promenades in the enclosed parade
ground. With a resourcefulness that inspires admiration tinctured by astonishment in the reader of his *Mémoires*, he contrived to borrow a few volumes of Young and Voltaire, which he
read and reread. The first gave him peace while saddening him
with its vivid word pictures of tombs and edifying but melancholy reflections on the vicissitudes of fate; Voltaire's winged
phrases lifted his spirits by their gaiety and wit.

The days dragged interminably. According to the *Mémoires*,
getting sufficient food became Barère's most pressing problem.
He had only what remained of the 500 francs in assignats that

his fellow Tarbais, Dominique Demerville, had hastily slipped to him when he was taken out of Paris. With what was left, he bought oysters, the succulent oysters which were the pride of Oléron, and enough milk to supplement the water and coarse bread that was his regular fare. Providence did not desert him, revealing its workings through a friendly old boatsman whose duty it was to bring mail and food from the mainland once a week. Through him the prisoner was able to receive smuggled food and to smuggle out letters.

The account is moving, even if made up of whole cloth. It was the triumph of Barère's sense of the pathetic over sober fact. In reality, as he testified in 1800, he had obtained from Demerville not 500 francs but 2,400. The money was put to other ends; he was in no danger of starving to death. The boatsman, if there was one, certainly must have smuggled out his letters, permitting Barère to get in touch with his friends. He wrote letters to Jean-Pierre, whom he had not seen since Thermidor, to his devoted cousin Hector, stationed nearby in Rochefort, and to the faithful Demerville in Paris.

The wave of retaliations against the terrorists was now reaching crest among the deputies as Fouquier-Tinville and fourteen jurors of the Revolutionary Tribunal went to the guillotine. Only a miracle, it was apparent, could save the prisoners at Oléron from their fate, but for Billaud and Collot there was no miracle. They were hastily embarked and unceremoniously shipped off to Guiana. Why Barère did not go with them remains a mystery. "You must have friends in the Convention," was Collot's thrust by way of adieu to his former associate. A deputy, when the news reached Paris that Barère had been left behind, caustically observed: "It was the first time that he missed the wind." To Demerville, Barère wrote hopefully that the Convention would soon restore him to liberty, but his respite was brief. His "friends in the Convention," or perhaps in Oléron had spared him deportation, but a new ruling ordered him to stand trial before the criminal court of the department of the Charente-

Inférieure, where there was slim chance that he would fare well. On May 23, forty-eight hours after the implementing order, he was removed to the abbey of Saintes on the mainland to await trial for his life.

The *Dublin Journal* of June 16, 1795, while not too well informed, wrote sharply about the new turn of events: "Perhaps no circumstance of the French Revolution shows the arbitrary tyranny and injustice of the Convention in a stronger light than the recalling of Barère to be guillotined after a Court of Justice had passed sentence on him to be banished." Yet for reasons on which one can only speculate, he was not recalled to be guillotined. Perhaps the unnamed friends delayed the opening of the trial; perhaps the committees of the Convention, despite the White Terror that raged now against the old Jacobins and Montagnards, were little sure of the outcome of legal proceedings. Whatever the reasons, the days went by without the trial, went by too with the government taking no action on his impatient pleas to ship to him the box of documents which had been sealed in his apartment.

He wrote again to Demerville, beseeching him to prod the deputies from the Hautes-Pyrénées into action and implored an ex-colleague of the Convention, Boudin, to intercede in his behalf. A petition was enclosed with the letter that he then wrote to Boudin. "I remain alone," the cringing and righteous letter read, "in these proceedings, alone exposed to the dangers of the debates, without having carried out any missions, without having done anything else than read reports printed by the order of the Convention, and signed government orders with the other members [alone] with intentions as pure and a heart as republican as those of my colleagues, Carnot and Prieur de la Côte d'Or, whom the Convention has exempted from its ruling. I need all my means of written defense. Three months of detention, despair, and misfortune have so enfeebled my mind and so exhausted my memory that I no longer have any recollections other than those of the principles of justice and humanity which the Convention made the order of the day. . . . Whatever fate the Revolution has in store for me, I shall not cease holding up to execration the assassin [Robespierre] of the national assembly and praying for the success of the great work which will allow France to enjoy a constitution and peace." The Committee of General Security finally ordered on July 26 that his sealed box should be sent to him at Saintes, where he received it several days later. It contained mainly his personal effects, not the papers he wanted.

Nonetheless he penned his *Compte rendu, adressé par Barère à ses commettans,* an abject attempt at self-exoneration. Fortunately for himself, no doubt, the *Compte rendu* did not reach its destination and the excerpts that were published posthumously as part of his *Mémoires* deserved the scorn with which they were received. In what concerned his own behavior, Barère took on the character of a pure and helpless dupe, "only the passive, involuntary instrument of wills that emanated from the Convention itself." Only "the innocence and purity" of his heart gave him strength to carry on and attempt to soften the rigors of measures that he had to accept lest he go to his ruin or at least became suspect. His old friend and first patron, the Duke of Orléans, was portrayed as an ambitious intriguer, harmful to liberty. Danton, with whom Barère had collaborated during the struggle between the Girondins and the Montagnards, became a master plotter, working hand in glove with Dumouriez to establish the general's dictatorship. And Dumouriez himself, the Dumouriez to whom he had once written in fulsome praise of his statesmanship, Barère now recognized as "a traitor and a royalist" in the service of Orléans.

His material circumstances were not difficult at Saintes, where at least he escaped from the agents of the White Terror. Though the civil authorities plagued him, so he alleged, by stationing in front of his room, a young tenor who every morning regaled the prisoner with the strains of *Le Réveil du peuple,* and curtailed the privilege he had been given to walk in the garden, he had

many compensations. He made friends with the jailer who allowed him to eat his meals with the family and, escorted by two
town officials, to take promenades which opened on the adjacent
fields. He was permitted to write and receive letters freely and,
even more heartening and useful, to receive visitors. Sympathizers from the neighborhood of Saintes paid calls, and his brother
Jean-Pierre was with him for several weeks. Madame de Guibert
came too, consoling him with her affection. Their friendship
went back to 1793, perhaps earlier, when Barère was already
dining in her home and attending the receptions that she gave
for men of letters. Were they then lovers? Most likely but impossible to state authoritatively. Barère was still pining for his
Sophie, he wrote Demerville, but Madame de Guibert was more
than welcome, as she was to be again later when he escaped from
Saintes and lay in hiding, as she was to be when she harbored
him in her home still later in 1799. Their relations were not
secret, for in 1798 he was sending her greetings to his uncle
Joseph and expressions of her pleasure at the thought of seeing
him again.

The months were slipping past and Jean-Pierre had to leave.
But in the two Vanderkands, naturalized Frenchmen of Dutch
extraction, Bertrand found new friends. They called on him
regularly, brought him the files of the *Moniteur,* and offered
him "money, clothing, and help of every sort." A detachment of
troops from the Hautes-Pyrénées, en route to a new post, was
permitted to pay him their respects and, without permission
presumably, volunteered to liberate him by overawing the garrison. Still, there were moments of bleak despair and in one of
them he wrote his own epitaph:

> Here lies Bertrand Barère a citizen of the Republic
> and a poor man.
> In Paris he found venal enmities, calumnious libels
> and the ingratitude of the French;

above the ocean beaches of Saintonge prisons
and zealots and, what is somewhat
rare in France, friends in adversity;
above his native Pyrenaean Tarbes
oblivion and ill-will;
in this tomb, awaiting justice at the hands
of posterity, he found peace.
The Republic will endure and it will flourish.

Fresh hope came, and in October 1795, after he learned that the Convention, thanks to Napoleon Bonaparte, had withstood the royalist threat of Vendémiaire, he was confident that he would be recalled to take his seat in the assembly. Like Aristides, Camillus, and Cicero—the comparison is his—he would return from unjust exile. Instead of the triumphant exoneration on which he counted, he received a crushing blow: on October 12 the Convention rescinded the decree for his trial and instructed the executive committees to have him deported—either to Guiana or Madagascar—there are two versions. This time there was to be neither delay nor interference. On October 23, two days after the Naval and Colonial Commissioner had received orders from the Committee of Public Safety, he reported back to the Committee of General Security: "The Committee of Public Safety has just ordered me to have a small corvette . . . armed at Rochefort to pick up the ex-representative Bertrand Barère, condemned to deportation by the law of 12 Germinal last and transport him to Guiana. I am writing this very day to the port administrators to inform them of the Committee's intentions, but to avoid delays in the proceedings, I beg you to have the deportee removed from the prison in Saintes and instruct your agents to conduct him under good and safe guard to the military commandant of Rochefort. As soon as he has been given over to the custody of that officer, we shall have him embarked on the boat destined for Guiana in such a way as to keep his stay from provoking any disturbance."

Barère did not sit by idly waiting to be removed from prison: he speeded up the careful preparations he was making to escape. The two Vanderkands were already at hand, cousin Hector turned up from Bordeaux, as did "a merchant" who was not named, and a young man simply referred to in the *Mémoires* as "F." There was, in addition, wrote Barère, "a good man whom I cannot name, but whose name is ever written in my heart." In the night of October 28, at eleven o'clock the "good man" gave the prearranged signal that all was clear, and Barère climbed down a rope ladder which his cousin had slipped in some days earlier and followed the nameless good angel through the cloistered garden of a convent adjacent to the Vanderkands' property. There the elder Vanderkand unlocked the gate that led into the open country and there Hector was waiting for him to lead him through the meadows to the banks of the Charente. A skiff was ready for him and the younger Vanderkand rowed them over. On the opposite shore Barère and Hector mounted a horse that "F" had tethered, and for twenty-four hours, with only a short break at dawn for rest, they rode for miles through woods and moors until they reached an inn at the village of Montendre. There the landlord carried the exhausted Barère to bed. "Never," he writes, "had I passed a calmer and happier night. . . . I breathed freely and it seemed to me that life was beginning again."

This was his version of the escape, written many years later, the version in which he gives blessings to the jailer, Fédy, for his "honest, kindly and considerate attitude." His account, however, differs from that of his jailer. Fédy made his deposition of the escape on the morning of the 29th. Barère must have escaped, he wrote, sometime between 8:15 and 9:15 that morning while he himself was away on his rounds, for when he returned he found the prisoner had fled. In the room next to Barère's he discovered a hole about eighteen inches square and under it a small wooden chair placed on an armchair. When he looked around outside he found fresh footprints on the trampled ground, also a letter addressed to Barère, which presumably the latter had dropped in his haste to get away.

His deposition was countersigned by "the two extremely honest" and generous municipal officials whom Fédy had already induced "to drop their work" and accompany Barère on his promenades. Was the generosity theirs or Barère's? Apart from the crucial discrepancy in the time of the escape, the deposition of the jailer otherwise taxes credibility. Would the planners have selected broad daylight to effect the escape? Could the hole eighteen inches square, that Fédy first discovered after the flight, have been cut without his noticing it before? In the chairs, the footprints, the fallen letter, there is something suggesting a crudely arranged stage set. If the two officials seem a little too eager in their immediate corroboration of Fédy's deposition, the district administrators did not share their readiness. Within a week the *Moniteur* published their simple statement that Barère had escaped from prison "on a dark night." Obviously, the jailer had been bribed.

What happened to Fédy, one does not know. But Barère, refreshed by his long sleep, was ready at dawn to carry on. His friends guided him to a village near the banks of the Dordogne, where a cousin of the Vanderkands was at hand to take him to a chateau back country of which he was the tenant farmer. The escaped prisoner remained there for two weeks, consoling himself again with Voltaire and "old moralists," impatiently awaiting word when it would be safe for him to proceed to nearby Bordeaux. Impatient though he was, he would have stayed longer, but he learned that the local gendarmerie had been alerted to his presence and had received orders to arrest him. So he fled through open fields to the Bec d'Ambey, where the Dordogne joins the Garonne, and where two simple and friendly sailors took him in charge. They had been told that the unfortunate refugee was one of theirs, an émigré seeking shelter in royalist Bordeaux from the revolutionary devils. More patiently than he, they waited for the tide of the Dordogne to turn and then rowed him through the calmer waters of the Garonne to the outer docks of Bordeaux. He lay hidden with the sailors overnight and with Hector's family the day after, and on the following night he reached journey's end. He found refuge in the home of a wealthy Bordeaux merchant, Jacques Fonade, who, for the next four years sheltered him, enjoining upon his family and his domestics the strictest secrecy. During all those years, Fonade "forgot his own danger, compromised his security, the repose of his nights, his credit as a merchant [and] gave me, through friendship and out of regard for misfortune, careful, noble, and free hospitality, all the greater in that it was without hope of a better future, either for me, for him, and his family." What he wrote in the *Mémoires* about the years "without hope of a better future" is greatly dramatized. Those were the years of the Directory from 1795 to 1799 when, the evidence clearly shows, he was tirelessly working with high hope for a better future.

Why exactly Fonade gave him shelter remains a mystery, even as during the Terror he had sheltered their mutual friend Isaac Tarteyron, then in the administration of the department of the Gironde, whom Barère had saved from prison. Fonade's precautions notwithstanding, word was being bruited about that the prisoner lay in hiding in or near Bordeaux, so Barère took no needless chances. The Convention had specifically excepted him from the amnesty that it accorded to other political prisoners three days after his escape, and twice again, in 1796 and in the following year, the new Council of 500 reaffirmed the exception. And for all Fonade's generous hospitality, Barère's financial embarrassment was great. Bribing Fédy could not have come cheap. He now wrote to Jean-Pierre: "I am without a sou. I am waiting for the 240 francs that you managed to pass on to the old friend who tells me that he has received them. I am borrowing a coat because this is neither the time nor the place for torn clothing. Besides, I cannot be fed like a tramp. So long as I have something left [meaning from his inheritance], you must send me four hams for the little household. That will be the basis of our cuisine for a long time." Though one cannot state with full certainty, the other member of "the little household" must have been Madame de Guibert. "She came to bring me further consolation when . . . I took refuge in Bordeaux," the *Mémoires* record.

Neither straitened circumstances, the dangers of his status, not even his "reading and reflections," kept him from continuing his obstinate efforts to return to public life. His political enemies in Tarbes had valid reason for alarm. The old feud between Barèrists and anti-Barèrists had broken out again, basically a power struggle between rival clans for political control of the department. During the Terror, for all of Barère's powerful position in the government and his influence in the popular society in Tarbes, his relatives and adherents had had a difficult time. His cousin Jacques, his uncle Joseph Carles, another cousin, Dintrans, and his relative, Jean Lairle, who had married Jacques Barère's sister, Anne, had all been stripped of power in local affairs. Jacques himself had been imprisoned, while Jean-Pierre, who awakened the suspicions of political extremists, had fled to Paris to solicit the aid of his famous brother. By the fall of 1794 their differences were seemingly composed and in the new harmony of the truce, the Barère faction had regained its position.

Not for long, however. Within a year the old rivalry flared up, and in mid-February 1796 a delegation of the department of the Hautes-Pyrénées to the Directory denounced the meetings that were being held at Lairle's home: "Tarbes, citizen Directors, is the commune where Bertrand Barère saw the light of day. . . . During the reign of the decemvirs his very numerous family and his partisans formed a sovereign dynasty in this department. Accustomed to power, burning with an inextinguishable thirst for domination, they cannot suffer any citizen to exercise public office unless he has put on their livery and ranged himself under their banner." After describing "the scandalous and insulting orgies" of the plotters, the letter went on: "The plans are first conceived by Bertrand Barère in his retreat in the environs of Bordeaux. They are carried out in Tarbes by his relatives and his faithful followers. He encourages them as best he can: 'Your reign is not over,' he told them in one of his letters, 'I have powerful friends in Paris; carry out my orders to the letter and soon. . . .' "

Perhaps the writers only affected to quote directly from his correspondence, but they certainly knew a great deal about what he was doing. In a small town like Tarbes news as well as rumors circulated fast and Barère's enemies knew that he was in hiding in the environs of Bordeaux and they knew who his adherents were. They knew that Demerville was among them, also his cousin Hector, and his cousin, Nicholas Carles, son of Joseph, then a section chief in the ministry of police in Paris. And of course it was true that Barère was hard at work, applying himself with unabated energy to keeping his supporters in line. It was on March 3, 1797, that he wrote cryptically to uncle Joseph in Tarbes, referring to "someone who gave me news about the whole family" and to whom he was confiding an answer. "We are," he continued, "at the moment of intrigues. My opinion is that J. P. [Jean-Pierre] should . . . keep quiet and help P. who prides himself on being useful to me in my misfortune. . . . We must then help those who will help us."

"P." was certainly Picqué, former deputy of the Convention and at the moment, like Barère himself, a candidate for election to the Council of 500, to which the latter's devoted constituents had nominated him. Barère had already pressed Demerville to see Picqué: "Urge Pic, who has balance, wisdom, means, and who once had some friendship for me, urge him to see what means are left for the unfortunate one. . . . Also see Ger [Gertoux, the father of the Directory's agent in the Hautes-Pyrénées who had taken the initiative against the Barèrists in Tarbes]. His son is against me. And what have I done to him! Is it a crime to have had him liberated, and justly so, in the month of August, 1793? Ah, if I had also been able to have him freed when the wicked Monestier of the Puy de Dôme persecuted him, as well as Dauphole and my entire family. Ger, the father, knows that I would have done it."

There was something pathetic, if not wholly admirable, in the way he labored from his retreat, hope against hope, to rehabilitate himself. Almost two years had elapsed since his flight, since the government of the Directory had replaced the Convention, and he still remained a refugee from justice. Besides, the men of the pen were not aiding his cause. Lecointre's accusations had a wide circle of readers. Dulaure's *Supplément* to the crimes of the committees was published, and the spiteful Courtois, who had earlier presented a garbled report on Robespierre's papers, was enjoying fresh success with his *Rapport sur les évènements du 9 Thermidor*. In the *Mémoires* of Louvet, whose attack on Robespierre Barère had refuted in 1792, it transpired that the "French Narcissus" had drawn an annual stipend of 12,000 francs from the Duke of Orléans. In 1795, the *Mémoires* of a proscribed Girondin, A. Meillan, while conceding to Barère both sensibility and "a sort of nobility of soul," portrayed him as an ambitious weakling, indispensable to whoever was in authority. From Riouffe's *Mémoires d'un détenu*, one learned that Barère was bloodthirsty and from the *Letters* of Barère's former friend, Helen Maria Williams, that he had cravenly abandoned his and her Girondin associates. Madame de Genlis, whom Barère knew so well in the early years of the Revolution and who had written enthusiastically of him, pointed out in a *Précis* of her own activities that he was "execrable." In 1796, Bailleul's *Almanach des bizarreries humaines* confidently predicted that "some day his name will be cited to little children to inspire in them horror of lies," while two years later the posthumously published *Tableaux* of the guillotined ex-priest and Christian mystic, Claude Fauchet, tersely likened him, in an improvement upon classical mythology, to a "three-faced Janus."

There was more in the same impressionistic style in the *Recueil d'anecdotes* of 1798 as well as in the English *Biograph-*

*ical Anecdotes.* In the following year, 1799, in the *Dictionnaire des Jacobins vivans*, he was portrayed as a "cold scoundrel . . . whose actions seemed to be guided by virtue, while [in reality] crime alone directs him." The famous chronicler, Louis Sebastien Mercier, in *Le Nouveau Paris* informed readers that Barère was "cunning," "dangerous," and a "scoundrel." Meantime, those who passed for historians, like the anonymous "Two Friends of Liberty," who were not always the same "friends," employed in their *Histoire de la Révolution française* such words as "insolent" and "scoundrel." The pages of the *Mémorial révolutionnaire* written by a rabid royalist named G. B. Vasselin supplied the edifying information that "Barère always had three different speeches for all crises—one for, one against, and one about—and often gave all three of them at intervals of two hours, according to whether the barometer was turning to rain, good weather, or variable." In his *Histoire secrète de la Révolution française,* F. X. Pagès divulged what was hardly secret any longer, that Barère was "a political chameleon . . . who changed his opinions as he did his clothing." It remained for L. M. Prudhomme, in a six-volume *Histoire des crimes commis pendant la Révolution française,* which began to instruct the public in 1797, to repeat the choicer morsels of Thermidorian tracts. It omitted neither the prostitutes of the Opera who flocked to Barère, nor his advice to Robespierre to guillotine all enemies systematically, group by group, nor yet the trousers, fashioned of the skins of his victims, which Barère had worn.

Barère for his part was busily writing in these gloomy months and years of hiding. In the "Pages mélancoliques," part of which appear in the *Mémoires,* he yielded to self-pity and covered sheet after sheet with reflections on the moral worth of suffering misfortune, but the dejection of so buoyant a person was not for long. The idea came to him "to paint Montesquieu through his own writing, so as to unravel the thread of his political conceptions . . . which he had been forced to hide and conceal in a thousand ways in his *Esprit des lois,* because he was living under the despotism of Louis XV, just as Tacitus wrote under the despotism of Domitian. When I had composed this work called *Montesquieu peint d'après ses ouvrages* I waited for a favorable opportunity to publish it." In early 1797, the favorable opportunity presented itself in the coming elections for a partial renewal of the deputies of the Council of 500. Barère became a candidate. The monumental discovery that Montesquieu only pretended to be a supporter of the monarchy, while in truth "his genius was always republican," might well impress upon the voters of Barère's department his own unswerving devotion to republican and constitutional institutions. "It is to your example, O Montesquieu! that I owe the courage which permitted me every day to suffer calumny and injustice; it is to your works that I owe those principles which make me hope for the strengthening of our constitution and the triumph of our Republic."

While he prepared the *Montesquieu* for the press, he also was working hard on another study which would elaborate in detail upon his conception of the republican institutions to which he was devoted. Some of the chapters he showed to Tarteyron, who then must have been visiting him, and Tarteyron, on whose "knowledge and wisdom" Barère counted, did not fail him: "He made some comments and even some corrections in the manuscript which I had entitled *De la pensée du gouvernment républicain*. The period of elections was approaching. The month of March [1797] could change my sad position through the effect of public opinion and thus force the Directory to end the persecutions of which I was the object."

Friends saw to it that the *Montesquieu* was published in Toulouse and the *Pensée* simultaneously in Geneva and Tarbes, and both on the eve of the elections. The former apparently had fewer admirers in Paris than either in Toulouse or Tarbes, for in a brief, ironic note a reviewer in the *Journal de Paris* of May 17 dismissed the *Montesquieu* as a work without ideas or talents and noteworthy only for the insolence of its preface. The *Pensée*, however, went through two editions, and one wonders why. As a profession of political faith it was reasonably consistent with what Barère had written in *Le Point du Jour*, but for the expression of his republicanism. There was not much in the new Constitution of the Year III that he praised in this work to which he could honestly object. Like the deputies who had drafted it, he too held that liberty and not equality was the first of the rights of man. He, too, in full conscience, accepted property as the base of all society. Except during the crisis of the Year II he treasured and advocated freedom of the press and religion, free trade and production, civil liberty. After the factions were crushed he confidently expected them all to be restored. In the days before the Terror he also believed in the separation and division of powers, though never, it is true, in a bicameral legislature.

In considerable measure then, he wrote what he believed. Yet neither of the two works rings quite true. They were not so much the expression of his political philosophy as tracts for the time, studied and calculated appeals for votes. When he wrote them, he had little real respect for either the existing constitution or the men in power. His private letters were truer gauges of his feelings than those published works. In one letter he qualified the Directory as "too weak, too ignorant to win public confidence ... a bastard constitutionalism ... a perfidious system of division among electoral assemblies. . . ." What he wrote, then, about the government of the Directory itself can largely be dismissed. What alone was important was the dedication of the *Pensée* to the citizens of the Hautes-Pyrénées and the preface in which he bid for electoral support. Despite all the injustice done him he remained "one of the most ardent defenders of the present government." He had been a revolutionary, he was now a constitutionalist, and "those two states, far from contradicting each other . . . support each other." There had been excessive concentration of power, but "so far as principles were concerned he had always been the same." As for methods and measures, "no man, whatever his strength and influence, however great his power or his talent, could have changed them or directed them according to his will."

The appeal for votes was passingly successful, and in April 1798, his devoted followers elected him to the Council of 500. "My dear brother," Barère wrote in an exultant letter to Jean-Pierre, "I finally breathe freely. . . . God be praised. . . . I thirstily drank up all the satisfying and flattering details. They have brought consolation to my heart which so many atrocious calumnies had withered. I have obtained the free and spontaneous votes of a free and grateful people. . . . O! my dear fellow-citizens, one can die in peace when he has seen his memory rehabilitated during his lifetime."

Jean-Pierre communicated the letter to the leading newspaper in Tarbes, *Le Journal des Hautes-Pyrénées*, and a minor Paris newspaper, *Le Révélateur*, reproduced it. But the Barères rejoiced too soon. While Gertoux wrote to the minister of the interior protesting the legality of the election, Barère's enemies in the 500 also bestirred themselves. "Who among you would want to sit alongside such a monster?" ran the debates on May 14, and "a medley of voices [answered] 'Not I, not I.'" On May 20, when the vote was called for, the election was declared null and void.

It had all been in vain. Perhaps he had a "presentiment" that his election would be invalidated, though like so many other of his souvenirs that one too seems an afterthought. Perhaps Tarteyron then really offered him help and money to escape to America and Barère did reply: "I have always sacrificed myself for my fatherland. . . . I prefer to die in France rather than live in America." Perhaps so, but he still hoped, it is more likely, that somehow he could remove the stigma from his name and return, if not to power, to public life. But from the developments of Fructidor (September 1797), when the republicans crushed the royalist plot to seize power, he derived no gain. Another year ended with his fate unchanged.

His "dear books" kept up his spirits; his writing too, for he had not laid down his pen. Even as he was appealing to the public in still another book, he had hopes that this time Jean-Pierre would prove the providential instrument of his vindication. To uncle Joseph he wrote on May 15, 1798: "What my friends . . . write shows the need of electing J. P. . . . . Yes, we must have him elected. He is a patriot, he will render services . . . and he alone, with the friends that he made on this trip [to Paris], can have me freed and my election upheld. . . . Elect J. P. and I am assured of everything."

So he thought or made a bold pretense of believing. Jean-Pierre was indeed elected by the steadfast followers, who meantime had not ceased addressing petitions in Bertrand's behalf, but like his own, Jean-Pierre's election, was invalidated. This was another harsh setback, worse than the preceding one of 1797 because it drew attention to his presence in Bordeaux. The Directors called for action against the tireless man who refused to remain silent. In the letter to his uncle he referred to new literary activities: "Dintrans has doubtless given you the first of the 25 copies of my work against the English. You will tell me what you think of it when you have read the other volumes. . . . The work is already succeeding very well. It will be read more in London than in Paris."

Writing at a pace that was remarkably rapid even for one who largely paraphrased his own earlier works, in 1798 Barère published a three-volume diatribe against the English. On the fly-leaf of the manuscript of *La liberté des mers ou le gouvernment anglais dévoilé*, which he presented in 1839 to the municipal library of Tarbes, he explained the circumstances of its composition: "I was hidden at Bordeaux in the home of M. Jacques Fonade, merchant, who for five years had courageously given me free hospitality . . . at his peril and risk. . . . I was forced to write down my thoughts during the day and hide the sheets each night for fear that the police of the Executive Directory would surprise me."

While he wrote, the Directory was busily laying plans to invade England, and in the shipyards at Brest, Cherbourg, and Dunkirk one heard the strike of the hammer and the buzz of the saw. Since public opinion had to be prepared to support the expedition, Barère would not miss the opportunity to get a lien on the government's good will by backing its campaign. Accordingly, he dedicated the new work to the "Army of England," as the fighting force was called which Bonaparte was to lead triumphantly across the Channel. Addressing himself to the "Conquerors of Europe," he wrote: "It will no doubt seem novel to dedicate a philosophical work to the army. It is also a novel event to see an army composed of citizen soldiers, statesmen officers, and philosopher generals. . . . The Greek republicans made themselves immortal at Thermopylae, but they fought only for their homes. The free Romans distinguished themselves in Carthage, but they fought only for their empire. You, French citizens, republican soldiers, you have fought at once for your homes, your liberty, the right of man, the independence of other nations, and peace of the continent. You are going to fight for the freedom of the seas." And he bade the triumphant soldiers of *la grande nation* to "receive the homage of a proscribed republican . . . [and] the tribute that misfortune pays to glory, the tribute that will not be refused."

The proscribed republican repeated what he had been saying and writing for almost two decades against the tyrant of the seas, the barbarous oppressor of all free peoples, the greedy monopolist of all trade and industry. If he was stating what he believed, he also wrote what he thought the public had to hear him say. He was stating what many of his compatriots, a century and a half later, still believed, when in 1942 an enterprising editor reissued *La liberté des mers* in a convenient résumé, this time too to whip up patriotic passions against the English. Again Barère failed to land on his feet. The cross-Channel invasion was dropped. Both Napoleon and the Directory had other plans in mind. The new literary venture brought him as little as the preceding ones, and like the preceding ones it cost him dear. "I have been obliged to sell almost the whole of my inheritance," he wrote a year later to a deputy named Briot, "in order to live or support my family, brother and sisters, or pay for the printing of my works." Almost 10,000 francs had gone into the literary enterprise and the general indifference to his publications could not have been greater.

Nor was he now secure in his hideaway. Some months after the publication of *La liberté des mers*, in midsummer of 1798, the royalist youth of Bordeaux raided Fonade's home and Barère barely escaped. He returned when he got word that the coast was clear, but the hunt continued in earnest. There was another raid on Hector's home in Bordeaux, where Bertrand was then visiting, but his luck still held. Finally, however, in the spring of 1799 he was advised by Demerville to quit Bordeaux altogether, and he decided to take the advice. While Demerville was letting him know that Madame de Guibert would harbor him, Barère was also asking his friend to sound out the possibility of having "the wife of the famous general of the Army of Italy" help him. Soon he was to appeal directly to Bonaparte himself. In June 1799, he made the decision to return and Demerville accompanied him on the trip to Paris, an uneventful journey except for the last day when suspicious officials held him up at the Clichy gate and Madame de Guibert herself was agonizingly late for her rendezvous.

In the end all turned out well and he was safe in her home in the little community of St. Ouen, then on the outskirts of Paris. Madame de Guibert would suffer no nonsense from search parties. Even if the mayor could see a stranger strolling around her garden and, if he looked harder, note the presence of unfamiliar visitors, the hostess was too important to be molested or even queried. The "famous general of the Army of Italy" was soon back in Paris from his Egyptian venture; and it was in Madame de Guibert's home that the aging Barère passed the months preceding Napoleon Bonaparte's return. Brumaire was close at hand, and with Bonaparte's seizure of power another new chapter opened for France, for Europe, and for Barère as well.

# ☒ X V I ☒

# *In the Service of Napoleon,*
# *1799-1807*

STOCKS went up on the Bourse with Bonaparte's coup, and the spirits of many Frenchmen soared with them. For Barère, if Brumaire brought no immediate relief, it brought hope. However, with the deportation order still hanging over his head and his old enemy, "the subtle dialectitian," Siéyès, one of the provisional consuls, he judged it expedient to move warily. He remained in hiding at the home of Madame de Guibert, "a truly heavenly soul," and looked about for ways of getting to the new master of France. Barère did not yet know Bonaparte himself, but judging it preferable, as the French proverb has it, to deal directly with God than with the angels, he succeeded in having a copy of *La liberté des mers* placed in his hands. He followed up this move by writing a long letter to "the citizen consul," which the *Moniteur* published on December 10, 1799 (19 Frimaire, Year VIII), twelve days after he had composed it "from my retreat."

"I, too," it began, "add my feeble voice to the friends of liberty who placed their confidence in your civic virtues and their hopes in the revolution of 19 Brumaire. . . . It is a great and courageous thought . . . to take control of the Revolution and end it for the benefit of the sovereignty of the people, the national representation, liberty and equality." He had not waited for Bonaparte's assumption of "supreme authority" to laud those civic virtues nor to write how much France needed a government sufficiently "strong in its structure and wise in the exercise of its powers" to check "the instability of the nation." Though he had tried earlier to rally his countrymen around the Constitution of the Year III, now he wished "a shorter one in which there will be a more frank division of powers [and] more

303

unity in the national representation, which is the principal
guarantee of liberty. . . ."

He then gave a summary of his views on the kind of constitution he desired for France, stating that as he looked forward to
its completion, he foresaw a day of "general forgiveness and of
concord among the French." He appealed to Bonaparte to consider the fate of "the unhappy author of the letter" and end his
long proscription by restoring his full freedom. "Once free," he
continued, "I shall have only one wish, to see the hero of the
eighteenth century, to see the Republic pacified under his auspi-
cious influence." He signed it, "With greetings and respect,
B. Barère."

If it seems strange that the quasi-official *Moniteur* should
give three columns to the letter of a proscribed and notorious
terrorist, the explanation is not difficult. Bonaparte wished to
have it published: he had not yet consolidated his authority and
was eager to have it known that the old revolutionists were
behind him. He was making overtures to a man who could be
useful. Barère was fulsome in his flattery, giving intimations of
future abjectness, but he did not conceal his political opinions:
"Revolutionary ideas are played out; reactionary ideas are
hateful. There is room only for liberal ideas and thinking which
would preserve our liberties and our rights." He was sincere in
his hopes that Bonaparte would end the war abroad and, to
France itself, bring order and tranquillity after a decade of
upheaval. His trust in Bonaparte was to fade, but not for some
years did he become disillusioned and realize that the general's
military ambition was destroying the opportunity afforded by
Brumaire to preserve the liberties of Frenchmen. What he wrote
to "the citizen consul" in November 1799, he then believed.

The call from Bonaparte was slow in coming. Though Siéyès
had been conspicuously retired to private life and could no longer contrive against him, Barère chafed over Bonaparte's failure
to respond directly to his appeal, so this time he addressed himself to the angels. The Third Consul, the old royalist Lebrun, he

did not know or know well enough to solicit for favors, but his relations were friendly with the Second Consul, Cambacérès, who was like himself a former Conventional and regicide. The Cambacérès card was worth playing. He had a still stronger card in the good will and friendship of Fouché, minister of police, and an old colleague from the days of the Terror. Fouché was too Jacobin for Bonaparte's taste, but since that indispensable man had taken the precaution on the eve of Brumaire to be useful to whoever won out, Bonaparte had allowed him to keep a key post, which he held on sufferance. Bonaparte counted on intelligence reports about the republican and liberal opposition from the imperturbable administrator whose determination not to give him a pretext to pounce down upon "the anarchists" he strongly resented but nevertheless accepted. And to Fouché, as he set up a ramified espionage service, Barère with wide contacts in republican circles, could be very useful. Through him Fouché could get the information that was passed on to Bonaparte, as much at least as he chose to transmit; and through Barère he could convey, when needed, timely warnings or discreet financial aid to the political malcontents. The minister was not prompted by sentimental memories when he responded to the overtures that Barère made. The two old revolutionists, who had already worked together, reached a new understanding for their mutual benefit.

Fouché lost little time in preparing an amnesty for men who could be useful to him in checking the Bonapartist reaction that he feared. On December 28, 1799 (7 Nivôse, Year VIII) Barère read in the *Moniteur* that his name was on the list that the minister of police had submitted to the consuls of the Republic two days earlier. He was a free man again, free to reside in Paris under Fouché's surveillance. In his first exultation he envisaged a brilliant, new career. Careers, as Bonaparte was making clear, were open to talent, and if other revolutionaries, such as Fouché and Talleyrand could become ministers, as Carnot, also on the list, was about to become, surely there was room at the top for him too. For such an ascent Cambacérès could be useful; and Bonaparte's colleague, as Barère tells the story, conveyed to the First Consul "the feelings of gratitude" which filled Barère's heart. Presently the latter was invited to call in person and present his respects at an official reception. When he entered the drawing room of the Luxembourg palace, it was already filled with officers, all waiting for Bonaparte to make his ceremonial entrance. The First Consul was in no hurry. He engaged one of the guests in conversation, meantime looking Barère over out of the corner of his eye. Then coming closer, but still deliberately addressing his question to Cambacérès, he inquired whether it was not in fact "citizen Barère" whom he saw.

"Yes, First Consul, it is I who comes to thank you for having restored my rights and my liberty, which I should never have lost." The philosophical reflection on the mutability of fortune that Bonaparte deigned to make by way of response did not break the ice of conversation. "Such is the inevitable effect of revolutions" was Bonaparte's observation as Barère recalled it. The former next inquired how old Barère was. "Forty-two years old" was the reply, "the proscription took away from me the seven best years of my life." While Barère's singular computation added two years to his proscription, it subtracted three from his age and may perhaps have influenced Bonaparte's more encouraging comment: "You can still be useful to France and its government for a long time."

Barère expatiated upon that theme, giving to his host the benefit of his own views on government. As the conversation dragged, he judged it wise to take his leave. "I thought I should withdraw when I noticed that he did not care too much for the truths I told him about . . . the rights of the nation." This interview, touched up as it is, must have been painfully unsatisfactory. Even so there was a crumb of hope, for Bonaparte had dropped a clear hint that he had something in mind for the future. A week went by. There was a second meeting, and, though there was still no specific assignment, Barère continued to inch ahead. Bonaparte divulged in a parenthetical aside that he had instructed Fouché to end all police surveillance over him.

If the door was ajar, the carpet was not yet fully unrolled, and while he waited for Bonaparte to disclose exactly in what ways he could still be useful to France, Barère knocked at other doors. Early in the new year he tried the door of Lucien Bonaparte, the minister of the interior, not overlooking the opportunity also to try the door of "Citizen Gaudin," the minister of finance. To the one he wrote that "Barère would like to speak to citizen Lucien Bonaparte for a few minutes. He knows the value of time [and] he asks for an appointment"; to the other he complained that "his needs cannot be put off." Apparently the subordinate administration paid him no attention. On the contrary, Fouché, "who welcomed me with friendship and frankness," bestirred himself and easily obtained for Barère the box containing his personal papers that the Committee of General Security had placed in escrow almost five years earlier.

He heard finally from Bonaparte toward the end of January, still not directly, but through Cambacérès. He was told that Bonaparte had an assignment for him, to write a refutation of the attack that Lord Grenville had made in the House of Lords on French policy in general and upon the First Consul in particular. After all his maneuvering this humiliating commission was an affront, but Barère had to make the best of his disappointment. He did not dare refuse what was in effect an order. He set to work and within a week dashed off a pamphlet, some eighty pages long, which was published under the title, *Lettre d'un citoyen français en réponse à Lord Grenville.*

In this work of pure patriotism, which in later years Barère cited as "evidence of [his] love for liberty and devotion to [his] country," the anonymous author gave his readers a lesson in international relations. It transpired that what Lord Grenville in his myopic and insular way chose to consider a policy of national expansion and aggression was in fact the generous response of France to the appeals of her neighbors. It was a gross error hence to regard the annexation of the Netherlands as a military conquest: "It is a union of two peoples . . . the free and spontaneous exercise of the Belgian people's right of sovereignty." As such, it stood in sharp contrast to British imperialism, which was "little different from that of Attila and Genghis Khan." As for Grenville's carping strictures about Bonaparte's military ambition, Barère found them ridiculous: "Bonaparte, general or consul, soldier or magistrate, will ever be the man of liberty and the pride of the French Republic. . . . In the midst of unparalleled disturbances, the benefactor of humanity [has not] ceased displaying an incorruptible love of justice and truth, a heart free of prejudice, party spirit, vindictive passions."

This contribution to historical understanding was published in an edition of 14,000 copies, and Bonaparte seemed content with it. He wrote to the author, again requesting the pleasure of his company. "I have to speak to you but first I want to thank you for the response to Lord Grenville. It is well done. Now you must write a journal for the army. You are loved there. They remember your reports and how you celebrated their victories. The army must be galvanized anew, I have fixed my eyes on you."

This invitation, too, was not what Barère had counted on. Though Bonaparte promised him all the material that he might need and full editorial liberty, he remained adamant: "I could not lower myself to the point of serving his government only to edit journals, while so many insignificant, vulgar, and servile men . . . held high offices in this government of parvenus." If Bonaparte's eyes were fixed on him, his own eyes were fixed on something higher, higher even than the post of prefect, which had been offered him and turned down. He had set his sights, so rumors held, on the ministry of foreign affairs.

While he pouted in wounded self-esteem, Bonaparte was off in Italy, soon to return with the glory of Marengo over his head. For his military needs the general could use the sword without anyone's help; for his political requirements a pen was needed. The republican pamphlets, which were many, censured him vigorously for his increasing political despotism, and he was particularly incensed by a brochure which analyzed the causes of his successful usurpation of power and prognosticated his imminent fall. How much his wrath was provoked by the accusation that he had usurped power and how much by the forecast that he would soon lose it is difficult to say, since the pages of the pamphlet, *Des causes qui ont amené l'usurpation du Général Bonaparte et qui préparent sa chute*, were uncut when it was placed in the hands of Barère. Again it was Cambacérès who served as go-between, and soon after Barère had received Bonaparte's personal copy he was at the Tuileries to find out exactly what the conqueror had in mind by way of rejoinder to it. According to what Barère jotted down on the flyleaf of the pamphlet, Bonaparte listened quietly to his brief summary of the contents and showed his feelings only once, when he was told that the author had compared him with Cromwell. "I am not a Cromwell," he expostulated angrily, "and I desire only the good of France and of Europe." At this point, Barère recorded, "the conversation ended and I wrote the response to the lampoon."

The rejoinder, like the refutation of Lord Grenville, was anonymous, but as in the case of the first pamphlet that Barère wrote, informed circles suspected that he was the author. The title was a long one: *Réponse d'un républicain français au libelle de sir Francis d'Yvernois, naturalisé Anglais, contre le Premier Consul, par l'auteur de la Lettre d'un citoyen français à Lord Grenville*. The refutation, too, was long, twice as long as the *Lettre à Grenville*. It was also twice as tedious, for, length apart, it was a carbon copy of the first work in exclamation marks. In exclamation marks also was his commendation of the master who was giving him orders and his appreciation of "the broad and liberal views which could belong only to a great soul and a superior genius."

Even as he began to write the *Réponse* early in October 1800, his mind was moving along lines of fear of what the "great soul" might do if he were assailed by doubts about his scribe's good faith. Barère knew that his security was precarious and that both Bourrienne, Bonaparte's personal secretary, and Talleyrand, the minister of foreign affairs, were on the alert for Fouché to blunder and fall into disgrace. Once Fouché was ousted, they could readily get at the leftist malcontents under his protection and get at Barère himself. The opposition to Bonaparte was broad and deep—on that score the daily reports from the office of the prefect of police leave no doubt—and Barère may have already surmised without having proof that his name had appeared on the lists of suspects that Bourrienne was placing before the eyes of the First Consul.

Innocent of overt plotting to overthrow Bonaparte, Barère was still in an exposed position by reason of his past record, and he was all the more vulnerable because of his close ties with various associates whom the police services of the Tuileries kept under close surveillance. Among the men under watch was his oldest friend and colleague of many years' standing, Dominique Demerville; among them too, and an intimate friend of Demerville, was the famous Roman sculptor Ceracchi. Ceracchi had just completed a terracotta bust of him, and out of sentiment Barère had imprudently appealed both to Bourrienne and Fouché on his behalf. He did not yet know, what he discovered soon after, that Bourrienne's agents, with the active knowledge of Bonaparte himself, were methodically contriving a mock plot to assassinate the First Consul in which they had deeply implicated Barère's friends. Nor did he yet know that they were planning to spring the trap on the plotters and their dupes without letting Fouché in on the arrangements until the last moment, intending in that way to prove him flagrantly derelict in his responsibilities.

There was much that Barère did not know, but also much that he feared if by ill chance he allowed himself to be incriminated by the actions of his republican and Jacobin friends. When with such fears in his heart he stumbled by accident on October 10 (19 Vendémiaire) on what seemed unmistakably a plot on the life of the First Consul panic gripped him. As he told the story in his declaration to the prefect of police late in the afternoon of the following day (a declaration of which there is no mention in the *Mémoires*), he had been struck in the course of a courtesy call on his ailing friend Demerville by the latter's marked nervousness and even more by a cryptic warning not to attend the performance at the Opera that night. There might be "a disturbance," Demerville told him. Protesting indignantly that only the English could be so base as to provoke disorder, Barère went his way. Later that day, when he reminded himself that Bonaparte and his family were to attend the performance of *Horace* at the Opera that night, he decided that he should get in touch with General Lannes, the head of the security police. At the same time he instructed his young cousin Dintrans, who was with him, to report to Fouché. Fouché by ill chance happened not to be in his office.

According to General Lannes, who also made a declaration to the prefect of police that same day, Barère did more than voice suspicion, he stated definitely that there was a plot to assassinate the First Consul. Lannes, to return to Barère's declaration, thanked the informant, assuring him with a composure that might conceivably have impressed Barère as forcefully as had Demerville's edginess, that appropriate action would be taken to safeguard the life of the head of the state. The appropriate action was taken toward six o'clock that evening, about two hours after Barère had left Lannes' office, when Ceracchi and "an accomplice" were arrested by police forces acting under Bourrienne's orders.

Barère had acted fast to save his skin. In panic fear he betrayed Demerville, who out of old friendship had warned him to keep out of trouble's way. From fear for his own security and to get a lien on Lannes' good favor, he had divulged a conspiracy that needed no disclosure. Bourrienne with the help of his secret agents, including a certain Captain Harel who served as stool pigeon, had staged it down to the last details. As the testimony at the trial of "the conspirators" two months later revealed, it was Bourrienne who had instructed Harel to keep the Demerville and Ceracchi group stirred up, provide them with pistols and daggers, and assure them that while they were rounding up disaffected sans-culottes for future political action, he would have four stalwarts at hand at the Opera to dispatch Bonaparte. The October 10 date had been set three days earlier. At the trial, too, General Lannes naïvely blurted out how much Bonaparte himself was privy to the arrangements: "There were to be four or five of them to assassinate me," were the outraged words of the First Consul when Lannes informed him on the night of the denouement that only two of the conspirators had been arrested.

Barère had acted fast, almost too fast for Fouché. By going to General Lannes in the afternoon of October 10 and then again in the morning of the 11th, he had made things extremely awkward for his own employer. Once, however, Fouché learned that the arrests had been made and that Barère had gone to Lannes, he quickly took the necessary steps to cover himself against any possible charge that he had been remiss in vigilance. When he called his blundering subordinate to his office toward 2 o'clock in the afternoon of the 11th, he had the situation well in hand.

Ceracchi was under arrest. Demerville had voluntarily come to the minister's bureau earlier that day, giving himself up possibly on his own volition, possibly because Barère had persuaded him that to appeal to Fouché's protection was the wiser course to follow. And as for Barère and himself, Fouché had undoubtedly learned that Barère was summoned to make a declaration before the prefect of police later on that same day.

Ever nimble, he quickly grasped the fact then that whatever was said in his own office would later be entered into the official record. So he had Harel on hand when Barère made his appearance and with due formality introduced Bourrienne's secret agent as "the man who has denounced the affair on which [Barère] is called to make a declaration." In that way Fouché covered himself against Bourrienne. He exculpated his own agent by having Harel's explicit declaration recorded that he had never seen Barère before in his life. Barère, in his turn, made a similar statement about Harel. The scenario was perfect: Fouché exonerated himself of negligence and Barère of plotting; only Demerville had no protector.

Demerville's disclaimers of guilt when he was interrogated by the police were pitifully vague and unconvincing. It could not have been otherwise; he was too deeply entangled in the coils of Bourrienne's intrigue. Barère wished an exonerating statement from Demerville in order to "remove from the head of a friend of liberty and a long proscribed republican the suspicions which in a free country should fall only over suspected or guilty men," and he obtained it, a contemptuous exoneration. After heatedly insisting that Barère knew nothing whatever of such plans as had been made, Demerville scornfully added: "I knew that he was too weak . . . to confide anything to him. He would have been capable of denouncing me." When he spoke he did not yet know that Barère had already done so.

Demerville went to the guillotine and Barère lived on to gather the reward of an informer. Thanks to Fouché, who suavely took credit for the arrests, he was permitted to remain in Paris and his name was stricken from a list of suspects which he claims to have seen. He also escaped the deportation order which soon fell on other and more notorious Jacobins. He was not spared Bonaparte's spleen and scorn. The two years which followed were difficult, and whatever he still received from Fouché for his articles in the *Moniteur* and the government-sponsored anti-English newspaper, *The Argus*, was wretchedly little. To raise funds to put off pressing creditors, he placed a lien on his house in Tarbes. Before he fell out with Demerville, they had worked together in a crude confidence game to fleece an ex-priest named Rioust by obtaining for their intended victim permission to open a gambling den in the capital. The venture collapsed and with it the prospect of an easy windfall. He collaborated with Louis Bonaparte on a pamphlet about the English parliament and translated two works into French, but the income was not great.

It may be that he picked up a little money during the brief interval of peace between England and France, when former enemy nationals flocked to Paris, and he confided to such distinguished visitors as Thomas Erskine and Sir Francis Burdett that Bonaparte was "the most ambitious, the most haughty, the most bloodthirsty, and the greatest enemy of liberty." Whether he received from them more than invitations to enjoy their hospitality in their own country is pure conjecture, but that his relations were cordial with English radicals is not in itself surprising. For the curious thing is that for all he wrote against England, he also admired the enemy that he condemned.

Was it in these years or later, it does not too much matter, that he made a confession which he intended for only his own eyes? He annotated his copy of a work, *Tableau politique de l'Europe*, published in 1802, and alongside the page where the anonymous author, actually a former Conventional, J. Eschasseriaux, expressed the conviction that France should increase her strength sufficiently to become a strong rival to England without, however, attempting even if it had the means to do so to destroy the island kingdom, Barère put down what he really believed on that score. "I think so too," he wrote, "although under political threats I have said the contrary in my reports and my writings. I am fundamentally convinced that the rivalry of London is very useful to the prosperity of France; that the maintenance of English power in Europe . . . [is] a natural and necessary counterweight. . . ."

If such were his true views, he was careful not to vent them in public in the last days of winter of 1802-1803 when it became evident that the renewal of the great struggle was imminent. When the English notables left Paris, Barère made plans to follow their example. At the end of his resources, he would leave the capital, retire to Tarbes, and end his days there in peace. Whatever he himself intended, Bonaparte had other ideas in mind for the man whose pen was so facile and whose contacts so numerous. He made no pretense on this occasion of consulting Barère. There were no gracious intermediaries, no cozening, no coaxing, no personal interview. He gave orders now, and in the last days of April 1803 Barère received his instructions:

"The First Consul having learned of Barère's departure for his 'pays,' desires him to stay in Paris. Each week citizen Barère will give a report either on public opinion or on the course of the government or on everything he may think interesting for the First Consul to know. He may write with perfect freedom. He will deliver his reports under seal in his own hand to General Duroc [the marshal of the palace], who will give them to the First Consul; but it is absolutely necessary that no one suspects this kind of communication, otherwise the First Consul will have it cease. He may also frequently insert articles in the journals which will tend to invigorate public opinion, especially against the English."

According to the editor of the *Mémoires*, Barère acknowledged the receipt of his orders: "I shall stay in Paris. I shall devotedly and sincerely do what the First Consul desires. I have nothing to refuse him who restored to me the greatest good of all, freedom."

On the new arrangements, the *Mémoires* themselves observe silence. Barère did not choose to record that in exchange for imprisonment or deportation, perhaps for the guillotine, he had accepted the freedom to crawl on his knees and do what he was instructed to do. What happened to the files of the weekly bulletins is a tantalizing mystery. They were extant as late as 1837, for in that year Barère wrote to his friend, Leonard Gallois, the historian, that they were ready for publication. "I am having my six-year [actually only four] correspondence with Napoleon, consul and emperor, copied," he wrote. "It will make two volumes in octavo. I need only a publisher to whom I shall either sell the publication rights or the literary property." Twenty years later, his editor reported that the correspondence had disappeared and all his efforts to trace it had been fruitless.

The nature and the worth of those reports are also a mystery. According to a Restoration publicist who consulted the file in 1825, the reports are vivid, instructive, honest, and prophetic in their warnings. That Barère should also hold a high opinion of them is not surprising. "When my political and confidential correspondence with the First Consul Bonaparte and the Emperor of the French, Napoleon I, is known," he wrote in his commonplace book for 1838-1839, "and published after my death, history which is always accurate and fair, will say that I told him the most forthright . . . truths that one could offer to a victorious conqueror who never listened to anybody. Surely posterity will not refuse me this praise, that I was almost the sole contemporary of Napoleon who dared to tell him the truth which he suffered so impatiently."

Perhaps it was so, there is no way of knowing whether Barère dared to tell him the truth or reported only what political prudence commanded. In any case, for the following four years he was a paid secret agent of the government. What he had earlier done for Bonaparte indirectly through Fouché, he then did directly for the emperor. For the moment with the new income from Napoleon to supplement whatever he was receiving from Fouché, things were looking up. His most pressing financial difficulties were over, and he could write to his relatives promising to reimburse Jean-Pierre and Cécile within six months for some 3,000 francs that they had advanced to pay off one of his debts. Fantastic stories circulated about his new affluence. According to H. R. Yorke, a renegade English revolutionist, he was receiving £1,000 per annum, a figure which Lewis Goldsmith, in his obituary of Barère, raised to 36,000 francs. Whatever his income may have been, he was living in style—"with a girl of his own"—if Yorke is to be believed.

He had funds enough of his own to found a newspaper, so Barère alleged. If the word of Méneval, Bonaparte's secretary, is to be accepted, both the inspiring idea and the sustaining funds came from governmental sources. Probably he and Barère were each telling part of the truth. The *Mémorial anti-Britannique. Journal historique et politique. Par M. B. Barère, membre de plusieurs Académies* did not flourish and its life span was brief, from September 26, 1803, to November 30, 1804. In the first issue Barère explained why he chose that moment for his venture. England had broken the peace, and it behooved thoughtful Frenchmen to understand the motives of "the tyrant of the seas." In his pages he would "conceal nothing about its political crimes, its perfidious diplomacy, its present situation, the abuses of its naval policy [and] the tyranny and the intolerance of its commercial and industrial system." Its readers were few and indifferent, and Bonaparte was contemptuous of the lifeless pages which repeated all that Barère had been writing for many years. "He [Bonaparte] found in it," wrote Méneval, "only declamations, arguments without substance and often, he said, inanities wrapped in sonorous phrases."

For several months after he became emperor of the French, Napoleon kept his peace and accepted the six copies on vellum that Barère sent him of each issue, then in a crushing two-line memorandum he had Duroc tartly inform the editor that a single copy on ordinary paper would be sufficient. After this ironic snub came the lash of the whip. At the end of November 1804, when his coronation was only a few days ahead and Napoleon no longer required the services of his anti-English propagandist, he gave Barère orders to liquidate the venture completely. The new Charlemagne was now more concerned with having his subjects think in the larger terms of the restored European empire which haunted his own thinking, than in damning the island kingdom. Barère's hackneyed tirades had outlived their usefulness.

Barère bowed before the imperial will. On December 2, the journal appeared under a new name, *Mémorial européen. Journal de politique et de littérature,* and his name no longer graced the title page. The disgraced editor laid a gloss of plausibility over the raw dismissal, explaining to his readers in a brief editorial note the imperative reasons for the change. "A new era is beginning," it read, "and the French empire is rising. A hero presides over its destiny and is taking steps to preserve and extend the benefits of civilization. . . . Politics, the sciences, letters and the arts of all Europe will henceforth be the subject matter of the *Mémorial*." Though Barère put up a bold front, the blow was a cruel one. It cut him off from the 500 francs per month that Méneval presumably had been paying him for his editorial services. He also stood to lose such funds of his own as he had invested in the venture, and apparently he did, two years later, when the *Mémorial* was absorbed by another journal.

Meantime another source of income had dried up. On Napoleon's instructions of September 9, 1804, Fouché had advised Barère to discontinue the unsigned articles that he had been contributing to other newspapers which enjoyed imperial protection: "Tell Barère, whose declamations and sophistries are not in accord with his colossal reputation, to stop writing in that style. He still thinks that one has to stir up the masses; on the contrary, they must be guided without their being aware." After a brief moment of affluence, the "man with little talent"—this was Napoleon's phrase—was again short of funds. He busied himself once more with translations and there were two more in 1804, one from the English and the other from the Italian. That same year he applied for a temporary editorial position with a publishing house. Nothing came of it. Nothing came from the publication of his newest denunciation of "the crimes of that pitiful, ambitious, haughty and greedy nation," for his anonymous *Les Anglais au XIXe siècle,* left the public unmoved. The brother of the emperor, Louis Bonaparte, also turned a deaf ear to the author when Barère solicited an audience in order "to bring his token of gratitude and devotion to the distinguished family to which he owed his freedom." The distinguished family by this time had had enough of wheedling.

The years were going by and Barère was in 1805 where he had been in 1803, more sick at heart than ever over the prospect of remaining in Paris. With imperial permission or without, he left the capital in the spring of 1805 and made his way to Tarbes. Things could be no worse there and possibly, while renewing his association with his brother and sisters, he could also patch up relations with the estranged and embittered wife whom he had not seen and from whom he had heard not a word since those distant days when she wrote him letter after letter entreating him not to vote for the execution of Louis XVI. Now it was he who made overtures. As local historians tell the story, for in the *Mémoires* Barère says nothing about his efforts, his wife spurned him with icy silence. After her refusal even to acknowledge the first letter from the man who had betrayed his king and his God, he wrote to her again to inform her that at a specified day and hour he would appear in front of the house that she inhabited at Vic. If he found the shutters open, he would understand that she had forgiven him his past. He rode down the main street of the small town, hopeful of the best, but curtains were drawn, windows shut tight, shutters grimly closed. He did not even dismount from his horse. He rode on and returned to Tarbes. They were never to meet again or hear from each other.

This stinging rebuff overlapped further political disappointments. More loyal to him than Madame Barère, his constituents in the Hautes-Pyrénées elected him to legislative office, first to the Imperial Senate and then to the Corps Législatif. There was no sequel to those marks of favor: the legal authorities nullified the elections. Utterly dejected, he returned early in June 1805 to the Paris that he loathed to eat the bitter bread of the emperor. His pen scratched rapidly over paper and one more anonymous booklet appeared, *De la conduite des princes de la maison des Bourbons depuis 1789 jusqu'en 1805*. In this panegyric, like the one which preceded it, *Les Anglais au XIXe siècle*, Barère discharged his task with his customary professional skill. He contrasted the lustre of Napoleon to the nullity and baseness of the émigré brothers and cousin of Louis XVI. For good measure he also dipped deeper into the historic past. From this research he discovered what he had not known in his earlier days, that of all the Bourbon princes who had sat on the throne of France, Henry IV alone was worthy of the plaudits of posterity and only because his talents compared favorably with those of Napoleon. "Illustrious conqueror," Barère apostrophized the most beloved of all French rulers, "a heroic genius, similar to yours, presides over the destiny of France. . . . The founders of empires, distinguished generals, beneficent rulers, and the great men of all ages form only a single family."

What Barère published, under instructions or out of uninstructed cravenness, extolled the "heroic genius" whose ire he dreaded. What he thought in private did not square with the printed text. "His countrymen," he acidly jotted down in notes for a book on the political errors of the French that he would have wished to write, "were always worshippers of new forms of power, always ready to grovel before new masters." Since it could not be otherwise, he too was crawling before the master. As he crawled, he also looked ahead. He was beginning to discount the future and make contacts which could prove useful when the emperor fell from power. Among the new friends whom he cultivated were resident Russian diplomatic agents in Paris, and soon he was confiding in them. To the private secretary of the Grand Duke Constantine, who was "eager to know my opinion of him whom all flatterers called a great man, a profound statesman, and a distinguished general," he stated categorically that the emperor of the French was doomed.

Since we have Barère's own account of this singular fashion in which he earned the emoluments that Napoleon gave him for his bulletins, presumably he saw nothing amiss in the irregular procedure. Possibly the Slavic friends gave him more tangible expressions of gratitude than their thanks. If such was the case, on these details the *Mémoires* also maintain silence. From the testimony of another new friend, however, whom Barère also briefed on the political situation, the evidence is clear that he did not disdain pay for the expression of his opinion that the days of the emperor were numbered. This new friend was the cultivated Spaniard, Eugenio Izquierdo, whom "The Prince of Peace," Manuel Godoy, had sent to Paris to win Napoleon's collaboration in his grandiose project of a joint Spanish-French partition of Portugal. The two men, who first met in 1804, became fast friends, seeing each other as often as twice a day to exchange confidences. Naturally, Izquierdo was delighted with a man so affable, gracious, and well informed as Barère, who in his bulletins to Napoleon bespoke the merits of Godoy's project. "We have in him," the envoy reported to Godoy in June 1805, "a writer who is completely devoted to us. His imagination is fertile, his talent in presenting things is unequalled." Izquierdo was not lacking in funds, as Talleyrand among other officials in high places had already learned, and for a writer of such talent and devotion to Spanish interests as Barère, a gift of 100 gold louis, the handsome sum of 2,400 francs, was not excessive as a mark of appreciation.

The naval disaster at Trafalgar wiped out the Spanish fleet, but Godoy persevered, and in the following year, 1806, his agent was back in Paris, closer than ever to Barère. The discomfited Portuguese envoy, Brito, reported the renewal of the great friendship with grudging admiration: "They exchange visits, write to each other, and consult each other regularly." Izquierdo undoubtedly was charmed by his French associate; grateful, too, for Barère's disclosures about rifts and intrigues in the Napoleonic entourage and constant and repeated warnings for him not to place all his trust in "his Corsican majesty." For that matter, since he was as astute as he was gracious, most likely Izquierdo did not place all his trust in Barère either. He did not have to be told, as Brito reminded his home office, that Barère was "an agent of the French government [and] I suppose his services are double."

In the meantime the double agent was making the best of the Spanish and French worlds, maintaining remunerative relations with Izquierdo and cultivating the French imperial garden. "Barère has paid off his debts, through the Spanish agent, it was learned," Brito observed tersely about the cordial friendship. For two more years, until late in 1807, Barère consorted with his friend and covered his tracks, so he thought, with weekly bulletins and honeyed translations which in verse and prose sang the grandeur of Napoleon. To Louis Bonaparte, whom for good reasons, no doubt, he considered an exceptionally valuable contact, he presented a copy of the collected edition of his prerevolutionary essays, inscribing the *Eloges académiques* to "the wise and beneficent prince, the worthy brother of the great Napoleon."

Barère was still sending his bulletins and working away on the 223rd number, when, in December 1807, Napoleon called a halt to the comedy. The emperor by now had had enough of double agents. What the Portuguese envoy knew, the ruler of France also knew. He had enough of Barère's reports. Through the aide-de-camp Duroc, on whom some of Izquierdo's manna had also fallen, he gave Barère the last of his orders. The words were mordant and deliberately discourteous: "I am instructed to write you, monsieur, that it has become useless to send me any bulletins, since His Majesty's busy schedule no longer permits him to read them. If, subsequently, things are different, I shall not fail to let you know." This contemptuous dismissal was the end. After seven years of spying, adulation, and hack writing, Barère was discarded. Napoleon threw him back on his own resources, not even bothering to keep him under surveillance.

# The Constitutionalist,
# 1808-1815

FOR the remaining years of the Napoleonic era Barère wore the desolate cloak of rejection. With political writing and activity denied him, he ground out more translations and stale compendiums, such as an edition of the letters of the famous bluestocking, Julie de Lespinasse, and a selection from the writings of Madame Necker, which the title page attributed to "M.B.D.V." If that transparent reference to "Monsieur Barère de Vieuzac" gave the measure of his nostalgia for the old days of the prerevolutionary era, it also reflected the tone of the new society where the reopened aristocratic salons of the Faubourg Saint-Germain shone. With his wide social contacts Barère was a welcome guest at fashionable gatherings, including most likely the salon of Madame de Staël in recognition of the tribute that he had paid her and her mother. His prospects were bleak, but his captivating charm still cast its spell over fellow guests. The aged Bernardin de Saint-Pierre, who many years earlier had played on the sensibility of the Old Regime youth with his mawkish *Paul et Virginie,* was enraptured by "the politeness, humanity, and wit" of a dinner companion whose identity their hostess tactfully did not disclose, and at a gathering at the home of Madame de Récamier, the old tutor of Alexander I, La Harpe, declared categorically that he recognized by "the tone and agreeable manners" of his unknown fellow guest "a man of the Old Regime." Barère of the powdered hair and silk stockings that he was then affecting saw no reason to reveal to the admirer that he was a Jacobin terrorist of odious repute. He visited with old friends, among them David and the great actor, Talma, obtaining from them tickets to the theatre and the opera. He attended public lectures, read widely, and collected old prints to sell at a profit.

"La dame Guillebert, *rentière*," as police reports referred to Madame de Guibert, may have helped provide for his needs, for they were probably still living together. More certainly, there were occasional remittances from Izquierdo, who stayed on in Paris and whom Barère saw regularly; and a little money dribbled in from the rental of a floor in his Tarbes home, possibly also from income on the St. Lézer property that he was still vainly trying to sell. Whatever he obtained from those sources, the total was slight and he lived a marginal existence in the political shades.

There was little solace for him in the works about the Revolution which were published during the Napoleonic era. The brief notice in Coiffier's *Biographie moderne* of 1800 showed an unexpected forbearance in merely recording that "to give an account of all the opinions and the work of Barère it would be necessary to mention all the operations of the Committee from the 31st of May till the 27th of July, 1794." Such impartial indifference was by way of exception. Lecomte's *Mémorial*, published a year later in 1801, repeated the choicer bits of the post-Thermidorian pamphlets. As for the historians who reviewed the course of the Revolution, like Lecomte they were all flatly outspoken in hostility, excepting the Viscount of Toulongeon. From Beaulieu's essays it could be gleaned that Barère was a turncoat and a weathervane. The numerous references to his career in Lacretelle's history of France, which went through four printings, were variations on the single verdict that Barère was "the habitual spokesman of all the base thoughts of the Convention" and a man who "put the most barbarous decrees in facile phrases." Molleville, who had been in the service of Louis XVI, conceded in his account that Barère was without question the deputy "who rendered the greatest services" to the Convention, but this observation was little more than a parenthetical aside to the author's opinion that Barère was one of "the great number of cowardly men without character or principles whom the Revolution in France pulled out of obscurity." The appreciation was harsher still in Fantin des Odouards' concise textbook for secondary school students. After repeating the stories of human tanneries, he gave his measured opinion that Barère's "art was to fuse vice and virtue, falsehood and truth, and find affinities between the actions of Domitian and the thoughts of Marcus Aurelius."

The English adventurer, H. R. Yorke, who informed his readers in 1804 that Barère "lives in good style [and] keeps a girl of his own," stated also that Barère was "allowed by the First Consul to share in the profits of a house of ill fame which he has founded." Four years later, in 1808, another English work, *Lives of the Revolutionists*, conveyed the information that Barère had "been dragged from obscurity by Buonaparte [and] has proved one of his warmest sycophants." Following these assessments there was almost complete silence until the end of the Napoleonic period, when in 1814 Robert's biographical dictionary again expounded on the theme of Barère's "duplicity," while a similar work edited by Robinet in 1815 dutifully characterized him as "pusillanimous" and "always on the side of the stronger."

These accounts, one may presume, hardly elevated Barère's spirits. Depressed by his reverses, financially embarrassed, he was also failing in health. One of his cousins, in order not to upset the relatives in Tarbes, refrained from making more than passing references in his reports of Barère's good health to a "humor" that affected his stomach. The physician who was treating the ailing man scorned such delicacy. His patient, he later testified had suffered for many years from a persistent rheumatic cold that affected kidneys and bladder, which made voiding difficult and painful and compelled him to take *bains de siège* for passing relief. The surgeon in attendance supplied corroborating details about the catheter that Barère had to use to avoid intolerable pain.

To make matters worse, the police began to badger him again. He had been careful not to give them a handle; indeed, by a kind of conditioned reflex, even after Napoleon had cast him into the outer political darkness, he continued to fawn, hoping no doubt that his words would reach the imperial ear. As late as 1810, when all was dark, he wrote to a young poet, acknowledging the receipt of a composition which lauded the emperor: "I receive with real pleasure, the precious gift of your *Napoléonide*. . . . It is a truly inspired work [and] your hero is that of all Europe, an honor to the human race. When you see him, you will be even more inspired for the second part of your work." Whether the hero of all Europe heard those words or not, the police remained on the alert and in the following year, when the electoral college of the Hautes-Pyrénées put his name down on a list of delegates to extend congratulations to the emperor, the Paris authorities summarily removed it.

Though he was taking no chances, he must have been indiscreet, for the prefect of police saw fit in 1812 to interrogate him about his anti-Napoleonic activities. Whatever Barère knew or had done, he did not disclose. Keeping closer watch over his own tongue, he also advised his friends, various royalist sympathizers among them, to do likewise. He agreed, as he exchanged views with Izquierdo, that the drama of the Russian campaign had shattered the empire and that Napoleon was insane, as Izquierdo had it, to try to grasp the European bull by both the Russian and Spanish horns. After the holocaust of the Grand Army in the frozen wastes of Russia, came the carnage in Germany in the spring of 1813 and the rout of the new army of fresh recruits in the Battle of the Nations at Leipzig in the fall. Then the long subservient and silent deputies of the Corps Législatif drew up a memorial itemizing Napoleon's violation of the constitution and sharply condemn-

ing him for his summary rejection of the terms of peace that
the allies offered France. Barère was convinced that "the emperor had lost his wits and would soon lose his throne."

While the allies were completing arrangements to invade
France, Barère cudgelled his brains how to escape from Paris.
He was of no mind to stick to the end with a cause that he had
never fully made his own; much less was he resigned to the
prospect, if he did stay on, of being seized by returning émigrés who could be counted upon not to forgive him his revolutionary past. Since he would not go down fighting for the imperial regime, when he was called to report for duty with the
National Guard, he pleaded old age and infirmity, as well he
might, and obtained exemption from service. In fact he succeeded in getting out of the menaced capital in the very days
when the allies crossed the Rhine and Napoleon was deploy-
ing his troops for the brilliant but hopeless spring campaign
of 1814. In the death of his cousin, Hector, and the necessity
of escorting the bereaved widow and young daughter to his
"only true *pays*, the Pyrénées," he found a pretext that the
municipal authorities were willing to accept. By mid-February
Paris was behind him, and along with other refugees he headed south for safety.

The narrative of his flight is fresh and striking, a vivid story
of the panicky exodus, clogged roads, confusion, and the curious mixture of relief that welled forth over the crumbling of
Napoleon's despotic rule and frightened uncertainty over what
the future would bring. He reached Bordeaux safely, but remained only a few days, not daring to expose himself longer in
that hotbed of royalism. The little party went on and finally
reached Tarbes. If he had any illusions that Tarbes would be
a haven, he quickly realized his error. The troops of Wellington were already within gun range of his native town and he
remained only long enough to embrace his family and turn
about to head north. Travelling alone now, he made his way
to Toulouse, where royalist sentiment was as intense as at

Bordeaux, but where for lack of alternative he had to stay for a long, precarious month, terrified every day that his identity might be discovered. From Toulouse, it was only a brief journey to Cahors, and from Cahors to Limoges, where the situation was no better. Cut off from news, there was nothing else to do but stay where he was. The Paris papers finally came through and he learned on Easter Monday, April 11, so he says, that Napoleon had abdicated and that the provisional government had invited the Bourbons to return. He changed his plans abruptly and made the decision to return.

Fear had led him to flee; a quick estimate of his chances determined him to return. If he stayed on in the capital of Limousin, sooner or later one of the fanatical royalists would discover who he was. It is not likely that he had forgotten how the royalists had tried to get at him in 1795. In Paris, on the other hand, something might conceivably turn up to his advantage. He had friends in the capital, royalists as well as former revolutionists, and he knew the rules of the political game. On April 25 he was back in Paris looking about for an opportunity to serve his country and himself. "With what pleasure did I at last see my books, my paintings, and my lodging again," he wrote in the *Mémoires*, meaning that no one molested him.

He found a course to follow which offered the personal security that he had not known for many years and placed no strain upon his political beliefs. He professed to be satisfied with the promise that Louis XVIII made in the Declaration of St. Ouen to give his subjects a constitutional government. Despite reservations that he made no point of voicing, he was reasonably satisfied with the Charter of 1814 which the Bourbon monarch promulgated soon after in redemption of the promise. The Charter of 1814 had its shortcomings, but its provisions were far more liberal than anyone could have hoped before the return of the pretender. If Louis XVIII would adhere to them while holding his ultra followers in check,

France had every reason to expect more from the liberal Bourbon monarchy than it had obtained from the government of the Consulate and the empire.

So reasoned Barère and so reasoned many notables who had given their allegiance to Napoleon and now accepted service under the returned Bourbon. Among them were Marshal Ney, who gave Louis XVIII his support, Carnot, who agreed to accept a high post in the new government, and Fouché, who was as prepared to be Louis XVIII's minister of police as he had been for the fallen emperor. When such illustrious ex-revolutionists and ex-imperialists saw where duty lay, Barère would follow their example if he could. A Rouget de Lisle, who had composed the immortal *Marseillaise* for the revolutionists of 1792, wrote a royalist hymn; Barère, the old rapporteur of the Committee of Public Safety, was seen wearing the fleurs-delys as his boutonniere.

To be sure, the *Mémoires* assert, he wished nothing for himself from the Bourbons, "neither their honors . . . nor their baubles, their ribbons, their crosses." But in 1814 it did not do to affront them with a needless display of disinterestedness, and soon he was writing a note to "an important person," asking for an audience with His Majesty. Cambacérès had arranged for him to meet the First Consul in 1800; though Bonaparte had not seen fit to follow his advice, perhaps Louis XVIII would be wiser. How could one serve France better than by inducing the king to let the dead past bury the dead past and consolidate the future by establishing a parliamentary regime. Barère would also utilize the occasion to inform the monarch that he had always been devoted to the descendant of Henri IV near whose birthplace in Pau he himself had been born. Louis XVIII missed his opportunity to hear sound advice and be moved by a display of allegiance. Barère was not accorded an audience. "By chance," as the latter delicately phrased it, he ran into an old acquaintance, Maurice Roques de Montgaillard, who forthwith introduced him to his own friend, Fauche-Borel, like himself a royalist agent and now returned to Paris with his king.

The mysterious Montgaillard was a past master of undercover operations. For years he had been involved in secret intrigues and negotiations, in conspiracies in and outside France. "No one can make out for sure," his biographer wrote, "in whose name he speaks and in whose interests he acts." He had betrayed the revolutionists to the royalists, whom he served from London after his emigration in 1792, and in 1797 he had been the soul of the Pichegru conspiracy against the Republic. After Brumaire he made a new career for himself, at least outwardly, as an agent of Napoleon. In 1814 he was one of the first to go over openly to the Bourbons. His path crossed with Barère's at this juncture, probably some years earlier, one suspects, and an idea was born of their chance meeting and conversation, that Barère should write a memorandum for the political guidance of the king. Though nothing came of Montgaillard's suggestion, Barère incorporated its cardinal thought in a brief anonymous account of the imperial despotism which apprized the subjects of Louis XVIII of their new good fortune and at the same time tactfully warned the ruler himself against pursuing the rule which had toppled Napoleon.

After this brochure, of which he did not give the title in his *Mémoires*, Barère penned another in the fall of 1814, also unsigned and unidentified, a variation on the theme in which he appealed to all shades of political opinion to stand fast around the government of the Charter. It was "a high person in court circles," Montgaillard cryptically informed him, who desired to have that pamphlet written. Either Montgaillard was intimating that the king desired it or else Barère retrospectively tried to convey that impression. Since there is nothing in Montgaillard's papers on this matter, either supposition is possible, or neither. It may simply be that Barère's elastic conscience suffered a twinge over this brochure, as well as over the unsigned articles that he contributed to the *Gazette de France* in the inter-

ests of national harmony, and that the whole story was deliberate mystification to salve it. In any case his *Mémoires* vehe-
mently protested his good faith. "Let those," he indignantly
wrote, "who from hatred or vengeance or habit slander me for
making myself agreeable to the Bourbons, read this work and
learn . . . to do me justice."

The policy that he pursued was crumbling before it collapsed when Napoleon dramatically escaped from Elba in
March 1815 and made his triumphal return to Paris. Barère
had overestimated the capacity of Louis XVIII and underes-
timated all the follies that the Bourbon government could
commit. If that first monarchical experiment failed, there was
nothing dishonorable in itself in Barère's desire for the great
reconciliation. Frenchmen had been divided for a quarter of a
century; France had been torn apart by passions and interests.
It was time for a new leader to proclaim that he had charity
for all and malice toward none. The irreconcilable few within
the country who had refused to accept the achievements of the
Revolution would have obeyed him and the returned ultra-
royalist émigrés would be kept within bounds. So one could
hope. There was wisdom in Barère's wish to avert new strife
by reconciling revolutionists and royalists within the frame of
a constitutional monarchy and a parliamentary regime. If
Louis XVIII could not control his subjects, Barère could not
refrain from currying favor and debasing himself to purchase
personal immunity. The justice that he asked for would have
been his if he had not made himself more "agreeable" to the
Bourbons than necessity required.

When Napoleon returned, though Barère certainly had not
foreseen it, he was in no great danger. He had held no office
under Louis XVIII and received no honors. How much he had
fawned on the king may have been suspected, but its extent
was not known, and all that he had written he had taken the
precaution of not signing. Besides, Napoleon could not afford
to be fastidious about the men whom he rallied to his stand-

ard. From all sides, he was learning how much the political atmosphere had changed since his abdication. He heard from the journalists, from his old administrators, from former political associates, that if he wished their support, he would have to renounce the ways of the dictator. So Barère had a large margin of safety for his future operations. When Cambacérès agreed to enter Napoleon's ministry, and upright Carnot, too, who had been dismissed by his emperor, Barère was also prepared to serve the larger interests of France. Paris had been worth a mass, France was worth one more shift in his personal allegiance. Perhaps he would have made that shift anyhow only to be safe, but he could make it with an easy conscience, for the emperor had repeatedly professed his intention to reign as a constitutional monarch.

Fouché, too, entered Napoleon's service for the last time. It was known that the minister of police had not wished the emperor's return and that the emperor was not happy in recalling the man he detested and feared. But Fouché was indispensable for the office which Napoleon gave him. No one else could discharge so effectively the responsibility of enforcing public order, as Napoleon knew from experience. Old Jacobins were behind the minister, it is true, but with his wide contacts among moderate revolutionists and the liberal wing of the royalists, he might perhaps also swing them over to Napoleon. Consequently, the emperor had to suffer the presence in the official family of a man he was convinced would seek to betray him.

Napoleon made concessions to public opinion, but not more than he had to. He rode through the narrow streets of the Faubourg St. Antoine and made addresses to its working-class population. Though his new ministry won him favor, fears remained that unless he sincerely submitted to the curbs of representative government, liberty would be as much menaced by him as by the Bourbons. Shortly after his return, the constitutionalists instructed Benjamin Constant to ascertain Napoleon's true feelings and intentions. Constant had already employed his powerful pen to attack the emperor's despotism. A long interview convinced him that Napoleon had not changed his authoritarian views but was only conforming to circumstances. Neverthless, Constant agreed to aid him in drafting an amendment, an "Additional Act" to the imperial constitution. In his mind was the hope that the promulgation of a liberal amendment might possibly keep the allies from attacking France and that even if the coalition attacked and the empire fell, the new constitution and the parliamentary regime would remain intact. The Additional Act was to prove a disappointment. Constant notwithstanding, it emerged from the Elysée, where it was discussed *in camera,* hardly distinguishable from the Charter, neither better nor worse. Drawn up behind the scenes, it was not discussed in public and not published until late in April when it was submitted to the secondary electors for ratification. If they did what was expected of them and approved the *fait accompli,* there were still elected representatives to the new Chamber which convened a few days later, on June 3, who were determined to modify the provisions of the Act. Barère was one of them. After twenty years in the political wilderness he was back at last in the parliamentary lists.

He was elected as deputy from the Hautes-Pyrénées, and he owed his election to the pressure that Fouché had put upon the secondary electors. How far Fouché's reservations went when he accepted service under Napoleon is an open question. Perhaps he was even then discounting the emperor's defeat and looking forward to becoming the strong man of a caretaker government to succeed Napoleon, preferably that of Napoleon's son. Whatever may have been his long-range scheme, he worked immediately behind the screen of his official loyalty to ensure the election of old revolutionists to the new Chamber of Representatives that Napoleon had promised to establish. In them he would have the nucleus of an opposition strong enough to curb the emperor in his dictatorial leanings.

Barère was one of the supporters on whom Fouché placed his hopes. Years after their last working arrangement, the two old actors of the Revolution renewed their contacts. The minister of police received Barère in audience, and Barère submitted to him a detailed memorandum of a constitutional regime in which the role of responsible ministers would be great. Fouché was pleased with the draft and encouraged Barère to stand for election, promising him aid in the electoral college. In Barère, Fouché had a veteran parliamentarian, skilled in debate; in Fouché, Barère had a powerful patron, a shield and a sword, on whom he could rely no matter what happened to the emperor. So he thought when he returned to parliamentary life.

He was already at work when his election came in May. Naturally, as he told the story in his *Mémoires*, he had not demeaned himself by joining the throng of "sycophants" who flocked to the Tuileries to welcome Napoleon. Nevertheless, "friends urged him to write and publish some thoughts which would induce the emperor" to live up to the loose promises about the constitutional regime that he had made at Grenoble and Lyons in the course of his triumphal journey to Paris. He chose first to address Napoleon directly and on March 21 wrote a long memorandum for the emperor's guidance. He was vain enough to believe that Napoleon would listen to him again. But 1815 was not 1800, and Napoleon remained silent. There was no acknowledgment of Barère's counsel. Not willing, even years later, to admit that Napoleon had scorned him, he obtained solace from the inference that his memorandum "must have been read by some secretary or political lackey."

Since the emperor had made no response to the personal appeal, perhaps strategically situated public pressure would make an impact, and Barère undertook the delicate task of expressing what public opinion desired. A news story appeared in the *Moniteur*, a long story, more than a full page, stating that under the title of *Théorie de la Constitution de la Grande-*

*Bretagne* he had translated the work of "a very distinguished English publicist [which] appeared in London in 1769," and that he had prefaced his translation with "some observations on the great interests which concern us. . . . " That story is intriguing for several reasons. First, that it appeared, of all places, in the official newspaper. Secondly, that it appeared on April 27, the very day that Napoleon's Additional Act to the imperial constitution was released to the public. Thirdly, that the writer, who signed himself "B," said virtually nothing about the translation and devoted almost all his space to Barère's observations about the constitutions that France had had from 1791 to 1814 and to his own favorable comments on the Act. Finally, that neither Barère in his book nor "B" had seen fit to say that the English original of the translation was a very brief passage from a long and once famous novel, *The Fool of Quality*, written by Henry Brooke who, the *Moniteur* notwithstanding, was not "a very distinguished English publicist." In its account, the *Moniteur* carried excerpts from Barère's commentary in which he reminded his readers that the French themselves "for twenty-five years had made so many efforts . . . to ensure the independence of the nation, establish its rights, regulate the prerogatives and the duties of the executive power, and make secure the throne which the sovereignty of the people had established and made hereditary in the sole interests of the nation." That point made, "B" quoted at length from Barère's sharp criticism of the Charter, which Louis XVIII had arrogantly presented to the people without any pretense of consultation or discussion. Then came excerpts from Barère's plea for the creation of a hereditary peerage *à l'anglaise*, in which he argued that in those élites of administrators, officers, men of affairs, and leaders in the arts and sciences, France would have not a reconstituted aristocracy but "a rock . . . against the waves of democracy and the torrents of despotism." And as for Napoleon himself, "B" quoted Barère that the emperor was "a great man and illustrious monarch whose return has delivered us from political proscriptions and dissension and who has shown himself the noble defender of national liberty and the rights of the citizen." "We foresee," the quotation continued, "all that we can expect by way of what is moderate and good from a new dynasty that has learned much from adversity."

Having thus given what Barère expected of Napoleon, "B" turned to the Additional Act. Barère—and he stressed the point—had not seen it in advance. Hence readers should be all the more grateful for his analysis of the British constitution which the Act followed "in all that is liberal and wise. . . . One will be able to appreciate that while it gives solid guarantees to power, it also gives pledges to public liberty on which the former rests." Though the French people may have some reservations, "B" quoted Barère, there would be general agreement that "of all the forms of government which have been offered to the French people since they reconquered their rights, none other can assure them fuller exercise of those rights and promise to last longer. It dexterously combines the forces of [public] opinion with those of power, of an assembly which gives consent with an authority which enforces it, of liberty which instructs and unity of action which governs."

There the *Moniteur* account ended. Together with Barère's small book of 104 pages, it was a cleverly mounted propaganda campaign intended for Napoleon's edification. Fouché had doubtless blessed it and, utilizing his powerful influence, obtained for it the maximum of publicity. "B," who could hardly be anyone other than Barère himself, had timed the article to appear with the publication of the Act; and in it he went as far as he dared or deemed politic to inform Napoleon that liberal France had confidence in him and would support him, but would do so only if he mended the error of his ways. France expected him to remember where his authority came from and not to forget that his throne rested upon the sovereignty of the people and had been made hereditary solely in the interest of the nation. With skill and subtlety, and with courage too, Barère stated the terms on which he would endorse the rule of the restored emperor.

In the following month, he wrote two additional booklets. In the one, *Considérations sur la Chambre des Pairs*, he repeated his arguments in favor of a hereditary peerage; in the other, *Les époques de la nation française*, he reviewed the history of France to prove that even under the most reactionary ruler of the past the principles of popular sovereignty had always been respected. Neither work had the impact of the *Théorie de la constitution*, and Napoleon did not alter the provisions of the Additional Act. He was far less concerned at that moment with meeting criticism than with completing military preparations to crush the allies before they could muster their strength in full force against him. Barère was disgusted, his *Mémoires* say, with the representatives of the electoral college who accepted the Act in the public ceremony arranged for that purpose. He professed pride in his efforts to win Napoleon over to the ways of a true constitutional monarch: "Those . . . works were proof of the freedom and independence of my political opinions." He had reason to feel proud of those efforts; he had cause, too, to think well of his role in the Chamber of Representatives, where he took his seat on June 3.

He took part in the debates for the first time on June 16, ostensibly on the constitutional question of the right of the subordinates of ministers to appear in the Chamber and answer interpellations for their superiors. Without openly opposing Fouché, for he insisted that any minister, "even if he were a peer," had the constitutional right to make recommendations to the representatives, Barère deftly made the point that the minister was responsible to the Chamber: "His presence is all the more necessary in that he alone can give all the necessary information and in appearing on the rostrum he guarantees his responsibility." If Fouché, the Duke of Otranto, did not miss the reference to peers, he probably did not fail to heed the intimation that Barère would not delegate all authority to his hands.

On the following day, when the Chamber debated Fouché's report to the emperor on the military situation, Barère spoke more openly still. It was the eve of the decisive day of the fighting at Waterloo, and Fouché, anticipating defeat, was taking a long first step toward establishing his emergency rule. To do so, however, he needed the formal sanction of the legislative assembly, for otherwise he would be placing himself in the same position as a dictatorial Napoleon. In Barère he had a supporter but a supporter with reservations and conditions. Barère upheld the constitutional propriety of having a minister take the initiative of making recommendations for action, but he insisted on the right of the assembly itself to take the necessary steps to implement them. Speaking in his old vein of the Year II, he urged his colleagues to refer Fouché's report to a special commission of the Chamber. In this "matter of having recourse to emergency measures (*un pouvoir extraordinaire*), it is the dictatorship of the law that we must establish and not that of a man." He was making his position clear: in the new committee of public safety that he advocated, Fouché would be a member, not its master.

Until definite word was received that Napoleon had been crushed at Waterloo, the Chamber refused to delegate its powers, but after the disaster there was no escaping the creation of an executive Government Commission. As strong man in the governing board, Fouché was powerful enough to force Napoleon to abdicate. He was not influential enough to have the allies recognize the King of Rome as his imperial father's successor. Fouché shifted his ground. If he could not be the power behind the throne to Napoleon II, he could make himself indispensable to Louis XVIII; and he made secret contacts with the agents of the Bourbon to end the fighting, with the Chamber's assent if possible, without it if necessary. His dis-

illusioned supporters complained bitterly, but he was not de-
terred from his course.

He carried on negotiations for an armistice, sending messengers to Wellington and Blücher to advise them to withdraw
their troops and defer their entry into Paris for three days.
When the terms of the capitulation that he arranged with the
allies came to the Chamber on July 3, he ran into difficulties.
On the 4th of July, the deputies drafted a Declaration of the
Rights of Frenchmen and of the Fundamental Principles of
the Constitution. A day later, when the Government Commission publicly announced its decision in a Proclamation to the
French People, the Chamber sharpened the language of its
first Declaration. If the deputies had to give in, they would do
so with dignity.

Barère took an active part in the discussions, taking the lead
to modify the Declaration and include within it a bill of rights:
"This will be your best legacy to future generations." In the
final draft, the Chamber solemnly pledged itself to continue
its sessions. Appealing for support to civilians and the National
Guard of Paris, it declared that whoever was to become head
of a new government had to swear to observe a constitution
voted by the representatives of the people. The principles of
that constitution were the liberty and the equality of all citizens, freedom of the press and of worship, taxation by consent. By its provisions ministers would be responsible and
judges irremovable. The tithe would be abolished, the sales of
nationalized lands declared irrevocable, and the national debt
would be honored.

The Declaration was formally transmitted to the allies and
the deputies of the Chamber released their emotions in an outburst of self-congratulation. As the *Histoire parlementaire* re-
constructed the scene many years later, it was a debauch of
feeling: "All the representatives rose, stretched out their arms,
hugged and embraced each other. . . . Citizens in the visitors'
galleries shared their emotion . . . and from all sides the cries

resounded: 'Long live liberty, long live independence. . . . Let the enemy come, we will show that we can die in our seats!' "

All was now lost except honor. On the 7th, the Government Commission informed the Chamber that the allies had agreed to recognize Louis XVIII as ruler of France and their troops had occupied the Tuileries. "In this state of affairs," the communication concluded, "we can only wish the fatherland the best. Since we are no longer free to deliberate, we believe that we should adjourn." In short, the Commission would set no conditions for the return of Louis XVIII. Though the representatives of the people renewed their protests and swore again not to break up their meeting unless brute force compelled them, by six o'clock in the evening, the presiding officer declared the session adjourned until eight o'clock of the following morning. The adjournment was the end; the Chamber never met again.

There was an epilogue, and in the final protest Barère stood solidly with the few. He was one of the fifty-three representatives who signed the formal minutes of the session of July 8 that the Chamber was not permitted to hold. They had come to take their seats, they stated, but palace gates were barred, the avenues patrolled by Prussian troops, and the commanding officer announced that he had been instructed to refuse all entry. The last words were dignified: "The undersigned, members of the Chamber . . . have signed the present *procès-verbal* in order to place the above facts on record."

Barère ended the imperial era as he had begun it, with a defense of the parliamentary regime. With a final flare-up of courage he expressed his political faith. He was back where he had been in Brumaire, but he no longer had Fouché to befriend him. This he did not yet know. He was also fifteen years older and the springs of action were wearing out.

# XVIII

## *The Bitter Bread, 1815-1830*

THE sessions of the Chamber ended that night of July 7, and Louis XVIII was back in Paris, this time to stay. Barère, no doubt, was as cynical about the overnight shift of loyalty to the Bourbon ruler as his colleague of the Chamber, Auguste Jal, later recalled, but his cynicism about the volatile allegiance of the public was linked to a false sense of his own personal security. He was unperturbed because his protector Fouché was now the Bourbon ruler's minister of police even as he had been of Napoleon. Believing that he was still Fouche's protégé, Barère was not at first disturbed by rumors that Louis XVIII was preparing a proscription list. In justice to Fouché, he did what he could without endangering his own standing to aid Barère and spirit him out of the capital—and on July 17, he obtained a passport for his old associate which granted Barère permission to reside in the Hautes-Pyrénées. Unfortunately, this friendly move, which would have solved all of Barère's difficulties, was countermanded by the head of the Prussian Kommandatur. General Pful refused to affix a visa to the passport, alleging, not without justification, that the presence of the French army south of the Loire made it impossible for him to assume the responsibility of endorsing a document which could permit the bard of revolutionary victories to whip up the ardor of the troops. This was the first reverse, and as it became more and more certain that the king was yielding to the joint pressure of the victorious allies and his émigré entourage and had made up his mind to turn the ranking imperial officers over to a court martial and to have the most notorious revolutionaries deported with or without the formality of a trial, Barère's composure began to crumble. On July 24 Louis XVIII signed the ordinance prepared for him. It was his desire, it ran, "to conciliate the interests of our people, the dignity of our crown, and the peace of Europe with what we owe to justice." In accord with those lofty principles it provided that the officers were to be arrested and held for trial while designated political undesirables were to place themselves within three days under police surveillance in specified centers and remain there until the two chambers ruled on their fate.

Barère read in the *Moniteur* of the 26th that his name was on the list. Although it is unlikely that he was as stupefied as he claimed, even if he were, his resourcefulness did not desert him. He contrived to have an audience with Elie Decazes, the prefect of police, and a day later, on the 27th, he wrote to Decazes enclosing his passport and entreating the prefect to use his great influence to have it visaed for the Hautes-Pyrénées. Pending action on the petition, Barère requested the prefect to grant him permission to remain in Paris, naturally under due police observation. His letter, apparently, was mislaid: "How did this letter come to my attention only today," the exasperated Decazes scrawled on the margin, not unreasonably irritated over having the delicate problem of Barère's future thrust into his hands.

While Decazes was weighing the request and the three days of grace were running out for compliance, Barère did not remain inactive. He bombarded Fouché with appeals, writing on the 29th, that he would obey the ordinance if he could, but it was absolutely impossible for him to comply with its terms and "change his place of abode." Fouché knew that he was old and in poor health, that he lacked financial resources, that he had lived in Paris for thirty years, that his life was endangered if he left it. In those circumstances, his letter ended, "M. Bertrand Barère begs Your Excellency to agree to authorize him to reside in Paris under his surveillance." Leaving nothing to chance, he enclosed two medical affidavits, each more than a year old to be sure but both emphasizing in the strongest terms that he suffered from persistent kidney and bladder trouble and required absolute quiet and rest for his recovery.

Decazes, to whom Fouché turned over the affidavits, scrupulously conducted his own investigation, ordering a third doctor to examine Barère. Dr. Renault gave his report on August 2: before he could definitely make up his mind, he wished Barère to be re-examined with the two doctors present. Meantime, he was of the tentative opinion that even in cases of emergency, a patient like Barère could be moved a short distance, providing it was in a comfortable carriage. For Decazes the report was sufficient. He saw his chance to get Barère off his hands. That very day, accordingly, he requested Pful to affix a visa to Barère's passport for the Hautes-Pyrénées. He reckoned without the stubbornness of the Prussian commander. The passport came back at once with the curt annotation: "Rejected; he may not leave for the Hautes-Pyrénées." Decazes was discomfited, but refusing to take the initiative of acting independently, he wrote to Fouché, on the 3rd, for instructions and requested "His Excellency, the duke of Otranto, to be kind enough to let him know his intentions concerning M. Barère."

His Excellency disclosed his intentions. He was going to drop ballast: Barère was expendable. Fouché would not impair his own status by permitting Barère to flout the royal ordinance. When the poor wretch learned that Fouché had given orders to have him rounded up and arrested for evading the July 24 ordinance, he fell into a panic. It was the ordeal of 1800 all over again, and this time there was no service for him to render which would earn the forbearance of the head of the state. Denied the Hautes-Pyrénées, where he would be safe, and unsafe in Paris if he showed himself, he went into close hiding. Most sensibly, too, because in the next half year the political air was as heavy with vengeance as in the terrible days of the Thermidorian reaction. In Naples the execution squad of the restored Bourbons shot down the swashbuckling Joachim Murat. In Paris a fusillade mowed down the loyal imperialist soldier, General La Bédoyère, who was soon to be followed to the grave by Marshal Ney, "the bravest of the brave." The capital swarmed with police agents and spies, and the newly elected deputies of the unbelievably reactionary *Chambre introuvable* took their seats determined to mete out exemplary punishment to conspicuous revolutionaries and adherents of Napoleon.

Worse was to come in 1816. The year opened with Chamber and Peers debating the so-called "amnesty" bill of December 9, 1815, which Louis XVIII had introduced to mollify persisting pro-Bonapartist sentiment. According to its provisions an amnesty would be extended to "all who directly or indirectly took part in the rebellion and the usurpation of Napoleon Bonaparte." The officers, however, who had been named in the ordinance of July 24 remained subject to its terms, while the political undesirables originally named were now ordered to leave France within two months of the promulgation of the new law. They were forbidden, too, to return to France without royal permission on pain of deportation.

Since Barère feared that only in Prussia would he be able to obtain entry if he obeyed the law—and Prussia was the last country in which a former revolutionary would wish to seek refuge—he chose to evade the new law as he had the ordinance. He made up his mind to try to escape elsewhere under false papers. If that decision in the existing circumstances was wise, his position was now more difficult and dangerous than it had been before. Should he be picked up by the police in flagrant violation of the new law, he faced certain imprisonment, possibly deportation to the penal colonies, perhaps the firing squad. So he scurried frantically from one hiding place to another.

Although his cousin Jacques took care to disassociate himself from the embarrassing relative, other cousins and friends rallied around. Barère stole from the apartment of one of his fellow Tarbais on the rue Montorgueil to another on a higher floor in the same building, where "the sister of a young man whom he had befriended" years ago took care of his needs. The second lodging, in turn, had to be given up. But there was always a friend, this time the same ex-colleague Picqué who had denounced him nearly twenty years earlier, and he found a third and final hideaway in a tiny fourth-floor apartment on the rue des Vieux-Augustins where he secreted himself until February 1816. There, too, the young man's sister, "whose name I write with happiness, Marguerite Lefauconnier, exposed herself to all the perils and all the pains of my plight." His *Mémoires* go on: "Each day she went to Nicholas Carles, my relative, who was living in my apartment on the rue Lepelletier and got what was needed, my mail and newspapers too. May this young person who with the consent of her honorable family had the courage to succor a proscribed man here receive the expression of my gratitude."

While he lay in hiding, on Fouché's order the police authorities cast a dragnet over Paris. Whether by chance or otherwise his police identification was misplaced, finally to turn up after having been buried among the papers of an inspector. Save for such details as giving Barère's age as sixty-eight, when he was sixty, and making him five-foot three inches in height, when all other descriptions called him tall, it was reasonably accurate, and sadly accurate in noting the marks of age and care. His face, as the identification gave it, was long, his nose straight, and his dark gray eyes sunken. He had a high forehead and black hair sprinkled with gray. His lower teeth were gone, his complexion sallow, and his legs spindly. With this doleful description in their hands and other pen pictures from their informants supplementing it, the police hunted high and low for him, by supreme irony also searching for his tormentor of 1795, Méhée de la Touche. Their two files were coupled.

The police searched for him in his apartment but only Nicholas Carles was there. Barère had left, having given notice to the proprietor that he would vacate it on January first. They hunted for him at the home of Madame de Guibert, "with whom he had long been living," the police report stated, and when they finally obtained her correct address, there was no trace of her sometime lover. By January 12, the precinct police threw up their hands: "We cannot find Barère anywhere and the place of his residence is an impenetrable mystery."

Meanwhile, the hunt was extended to the Hautes-Pyrénées and the neighboring departments. Fouché no longer directed it. The ultra-royalists had compelled Louis XVIII to dismiss him, and Decazes was now the minister of police. The police file on Barère would be ludicrous were it not concerned with the life of a wretched fugitive. Rarely were so many errors of fact and false rumors so painstakingly assembled and soberly analyzed. The minister of police in Paris wrote to the prefect of the Hautes-Pyrénées, who conscientiously supplied a store of misinformation in his reply. The prefect of the Hautes-Pyrénées wrote to his colleagues in the Basses-Pyrénées, in the Gironde, in the Haute-Garonne, and in the Lot, they to him and to each other, all to Decazes as regulations required. The local gendarmerie ran around in circles: Barère was certainly somewhere in or about Tarbes, however, his family and friends were thwarting all efforts of the authorities; he was with friends in Bagnères de Bigorre, but had slipped out by a secret passage just before the police had arrived. He was seen in Bordeaux; no, he was concealed, it was now certain, in the chateau of his friend Isaac Tarteyron. By February the gendarmerie reported that he really was in the Hautes-Pyrénées after all, but "in order to deceive the authorities," registered letters kept coming from Paris addressed to his family so as to give the impression that he was in the capital. Then the police reported that he had turned up in Prussia; after that he was in London; and in July of 1816, they quoted the Belgian press to the effect that he was in the Low Countries. As late as 1821, after Barère had in fact been living in Belgium for five years, an office memorandum in the Paris police files solemnly gave the information that he had taken refuge in Prussia, adding lamely that "the ill fame of that person is so notorious that there is no need to go into any details on his score." The police might have spared themselves much trouble if they had reached that conclusion earlier and centered their search in Paris.

Barère did not tempt fate too long in Paris. Since he had no way of getting to the Hautes-Pyrénées, and staying on in Paris could only ultimately end in his being detected, he focused his efforts on escaping from France under false papers. As he tells the story, it was a friend of Nicholas Carles', a former secretary of Fouché's, who contrived somehow to get a passport for him made out in the name of "Barère de Roquefeuille," permitting the bearer to leave France. It is more probable that Decazes knew about the transaction and deliberately winked at the transparent deception, reluctant to have Barère apprehended but relieved not to have him on his own hands any longer. Friends providentially turned up to help and on March 1 secured passage for him and Marguerite in a public coach headed for Belgium. The escape from France was uneventful. Within a week they were in Mons, safely lodged in the apartment of a minor municipal employee who discreetly kept to himself what he knew about the identity of his lodgers.

Barère immediately burned up his passport. Even if he were picked up now it would be by the Belgian authorities, and he would have escaped the Prussians whom he so dreaded. If the mayor of Mons was not too friendly, the police commissioner, to whom he disclosed his identity, refrained from molesting him, and the governor of the province by his forbearance countered the efforts of the Brussels police to have political refugees like Barère deported to Russia or America. In that summer of 1816, Decazes and Richelieu, the latter then minister of foreign affairs, when they picked up reports that Barère was somewhere in Belgium, instructed the French chargé d'affaires to cooperate with the Belgian police in whatever the latter chose to do. Nothing came of their move, either because King William personally interceded for Barère, as the latter claimed, or because the mayor of Mons, according to another account, sheltered the refugee.

After the first year, Barère had little to worry about concerning his security. In fact, for a moment in 1819 his hopes were high that he might benefit from an amnesty that allowed some of the refugees to return to France, but a memorandum in the hand of Decazes, now minister of the interior, specifically advised Louis XVIII not to extend grace either to Carnot or Barère. The uneventful years went by in the small provincial town, and by 1822, Barère had resided at Mons for six years. He was now entitled, under the terms of a new civil law, since he had proven his intention to settle permanently in the kingdom, to the rights of Belgian subjects. He lived quietly during those years, "going to cafés, occasionally attending the theatre and concerts," but prudently refraining from all political activities. His life was secure, but it was dreary and monotonous. They were terribly lonely, he and Marguerite, and his health grew worse. Mons certainly was no place for him with his catarrh and rheumatism and bladder infection. After the unusually severe winter of 1821-1822, when he could benefit from his new civic status, he applied to the authorities for permission to move to Brussels. Brussels was gay and alive; in the Belgian capital many old revolutionaries, fellow-exiles like himself, had settled. Perhaps in Brussels, with the help of "the colony," some way would be found for him to supplement his now almost exhausted resources.

He had no real difficulty in getting permission to take up residence in Brussels. Although it took some time to overcome the misgivings of the attorney general of the high court of Brussels and the minister of justice at The Hague, on May 25, 1822, King William intervened and issued a royal warrant authorizing a provisional stay of three months. A minor flurry arose when Barère failed to register immediately with the police on his arrival on July 1, and the agitated attorney general cautioned the municipal authorities on July 4, "not to overlook the fact that this foreigner . . . merits particular surveillance." The mayor of Brussels assured him, however, that all was well and that Barère was living in an apartment in Section 7, No. 347, on the rue de la Montagne. The incident was closed.

Before the three-month period expired, he petitioned the king for permission to make Brussels his permanent home. Again there were delays, for the minister of justice advised the king to turn down the application. The monarch quietly disregarded the advice and on October 9, "M. Barrère de Roquefeuille," had the precious credentials in his hands. "Monsieur," the mayor's accompanying memorandum stated, "His Excellency, the Governor, informs us that by the resolution of September 18 last, His Majesty has accorded you permission to stay in Brussels until further notice with the right to have your books and personal effects shipped to you."

Barère de Roquefeuille remained in Brussels almost eight years to a day. His health did not improve, his financial embarrassments increased, and he complained endlessly. But the resignation of old age tinctured his lamentations and in his sadness there was mellowness. In one of the last memoranda that he penned, he wrote half-joyously, half-sadly, "Brussels! This is the only place where I ever lived happily. In my extreme old age I still cherished the hope of seeing it again and finishing my days there. . . ." He took many walks through historic Brussels, sauntering with Marguerite through the beautiful Royal Gardens, inspecting public monuments, churches, and famous private homes. On countless slips of paper that were never lacking, he recorded observations about the agriculture and the coal-mining industry of the small kingdom, the high civic spirit of the Bruxellois, their cleanliness and hospitality, their philanthropic and charitable institutes, their orphanages and the homes for the aged. His notes pulsate with life, recalling, after the passage of four decades, the vivid pictures he had once drawn of Paris on the eve of the Revolution.

A celebrity, Barère was sought out by visitors, diplomats and military attachés, financiers, men of the theatre, agents of publishers, and important travellers from abroad. He got to know some Belgian deputies, for the Estates General met alternately at Brussels and The Hague, and to his delight he found he was free to talk politics with them. English visitors solicited interviews, inviting him to dine out. He tells how one of them, Sir Richard Phillips, pressed him in 1825 to retire to England, offering him the hospitality of his own home, a library, and the services of his publisher. He would be well received there, the insistent baronet declared, and the publication of his memoirs would add fortune to his fame. Barère was grateful but unswayed by the invitation. He thought he hated the English, but as his good and kind friend Baudot astutely remarked, "he hated nothing, neither men nor institutions." What kept him from accepting, Baudot thought, was his poor health and his age.

What sustained him most was the affection of Marguerite and the good will of "the colony." Of Marguerite Lefauconnier, his "guardian angel," little can be told: what she looked like, when she first met him, by what promptings of the heart she spent the last twenty-five years of her life with him, sharing the rigors of his exile in Belgium and the sorrows of the last decade in Tarbes. In 1815 she was forty-three years old; she died in September 1840, a few months before his own death, attended to her last days by his unfailing gratitude and love. With the charming old-world gallantry that was his, he always referred to her in his letters and in conversation with their friends as "Mademoiselle Lefauconnier," or "My companion"; with rare tact or perhaps with circumspection he never failed to refer to their son, Henry Alfred, other than as his "nephew."

They were not many in the colony, those aging deported or runaway revolutionaries, but adversity kindled in them memories of the past and linked them together in their decline. The compassionate Marc-Antoine Baudot was one of them, unyielding in his scorn for the more affluent "magnates" like Cambacérès and Thibaudeau, who lived well in exile, and unwavering in his loyalty to the true heroes of '93 and '94. Barère, he thought, was not undeserving of the opinion of his compatriots in the Pyrenees who held him a great man. "Barère was gentle, affable and conciliatory," he wrote. The caustic octogenarian, Marc Guillaume Vadier, garrulous and ebullient to his death at the age of 91, was a pillar of the group. The amnesty law of 1816 had forced the old terrorist of the Committee of General Security to leave Paris, and like Baudot and Barère he too kept the faith. At first there was a cloud between Barère, Vadier, and his friend, Buonarroti. As the years went by, Barère won Vadier's esteem and the affection of Buonarroti. In his last years he had no warmer friend than that dynamic and warmhearted living link between the revolutionary utopian communism of Babeuf and the Marxist communism of the nineteenth century.

Up to Vadier's death in 1828, his daughter Victorine lived with him and his second wife on the rue des Douze Apôtres, where the group so often came together. With them all, with Victorine and her husband, the lawyer Tussau, Barère was joined by bonds of mutual esteem and affection which remained unsevered to the end. Of them all, none was now so dear to him as the celebrated Jacques Louis David with whom he had cooperated as friend and fellow propagandist in the great days of the Terror. As though following a sacred ritual, Barère and the famous painter walked together almost every day in the Royal Park, exchanging memories of a happier past. After dinner, weather and health permitting, the men of the colony foregathered at the Café des Mille Colonnes to talk over the day's happenings. One of the visitors to Brussels who was invited to join them was particularly captivated by the old revolutionist: "Barère monopolized the conversation, talking and listening with the gracious and slightly superior politeness of a man of the Old Regime. Seeing this foreigner, chatting in that way, going out to the theatre and social gatherings in irreproachable attire . . . no one would ever have been able to recognize the terrible *rapporteur* of the Committee of Public Safety." Other visitors too yielded to the charm of the "old man of medium height and sallow complexion but with a lively eye, a gracious smile, exquisite politeness."

Solicitude and the devotion of Marguerite enveloped him; but there were moments when despair was almost unbearable. "Twenty times during my exile," he wrote, "the pen fell from my hands as I thought of my contemporaries, of their natural ingratitude, and their constant indifference. And so I interrupted the writing of my memoirs, having neither esteem nor fear, neither hope nor concern for this reactionary, servile, and venal generation. I went back to work only by directing my thoughts to the youth, the hope of the fatherland, and to the people, that is to say, the lower classes, the sincere and disinterested friends of public liberty." Tired and dispirited, poignantly yearning and dreaming in his vigils for the native soil that he thought he would never see again, the pathetic displaced person foiled despair by writing, by endless writing. He consoled himself with reflections on old age, the human scene, the heart of man, the immortality of the soul. As he had done, three decades before, when he lay in prison in Saintes, he turned for consolation to the comforts of religion, writing a commentary on the Psalms and taking solace in the teachings of Jesus, "the legislator of democracy."

The bitterly cold winters were almost too much for him. Both Baudot and Buonarroti were full of concern about "our friend Barère" in their letters to Vadier's daughter, who with her husband was now in France. During the rigors of 1828-1829 he stayed in bed to keep a little warmth in his poor body. By midsummer of 1829 Buonarroti reported happily that he was "completely recovered," and Baudot thought so too, find-

ing him, "a little depressed [but] ever charming." Charming
no doubt he was, for he could not change his nature. He could
not change the weather either and the following winter was
no less severe. On January 15, 1830, he wrote to the Tussaus
that the cold Siberian winter was unbearable and were it not
for the constant care of "Mademoiselle Lefauconnier" he would
long have been dead. When winter broke up, Buonarroti wrote
with relief, as he had in the preceding year, that the worst was
over: "He is now enjoying the spring  and no longer frightens
his friends." That is what Buonarroti thought, but Barère in
his letter at the end of that same month of May thought otherwise. He wrote to his "very dear and loyal friends" that he had
again stayed in bed for four months: "Spring has returned, but
neither my strength nor my health. I am vegetating, that's the
lot of my age."

Along with dejection and physical frailty, there remained
acute financial stringency. As he wrote to Jean-Pierre in 1822,
he never knew in advance what he would have to live on or
whether he would have enough to last out the next half year.
His own letters of the preceding summer are not available;
those of his brother show that Jean-Pierre's concern was great.
The latter wrote of his "great anxiety [about] the brother
whom I love and esteem more than any one else in the world"
and how happy he had been with "the visit of a young lady"—
the reference was to Victorine—who gave him firsthand news
of the exile. Bertrand would always have a home in Tarbes,
"if ever he is returned to us." Meantime, Jean-Pierre went on,
he was doing his utmost to get Bertrand back but one should
not expect too much help from "men filled with hatred . . .
against the Revolution."

As for financial help, the outlook was not bright. Jean-
Pierre was sending him a draft of 600 francs payable in Paris,
which was probably Bertrand's share of the rental of the old
family home in Tarbes. Otherwise there was little good to report, quite the contrary. The St. Lézer property continued to

be a heavy drain and the costs of keeping it in good repair were prohibitive. There had been an offer of 2,000 francs, which he refused to accept for only two years before he had been offered 8,000. Violent storms had hit the Argelès valley, but fortunately the Anclades property had escaped serious damage. He had tried also to get something from the enormous profits of the resale of the St. Paul property that Bertrand had given up for a pittance. The court at Bagnères had ruled against his petition. Even worse, "cousin Lili"—that was Hector's widow—and her son-in-law were making trouble, insisting that Bertrand repay them mortgage money that Hector had advanced to him in 1795, in "worthless assignats," Jean-Pierre caustically added. Bertrand should not be a fool or a weakling: "I know that you had made loans to Hector and never asked for a reckoning." Why did not Bertrand for his part demand a statement from Lili on the sales of *La liberté des mers* on which he had not received a franc? Jean-Pierre had even tried to have Bertrand's estranged wife pay back the money that had been advanced to her family at the time of their marriage, but she had not deigned to answer his second letter after denying the claim in her first curt and unpleasant reply.

Things grew worse in the following years, and between 1828 and 1830 Barère twice changed lodgings in Brussels, either because he was evicted for non-payment of rent or because he had to look for cheaper quarters. From what one can gather, and the fragmentary correspondence between him and his relatives does not throw much light on the situation, by that date he was not receiving anything at all from the rental of the downstairs apartment of his home in Tarbes. Judging from the records of later court proceedings it seems likely that not only sister Cécile, who held a mortgage of 15,000 francs on the house as her share of the parental heritage, but Jean-Pierre too, who was still living in the upper story, already considered the house their own. Whatever the reason may have been, the devoted brother stopped writing by 1830, and Bertrand was greatly upset. "One thing fills my thoughts," he wrote in a letter that was otherwise exultant because the July revolution had opened to him the prospect of returning to France. "It is your silence. . . . Are you ill? Has some misfortune befallen you? . . . I do not know what to think and fear." Perhaps he suspected the reason; if he did not, he found out soon enough when he did come back to Tarbes that it was indeed absence not presence which made the heart grow fonder. The brother and the three sisters had staked out squatters' rights to his home.

There was one way out of his nightmare, but he did not dare take it. His morbid fears of being deported kept him from accepting all the offers he received to sell his manuscripts. When he was dead would be time enough, he repeated over and over to Baudot; he wished to end his days in peace. Those fears of deportation were probably groundless; they were not less frantic for being implausible. As a matter of fact, the police were harrying him, and he may even have locked himself in at night, as he alleges, against possible house search and arrest. There is nothing to show that he was anonymously contributing political articles to the Brussels press, but since insinuations were raised to that effect, he wrote to the king to protest his innocence. He persisted in not taking the way out. Had he accepted any one of the offers that were made for the manuscripts, he would have had more than enough for his needs. A firm of German publishers, Treuttel and Würtz, were willing to go as high as 50,000 francs for the whole and the Parisian publisher, Baudouin, offered him 10,000 francs a volume. He turned down all offers, convinced that they were traps that the French police in connivance with the Belgian were setting for him to have the needed pretext to expel him.

Though he also refused to sell the precious books that he had shipped from Paris to Mons and from Mons to Brussels, there were still some oil paintings and *objets d'art* on which something could be realized. In January 1828, he sold a Houdon bust of Mirabeau to the great Paris banker, Jacques Lafitte, and the 600 francs he received in payment tided him over and paid off current debts. Then Marguerite twice performed a miracle and turned up ready cash. He repaid her scrupulously by liquidating more of his tangible art assets. On February 1, 1828, by a notarized declaration he bequeathed to her "six silver services marked with my arms . . . as well as two gold [repeater] watches . . . and eight small silver coffee spoons, in payment of the sum of 900 francs which . . . Mademoiselle Lefauconnier advanced to me in Brussels for my maintenance and expenses." Three months later in that same year, on May 3, he ceded to her two paintings, one, Leonardo da Vinci's "The Amours and Leda," most certainly a copy, and the other, "Diana's Repose," by an artist whose name is undecipherable, both of them, his attestation read, in his room on the first floor, on the rue Neuve where he was living. "This bequest . . . is made in compensation and payment of the sum of 800 francs that the aforesaid Mademoiselle Margeritte [sic] Lefauconnier advanced and provided for my expenses during my exile in Brussels in the month of February of this year, the money coming from the inheritance of her older brother, Pierre Henry Lefauconnier, deceased in Paris."

Privation, ill health, old age, the trying winters, nerves on edge, would there be no end? There was no end to his afflictions; only one additional pain to bear, the stubborn refusal of contemporary writers to clear his name. Many of the old pamphlets and memoirs of the Thermidorian reaction were reprinted, Vilate's thesaurus of vilification and Louvet's diatribe among them. Though Dumouriez in his *Mémoires* recalled "the gentle, amiable and esteemed" young deputy whom he knew in the days of the Constituent Assembly, an editorial footnote reminded the readers that "We find his name on almost every shameful and sanguinary page of the Revolution." Thibaudeau, who had tried hard to have him deported, did not conceal his hatred for a fellow exile. Granted that in the posthumously published souvenirs of Durand-Maillane, a Girondin turned royalist, there was grudging acknowledgment that Barère had been "ill-rewarded for his zeal and his toil," that was not much by way of rehabilitation.

The makers of biographical encyclopedias meantime continued to pour the old sour wine of defamation into new bottles. He received short shrift in the *Biographie moderne* of 1815 and his name was included that same year in the *Dictionnaire des girouettes*. To be sure, in the following year the *Dictionnaire des braves et des non-girouettes* listed him among the men who were not weathervanes, but the brief treatment of his career, while it conceded that he was a good patriot, added that his patriotism was born of fear. The notice in the *Biographie des hommes vivants* (1816-1819) did not concede that much, contending that "his associates of the Committee of Public Safety had profound contempt for him," while the *Biographie nouvelle des contemporains* of 1820 pointedly contrasted his "gentleness" during the early days of the Revolution to his behavior during the Convention, "when human pusillanimity was never carried so far."

The proto-historians of those years did not enhance his reputation, neither H. Lemaire in a three-volume *Histoire de la Révolution française* of 1816, nor R. J. Durdent in a seven-volume *Histoire de la Convention nationale* (1816-1817), which carried repeated references to his "perfidious" speeches and relied heavily on Vilate for his private life. The brief *France sous le règne de la Convention nationale* by the arch-royalist, Conny de la Faye, echoed most of the horror stories of 1795, also using Vilate as its source. Among the historians more worthy of respect, Madame de Staël did not so much as mention his name in her *Considérations* of 1817, which, in the prevailing mood was probably more blessing than insult. The sober treatment in Mignet's *Histoire de la Révolution française* balanced recognition of his irreproachable personal life and moderation of spirit with regrets over the weakness of character that led him to condone the dictatorship. Thiers, who also published his detailed history of the Revolution in those mid-years of the twenties, found little good to say about Barère, making much, on the contrary, of his scandalous and profligate life.

What those liberal historians in their detachment lacked, the royalist J. G. M. Roques de Montgaillard, old friend of Barère, possessed—the warmth of human charity. In the fourth volume of the nine which he consecrated to the history of his country, he made almost all the statutory references to the horrors and the madness of the Terror and Barère's unhappy talent for dressing crime in pleasing colors. Then musing sadly over the evil that the revolutionary cyclone had inflicted upon men whose hearts were pure but whose characters were weak, he paid affectionate tribute to the Barère that he had known. "Yet," he wrote, using the historical present, "Barère is naturally gentle, his ways are polished, his heart is good. . . . Cupidity, avarice, ambition do not hold him in grip. . . . Capable of the most noble resolution, the most generous deeds, he hides the proscribed and exposes himself personally to great dangers. He saves the lives of several of his compatriots [of the Hautes-Pyrénées], of a host of royalists. All nobles, all suspects who solicit his protection, his generosity, are shielded against proscription. . . . He sacrificed, scattered the larger part of his ancestral fortune for the Revolution. In control of immense resources . . . he returned that credit intact to the Committee. . . . He was cast into exile in 1816, poor, almost naked." These pages Barère also read, as he had Mignet and Thiers, which he found detestable; yet for their crumbs of fairness, he had no praise.

All avenues of escape from his plight seemed blocked and he had practically given up hope for a kinder future when the news of the overwhelmingly anti-government elections of 1828 rekindled his spirits. Drawing upon a seemingly inexhaustible fund of vitality, he took up his pen and on March 29 he was writing to General Lafayette advising him that it would be worthy of "the elected and national Chamber of 1828" to rescind the proscription of 1816 and by a general measure legalize the return of every Frenchman who had been banished or exiled without trial. Though he could not know whether or not that national Chamber, "which is the hope and bulwark of the country," would pass that enabling legislation, he owed it to himself, his fellow exiles, and the honor of France, to write to "the friend and companion in arms of the immortal Washington." After the appeal to Lafayette who, he was sure, had not forgotten their old relations during the Constituent Assembly and Napoleon's Hundred Days, he showered others with letters in 1829 and 1830, in all of them begging for a passport to return to France.

The news of "the three glorious days" of July 1830, when the hated regime of the returned Bourbons collapsed, filled his cup: "The finest page in the history of France; I still believe that I am dreaming when I think of those unforeseen events which overthrew tyranny like a bolt of thunder. . . . I shall quit life without regrets now, after having seen Frenchmen free and happy." This was in mid-August and for almost another month he wrote letters in that vein, not forgetting practical things in his joy, such as being remembered to Lafayette, "the great citizen who has given proofs of his devotion to liberty in the two worlds," and asking that a friend find him lodgings in Paris where he was confident he would soon be.

The breathless expectations were not deceived; the miracle of the revolution was real and the July Monarchy did extend an amnesty to the proscribed terrorists. Precious passport in hand he was free once more to go where he willed, free to return home. In September 1830, he was back in Paris, planning to make the capital a way station on the long road to Tarbes. He thought that his tribulations at last were over. Soon he would be with his family, sheltered against want, surrounded by the love of his relatives. In his seventy-fifth year the indestructible old man prepared to tie together the broken threads of his life. He still looked to the future.

# ✠ X I X ✠

# *The Last Years,*
# *1830-1841*

IF THE future to which Barère looked forward proved the final disillusionment in a long series of disappointments, he already had some misgivings before he left Brussels. The July revolution had opened prospects for sweeping changes in the political scene but they were not being realized. As Barère recorded in his notes, the inexperienced deputies, who were his hope for the future and the hope of his country, were as weak and inept as the Girondins. They were political cobblers, he sneered, patching up the worn-out ideas of 1814. The expectation that under their guidance France would complete the democratic program of the great Revolution of 1789 died as quickly as his spirits had soared over the dramatic news of the overthrow of the government of Charles X.

He found lodgings near the Marché St. Honoré, not far from the old monastery where the Jacobins had held their meetings. Whatever that portended, his infirmities decided his immediate course before he could act. Excitement and exertions sapped his strength and he took to his bed, physically and emotionally prostrated from the strain of his return. When, after four months, he recovered sufficiently to follow the parliamentary debates, he could only look on as a spectator from the visitors' galleries, listening to phrases that disheartened him by their vacuity.

It had been fifteen years since Barère had seen Paris. At no time, not even when his renown was at its height, had he been completely at his ease in the ways of "the great Babylon," his sardonic term for the capital. There had always been something of the provincial's disapproval in his response to the excitement and the charm of the city of light. The rejected and ailing old man now found Paris utterly hateful, all the more perhaps because the outbreak of the cholera epidemic forced him to stay on, not for the brief moment that he had contemplated to break his journey to Tarbes but for almost two years.

In the course of those years he wrote sketches of Parisian life and ways, entitling them *Le Tartare à Paris, tablettes parisiennes.* As the title suggested, *The Persian Letters* of Montesquieu, whom he greatly admired, were his model. Though Usbek and Rica were the prototype of his Tartar, they had failed to communicate their vivacity and wit to their fellow Oriental traveller. Barère's mouthpiece was a carping and querulous fellow who scolded his monotonous way through the 625 folios generously placed at his disposal. He walked along the streets of the capital, the outlying suburbs too, entered many shops, but saw nothing save bagatelles, playthings, and toys. It was as though Paris were inhabited by grown-up children. All was affectation and artifice; the conventions of social intercourse crushed the soul and the body alike. The real god of the Parisians was gold, the players on the human scene imposture and lies in carnival dress. For people of quality, there was a closed universe of their own where they worshipped the luxuries of dress, dwellings, and adornment; the remainder of the population, scorned and rejected, lived outside it. And so the account ran from its opening words, "Paris, center of the richest mine of vices, shortcomings, things ridiculous, strange and corrupt manners," to the end of its scolding.

The Tartar-Barère was too bitter to temper vituperation, too alienated for irony, too old and set in his ways to have eyes for the painters whose heroic canvases went beyond neoclassicism, to listen to the music of a revolutionary Berlioz, to read the masterpieces of the rebellious romantic poets. Steeped in classical authors, Barère's Tartar did not so much as mention the literary battle over Victor Hugo's *Hernani* or the protests of Musset against old classical forms. Before he left the capital in mid-1832, Barère dropped the disguise and said farewell to Paris in petulant doggerel that makes up in exasperation what it lacks in art.

> Farewell Paris, joyous site
> Of love and play and laughter light.
> Farewell Paris, seat of sorrow,
> Where good men dread to face the morrow.
> I've had enough of empty praise,
> Of your pleasures and your ways,
> Of your sycophants bold,
> Of your writers cold,
> Of your many upstarts shameless,
> Of your feted idlers, aimless.
> Farewell! I shall seek with all my might
> Men in France who are upright.

So he wrote of Paris in the disappointment of his return. Actually, he loved the sophistication he professed to despise, he was wretched because he could no longer enjoy it. In a letter of these very years he gave praise to Paris in spite of himself as "the best of possible cities, the center of the most refined and highest civilization," and a few years later in 1836, when in its turn Tarbes depressed him, as well it might have, he wrote to the young son of the old revolutionary general, Pelleport, "One can live only in the great, new Babylon [but] you must be young, strong and rich. . . ."

If complaints gave relief, once Barère regained his strength he refused to accept the status of a superannuated actor. He took steps, while he was still in Paris, to have his name put on the lists as a duly qualified voter of his department, and presently he announced himself as a candidate for election to the departmental council of the Hautes-Pyrénées. From Paris he made a first preliminary electoral appeal, an *Adresse* to his former constituents which freshened their memories on the last political activities in which he had engaged when the empire fell and the Bourbons returned. He recounted how he had protested the establishment of the hereditary peerage (which was not true), challenged the constitutionality of Louis XVIII's Charter, and attacked "the shameful restoration . . . which had been imposed upon France by bayonets." Back in Tarbes, where he campaigned actively, or as actively as a man of his years could, he had reprinted the *Observations* that he wrote in 1789 on the decisive part he had taken in establishing the department of the Hautes-Pyrénées. He prefaced the old tract with a new introduction and bid directly for political support in this *Notice*.

The magic of a name that had won him so many elections before did not fail him on this occasion, and "Bertrand Barère, proprietor," was returned to the council general of the Hautes-Pyrénées in the 1833 elections. The prefect of the department made his report on February 14, 1834, to the minister of the interior: "The result of the elections is extremely satisfactory, for among the elected councillors, there is only one who may be considered an enemy of our institutions. That is Barère whose election is the sole noteworthy fact." Noteworthy indeed, since Barère had not concealed his views on "the bragging of priests and royalists" in one of his letters to Tussau.

Though there was little he could do in his councillorship beyond voice or write down his complaints, he clung to "the shield of his old age" almost to the end of his life. The position gave him a margin of political security along with a great deal of emotional satisfaction. He sputtered in his little memoranda about the chicanery of the government and the reactionary spirit of his contemporaries. In foreign policy the deputies fumed against the treaties of 1815, but pursued a policy of peace at any price, serving as gendarmes of the Holy Alliance. In domestic affairs their liberties were on paper. While they did lip-service to popular sovereignty, the government effectively controlled elections: "They take pride in two revolutions made by the working classes and the youth, but those who contributed nothing to them exploited the revolutionaries. The brave were in the grave, the profiteers in power." If the ineffectiveness of the left-of-center liberals depressed him, the smugness of the Doctrinaires, the more conservative liberals who followed Guizot, infuriated him: "They are an arrogant and inexorable party with hatred and contempt for all social institutions that liberty inspires, a sect of persecutors and enemies of all the noble needs of the times, a faction recruited from the upper and middle classes of society possessing fervent but stupid auxiliaries [in] credulous men, ignorant and fanatical men who are full of fear. This faction of the [political] opposition has faith neither in the country nor in liberty; it denies the moral and intellectual movement which is agitating France and it would govern only through the peace of the grave." His spleen was great, his judgment of the Doctrinaires not inaccurate.

Very crotchety, however, he wanted it both ways, to damn the government and get honors from it. He was outraged that he was not named to the Legion of Honor. With heavy irony he wrote to Pelleport in 1836, "As for me, who committed the crime of celebrating the great deeds of the French soldiers and the triumph of our armies of 1793 and 1794, no doubt I am not going to be named." If those outbursts were expressions of thwarted expectations, still there was something wonderful about his rancor. The fervor of the Year II was not extinguished in the crusty octogenarian of the 1830's. After serving six years in the council of the department, when he was eighty-four years old he judged it time to withdraw from political life. Though he took pains to inform his cousin Dintrans in November 1839, that he was not going to resign his position to make room for a reactionary, in February 1840, he finally resigned, writing again to Dintrans, "I am quite content henceforth to be nothing in the political world. [It was proper] to have an interval of rest, meditation and prayer between mortal life and life eternal." He retired from politics more than a half-century after he began his career, on his own immediate terms and with a flourish.

He was still reading widely, still writing his garrulous notes in these years, still "the register-man," that one of his Belgian friends had called him, but his time had certainly come as the new decade opened. Tussau thought that his health was good and one of his few friends in Tarbes reported that he had no serious infirmities, which was no doubt so, but he was very old and his life force was slowly ebbing. Even walking was becoming difficult; and he sat in his armchair, wrapped in a heavy blanket, waiting for death to take him. He could bear the presence of "the litigious and envious Tarbais, greedy and pretentious"; he accepted his fate to frighten children who ran from his presence "as if they had seen the devil."

It was the ingratitude of his close relatives that had hurt him most deeply. It was their greed and inhumanity which rankled in those last years. The claims of cousin Lili were an old story, but he had not expected that his brother and his sisters would also take advantage of his misfortune. The return of the exile was more than an unexpected shock to them; it was an affront. Not only had he come back, but he returned with an alien woman, and it was in her interest that he contested the squatters' rights the clan had established to the parental home. He was nearing eighty in 1834, a poor wreck, when Jean-Pierre and sister Cécile, the widow Lassalle, filed suit to have the court declare them the rightful proprietors of the home that they had been occupying for more than thirty years. Since their claims were flimsy, they must never have believed that he would either have the strength or obtain the means of contesting them. The providence on which he counted again came to his rescue, and a friendly and able young lawyer, Maître Lebrun, volunteered to take the case without a fee.

The appellants claimed that between 1801 and 1803 Barère had consented to the sale of his house on the rue Bourg Vieux in return for 15,000 francs, the amount of his debt to them jointly. If the court ruled that the house had not been sold, then they filed for reimbursement of the debt, petitioning in that case to be allowed to remain in possession and be declared co-proprietors by virtue of the fact that Barère had never given them their share of the patrimony. In rebuttal the defense introduced evidence which attested "in the most positive and categorical way" that the house had never ceased being Barère's. Among "the prodigious number of documents" was a letter dated 1823, that its recipient, Jean-Pierre, did not challenge, in which Bertrand had written that his younger brother "was making use of my house, my furnishings, my books. . . ." As for their claim to a share of the legacy, even the appellants' attorney was forced to admit that Bertrand alone, by virtue of the father's bequest on the occasion of his marriage, was the sole heir and proprietor of the paternal home.

The court threw out the claim, holding that Bertrand was in fact the proprietor, and ordered the claimants to vacate the premises forthwith. It also dismissed the claims for reimbursement and condemned them to pay the expenses of the legal proceedings. Immensely grateful to Maître Lebrun, Barère wrote to his "honorable defender," presenting to him in lieu of the money that he did not have and in place of the fee that Lebrun would not take, a framed oil painting which he cherished. It was the one that "the immortal David" had made of him at the trial of Louis XVI.

It was a great triumph, this verdict of August 9, a fine birthday present. The house was his to use as he judged proper and honorable, and by a notarized declaration six months later, on December 31, he made his intention clear to use it to reimburse Marguerite for almost twenty years of "care, help and service that she had rendered him in good health and ill" from 1815 to the present. He owed her, this was his scrupulous reckoning, 7,500 francs calculated at the rate of 400 francs per annum. Since he lacked the financial means to give her that feeble mark of his deep devotion "because of the lawsuits that his collateral relatives had filed against him," he was herewith making arrangements to have that sum paid to her in two equal instalments after his death, with interest of course, and without prejudice to any additional money that would be due her for services after the date of the declaration. As security, he had the house and adjacent grounds at No. 36, rue Bourg Vieux, a garden on the rue des Petits Fossés also in Tarbes, and "a farm . . . situated at Anclades, commune of Lourdes, consisting of buildings, arable land and meadows."

Marguerite did not outlive him, fortunately for her own security. His generous provisions could not be observed. Sometime after February 1837, he was forced "to put the paternal house up for sale." Perhaps earlier still he lost the St. Lézer property to the collaterals, when exactly one cannot say, for the court records of the proceedings at Lourdes, where the verdict was rendered, have disappeared. In the spring of 1835, soon after he had provided for Marguerite, he mentioned in a letter to Merlin de Douai that he had lawsuits on his hands, while later that year Buonarroti received a letter from Tussau informing him that "poor M. Roquefeuille is not happy; he has lawsuits to contest against greedy collaterals who would strip him of what still remains from all the misfortunes that have struck him." "Not happy!" He was outraged to the depths of his feelings. "My Family," he put at the head of a terrible apostrophe:

> Get thee gone, relatives with hard litigious hearts!
> Get thee gone, covetous and ungrateful collaterals!
> Providence is not for you!
> Get thee gone and curses on you!

In the meantime, while the family house was still his and Marguerite provided for, he also made provision for their son. His declaration was breathless, scorning grammar and orthography: "To pay homage to the truth and to avoid all disputes, I, the undersigned Bertrand Barère de Vieuzac, resident of Tarbes in my house on the rue Bourg Vieux, declare that all furnishings designated and described below and to be found in the room on the ground floor of my house, belong in full ownership to M. Henry Alfred Lefauconnier, native of Paris, married at Tarbes, and living with me. . . ." Then with great meticulousness he itemized the treasured possessions that he was bequeathing: "A walnut bed, three mattresses, a pallet, a pillow, a cover or quilted coverlet of crimson or amaranth cloth, a mahogany clock, a large painted and gilt old Sevres cup, a small Sevres soup tureen, two armchairs in Aubusson point, a square walnut table, a walnut wardrobe, a framed engraving of Ossian with a gilded border, two small paintings on wood, a pair of andirons, a shovel and tongs, an old silver watch, also twenty-two soup bowls with their lids, two plates, six coffee cups and six saucers, all in old Sevres porcelain, a large landscape painting on canvas." He had forgotten something, and he added in a postscript: "Plus a round mahogany table and two little oval sketches framed in gilded copper, these two objects having been omitted in the above inventory of the furnishings belonging to M. Henry Alfred Lefauconnier, drawn up at Tarbes, the same day of the first of February 1837."

Whatever it was, visceral urge, *noblesse oblige*, or sense of justice, that drove him to ensure the future for Marguerite and her son, vital forces kept him from selling the manuscripts of his memoirs while he was alive. The fears by which he had been obsessed in Belgium still remained and he begged for pensions from officials of a government he despised. For some years he received a pittance from the ministry of justice, judging from available fragmentary evidence, though it is probable that it did not come regularly. There was a letter to the keeper of the seals, dated New Year's Day, 1838. "Monsieur minister, it is to you that I owe the grant-in-aid of five hundred francs as a former magistrate. Aged eighty-three, I hope you will agree to continue this grant which is necessary for me for the year 1838. I beg you to accept my good wishes at the beginning of the year for the continuation and the prosperity of your ministry. I am, with respect, monsieur minister, keeper of the seals, your very humble and very obedient servitor, B. Barère de Vieuzac." From the reminder to himself which can still be read through the erasure, "to send on January 1, 1838," it was clear that the begging appeal had been composed earlier and he was waiting for the most favorable moment to mail it. Fortune was with him on this occasion; an annotation in another hand in the upper left corner of his note reads: "To continue 500, January 23, 1838." Two years later, in all likelihood, he was less fortunate for on February 21, 1840, there was a complaining letter to Dintrans that he should be receiving help as an ex-magistrate.

Before that date he had obtained a small pension from the ministry of the interior in his capacity as a former man of letters. A communication to Thiers in June 1834, dripping with honeyed dishonesty, heaped praise upon "the distinguished historian," whose volumes on the Revolution Barère had dismissed in a private gibe, and reminded the minister that he had been led to hope that Thiers would grant him a literary pension now available. The reminder was not needed. Thiers had already taken favorable action, but his decision must have crossed in the mail with Barère's appeal. A rough office memorandum with the annotation on it "to copy" reads as follows: "My attention has been called to the financial position of M. Bertrand Barère, former member of the National Convention, and I desire to relieve it. You will find herewith in consequence a draft of 800 francs which I beg you to remit to him and have him sign a receipt drawn up in this way: 'I have received from monsieur the minister of the interior a sum of 800 francs in compensation for my former political position and my actual financial condition.' "

Barère also received this pension during the two following years, but there is no clue from his letters confirming the receipt of the money as to whether a quid pro quo was part of the arrangement. It is alleged that the secret files of the ministry for 1836 listed his name among "the espionage agents or journalists working for the regime." Presumably he was drawing 400 francs per year for his services. If some understanding was reached for him to serve the government of Louis-Philippe in the same role that he had once discharged for Napoleon, which is not in itself impossible, the evidence to prove it is meager. In any case the government had the worst of the arrangement. At the age of eighty-one Barère lacked the strength if not the inclination to stoop.

Most important of all, he was receiving a regular pension of 1,000 francs drawn on the privy purse of the king himself. As Carnot, the editor of the *Mémoires*, tells the story, Louis-Philippe, in 1833, made indirect contact with his father's old friend and revolutionary associate, ostensibly seeking explicit information from a man in a position to give it about the circumstances of the death of his father, the Duke of Orléans. In reality, according to Carnot, Louis-Philippe was tactfully using a pretext to befriend Barère financially without offending his sensibilities by open charity. If such were the case, and the request for information a subterfuge, the delicacy was matched by Barère's own sense of what was fitting and appropriate for him to tell the ruler whom he had known well as the young Duke of Chartres. In a memorandum now no longer available but which Carnot says he saw, Barère refrained from saying that what in his judgment was perhaps the greatest single factor in undermining the Duke of Orléans' standing as a good patriot and ensuring his condemnation to the guillotine was his son's defection to the Austrians in the spring of 1792.

Solicitous of royal feelings, Barère diplomatically fixed the blame for the tragedy upon the plotting of the Machiavellian émigrés whose sentiments toward Orléans were notoriously less cordial than the normal affection of cousins for each other.

There is certainly more to the story as Carnot gives it. One would wish to know the identity of "the former employee of the Committee of Public Safety" who from his post in the king's cabinet called his royal master's attention to Barère's needs. If the heart of Louis-Philippe was in fact touched by memories of the old man whom he remembered from his youth as the handsome guardian of "la belle Paméla," his father's natural daughter, one would still wish to know what else Louis-Philippe remembered, how much he himself knew of the relations between Orléans and Barère. Most of all one would wish to have details about the mysterious relations themselves. Whatever the reasons for his generosity, once the friendly contact was established, the relations between prince and pauper remained cordial to the end.

Though the direct evidence is scant, there can be no doubt that Barère received the pension regularly. On January 9, 1837, he wrote to Baron Fain, requesting the intermediary between himself and the king to transmit his thanks and devotion to His Majesty; in February 1840, he wrote to Dintrans, expressing his appreciation of "the agreeable things you report concerning monsieur, the Duke of Orléans [the king's son] to whom his august father had spoken about me." The likelihood exists that Barère received more than the annual pension, for on June 9 of the same year, he sent a complaining letter to Dintrans: "I wrote to His Majesty on his birthday; at a similar period of the year I had received *a generous response*." This year, seemingly, His Majesty was remiss, for Barère wished Dintrans to intercede again: "I lack the means to survive the year 1840."

From those several pensions he was receiving at most between 1,900 and 2,300 francs a year, a total considerably less than the 3,000 francs that the election rolls of 1833 indicated as his annual income. And after 1833 he had lost the income from most of his real property. The total was wretchedly small to defray the living expenses and medical care for himself and the Lefauconniers. His begging letters were abject, but beggars have no choice.

There was an unexpected increment, even if he could not live on it: the income of good will from writers about the Revolution. From them he fared better than he had for many years. The publications which in one way or another referred to his revolutionary past were few in this decade, and only in the *Memoirs* of General Dumas and the *Biographie universelle* were the allusions unreservedly hostile. The dour Carlyle held him at arm's length, it is true, calling him "an indispensable fellow in the great Art of Varnish," but even in his ironically contemptuous evaluation there was an undertone of friendliness: "Ingenious Barère is one of the usefulest men of this Convention in his way. Truth may lie on both sides, on either side, or on neither side; my friends, 'Ye must give and take: for the rest, success to the winning side.' This is the motto of Barère. Ingenious, almost genial, quick-sighted, supple, graceful, a man that will prosper."

In his *Recollections of Mirabeau*, Dumont considered Barère "of a mild and amiable temper. . . . [His later course was] less the effect of an evil disposition than that of a timid and versatile character. . . ." The *Encyclopédie des gens du monde* denied that impulses of self-aggrandizement prompted him during the days of the Constituent Assembly and was outspoken in its appreciation of his constant zeal for the revolutionary cause. It defended him against the charges that cowardice alone had swayed him during the Convention. During the crisis of 1815 he was outstanding for his "wisdom and moderation," and it wrote almost lyrically of how the sexagenarian bristled with martial fervor when the enemy was at the gates of Paris. Among French historians, the Christian socialists, Buchez and

Roux, devoted many favorable pages to him in their valuable and widely read *Histoire parlementaire*. Leonard Gallois, in his monumental *Histoire de la Convention nationale,* while characterizing Barère as weak, also stressed his astounding and many-sided contribution. For Gallois' assessment in particular Barère was grateful, and he wrote his thanks to the defender of his good name.

While he begged for remittances to sustain himself and his dependents, he was also meeting payments on various debts, "principal and interest." One dated back forty years to the time that he had borrowed 16,000 francs from his father's friend, Abbé Gauderat. There was another that he owed to his "dear old friend" of the days of the Terror, Dr. Souberbielle, to whom he wrote in April 1839, happy that providence had prolonged his days to permit him to arrange for semi-annual payments of "a sacred debt:" "You were very generous to me in my need long years ago." To meet those obligations he sold remaining objects of art that a friend was keeping for him in Paris. With the obsessive miserliness of the aged living precariously on doles, he concealed his assets and hoarded little savings that he put aside for Marguerite. And finally with the utmost reluctance, he resigned himself to selling a great stock of his manuscripts. There were enough, his letter of July 22, 1836, to Leonard Gallois indicated, to make forty octavo and duodecimo volumes of political, philosophical, and literary studies, three more of political maxims, and two of his secret reports to Napoleon. "I shall deal only on a strictly cash basis . . . on account of my age and because I have no direct heirs," he wrote. "My memoirs [however] call for other arrangements. I shall finish them if my health, which is that of a man past eighty, will permit."

Health did permit and other arrangements were made. In Belgium he had been obsessed by fears that publication of his memoirs during his lifetime would lead to his deportation; in Tarbes he was afraid that the definitive manuscript which he was preparing for posthumous publication would be mutilated and denatured. With fixed resolution, utmost secrecy, and close attention to details, he looked about to find an editor whom he could trust. He found not one but two editors whose good will and integrity reassured him that posterity would receive his appeal as he himself was couching it.

One was the sculptor David d'Angers, bearing the same name as Barère's cherished friend but not related to the great painter. It is not known when or how they first met, most likely during the Belgian period, and by the time Barère was back in Tarbes they knew each other well. The other was Hippolyte Carnot, the son of his colleague of the Committee of Public Safety, Lazare Carnot, for whom Barère's affection was even greater than his regard for David. On the chronology of their acquaintance a little more is known. They saw each other for the first time in Paris during the Hundred Days and their friendship was sealed in Belgium where Carnot visited his father's old colleague. It was the young Carnot who welcomed Barère to Paris in 1830. After seeing him several times in Tarbes and after many interviews and much urging, Carnot was prevailed upon, jointly with David, to undertake the task which Barère pressed upon them.

They reached a preliminary understanding in 1837 and in the spring of the following year were actively corresponding and working out the final details. On March 7 Barère wrote to David, gratified that the two men had accepted his proposals to buy the literary rights to his political manuscripts and autographs. Although his attorney advised that there might be some legal difficulties if the private deed of sale were signed by him in Tarbes and by them in Paris, he would not permit them to send a proxy through the mails. Aware better than they how little the privacy of the mails was observed in his home town, he would not have "the litigious and envious" Tarbais learn about his affairs. So he wondered whether Carnot could come to Tarbes again to sign the private deed. There was also a mild reproach in the letter: David had spoken too freely to a M. Montaut, who had been keeping the precious manuscript in his home. To be sure, Montaut had been kind, but Barère was not altogether certain of his discretion. This warning apart, he was very happy over the agreement, happy that the proceeds from the publication would benefit "the two persons who are tenderly watching over [my] old age with steadfast and affectionate care."

By that time, it appears, the manuscript of "Le dernier jour de Paris sous l'Ancien Régime," was already in David's possession, for in a subsequent letter Barère enclosed brief addenda to the text and authorized David and Carnot "to delete, change and abridge" whatever they judged best. It was then, after he had received two letters from them, that he wrote a long and grateful response on May 18 to the "faithful, enlightened and upright patriots" in which he again enjoined upon them the utmost secrecy and gave his final instructions about publication. The private deed of sale was to be made out in triplicate but without specific mention of any sale price, "such, for instance, as 12,000-15,000 francs." Only the word "receipt" was to be written in the deed. His attorney was sure that a contract thus drawn up, while not requiring registration, would give them legal protection. As for the profit they might make from their editing of his manuscript or its resale he hoped that they would agree to divide half of it between themselves and have the other half divided among the Lefauconniers and Montaut. If they did not object, he would confirm the understanding under separate cover.

He explained at length and with intense emotion, also with a pinch of falsehood, why he was acting in that extraordinarily secretive manner: "I have no children, only collateral relatives, and their share [of his estate] was in my real property." He had taken steps to provide for his heir and have the remaining debts paid off from the sale of his personal and real property. He had not even mentioned in his will how he was disposing of his manuscript so as to leave no "public trace either to the authorities or claimants. . . . My thoughts and my intellectual works are my exclusive and sacred property. . . . They are *works beyond the grave,* according to Chateaubriand's expression. I am entrusting them to your keeping to avoid having them spoiled and altered by ignorant, petty, ambitious men of our day." Then came a blast against Parisian editors and publishers: "Swindlers . . . who change and denature everything, *arrangers of memoirs* who substitute their venal passions for truth and principles."

The letter reached them without delay, and they answered on May 23, accepting the arrangements which they pledged themselves to carry out with "religious piety." On one condition, they added. The generous terms concerning their share in the division of royalty rights, they pointed out, were excessive, and they felt free not to take advantage of "the goodness of your heart." At the bottom of their letter another hand affixed a note: "All the proceeds were sent to the heirs of Barère." The long, drawn-out negotiations came to a close with Barère's letter of June 7 in which he confirmed the arrangements.

The *Mémoires* were published between 1842 and 1844, and if their reception was mixed, the fault was not that of the editors. Carnot, busy with other matters, did not himself prepare the manuscript for publication. He turned over the routine work of making a fair copy for the printer to two professional journalists, who worked under his supervision. With the exception of one section, such changes as were made were stylistic emendations not affecting the substance of the manuscript. The published *Mémoires* were pure Barère, as pure as the copy he left. The details they supply about his person and family, like those concerning his public career, are precious, but their use calls for constant vigilance. The many minor errors that stem from lapses of memory are not serious flaws and may be forgiven him. The willful omissions and distortions, exceeding even the generous quota that by convention is allotted to writers of memoirs, are more serious. In a way, one can almost regret that Barère did not take the manuscript to the grave with him. In the great days of the Year II he had lied patriotically, in the grand manner, deceiving millions, but lying impersonally for the Cause, the Goal, for the Revolution whose interests transcended the morality of individuals. In the *Mémoires*, when he lied, he did so abjectly and cravenly, about himself and to himself. In that self-deception there would have been no harm, if only he had burned his pages after he had written them. The protracted dialogue between the shattered wreck that he was and the heroic figure he might have been and the upright man he convinced himself he was, served its purpose in the writing itself. The words he put on paper warmed him as he wrote them. The self-righteousness of his apologia, the false modesty and disinterestedness, the carping complaints and the petty pinpricks were a requiem for a broken life. They were not true to his better nature, nor the certificate of his achievement. They were the balm for failure, a release for dejection, relief from pain and despair he could not escape. They made reality bearable; with that boon he might have been content.

As for the staggering mass of other papers that remained, Carnot made scant use of them, dipping in them only enough to round out his running story of Barère's life in the "Historical Introduction" that served as a preface to the *Mémoires*. They were myriad, those scratchy memoranda, some on small slips of paper, others on large folios, many almost impossible to decipher, that filled the two large wooden packing boxes which finally made their way to the departmental archives in Tarbes. At a rough estimate, there are well over 20,000 separate entries in the *Fonds Barère*. Carnot, a decade after he had discharged his responsibility, was asked about their value. He wrote back: "You ask me if these papers, which I looked at when the *Mémoires* of Barère were published, could be gone through again with an eye to a new work. I do not think so, or at least, the few interesting things that one could extract would hardly be worth the trouble. They are only notes, extremely numerous, but completely disorderly." Carnot was a busy man. Perhaps under the pressure of other obligations, he dismissed their worth too cavalierly. The memoranda are no longer in the disorder that appalled him, but it may be, though now inventoried and calendared, they only reveal more clearly how repetitious and prolix they are and how banal he was in thought. Yet, to characterize them in a phrase as banal as they themselves were, the whole is greater than the sum of the parts. The endless platitudes weave a pattern and recreate the mood of their composition.

Many of the bundled notes can be dated with reasonable accuracy, either from internal evidence or because Barère supplied the year in which he wrote them. Most were begun in the Belgian exile a few earlier, some completed after he returned to France. What it pleased him to call "Méditations" is the small coin of the Enlightenment in which he was nurtured, a blurred carbon copy of the tenets of the Age of Reason. The testament of an unoriginal mind, they also reveal that his interest in things of the spirit did not flag. His industry remained prodigious. In the 1820's he began a scrapbook, "Notes on books to study, consult, abstract and procure in the large public libraries"; in the late 1830's he was still recording titles of books in French, Italian, and English that he should read. Thousands of notes showed how earnestly and seriously he kept improving his mind. "Senilia" was his own generic classification for some forty packets of "Studies, excerpts, souvenirs, thoughts, notes, maxims, historical sketches." The term, one must admit, is appallingly accurate.

He copied long quotations from French and English writers of the seventeenth and eighteenth centuries, expounded his views on the theatre, discussed the role of women in society, and speculated on the relations between order and liberty. He filled notebook after notebook on belles lettres, politics, history, economic developments, the social order, and religion. On religion, particularly, there was a great deal—on the Supreme Being, on providence, which had all but become an instrument designed for his special benefit, on the efficacy of prayer, on organized Christianity, and the priesthood. To the end of his days the apostate Christian who had turned revolutionary deist vented his dislike of the clergy: "They seek to dominate in 1833 as they did in 1789. . . . In every century and in every country priests have religiously seized precious metals while preaching against avarice and the corruption that wealth brings." In Belgium, he had written: "My religion is exclusively love of my fellow beings," and ten years later in 1830, he reflected on the social ethic of Jesus, "the legislator of democracy." There was much also from the bourgeois liberal on the evil influence of the aristocracy, which he coupled in a common aversion with the clergy: "The aristocracy has a very special political theology. Its existence is the very contrary of the social contract. Its god is exclusive domination, its cult royalty, which it manipulates for its sole profit. Its priests are those of the altar, those of the throne . . . those of police spies and the informers of the Inquisition."

Nothing impaired his intense concern with current politics. He began a file, "A little chronicle for the year 1838," and then another, "Begun on October 8, 1839." His hand was firm in the notebook dated January 1, 1840, still firm on the one "Begun on April 25, 1840." He wrote notes on the Near East crisis in the midsummer of 1840, full of contempt for Guizot's diplomacy of appeasement and bristling against imperialistic England. He was still writing on January 6, 1841, a week before he died, very hopeful that a French-Russian alliance would save the European continent from becoming "the instrument of English ambition."

The Revolution and the Napoleonic era engrossed him. He began a half dozen histories of the Revolution and he completed a rambling account of Napoleon, long in its 1,377 folios, scant in worth. In a file marked "The Military Pantheon," he gave his appreciation of the revolutionary and imperial officers, and in the one entitled "The Men of My Time," from which Carnot plucked enough to compose the fourth volume of the *Mémoires*, he appraised his civilian contemporaries with something less than charity. His shifts of judgment concerning Robespierre and Napoleon reflected in the main the changes in his own political status. Either in 1795 or 1796, when he blamed the former for his own disgrace, he characterized Robespierre as "a tyrant, without talent, without courage, without political knowledge. . . ." Twenty years later, Robespierre was still "obdurate and obstinate [with] sardonic smile, often terrifying, [whose] words were studied, often enigmatic, obscure. . . ." But in 1830, when Barère was pinning his hopes for himself and France on the new revolution, he wrote otherwise: "During the Convention he steadfastly supported the cause of liberty and the rights of the nation"; and in 1832, he cried out to the younger Carnot: "He was a disinterested man, republican to the soul . . . a pure man, upright, a true republican."

The reactionary politics of the July Monarchy, which altered his opinion of Robespierre and more than ever made him regret what he had done in Thermidor to overthrow the Incorruptible, also changed his conception of Napoleon. In 1818 the fallen ruler was still, in Barère's judgment, "the greatest enemy of liberty"; as late as 1827, he was still "a political adventurer, a mad conqueror." But in 1838, against the backdrop of a Louis-Philippe, Barère was convinced that Napoleon was "a great soul . . . not conquered but betrayed"; and in December 1839 he summed up the career of that great explosion of human energy as "a great life . . . the finest page of modern history." The farther the Revolution receded as a reality, the more ardently Barère's rambling notes defended its values and its principles.

With final arrangements for the publication of his memoirs completed, a heavy load fell from Barère's heart. It was then that he resigned his councillor's seat and withdrew from political life. Other lifelong habits persisted. He kept recording his thoughts on the current political scene and thinking, we can be sure, of his own past, composed an ode in honor of Gutenberg and the invention of printing from movable type, "a divine art ... that every day fulfilled a sacred mission." Where the zest and energy came from is a mystery, but the incredible scrivener entered his name in a literary contest, and he still kept up his correspondence with a few remaining friends. To Pelleport he wrote a delightful letter on May 30, 1839, ironically teasing a man many decades his junior for risking the danger of steamboat rides: "Leave these experiments, and railroads too, to the enthusiasts and the simpletons of our age. . . . As for me, old and sick, poor and forgotten, I think like Voltaire who said, when he reached my present age: 'an old man's life, a sickly life. Old age is premature death with a few moments of resurrection.' "

The ineffable charm did not leave him, he still entranced all visitors. "The most seductive monster I ever saw," was the astonished comment of a lady admirer after discovering that she had been conversing with the terrible *rapporteur* of the Committee of Public Safety. Another caller threw up his hands in amazement: "You cannot imagine how engaging and charming that man is." The graciousness and the endearing charm remained, but the end was near. Almost all the old revolutionary associates were gone, cousin Jacques died in 1837, Jean-Pierre in 1838. The time had come for him to draw up his final accounts with life. To pay off the last of the creditors and have a little something left over for Marguerite and her son, he sold the Biéouzac property to the Lassalle nephews, the sons of sister Cécile. He had to give up the house on the rue Bourg Vieux, moving with Marguerite to furnished quarters on the second floor of a house nearby on the Place Maubourget (the present Place Verdun). On June 16, 1840, he drew up his last will and testament.

"THIS IS MY WILL," he wrote at the head of the document which Maître Dalléas notarized as he had the bequest to Marguerite four years earlier.

Without parents or descendants, I hereby name as my sole heir and legatee of all my property, monsieur Henry Alfred Lefauconnier, born in Pau [he meant Paris] on November 10, eighteen hundred ten, now resident in Tarbes and living with me, all real and personal goods, securities, yearly income, contracts, petty cash, books, and specifically, all the papers, manuscript notes, memoirs, literary properties, translations, historical notes and literary works that I shall leave at my death, for the aforesaid monsieur Henry Alfred Lefauconnier to enjoy in full ownership, to do, to dispose as he sees fit [undecipherable] from the day of my death without any reservations. Such is my last wish, annuling by the present any other will that I could have made and adhering to this one on condition that the aforesaid m. Alfred Henry Lefauconnier [*sic*] pay and discharge, on account of what I am leaving him, my debts, my legacies and all expenses [and] whatever legal costs of the provisions herewith: I bequeath and leave one hundred francs to the poor and needy of the commune of Seméac in the vicinity of Tarbes, I leave a hundred francs to the needy inmates of the Tarbes prison, I leave and bequeath two hundred francs to the indigent families of the city of Tarbes, these several sums bequeathed by me shall be payable one year after my death. I bequeath and leave to Mademoiselle Marguerite Lefauconnier born in Paris the sum of four thousand francs payable within two years, and this to begin from the day of my death without prejudice to what I owe her by the attestation of December 31, 1834, drawn up before maître Jean Pierre Daléas [*sic*], duly registered notary in Tarbes. I expressly prohibit an autopsy whether in my apartment or elsewhere and in the cemetery. I count on my aforesaid heir m. Henry Alfred Lefauconnier to have my burial services simple. I desire my coffin to be accompanied to my last resting place by six indigent old men each of whom will be given five francs with the taper and that fifty francs shall be distributed to the poor by my above named heir on the day of my funeral.

Executed in Tarbes, written, dated and signed in my own hand, the sixteenth day of the month of June, eighteen hundred and forty.

B. BARERE DE VIEUZAC
Former deputy.

If the will was drawn up with breathless urgency, needless repetitions, and scorn of grammar, it was written, dated, and signed with compassion and solicitude for the disinherited of the world he was leaving. Excepting the 4,000 francs for Marguerite, which he doubtless secreted, the bequests were poignantly small. But the "former deputy" who, more than a half century earlier, had given his services gratis to needy clients, renounced his feudal rights without compensation, and supported the attempts to provide the poor with land and schools and government aid, died as he had lived, an eighteenth-century man of feeling.

Marguerite did not live to benefit from any of the provisions Barère made to ensure her well-being after his death. When she died on September 1 there was nothing left in life for Bertrand Barère. With his son and hers, who even then may have been afflicted with the mental disorder of which he died in 1847, his bonds were affectionate but not close. He was still following politics and making entries in his papers on January 6, 1841, but on the following day he suffered one of his recurring catarrhal attacks. His bronchial tubes swelled and he took to his bed. The congestion this time did not subside, and after five days, when he had lost the power of speech, he agreed to have a doctor called. He gave his consent in writing, his pen for the last time serving his needs. The night of the 12th was comfortable, he slept well, but when he was being dressed the following morning for the doctor's visit, he lost consciousness. There were only two strangers with him in his final agony, the landlord of his shabby little room and a friendly café keeper from nearby. In ten minutes it was all over. The clock marked nine and the exhausted old man breathed his last.

# Epilogue: The Historical Verdict

BARÈRE died hopeful in spirit, warmed by the glow of self-exoneration, confident that posterity would be kinder to him than had been his contemporaries. The obituaries were promising. Two days after his death, Maître Lebrun, now the leading barrister of Tarbes, delivered the funeral oration in the cemetery of the parish of Saint-Jean where Barère had been baptized. His auditors were few; in death as in life Barère had many fellow townsmen who execrated him. Lebrun spoke briefly and with sincere affection for the man whom he had already befriended. Passing rapidly over Barère's sorry reputation, he paid his respects to the man's charm and unfailing exquisite graciousness, emphasizing that the opportunity had been given him which was denied to others "to probe into the soul of the man whom political partisanship had so long and cruelly tormented." He was certain, as he saluted the body in the name of France that "before the tribunal of posterity . . . stripped of contemporary passions and calculations," Barère would one day take his rightful place in history and be recognized for the great man that he was.

With his love for the fulsome phrase, Barère would have garnered those flowers of rhetoric. From the English obituaries there was a crumb of comfort. Perhaps not from the notice in the *Annual Register* which characterized him as "one of the most conspicuous actors of the first French Revolution," for "conspicuous," however well intentioned, was not the happiest of words, but certainly from the London *Times*. The anonymous author who signed as "A Cosmopolite" deemed him "an extraordinary man possessed not only of sound talent but endowed with great wit and the refined gentlemanly qualities of the Old Regime." Since the writer was unquestionably his friend, Lewis Goldsmith, with whom Barère had been associated in sundry journalistic ventures for which Bonaparte had paid well, the exoneration of his double-dealing was not free of special pleading, but one wonders whether Barère would have minded the tarnished source of the tribute.

In his native country he was more honored by neglect or indifference than either praised or abused. The provincial press was largely silent, and its tone was that of the reactionary *Gazette de Languedoc*, which in recording the public figures who had died in 1841 placed his name at the bottom of its list among the regicides in a special category of "some more or less odd celebrities." In Paris, where public interest was passionately fixed upon the diplomatic crisis in the Near East abroad and the labor agitation in the capital itself, his death passed all but unnoticed. Four of the six leading dailies carried the briefest of notes and another ignored it entirely. It was only *Le National*, the liberal Catholic and prorevolutionary newspaper edited by Jules Bastide, that reviewed the career of the old revolutionary. It may have been Bastide himself, who had met Barère after the exile in Belgium, who wrote the sympathetic account which deplored the ingratitude of Barère's contemporaries, commiserated over the long suffering of his last years and, recalling his dedicated services to the Convention, appealed to its readers to withhold, until the promised *Mémoires* appeared, judgment of a man who was distinguished by "the elegance of his mind, the charm of his conversation, his native kindliness."

The tribunal of posterity on which Lebrun placed store gave a more positive verdict when the *Mémoires* were published. Still the verdict was not what either Lebrun or Barère counted on. Like *Le National*, which had called for forbearance until Barère could speak for himself, the influential *Le Temps* agreed, when Carnot's *Notice historique sur Barère* was published in the spring of 1842, that soon Barère's own words would make possible "the definitive ruling of inflexible history." The first ruling, in September 1842 in the pages of the widely-read *Revue des Deux Mondes*, when only one volume of the *Mémoires* had appeared, blasted Barère's appeal, stating categorically that in them was not "a single page truly worthy of history [only], sterile and often inexact repetition of facts already known." As for Barère himself, he was "a vulgar actor ... pushed forward by ambition and fear ... incapable of strong conviction ... a man whom one might have perhaps berated less, but [still] unworthy of being rehabilitated by history." And the *Gazette de France* was of similar mind when several months later in mid-1843 it mixed contempt and pity in its notice: contempt for the man who had betrayed Demerville, revealed state secrets to Izquierdo, and cringed before Louis XVIII and Napoleon; pity for a weakling "who committed evil ... without inclination or conviction."

Again *Le National* broke a lance on Barère's behalf and three long articles between the end of 1843 and the beginning of 1844 endeavored to explain how Barère's life could have been great but instead proved a sad and dismal failure. Without denying the lapses of his career after Thermidor, the author, who signed himself ironically "Old Nick" and made himself the devil's advocate, appealed to readers to recall that the abject sycophant of the last years was a man of taste and elegance who had labored to destroy ancient abuses, dedicated himself with "patriotic devotion and generous self-oblivion" to the Committee of Public Safety, and had been "the resounding echo of all the military ardor and enthusiasm" of the Year II.

The melancholy mellowness of that judgment was ill-remembered. What was long remembered was the fulminating verdict that Macaulay delivered in the columns of the *Edinburgh Review* in April 1844. His terrible judgment has been quoted in the Preface. The vindictive boast with which he terminated his demolition is also worthy of note, not for its acumen or charity but for the accuracy of his prediction: "By attempting to enshrine this Jacobin carrion he [Carnot] has forced us to gibbet it; and we venture to say that, from the eminence of infamy on which we have placed it, he will not easily take it down."

It is true but irrelevant that Macaulay's knowledge of the subject was not exhaustive and that with his angular morality he was not well qualified to judge the personality and the political behavior of a supple Gascon. He did, however, judge Barère and his opinion carried great authority. Neither the editor himself nor other writers for a long time to come took down Barère from the eminence of infamy on which the pundit of Whig liberalism had placed him.

Additional memoirs and journals of Barère's contemporaries were belatedly published in the course of the next three decades, fortunately in decreasing numbers, for they added little in information or fresh understanding. Old grievances of Girondins were retold, chatty trivia of unimportant moments in his life found publishers. Carnot, in the souvenirs concerning his illustrious father, told again that the great "Organizer of Victory" thought well of his colleague's services but was otherwise not enthusiastic about Barère. The posthumous memoirs of Baudot said in print what the generous Montagnard idealist who had been close to Barère in their Belgian days had frequently expressed orally about the gentleness, charm, and good nature of his fellow exile.

There were also several sets of biographical dictionaries intended for the large reading public, some new, some in new editions, all compilations of hack writers whose facility surpassed scholarly qualifications. The tone was generally unfriendly. If the lurid exaggerations of the Thermidorian tracts disappeared from their pages, the explanation was consistently advanced, with minor variations of distaste, that Barère's political behavior derived from the weaknesses of his character. The article in the *Galerie historique de la Révolution française*, after judiciously linking his career with both the grandeur and the baseness of the Committee of Public Safety so that "the memory of the days of sorrow which so often veiled the sun of our liberty is attached to his name," in the end reached the familiar conclusion that in consequence of his wooing each faction when it was in power and abandoning it as soon as it was overthrown "he made himself odious to all." In similar fashion the widely read compendiums, the *Nouvelle Biographie générale*, edited by Dr. Hoefer, and *Biographie universelle*, edited by L. G. Michaud, had as leitmotivs of the articles about him his "fear" and his "cowardice." After a lapse of half a century or more, two brief inconsequental works appeared in the early 1850's, when panic fear of the "reds" of 1848 had not yet abated, which reverted to the favorite themes of Méhée *fils* and Vilate.

General histories of the Revolution did not lack for readers, particularly in the turbulent days immediately before and after the revolutionary upheaval of 1848. The fiery Esquiros, whose heroes were the Montagnards, regretted much that Barère had done and was of the persuasion that he was more a chameleon than a statesman, yet this author too, acknowledged that Barère was gentle, softhearted, lively in imagination, quick in understanding, a man "warmed in the Midi sun." The three histories which most caught the imagination of Frenchmen were in varying degree all of the political left and yet for reasons not difficult to understand found little good to say of a man who had been of the left. In the sustained love song which the poet-philosopher-historian Lamartine addressed to the Girondins, Barère figured as the traducer of heroes whose nobility of character and loftiness of motives the author depicted in exalted prose. Michelet refrained from picking up the old canards about Barère's depravity, but in his animated tribute to "the people" and to Danton, in whom all the great popular virtues were embodied, he found opportunity to dub Barère "a turncoat," "the patented liar of the Committee of Public Safety," "a charming fraud and charlatan, an improviser from the Midi." Louis Blanc was made of sterner stuff. For that doctrinaire champion of the working classes who saw Robespierre as the conscience of the Revolution even as Michelet had seen Danton, Barère was utterly abhorrent, everything that Michelet thought of him and a cruel licentious betrayer as well.

When prorevolutionary historians were of one mind in finding Barère unworthy, it was natural for conservative scholars and those whose sympathies were royalist to think even less well of a man who had been a Jacobin of sorts. For the ardently royalist Barante, writing in the years when conservatives feared the worst for their country if the levellers of 1848 should again get the upper hand in 1852, Barère was a nimble-witted blotting paper: "Just as one dictated the words he should write to a secretary, so the ruling power dictated to Barère his judgments, his opinions, his friendships. It was a trade that he plied [and] he was always ready." A decade and more later, an able and hostile historian of the Terror, L. Mortimer-Ternaux, wrote of Barère's "sad fame that was well-deserved for his cowardice, his betrayals, and his double-edged reports," while the Prussian scholar, von Sybel, gave the verdict that no one in all France for a moment questioned the truth of the charges that Lecointre had preferred against Barère at the height of the Thermidorian reaction.

During the days of "the Liberal Empire" of Napoleon III, the revolutionists of 1789 had a better press. From Hamel, who attempted, not without some success, to rehabilitate both Robespierre and Saint-Just, came little for Barère, whom the biographer of the two Montagnards disliked particularly for his share in the proceedings of Thermidor and condemned more generally for his distorted *Mémoires*. Yet the reputation of Barère benefited by the new political temper. A small book was published under the ironic title of *Le vandalisme révolutionnaire* which made the point that the hated and hateful terrorists, including Barère, had made notable contributions to the scientific progress of France. The popular novelist and playwright, J. Claretie, recalled for his readers that Barère was one of the last, intransigent Montagnards in whom "the sacred fire of the Revolution burned."

Thus the years of monarchy and empire closed as they had begun—on a mixed note. Barère had writers to exonerate him of the worst charges, but he still had more detractors than well-wishers or champions. The writing had been largely on the levels of hagiolatry or witch-hunting. It was still too soon for dispassionate inquiry into the revolutionary experience. In many ways it remained too early even during the next great period of investigation, from 1870 to 1914, but nevertheless both treatment and conclusions underwent important changes in the years which followed the proclamation of the Third Republic in 1870.

From such few memoirs as were published or republished there came little to modify the familiar approach or still more familiar conclusions. The pamphlets of Vilate and Méhée *fils* appeared in a royalist compilation in 1878 when the continued existence of the new republic was still problematical. Old Girondin memoirs came out in new dress but with hackneyed accusations that Barère was "a eunuch in politics" and more in that vein. The memoirs of Napoleon's subordinate, Méneval, furnished details on Barère as the journalistic hack of the First Consul and the emperor. Barras, sometime Director after 1795 and an inveterate liar, elaborated upon the Demahi story originally given by Vilate. Then there were personal recollections, all posthumously published, ranging from minutiae to sober evaluation. Madame de Chastenay recalled the gracious Barère of the Constituent Assembly and a fellow deputy, Auguste Jal, commemorated him during the Hundred Days as a "witty, gay, and clever talker . . . in silk stockings and powdered hair." Choudieu, a Convention colleague in exile in Belgium with Barère, dipped into his memories to defend a "gentle" and "affable" man whose enemies, "unable to find anything reprehensible in his conduct . . . had recourse to the weapon of cowards, defamation."

While memoirs and journals abounded in reminiscences of the man, the encyclopedias and biographical dictionaries repeated what similar works had published before. The *Encyclopaedia Britannica*, in its ninth edition of 1889, paraphrased Macaulay in holding that Barère's career was "unparalleled for meanness, cowardice, lying and atrocious cruelty," and a score of years later, the eleventh edition informed readers that he was "thoroughly unscrupulous, wholly free from any guiding principles

# Epilogue

[except] to be on the side of the stronger." Among the corresponding works in French, there were variations on the verdict pronounced by Aulard, dean of French revolutionary students and incumbent of the recently established chair of the history of the French Revolution at the Sorbonne, that Barère was a "scoundrel and pedant," a "poltroon," as "vain and touchy as a ham actor."

When at the turn of the century, Aulard, in his great political history of the Revolution which had canonical authority among republican readers for a generation, piled up instance after instance of Barère's unworthiness, the prorevolutionary historian found himself in the company of antirevolutionary scholars. Sorel was not of the camp of the antirevolutionary scholars, but he was as conservative in his political sympathies as Aulard was liberal. Yet for him too Barère was unsympathetic, "a born valet." In the eyes of Taine, foremost critic of the revolutionists and of their presumed ideological masters among the philosophes, Barère was detestable and contemptible, "the betrayer of all factions"; while a half generation later, the intellectual son of Taine, the ironic, well-informed, and witty Louis Madelin, in his history of the Revolution which the French Academy honored with a prize award, sneered at Barère as "the trimmer [who] always appeared at the scene at the decisive moment . . . to deal the last treacherous blow." A year earlier, in 1908, the *Cambridge Modern History*, which may not reasonably be charged either with wit or irony, contributed to English understanding by explaining that Barère had acquired "a most sinister influence over his colleagues" by reason, among other things, of his dexterity in concealing his motives and in explaining away the apparent inconsistency of his words.

It would hardly do to say, if one limited himself to the works above, that the tide had turned in Barère's favor. Yet a countercurrent, a trickle of opinion in his favor, was beginning to flow. The first historian of professional standing to challenge the prevailing interpretation was the English-born scholar, H. Morse

Stephens, who was teaching in the United States. Macaulay, held Stephens, was entirely justified in calling attention to the inaccuracies, particularly the falsehoods, in Barère's *Mémoires*. But he was entirely mistaken in his conclusions concerning the personality of the man and the nature of Barère's services. The gist of Stephens' own conclusions is contained in this excerpt: "Barère was a typical Gascon, with a keen imagination and a fund of fluent eloquence, easily influenced by those about him and quick in assimilating the ideas of the majority. [While he was the spokesman of many different parties] it is hardly fair to rail at Barère as a double-dyed traitor; he was no more of a traitor than the vast majority of the Convention, or indeed of all Frenchmen, but his peculiar power of assimilating ideas and his faculty of eloquence made him conspicuous in the tribune, and therefore in French history, as a man who often changed his ideas."

With those words Stephens introduced a draft of fresh air in stale corridors. A few years later, when he devoted a section to Barère in a critical edition of the speeches of important revolutionists, he let loose the blast against his fellow historians that no well known participant of the French Revolution, with the possible exception of Marat, had been "so persistently vilified and deliberately misunderstood as Barère."

Whether because of Stephens' call for new study or because the moment was ripe or because of both his challenge and the times, the critics of Barère's critics made themselves increasingly heard. The *Mémoires* were translated into English and in the main they were well received, most of the reviewers holding to the view of *The Spectator* that in English eyes Barère seemed not very dissimilar from many other men whether French or of other nations. This last decade of the expiring nineteenth century also saw the old and temporarily stilled controversy over Barère reopened in his natal city. In 1889 a principal street was renamed in his honor. The strife which divided all France over *l'affaire Dreyfus* had its local counterpart in Tarbes where *l'affaire Barère* pitted republican and prorevolutionary sympathizers of Barère against conservatives and reactionaries. There were manifestoes and meetings, heated exchanges in the newspapers, and the storm raged for several years. In the end the Barèrists gained their objective: on June 14, 1896, amid jeers and outraged protests, they celebrated the erection of a statue of their townsman in the cemetery of Saint-Jean where almost a half-century earlier Lebrun had proclaimed him a great man.

The controversy did not end with the triumph. A decade later, Fernand de Cardaillac, a leading local student and well-wisher of Barère, returned to the lists with a brief, balanced study which showed how much the passage of time could blunt the ancient rancors. Without palliating the weakness of Barère and his inability to resist the passions which the Revolution had released, Cardaillac exonerated him of the charge of cowardice and double-dealing and maintained that Barère was "a mass of contradictions" who even in his lowest moments remained true to the ideal of popular sovereignty, convinced in his own mind "that he was fighting for justice, liberty, and equality."

Pouchet, a student of the sciences during the Revolution, wrote in admiration of Barère's interest and participation in the cultural renovation of France during the Terror: "We are overwhelmed by the prodigious faculties of Barère, to whom nothing seemed alien." And in the first years of the new century he received a warm tribute from the pen of the great scholar in politics, the socialist leader, Jean Jaurès. Barère's name is strewn over the pages of Jaurès' history of the Convention, his personality and his procedure analyzed with learning leavened by sympathy. That Barère on many occasions was not true to the better side of his nature, Jaurès readily granted, agreeing too that the *Mémoires* were replete with inaccuracies and falsehoods. He also found documentary value in them and made an effort to enter into the psychology of an embittered old man pathetically composing an apology for his career. Jaurès' judgment was no doubt also colored by his political convictions, by his ardor to keep intact the unity of the endangered Third Republic against its enemies from the right. Allowing for his republican leanings, his estimate of Barère's position is level-headed and penetrating. "Barère," he wrote, "was above all the man of the Convention and through all his sinuous tactics it is that which gives unity to his revolutionary action, honor and dignity to his life. It [the] Convention was for him the supreme force and the supreme means of survival and security. Everything that tended to weaken it, to dissipate its strength, to subordinate it, was equally harmful. To keep and increase the prestige of the Convention was for Barère to save the Revolution itself. He held that conviction more deeply than any of the men of that time."

The solid bases for investigating Barère's career were thus being laid during the first four decades of the Third Republic. The last volumes of the *Archives parlementaires* were making it possible to follow the debates carefully and critically, the procedures of committees and clubs could be traced, the archives were yielding their secrets about leading deputies and different aspects of revolutionary activities. After the brief interruption of the World War scholars returned to their studies, first under the impress of Aulard and Mathiez, later under the guidance of Lefebvre. None of the many new and valuable monographs were primarily concerned with Barère, nor did the biographies of his associates of the Committee deal at length with him. Yet the exhaustive researches on such diversified facets as cultural nationalism, propaganda, scientific renovation, price and wage policy, control of foreign trade, religious strife, political tensions and power struggles, all provided data concerning Barère and cast light on his actions.

The light that those researches cast on his actions was far from dazzling all the scholars who projected it. Dislike of his personality traits and condemnation of his behavior did not disappear from the world of historians. True, there was only Launay in his biography of Barère to disinter the black legend of the Thermidorian reaction, but more solidly grounded writers than he evinced distaste in varying degrees. One cross section of the special studies and the biographies would show Ording, the student of the Police Bureau, characterizing Barère as "an amiable and supple political charlatan," and Guérin, the ortho-dox Marxist investigator of the class struggle in the later Revo-lution, holding that Barère for all his great ability was still "vile" and "a wanton," seemingly not so much from his native defects of character as from an impersonal nexus between his acts and his defense of the interests of the bourgeoisie. Two biographers of Robespierre, the English scholar Thompson and the French student Walter, were in substantial accord that Barère was "cunning," "evasive," "equivocal," and "amphibious"—an as-sessment in which Curtis, an American biographer of Saint-Just, concurred. Detractors in Tarbes during these years did not let down their guard against their notorious fellow townsman. A brief article in the *Dictionnaire de biographie française* inclined little in the direction of admiration.

Some of the important studies, such for example as the biog-raphies of Carnot and David, displayed no particular interest one way or another in assessing Barère. But another cross sec-tion of the historical literature would disclose the opinion that Barère had not fared well at the hands of earlier writers. De-ville's study of the Commune of the Year II furnished data that once Barère had made up his mind he had acted with realistic intelligence, forcefulness, and courage in the Thermidor climax. Kuscinski's *Dictionnaire des Conventionnels* regretted that "by a strange fatalism [Barère's name] has been saddled with all the misdeeds and all the crimes of the Terror." In an early study the present writer expressed the opinion that Barère was the emol-lient of revolutionary passions and, while a pliant politician, also a participant who remained undeviatingly loyal to the basic principles of 1789. G. Bruun, another American biographer of Saint-Just, did not slur over Barère's evasiveness yet credited him with "imagination and a gift of fervent eloquence, much sagacity," while R. R. Palmer, in his detailed study of the Committee of Public Safety, wrote with sensitivity and understanding of a man whom he considered one of the most useful and valuable members of the executive government of the Terror. From Bouchard's biography of Prieur as well as that of the Italian scholar Galante-Garrone, who examined the career of Buonarroti, there came additional disclosures of the esteem in which Barère was held by his associates. Thus, just as aversion to Barère knew no national frontiers, so the inclination to judge him more favorably was international in scope.

The spectrum was similar in the well-known general histories. Among English historians the benevolent neutrality of Goodwin coexisted with the unfavorable opinion of Thompson, who elaborated in his history on the judgment that he had earlier expressed when he wrote on Robespierre, that Barère was "a trimmer," "a time-server," "always the first rat to desert a sinking ship." Allowing to him the virtues of intelligence and dedication to his duties, even of clemency to his political opponents, Thompson insisted nevertheless that with Barère all was calculated: "self-interest marched under the same flag as absence of principles."

The general French histories in the main were less severe if not more friendly than that of Thompson. If Mathiez, a man of the left, was at one with Gaxotte, a historian of the extreme right, in seeing Barère as "feeble" and "a waverer," their contemporaries did not expatiate upon his defects. Whether one scans the volumes of Sagnac and Pariset in the Lavisse series or the chapters on the Revolution that Labrousse contributed in the study of the eighteenth century written with Mousnier, he is struck by a notable absence of hostility. And in the most detailed and greatest of all modern histories of the Revolution, Lefebvre departs only once from his many balanced references to Barère's services: "As always he sniffed the wind," is Lefebvre's parenthetical comment on Barère's course on the eve of Thermidor.

With American historians Barère found a more hospitable reception than the welcome given him in the Old World. Of four well-known histories of the French Revolution published in the United States since the end of the first World War, one alone adhered to the older view that Barère was "sly," "voluble," "an almost flawless weathervane." In the judgment of the other three writers, his merits took precedence over his defects. He was described as "indefatigable," "eloquent," "affable," "concilia-tory," "a man thoroughly at home in parliamentary corridors."

The causes of this more favorable appreciation are several. It may be that American scholars, by the nature of their educa-tional conditioning as well as by their geographical remoteness from French politics, are relatively immune to the inherited partisanship which has marked much French scholarship con-cerning the most controversial subject in the modern historical experience of France. Perhaps in the open spaces of the New World across the Atlantic, where the pragmatic temper is pro-nounced, corridors are more ample than in Old Europe and be-ing at home within them, free to maneuver within them, is not synonymous with original political sin.

Yet in France too, if a century and a quarter after Barère's death scholars remain divided in judgment, historical research has not been in vain. The once glaring gap has been considerably narrowed, the ground cleared of many errors of fact, terrain once dark lighted up by research. With the passage of time old par-tisanship has been diluted; deliberate misunderstanding and willful misrepresentation are largely of the past. Of the long abuse to which Barère was subjected there are at worst inter-mittent echoes. It is no longer denied that he was honest in his personal life; the charges have been dropped that he was licen-tious, unscrupulous and cruel, that he was in fact a weakling who did evil without inclination or conviction, or alternatively, a sinister influence upon his associates to whom he was odious.

Where disagreement persists, it derives less from what he did during the Revolution than from the interpretations that are placed on why he conducted himself as he did. The difficulty lies in what seems at first a paradox: that the same procedures brought him, under one set of circumstances, esteem and admiration, and on other occasions, stinging criticism, suspicion, and aversion. A sympathetic commentator, groping for a clue, wrote that Barère was "a mass of contradictions." The intent of the explanation is generous, the substance erroneous, for in temperament and qualities of mind Barère was not ambivalent. He was of a piece. Ambitious as well as amiable, making the best of two worlds, he sought to keep things on an even keel. When his native graciousness and reluctance to give offense or hurt involved nothing fundamental in human relations, those attributes earned him acclaim. When basic issues came to the fore, the same predilection to avert strain or conflict among opposing groups or individuals and remain on good terms with all created estrangement. Inevitably, tactful urbanity and well-wishing appeasement took on the aspects of evasiveness and equivocation, when not of cowardice.

Not only softness of character but also the quality of his mind inhibited unreserved commitments. That he was highly intelligent, with a well-stored fund of knowledge, and in his thinking disciplined, all who knew him were agreed. However, often for the better, too frequently for the worse, and far more than most men, he could not escape looking both ways. He could not see truth embodied in one point of view or associated with one faction or one individual. Truth, loyalty, the good were not single, precise, angular and sharp: they were rounded and fluid, their essence in nuances. The operative truth came from accommodating divergent views. No position once taken remained invariably right, no adherence once given was irrevocable. The tyranny of absolute belief was more to be feared than the evil of total error. All rigidity of the spirit distorted truth; absolute rigidity distorted absolutely.

On the level of abstraction this capacity for seeing the protean faces of truth was admirably lofty. On the level of reality, when careers could be abruptly terminated or lives forfeit, when loyalty was not militantly and jealously given, revolutionists did not prize tempered support. For them Barère was not flexibly honest: he was a false adherent, a trimmer. Those traits, however, were not accessories to conduct, props for a performance that he put up and took down. They were integral with his being. They constituted the essential components of his conviction, convictions, moreover, which he modified by delicate gradations as he responded to the impress of changing circumstances.

In the last years of the Old Regime he moved from traditionalism to conservative reformism, and then to reforming liberalism. He became a convert between 1788 and 1789 to the idea of a revolution by consent. In the course of the following two years, from 1789 to 1791, he shifted from bourgeois liberalism toward the democratic left, and when the Constituent Assembly ended he was close to Robespierre in his views. As his thinking was taking that new direction, he tried, as the *Journal de Perlet* put it, "to reconcile principles with politics and national interests." What he did and wished to do won him advancement and almost unanimous approbation. The experience of those thirty months imbued him with the conviction that the indirection he had practiced to conciliate disputes was the stuff and texture of effective political conduct. In everyday relations one had to maneuver, retreat when required from weak positions, even give them up to fall back upon stronger grounds, not to give battle when open struggle could be avoided and ends gained by negotiation and temporizing.

Barère continued in that path and tactic when he took his seat in the National Convention, but as the margin of personal security narrowed in that arena of gladiators, his role little by little was played out. He failed in his efforts to mediate the duel between Girondins and Montagnards. The harmony he hoped for within the new assembly was not attained, the unity between Paris and the provinces not gained. Still valuable despite failure, he also became vulnerable. He was too much a Montagnard for the Girondins; for rabid Jacobins he was too lukewarm.

# Epilogue

Mistrust did not end when Barère made his farewells to conciliation and became a terrorist. Moderates felt he had betrayed them; the intransigents of the left were not wrong in sensing that he, the "Anacreon of the Guillotine," was at heart only a reluctant terrorist. They had good cause to suspect that the fervent apologist for total force secretly deplored, even abhorred, the coercion that necessity gave him no alternative to avoid. Accredited spokesman of the Committee, he expounded and defended policies he did not wholeheartedly endorse. He spoke often and well, but he spoke too often for his own good and too glibly.

During the Thermidorian reaction and for many years after, all men with grievances—Old Regime monarchists, constitutionalists of 1789, Girondins, the followers of Robespierre, and renegade terrorists—poured contempt, indignation, and hatred upon the head of the associate who once had been with them but never fully of them. In the endless reviews of the Revolution he became stigmatized as the great betrayer. That judgment is patently unfair. He was never the political eunuch of those hostile accounts, devoid of principles and swayed only by fear and calculation. Never swept by the passionate hatreds of the Revolution, for all his deviousness he was loyal to the revolutionary credo. For a moment he tasted power; his prestige was high; his renown wide. For a moment only life lifted him above himself. After Thermidor, except for brief intervals when he enjoyed relative security, he was a pitiable man. His softness became cowardice, his goodness turned into injured righteousness, and manliness eroded, giving way to servility. Broken in life and his memory pilloried, he paid heavily for evil he was not strong enough to prevent, the evil he did, and the evil he condoned.

*Note on*
*Sources*

# A GENERAL NOTE ON SOURCES

## Archives and Manuscript Collections

AIDS AND GUIDES: P. Caron, *Manuel pratique pour l'étude de la Révolution française*, rev. ed., Paris, 1947, is indispensable. For Paris archives, especially the Archives Nationales, see A. Tuetey, *Répertoire général des sources manuscrites de l'histoire de Paris pendant la Révolution française*, 11 vols., Paris, 1890-1914. *Exposition Bertrand Barère, 1755-1955*, Tarbes, 1955, with a Foreword by J. Mangin: a check list of source materials, principally dated manuscripts and printed works by Barère.

The standard guides to archives outside Paris, listed in Caron, Nos. 54, 102, 132, are of slight use for Barère material. Aulard's article, "Les archives révolutionnaires du Sud-Ouest," in *La Révolution française*, XIII (1887), 481-523, is helpful.

PARIS: The great archival repositories with their wealth of material on the Revolution have relatively little on Barère himself. In the Archives Nationales (hereafter A. N.), the most rewarding of the numerous files, given below under Notes, are the official reports of police and political authorities relating to the following difficult moments in Barère's later career: the period from 1795 to 1799, when he successfully escaped deportation; in 1800, when he denounced Demerville to the police; from 1815-1816, when he was again in hiding; from 1830 to his death. There is also scattered information concerning his family and followers in Tarbes and his relations with Madame de Mailly. The most useful single file is $F^7$ 6678. *Affaires politiques. Police Générale*. Dossier de B. Barère de Vieuzac, ex-Conventionnel.

In the Bibliothèque Nationale, Département des Manuscrits, Nouvelles acquisitions françaises (B.N.Mss.), the *Fichier Charavay*, a convenient compendium of the sales *Bulletin de la Maison Charavay*, lists many dated autograph letters of Barère, often with excerpts of the contents. In addition, there is scattered material, including letters, relating to the editing and publishing of the manuscript of his *Mémoires*, also of notes for inclusion in the published text.

The Archives de la Préfecture de la Police (A.P.P.) are very helpful on the Demerville "conspiracy," Madame de Mailly and Travanet, and the manhunt for Barère in 1815-1816.

The Bibliothèque Historique de la Ville de Paris (B.H.V.P.) has a number of autograph letters especially for Barère's last years.

While the Archives des Affaires Etrangères are unrewarding, the Bibliothèque de l'Arsénal has the manuscript, Ms. 5007, of the first three volumes of the published *Mémoires*, except for Barère's diary of 1788, "Le dernier jour de Paris," which is lacking. In a letter to the late Georges Lefebvre dated January 17, 1949, Professor Marcel Emérit of the University of Algiers raised the question of the authenticity of the published *Mémoires*. He cited a letter (Ms. Arsénal, *Fonds Enfantin*) of May 24, 1842, from a professional journalist, from which he concluded that Barère's manuscript notes were "arranged." Those doubts are not justifiable. Carnot, it is clear, entrusted the preliminary task to two journalist assistants, but carefully supervised the final editorial work. For an account of how he worked, see his "Historical Introduction" to the *Mémoires*, I, 3-7, 12-17, 21-26; also L. Caddau, "Trois lettres inédites de Lazare Hippolyte Carnot," in *Revue des Hautes-Pyrénées*, XII (1917), 5-11.

With one exception, folios 383-385, Carnot respected the Arsénal manuscript of "almost 800 pages of fine writing" that Barère had prepared. His emendations are largely stylistic, and he did not abuse the discretionary powers that Barère gave him to make deletions or weave where he could the many documentary memoranda into the text, "either textually or in the form of analyses." Where he used "interesting fragments" from the other Barère manuscripts, he indicated their source, as he did when he added sections that Barère penned after he had prepared his own final copy for the editors. My conclusions concerning the authenticity of the first three volumes of the *Mémoires*, based upon collating the Arsénal manuscript with the published text, are substantially those of the Associate Archivist (letter of January 20, 1957, to M. Mangin, in my possession): "In general the text is the same." Such were the conclusions, too, of M. Souviron (*Bertrand Barère, 1755-1841*, Pithiviers, 1906): "I noted some changes and some deletions but of little importance." The manuscript of the fourth volume of the *Mémoires* is not in the Arsénal Library but in the *Fonds Barère*, No. 60, in the departmental archives of the Hautes-Pyrénées (see below). But the printed text represents a small part of the 525 folios which Barère called "Les hommes de mon temps." Most of Barère's vignettes are abridged in the printing, many omitted. The original manuscripts on Danton and Robespierre have disappeared. Where there was more than one sketch of the same person, Carnot chose the one he saw fit to include. Collating the manuscripts of the vignettes with the published version again leads to the conclusion that Carnot did not denature either the letter or the spirit of the manuscript.

TARBES: Archives Départementales des Hautes-Pyrénées (A.D.H.P.). The enormous mass of Barère papers (*Fonds Barère*) have been inventoried and calendared by the present archivist, M. Jules Mangin. See his summary index in *Catalogue général des Manuscrits des Bibliothèques publiques de France*, LI, Paris, 1956: *Manuscrits conservés dans les dépôts d'Archives Départementales* (*Supplément*), p. 336 ff.; also "Le Fonds Bertrand Barère aux Archives des Hautes-Pyrénées," in *Annales historiques de la Révolution française*, No. 129 (Nov.-Dec., 1957), 508-509. For how those papers got to the Archives, see Caddau's "Trois lettres" above, also "A propos des *Mémoires* de Bertrand Barère," *ibid.*, XVII (1922), 234. Other materials relating to Barère are in the following files: *E 55 Familles.*

## Note on Sources

*Barère de Vieuzac; Greffe du Tribunal Civil* . . . 9 août, 1834; and the *Fonds Fontan*. Those papers of the late nonagenarian, Dr. Fontan, contain much information on Barère's family, but as M. Mangin wrote on January 18, 1953, they are "in great disorder . . . and difficult to use."

The Bibliothèque Municipale of Tarbes (B.M.T.) has the published text of Barère's legal briefs, many annotated in his hand. The three bound quarto volumes which he entitled *Mémoires de B. Barère* are not to be confused with his posthumously published memoirs. The B.M.T. also has a number of variant manuscript drafts of his prerevolutionary *Eloges*, while others are in No. 36 of the *Fonds Barère*. For material from individuals and private collections, see Notes on chapters below.

OUTSIDE FRANCE: There are only a few documents relating to Barère's stay in Mons and Brussels. See the Algemeen Rijksarchief at The Hague, *Secretariat of State*, secret file, also Archives de la Ville de Bruxelles, *Police des Etrangers, 1822.*

### Published Sources

AIDS AND GUIDES: For guidance to the sources on the Revolution—debates, acts, decrees, and laws, club and committee records, press, pamphlets—see Caron above; M. Tourneux, *Bibliographie de l'histoire de Paris pendant la Révolution française*, 5 vols., Paris, 1890-1913; G. Walter, *Répertoire de l'histoire de la Révolution française, Travaux publiés de 1800 à 1940, Personnes*, Paris, 1941, and *Lieux*, Paris, 1951; and A. Martin and G. Walter, *Catalogue de l'histoire de la Révolution française*, 5 vols., Paris, 1936-1955. The most up-to-date bibliographical references are in G. Lefebvre, *La Révolution française*, the printing of 1957, while current publications are listed and critically evaluated in periodic retrospective review articles in *Revue historique*. R. R. Palmer's critical bibliographical article,

## Note on Sources

"Fifty Years of the Committee of Public Safety," in *Journal of Modern History*, xiii (1941), 375-397, is very helpful.

SOURCES: J. B. Duvergier, *Collection complète des lois, décrets, ordonnances, réglements et avis du Conseil d'Etat . . . de 1788 à 1824*, 24 vols., Paris, 1825-1828. The parliamentary debates, reports, enactments of the assemblies are in the official proceedings: for the Constituent Assembly, *Procès-verbal de l'Assemblée nationale*, 75 vols., n.d., with a table of contents in 5 vols. (1806); for the National Convention, *Procès-verbal de la Convention nationale*, 72 vols., Paris, 1792-an IV (1796), as yet without a complete printed table of contents. The later official collection, *Archives parlementaires de 1781 à 1860 . . .* Première série, 82 vols., Paris, 1867-1914, ed. by J. Mavidal and E. Laurent, which ends with the session of January 4, 1794, is valuable, especially in its last volumes, where the text of the *procès-verbaux* is not blended with digests from different newspapers. The most useful and convenient of all the contemporary newspaper accounts of the debates is *Réimpression de l'Ancien Moniteur*, 32 vols., Paris, 1863-1870, with two volumes of tables (hereafter *Réimpression*). In addition, there is much of value in the extraordinary compendium edited by P. B. J. Buchez and P. C. Roux, *Histoire parlementaire de la Révolution française*, 40 vols., Paris, 1834-1838. For Barère's activities as a club member, there is F. A. Aulard, *La Société des Jacobins*, 6 vols., Paris, 1889-1897; for his committee assignments, the same historian's great *Recueil des actes du Comité de salut public*, 28 vols., Paris, 1889-1951, i-xv, and J. Guillaume, ed., *Procès-verbaux du Comité d'instruction publique de la Convention nationale*, 6 vols., Paris, 1891-1907. Public opinion, reported from the accounts of police observers and the press, in P. Caron, *Paris pendant la Terreur*, 4 vols., Paris, 1910-1949, and in the three following works edited by Aulard: *Paris pendant la Réaction thermidorienne et sous le Directoire*, 5 vols., Paris, 1898-1902; *Paris sous le Consulat*, 4 vols., Paris, 1903-1909; *Paris sous le premier Empire*, 3 vols., Paris, 1912-1923.

FOR BARERE: Besides the manuscript and published sources given above, the *Catalogue général des livres imprimés de la Bibliothèque nationale, Auteurs*, VII, Paris, 1891, pp. 698-718, for a check list of Barère's publications. This list includes the works he translated, the official reprints of his most famous reports and speeches from the floor, and his refutation of the charges preferred against him during the Thermidorian reaction. Neither this listing nor vol. I of the *Catalogue* of Martin and Walter is complete. For his own *apologia*, above all *Mémoires de B. Barère . . . publiés par Mm. Hippolyte Carnot et David (d'Angers)*, 4 vols., Paris 1842-1844 (hereafter *Barère*), which have been translated into English as *Memoirs of Bertrand Barère*, 4 vols., London, 1896. His participation in the achievements of the Constituent Assembly and the evolution of his political views are best followed in his newspaper: *Le Point du Jour, ou Résultat de ce qui s'est passé la veille à l'Assemblée nationale*, 26 vols., Paris, 1789-1791. The 815 issues covered the period from June 17, 1789, to October 1, 1791. In 1790 Barère published a volume covering the period from April 27, 1789, to June 17, but it is a retrospective compilation which lacks the value of the original.

## Contemporary Writings

While Barère's contemporaries were relatively silent on his work as deputy of the Constituent Assembly, beginning with the National Convention he was the subject of much comment in the daily press, in the speeches on the assembly floor, and in meetings of the Jacobins. After the overthrow of Robespierre, the pamphleteers and newspaper editors of the Thermidorian reaction attacked him savagely. Much of the billingsgate of 1794-1795 was reprinted in later years, when memoirs of participants began to appear, with them biographical dictionaries and the writings of the proto-historians of the Revolution. As contributions to historical knowledge or understanding of Barère, the worth of those publications runs the gamut from none to slight. The greatest value of those distortions lies first in revealing what their writers believed or professed to believe at a given moment concerning Barère, and secondly, in tracing for the student the origins and development of the black legend which placed Barère during his lifetime in the unenviable position of attending the funeral of his reputation. I have used them for what they are worth and cite them at appropriate places in the text and the Notes on chapters. The most important articles, studies, histories, memoirs, biographical dictionaries published after his death, are evaluated in a final chapter and listed separately in the last section of this bibliography.

## Modern Authorities

For the political background I have relied throughout upon the histories of the Revolution by the modern masters: F. A. Aulard, *The French Revolution. A Political History*, tr. from the French, 4 vols., N.Y., 1910; P. Sagnac, *La Révolution* (*1789-1792*) and G. Pariset, *La Révolution* (*1792-1799*), volumes i and ii of the Lavisse series, "Histoire de la France contemporaine," Paris, 1920; A. Mathiez, *The French Revolution*, N.Y., 1928, and *The Thermidorian Reaction*, N.Y., 1931, both in translation; J. M. Thompson, *The French Revolution*, London, 1943, and G. Lefebvre, *La Révolution française*, vol. xiii of the "Peuples et Civilisations" series, 2nd ed., Paris, 1957.

The course of the Revolution in the Hautes-Pyrénées is traced in detail in a series of studies by Abbé L. Ricaud: *La Bigorre et les Hautes-Pyrénées pendant la Révolution*, Paris, 1894; *Un régime qui commence*, Tarbes, 1911; *Un régime qui finit*, Paris, 1905; "Girondins et Terroristes," in *Bulletin de la Société Académique des Hautes-Pyrénées*, 2e série, partie locale, iv (1897-1900); 1573-1614, 1710-1748, 1767-1790; "Les représen-

tants en mission dans les Hautes-Pyrénées pendant le gouvernement révolutionnaire," *ibid.*, 307-435. Details about Barère's
family are in J. Bourdette, *Notice des seigneurs de Biéouzac,*
Toulouse, 1903; also F. de Cardaillac in *Revue des Hautes-
Pyrénées,* VIII (1913), 329-341.

Studies and biographies of Barère's colleagues of the Conven-
tion are legion. I have made extensive use of A. Kuscinski,
*Dictionnaire des Conventionnels,* Paris, 1917, which covers
Barère and all his associates. For Robespierre, J. M. Thompson,
*Robespierre,* 2 vols., Oxford, 1935; G. Walter, *Robespierre,*
Paris, revised edition of 1946; M. Bouloiseau, *Robespierre,* in the
"Que Sais-Je" series, Paris, 1957; L. Jacob, *Robespierre vu par
ses contemporains,* Paris, 1938, and the relevant volumes of the
*Oeuvres complètes de Robespierre* series published by the
Société des Etudes Robespierristes, beginning in 1910. On
Saint-Just, G. Bruun, *Saint-Just, Apostle of the Terror,* N.Y.,
1932, and E. N. Curtis, *Saint-Just, Colleague of Robespierre,*
N.Y., 1935. For Danton, Mathiez's valuable studies: *La corruption parlementaire sous la Terreur,* Paris, 1917; *La conspiration de l'étranger,* Paris, 1918; *Danton et la paix,* Paris, 1919;
and *Autour de Danton,* Paris, 1926. H. Wendel, *Danton,* tr.
from the German, N.Y., 1935, is useful, while Lefebvre's brief
appreciation of Danton, reprinted in *Etudes sur la Révolution
française,* Paris, 1954, pp. 25-66, is a model of balanced judgment. For biographies of Barère's colleagues of the Committee
of Public Safety: M. Reinhard, *Le grand Carnot, l'organisateur
de la victoire (1792-1823),* Paris, 1952; A. Montier, *Robert
Lindet,* Paris, 1899; L. Lévy-Schneider, *Le Conventionnel Jeanbon Saint-André,* 2 vols., Paris, 1901; G. Bouchard, *Un organisateur de la victoire, Prieur de la Côte d'Or, membre du Comité de
salut public,* Paris, 1946; D. L. Dowd, *Pageant-Master of the
Republic, J. L. David,* Lincoln, Neb., 1948; and R. R. Palmer,
*Twelve Who Ruled,* Princeton, 1941, an outstanding study of the
Committee of Public Safety, which devotes much space to an
understanding treatment of Barère.

## Note on Sources

For the period of the Convention treated in Chapters VII-XIII, I have relied upon many recent monographs which have extensive references to Barère. For economic and social developments, Mathiez's *Girondins et Montagnards*, Paris, 1930, and *La vie chère et le mouvement social sous la Terreur*, Paris, 1927; D. Guérin, *La lutte de classes sous la première république*, 2 vols., Paris, 1946; A. Soboul, *Les sans-culottes Parisiens en l'an II*, Paris, 1958; C. Richard, *Le Comité de salut public et les fabrications de guerre*, Paris, 1922; F. L. Nussbaum, *Commercial Policy in the French Revolution*, Washington, 1923. Both C. Brinton, *The Jacobins, an essay in the new history*, N.Y., 1930, and D. Greer, *The Incidence of the Terror*, Cambridge, 1935, are useful on the psychology of the terrorists. In A. Ording's study, *Le bureau de police du Comité de salut public*, Oslo, 1930, and P. Sainte-Claire Deville, *La Commune de l'An II*, Paris, 1946, one can follow the dissensions within the Committee and Barère's efforts to patch up a truce. J. Fayet, *La Révolution française et la science*, Paris, 1960, gives many details concerning the Committee's plans for the France of the future in which Barère fully cooperated.

*Notes*

## Chapter I

Barère's own writings should be used with caution, yet his account of his family background and his earliest years is the best single source of information: *Barère*, I, 26-31, 203-243, and *Défense de B. Barère. Appel à la Convention nationale*, Paris, an III. See also J. Bourdette, *Notice des seigneurs de Biéouzac*, Toulouse, 1903, pp. 139-179, 265-269, and the brief article of Ch. de Pouey, "Où est né Bertrand Barère," in *Bulletin de la Société Académique des Hautes-Pyrénées*, 2e série, partie locale, IV (1897-1903), 1-11. I am indebted to Madame A. Mayonnade de Naïs of Tarbes, a collateral descendant, for the genealogy of Barère's family as well as that of his wife. The transcript of the baptismal certificate is in A.D.H.P., but otherwise the file *E 55 Familles, Barère de Vieuzac*, and in A.N., $F^7$ 9175, dossier 37367, adds little information. The nonagenarian who (in the spring of 1928) told me the anecdote of his nursemaid was the late Théodore Fontan; and the letter in my possession relating to "the little girls" was written to me by the late Léon Ducasse on November 8, 1928.

For the prevailing modes of thought during Barère's early years, there is much of value in A. Mornet, *Les origines intellectuelles de la révolution française, 1715-1787*, Paris, 1933, and P. Sagnac, *La formation de la société française moderne*, Paris, 1946, II, Livre III. For his boyhood and school years, A. Combes, *Histoire de l'école de Sorèze*, Toulouse, 1847, and J. Fabre de Massaguel, *L'école de Sorèze de 1758 au 19 Fructidor, an IV*, Toulouse, 1958, were useful.

For the law studies at the University of Toulouse, see L. Vie, *L'Université de Toulouse pendant la Révolution*, Toulouse, 1905, pp. 15-16; A. Deloume, *Aperçu historique sur la faculté de l'Université de Toulouse*, Toulouse, 1905, pp. 135-140; Bibliothèque universitaire de Toulouse: *Registre des actes en droit*, Nos. 5 and 6, Mss. 52, 72, 73, 77, and R. Gadave, *Recueil des documents sur l'histoire de l'Université de Toulouse*, Toulouse, 1910, No. 1316.

# Notes

The purchase of the royal councillorship at Tarbes: Bourdette, p. 169, and Archives départementales de la Haute-Garonne, *Archives civiles*, série B, III. His installation into that office in *Inventaire sommaire des archives départementales* [of the Hautes-Pyrénées] *antérieure à 1790*, série B, Tarbes, 1904, I, 315.

The legal briefs, in the three volumes entitled *Mémoires de Barère* in B.M.T. given above. Barère's strong feelings against the Chevalier of the Order of Malta did not keep him from editing the love letters under the title of *Le chevalier de Reys peint par ses lettres* (n.d.).

## Chapter II

As above, *Barère*, I, 203-243, also *Fonds Barère*, No. 31, for his interest in the problems of social welfare.

The most detailed study of the prize contest essays is J. Duffo, "Quelques ouvrages de jeunesse de Bertrand Barère," in *Le Semeur* (Tarbes), Feb.-June, 1937, though the appreciation is marred by the open hostility of the author. Of the *Eloges* which were published before the Revolution, the *Louis XII*, 1782, the *Furgole*, 1783, the *Séguier*, 1784, and the *Rousseau*, 1787, were included in the *Eloges académiques*, Paris, 1806; the *Amboise*, the *Pompignan*, and the *Montesquieu* were published for the first time in the later collection. The "Discours sur cette question: la navigation a-t-elle été utile ou nuisible," was not published and the manuscript is in *Fonds Barère*, No. 36. This file also contains the manuscript drafts of the *Louis XII*, the *Amboise*, the *Pompignan*, the *Rousseau*, and the *Montesquieu*. There are two additional manuscripts of the *Louis XII* in B.M.T., *Ms. 65* and *Ms. Kc 249*; one of the *Séguier*, *Ms. 65*, one of the *Montesquieu*, *Ms. 65*, and one of the *Pompignan*, *Ms. Kc 249*. The prevailing anti-English cast of thought, in Frances Acomb, *Anglophobia in France, 1763-1789*, Durham, N.C., 1950, especially chs. iv and v.

On Barère's marriage, there are the marriage contract in the archives of *Maître* Darget at Vic; Bourdette, pp. 170-173; G. Lenôtre, "Madame de Vieuzac," in *Le Temps* (Paris), August 24, 1929; *La Liberté des Hautes-Pyrénées* (Tarbes), July 26, 1894; and A.D.H.P. *Fonds Fontan* contains Jean-Pierre's letter of August 2, 1821, on Barère's assumption of the debts of his in-laws.

His election to the Academy of Floral Games is in *Barère*, I, 32-33, and Bourdette, p. 269. The Curator of the Academy reports that Barère's inaugural address is not to be found, also that his seat was declared vacant on January 7, 1806.

There is little on Barère's activity as a mason. Though his name does not appear on the manuscript file of the "Encyclopédique" lodge of Toulouse in the B.N. Mss., see, however, J. Gros, "Les loges maçonniques de Toulouse de 1740 à 1870," in *La Révolution française*, XL (1901), 234-270.

## Chapter III

For the political background of 1788-1789, apart from the general histories, M. B. Garrett, *The Estates General of 1789*, N.Y., 1935; L. Gottschalk, *Lafayette between the American and the French Revolution*, Chicago, 1950, chs. xxi-xxv; and the suggestive article of B. C. Shafer, "Bourgeois Nationalism on the Eve of the French Revolution," in *The Journal of Modern History*, x (1938), 31-50. Condorcet's letter to Mazzei is in R. Ciampini, *Lettere di Filippo Mazzei alla corte di Polonia*, Bologna, 1937, pp. 54-55.

From Barère himself, *Barère*, I, 203-243, also 24-41 for the electoral procedure in Tarbes and 341-438 for his diary of 1788-1789, which are to be compared with his later recollections of the same period, 231-238.

How Barère's *pays* of Bigorre voted and how the inhabitants felt about the political developments is recorded in Bourdette, pp. 174-175; Abbé L. Ricaud, *La Bigorre et les Hautes-Pyrénées pendant la Révolution*, Paris, 1894, Books ɪ and ɪɪ. G. Balencie, *Les cahiers de doléances de la sénéchaussée de Bigorre pour les Etats généraux de 1789*, 2 vols., Tarbes, 1925-1926, is a work of great value, not alone for the cahiers but for conditions in Bigorre. See vol. ɪ, Introduction, and ɪɪ, 583-589, for the hostility of the Third Estate to the two upper orders. There is also the monumental work of A. Brette, *Recueil de documents relatifs à la convocation des Etats généraux de 1789*, Paris, 1894-1915, ɪ, 457-459, 484-485, ɪɪ, 206, 481 ff., and ɪᴠ, 130-141. The printed text of the general cahier of the Third Estate, with some minor textual variations from the manuscript in A.N., BA 80, *Sénéchaussée de Tarbes en Bigorre*, is in *Archives parlementaires*, ɪɪ, 359-365. Barère's role in the final drafting of that cahier, in Brette, ɪᴠ, 137-138, Balencie, Introduction, and Ricaud, pp. 5-18.

## Chapter IV

Additional material for the background in early 1789, is in G. Lefebvre, *The Coming of the French Revolution*, tr. by R. R. Palmer, Princeton, 1949, and A. Soboul, *1789. "L'An un de la liberté,"* 2nd ed., Paris, 1950.

For Barère himself, *Barère*, ɪ, 245-277, and the files of *Le Point du Jour*, on which I have relied most of all for my treatment of his activities from 1789 to 1791. Since his own newspaper is so full for those two years, I have depended less on the accounts of parliamentary debates in the *Réimpression* and the *Archives parlementaires* than I do for the later period.

For Barère as a journalist: A. Söderhjelm, *Le régime de la presse pendant la Révolution française*, Helsingfors, 1900, ɪ, 86, 90, 95, 112, 123, 139; E. Hatin, *Histoire politique et littéraire de la presse en France*, Paris, 1860, ᴠɪ, 272-274; L. Gallois, *Histoire des journaux et journalistes de la Révolution*, Paris, 1846, ɪɪ, 1-16; G. Lefebvre, A. Soboul, Marc Bouloiseau, and others, eds., *Oeuvres complètes de Maximilien Robes-pierre*, Paris, 1950, VI, Introduction; A. Aulard, "Le carnet de Barère," in *La Rev. fran.*, XLIV (1903), 497-500. Both Hatin and Gallois state that Barère was associated with Louvet de Couvray in founding the *Journal des débats et des décrets*. The statement that Barère made great financial profit from his newspaper is in A. C. Duquesnoy, *Journal sur l'Assemblée Constituante*, Paris, 1894, I, 491. Mazzei's good opinion of *Le Point du Jour* is in Ciampini, p. 154.

For David's painting of the Tennis Court Oath, pp. 36-40 of Dowd, given under Modern Authorities above. Barère's letter to his constituents on the events of June 23, in G. Hubbard, "Deux lettres autographes de Barère de Vieuzac," in *La Rév. fran.*, V (1883), 168-173. His opinion of the murder of Foulon and Berthier, in *Fonds Barère*, Nos. 20 and 21, and his note-book on the course of events from the end of August to early September, in A.N., AB, *xix, 600*. For his participation in the debates on the Declaration of Rights of Man and the first articles of the constitution, in addition to *Le Point du Jour*, also the pamphlet of 1790, *Etrennes du peuple . . . précédée d'une notice aux nations*. Bourdette, pp. 191-195, gives the text of the letters of August 8, 1789, and September 7, 1790. In his memoirs Barère incorrectly dates the sacrifice of his councillor-ship on August 4, 1789, and puts its purchase price at 12,000 livres; the contemporary accounts in *Le Point du Jour* and *Journal de Perlet* both give the date as September 25 and the value as 8,000 livres.

### Chapter V

As before, *Le Point du Jour* and *Barère*, I, 278-339, and the parliamentary debates in *Réimpression* and the *Archives par-lementaires*. The official text of his report on the restitution of the estates of the Huguenots and those for the Committee of Domains are in *Archives parlementaires*. There, too, his speech of February 28, 1791, on the respect due to the law (which he filed with the secretary of the assembly but did not deliver) and his comments of May 19, 1791, on Robespierre's self-denying ordinance.

For the establishment of the department of the Hautes-Pyrénées, the following three publications of Barère: *Observations présentées à l'Assemblée nationale par M. Barère de Vieuzac, député du Bigorre, sur la nécessité de faire de ce pays d'Etats un département, dont la ville de Tarbes soit le chef-lieu, 21 décembre, 1789*, Paris, n. d.; *Lettre de monsieur Barère de Vieuzac aux communes de Bigorre, ses commettans*, Paris, 24 décembre, 1789; *Notice sur l'établissement du département des Hautes-Pyrénées en 1789 et 1790*, Tarbes, 1834. The appreciation of his efforts in L. Ricaud, *Un régime qui commence*, Tarbes, 1911, pp. 5, 28-29, 57-62, 78-80.

His membership in the Jacobins and his adherence to the Société de 1789, in Aulard, *La Société des Jacobins*, I, lxvi-lxviii, 407, 516, and A. Challamel, *Les clubs contrerévolutionnaires*, Paris, 1895, pp. 391-431. The flight of the king and the Champs-de-Mars "massacre," in Challamel, 287 ff.; Aulard, *Jacobins*, III, 122, n. 2; and *Oeuvres complètes de Robespierre*, VII, 58-92. The letter to his uncle on April 16, 1790, in L. Gershoy, "Three Letters of Bertrand Barère," in *Journal of Modern History*, I (1929), 72, and that to Mailhe of January 24, 1791, in J. Adher, "Lettres de Barère et de Mailhe," *La Rév. fran.*, XL (1904), 78-80.

For his attitude toward the free Negroes, in addition to *Le Point du Jour*, the interesting brief study by R. Masso, *Bertrand Barère et les questions coloniales, 1789-1840*, Auch, 1957.

His relations with the Duke of Orléans and Mme de Genlis, *Barère*, I, 73, 294-302; L. Ellis and J. Turquan, *La belle Paméla*, London, 1924, pp. 201, 206-208; and J. Harmand, *Mme de Genlis. Sa vie intime et politique, 1746-1830*, Paris, 1912, pp.

220-222, 261. His relations with Mazzei in Ciampini, pp. 154, 172, 192, 249, 287.

The contemporary Parisian press provides much less on Barère for this period than it does for the Convention years. The two leading royalist newspapers, *Les Actes des Apôtres* and the *Journal général de la Cour et de la Ville*, ignored him almost completely. Of the leftist press, Marat's *L'Ami du peuple* made scattering references, in the main uncomplimentary, especially on the score of his reports on the royal domain. Among the journals of moderate revolutionaries the weekly *La Feuille villageoise* did not refer to him, while there were only passing brief and neutral references to him in Prudhomme's *Révolutions de Paris*, Brissot's *Le Patriote français* and *Journal de Perlet*. The first organ of the Jacobins, the weekly *Journal des Amis de la Constitution*, had only a single entry concerning Barère for the period from November 30, 1790, to September 20, 1791. There are many references, none of them hostile, and especially to his stand against the parlements and his reports on the royal domain, in the weekly *Annales patriotiques et littéraires de France* of L. S. Mercier. But the fullest and most favorable treatments are in Mirabeau's *Le Courrier de Provence*, and Gorsas's *Le Courrier des départemens*, and *Courrier français*, edited by J. C. Poncelin de la Roche-Tilhac. There was praise for Barère in two biographical dictionaries, *Le petit dictionnaire des grands hommes de la Révolution*, Paris, 1790, and J. P. Luchet, *Les contemporains de 1789 et 1790*, 3 vols., Paris, 1790, I, 93-95. Among the memoirs published later which showed the esteem in which Barère was then held, E. Dumont, *Recollections of Mirabeau*, London, 1822, p. 199; Madame de Chastenay, *Mémoires*, 2 vols., Paris, 1896, I, 113; and *Mémoires de Dumouriez*, Paris, 1822, Bk. III, ch. iv.

The present writer has covered this period in "Barère in the Constituent Assembly," in *American Historical Review*, XXXVI (1931), 295-313.

# Notes

## Chapter VI

As above, *Barère*, ɪ, 64-120, and ɪɪ, 1-36. The data on the real estate transactions in Barère's memoirs are far from complete and are to be supplemented by the miscellaneous information in A.D.H.P., *E 55 Familles, Barère de Vieuzac*.

The letter to Dumouriez in the spring of 1792 is in Bibliothèque historique de la Ville de Paris, *Collection Liesville*, which Professor Louis Gottschalk kindly called to my attention.

Barère's relations with the Jacobins of his natal city in J. Duffo, "Sur la Société des Amis de la Constitution à Tarbes," in *Bull. de la Soc. Acad. des Hautes-Pyrénées* (1929), 42-55.

## Chapter VII

For Chapters ᴠɪɪ to xɪɪɪ, consult the titles listed under Published Sources and Modern Authorities in the General Note. *Barère*, ɪ, 53-121, and ɪɪ, 37-241, 285-423, covers the National Convention from September 1792 to the downfall of Robespierre in Thermidor 1794. As before, the debates are in *Réimpression* and *Archives parlementaires*.

For this chapter see also the official text of Barère's decisive speech of January 4, 1793, in the *Archives parlementaires*; Aulard, "Note sur le portrait de Barère par David," in *La Rév. fran.*, ʟxɪᴠ (1921), 170 ff.; H. R. Yorke, *France in 1802*, 2 vols., London, 1804; and John Moore, *A Residence in France*, London, 1794, ɪɪ.

## Chapter VIII

As above. The *Réimpression* carried only brief excerpts of Barère's final attempt to mediate the Girondin-Montagnard struggle on May 29, 1793, and his speech is to be consulted in the official reprint or in the *Archives parlementaires*. For

# Notes

Danton's share in that attempt, F. Bornarel, "Danton, collaborateur de Barère," in *La Rév. fran.*, XIX (1890), 185-188. Also, R. M. Brace, "General Dumouriez and the Girondins, 1792-1793," in *American Historical Review*, LVI (1951), 493-509; P. Caron, "Trois lettres de Jeanbon Saint-André à Barère," in *La Rév. fran.*, LXII (1912), 356-366; Aulard, "La diplomatie du premier Comité de salut public," in *Etudes et Leçons*, Paris, 1902; Gottschalk, *Jean Paul Marat*, N.Y., 1927.

## Chapter IX

As above. Soboul's *Les sans-culottes* is particularly helpful.

## Chapters X and XI

In addition to the references above, M. Reinhard, "La guerre et la paix à la fin de 1793," in *Annales historiques de la Révolution française*, No. 131 (1953), 97-103; for the economic war against England: besides Nussbaum's *Commercial Policy*, P. Foner, ed., *Complete Writings of Thomas Paine*, N.Y., 1945, II, 1332-1335. The account of the work procedure of the Committee of Public Safety is based on *Barère*, I, 78-93; Bouchard's *Prieur*, particularly Prieur's own *Révélations* in the Appendix; Reinhard's *Carnot*; Guérin's *La lutte de classes*, I; Palmer's *Twelve Who Ruled*; and J. M. Thompson's "L'organisation du travail du Comité de salut public," in *Ann. hist. de la Rév. fran.*, X (1933), 454-460. The attacks on Barère by the Paris radicals are itemized in Guérin, I, 358-361. Barère's retrospective lament over the needless bloodshed is in *Fonds Barère*, No. 48.

For the opposition to the Committee of Public Safety, the special studies given in the General Note, especially Richard and Soboul. G. Rudé's study, *The Crowd in the French Revolution*, Oxford, 1959, and R. Cobb, "Quelques aspects de la mentalité révolutionnaire (Avril 1793 -Thermidor An II)," in *Revue d'Histoire moderne et contemporaine*, vi (1959), 81-120, throw great light upon the thinking and the behavior of the sans-culottes. Also Mathiez, "Les décrets de Ventôse . . . ," in *Ann. hist. de la Rév. fran.*, v (1928), 193-219; Lefebvre's essay on the Ventôse decrees in *Questions agraires au temps de la Terreur*, 2nd ed., 1954, pp. 4-59; and the same author's "Le commerce extérieur en l'An II," in *La Rév. fran.*, lxxv (1925), 133-155 and 214-243. For the Food Commission, P. Caron, ed., *La Commission des subsistances: Procès-verbaux et actes*, 2 vols., Paris, 1924-1925. The campaign for clemency in the winter of 1794, in H. Calvet, ed., *Camille Desmoulins: Le Vieux Cordelier*, Paris, 1936.

## Chapter XII

Aulard's *Recueil des actes*, xi-xv, is the basic source for the comprehensive effort of the Committee, in which Barère was so active, to lay the bases of new republican institutions. The monograph of J. Fayet, *La Révolution française et la science, 1789-1795*, utilizes J. Guillaume's *Procès-verbaux du Comité d'instruction publique de la Convention nationale*, 6 vols., Paris, 1907, and complements the earlier work of G. Pouchet, *Les sciences pendant la Terreur*, Paris, ed. of 1896. There are valuable suggestions on Barère's role in the self-conscious formulation of cultural nationalism in Dowd's study of J. L. David, already cited, which makes use of L. Tuetey's *Procès-verbaux de la commission temporaire des arts*, 2 vols., Paris, 1912-1918; and the same author's article on "Art as National Propaganda in the French Revolution," in *Public Opinion Quarterly*, xv (1951), 532-546.

The bare facts of the sinking of *Le Vengeur* out of which Barère elaborated his report, in the article signed by L. R., "L'histoire et la légende," in *La Rév. fran.*, i (1881), 407-419.

## Notes

### Chapter XIII

Barère's account as above in Chapter VII. The works of Ording, Soboul, and Deville, given under Modern Authorities, are especially useful for the last months of the "Great Committee." Mathiez's article, "Les séances du 4 et 5 Thermidor, an II," reprinted in *Girondins et Montagnards*, pp. 139-170, is serviceable, as are his essays on the attempt to discredit Robespierre as a religious zealot: "Le rôle de Barère et de Vadier au 9 Thermidor, jugé par Buonarroti," in *Annales Révolutionnaires*, IV (1911), 96-102; "La politique de Robespierre et le 9 Thermidor expliquée par Buonarroti," *ibid.*, III (1910), 481-513; and "Catherine Théot et le mysticisme chrétien," in *La Rév. fran.*, XL (1901), 479-518. Buonarroti's notes on this question, in B.N. Mss., Nouvelles acquisitions françaises, No. 20804. The biography of Vadier by A. Tournier, *Vadier, président du Comité de sûreté générale sous la Terreur*, Paris, 1896, adds little to our knowledge concerning Barère.

Barère's refutation of the charges that were made during the Thermidorian reaction is in *Réponse des membres des deux anciens Comités*, which is reprinted in *La Rév. fran.*, XXXIV (1898), 57-80, 154-179, 243-282.

### Chapter XIV

The background for the reaction after the overthrow of Robespierre is in the general histories; also in Lefebvre, *Les Thermidoriens*, Paris, 1937. See Aulard's *Paris pendant la Réaction thermidorienne et sous le Directoire*, Paris, 1928, I, for excerpts from the press and police reports. Though the parliamentary debates are reported sparsely in the *Réimpression*, the account in *Histoire parlementaire*, XXXVI, helps fill in the gaps. The best account of the developments culminating in the order for Barère's deportation is in K. D. Tønnesson, *La défaite des sans-culottes*, Paris, 1959, chs. viii and ix.

# Notes

From Barère himself, *Barère*, I, 121-149, II, 242-284, 423-427.
The official accusations against him, L. Lecointre, *Les crimes
de sept membres des anciens Comités*, and J. B. Saladin, *Rapport au nom de la Commission des 21*, were both published in
the fall of 1794. The disclaimers of the accused, apart from the
*Réponse des membres des deux anciens Comités*, already
given, are: *Second mémoire des membres de l'ancien Comité
de salut public; Réponse de B. Barère . . . au tableau des
persécutions déposées contre lui par Dubois-Crancé; Observations de Barère sur le rapport . . . par Saladin; Réponse . . . aux
pièces communiquées par la Commission des Vingt-Un*; and
*Partie de la défense . . . présentée dans la séance du 5 Germinal*. They are all of 1795.

Barère's replies to the more personal accusations in *Les
Alors . . .* and at greater length in *Défense de B. Barère. Appel
à la Convention nationale*, Paris, an III. Those accusations appeared in the contemporary press and in a great many pamphlets which vied with one another in irresponsibility. With respect to the grotesque variations that appeared in the newspapers on the related themes of Barère's cruelty, eroticism,
profiteering, and treason, a reader would find a symphonic
treatment in Fréron's *L'Orateur du peuple* and Tallien's *L'Ami
des citoyens*. If there is a common source for the defamations
that characterized the brochures, it is certainly to be found in
J. Vilate, *Causes secrètes de la Révolution du 9 au 10 Thermidor*, and the two pamphlets of Méhée, *fils*, *La queue de Robespierre* and *La grande queue de Laurent Lecointre*. It is interesting that the catalogue of the Bibliothèque Nationale attributes the *Vilate* to the great fancier of eroticism, Choderlos
de Laclos, the author of *Les liaisons dangereuses*. Other representative brochures, which must have circulated widely if
one is to judge from the copies available in library collections,
include *La famille Barère démasquée; Rapport à faire par
Barère au nom de l'opinion publique; La grande queue de*

## Notes

*Barère; Leurs têtes branlent; Le cri de l'humanité; Le club infernal;* and *Première séance des Jacobins aux enfers.*

On the allegation of the tanneries, see Aulard above, I, 510; L. Combes, *Episodes et curiosités révolutionnaires,* Paris, 1872; and H. Wallon, "Culottes de peau humaine," in *Revue de la Révolution,* IX (1887), 177-183.

The malicious nonsense of Vilate concerning Madame de Mailly and Barère can be checked against the depositions of the lady in question and her lover, M. Travanet, in A.N.[7] 4775[33], dossier Travanet; F[7] 4743[3], dossier Héron; F[7] 4641, dossier Charpentier; F[7] 4774[30], dossier 5; and A.P.P., AA 14, AA 27, and AA 29.

### Chapter XV

*Barère,* I, 121-149, II, 285-423, and III, 1-86. As before, the *Réimpression* for the parliamentary debates. The political background in the general histories and Lefebvre, *Le Directoire,* Paris, 1946, for the capital, and in the studies cited above of L. Ricaud for the Hautes-Pyrénées. Public opinion in the capital in Aulard's *Paris pendant la Réaction thermidorienne et sous le Directoire* given under Published Sources.

The quotations from the letters to Demerville come from Aulard, "Une correspondance inédite de Barère," in *La Rév. fran.,* XLIX (1905), 264-266, in which the author calls attention to the collection of 113 unpublished autograph letters that Barère wrote from 1795 to 1829 which M. Noël Charavay then owned. More than one hundred of those letters were addressed to Demerville between 1795 and 1799. The late Léon Ducasse, *procureur de la République* at Toulouse, did his utmost through governmental channels to find out what happened to this collection, but finally wrote to me: "Despite my persistent inquiries and endeavors, I have lost all hope . . . and I conclude that these letters are definitively not to be found." The letter from Bertrand to his uncle Joseph, in L. Gershoy, "Three Letters of Bertrand Barère," in *Journal of Modern History,* I

(1929), 67-76, and the letter to the deputy Briot in 1799, in M. Dayet, "Une lettre de B. Barère," in *Ann. hist. de la Rév. fran.*, v (1928), 561-566. Barère's testimony of 1800 concerning the 2,400 francs that Demerville gave him in 1795 is in A.P.P., AA 270, *liasse Barère*. The Convention order for Barère to stand trial, in A.N., BB³ 30 and F⁷ 4651, Nos. 12-122; the new order for his deportation and the jailer's deposition on his escape from prison, in AF⁷ 6678, Nos. 45-55; for the activities of his family in Tarbes, F¹ᶜ III, Hautes-Pyrénées, No. 9. See J. Labougle, "L'Epitaphe de Bertrand Barère," in *Bull. de la Soc. Acad. des Hautes-Pyrénées* (1944-1945), 1-4, and the B.M.T. for manuscript drafts of the *Montesquieu, De la pensée,* and *La liberté des mers.*

The evaluations of Barère's personality and role were almost uniformly hostile during the years of the Directory. The post-Thermidor accusations of Lecointre, Dulaure, and Courtois are cited in the text. References to the *Mémoires* of J. B. Louvet, first published in 1795, are to the 1899 edition, I, 18-22; to those of A. Meillan, also of 1795, to the 1825 reprint, p. 8; to H. Riouffe's *Mémoires d'un détenu*, originally 1795 also, to p. 466 of the 1823 edition; to H. M. Williams, *Letters . . .*, 4 vols., London, 1795-1796, I, 181-183. The quotation from Madame de Genlis' *Précis*, Hamburg, 1796, is in Barère's *Mémoires*, I, 38 and note. Representative collections of biographical anecdotes include J. C. Bailleul, *Almanach des bizarreries humaines*, Paris, 1796, p. 38; C. Fauchet, *Tableaux des principaux évènements*, Paris, 1798, p. 78; *Recueil d'anecdotes . . .* , Paris, 1798, pp. 424-426; *Biographical Anecdotes of the Founders of the French Revolution*, London, 2nd ed., 1799, I, 429; *Dictionnaire des Jacobins vivans*, Hamburg, 1799, pp. 16-17; L. S. Mercier, *Le nouveau Paris*, 6 vols., Paris, 1798-1799, II, 90. In the *Histoire de la Révolution française par Deux Amis de la Liberté*, see vols. x, 77, 78, 232, XII, 318, and XIII, 20, which were published between 1795 and 1799; L. M. Prudhomme, *Histoire des crimes commis pendant la Révolution,* 6 vols., Paris, 1797, v, 43-44, 52, 65, 99, 109, 111, 113-114, 153, and vi, 48, 484. The *Mémorial révolutionnaire de la Convention* is by the rabid royalist, G. V. Vasselin, 4 vols., Paris, 1797, ii, 181, 186, iii, 16-17, 22-25; see also F. X. Pagès, *Histoire secrète de la Révolution française,* 7 vols., Paris, 1797-1802, ii, 202.

## Chapters XVI-XVII

*Barère,* i, 149-167, and iii, 86-229; also his published writings which are cited in the text. The political background is in the histories of G. Pariset, *Le Consulat et l'Empire* and Lefebvre's *Napoléon,* both given under Modern Authorities; also in Aulard's *Paris sous le Consulat* and *Paris sous le premier Empire,* given under the Published Sources. On Barère's relations with Louis XVIII and with Napoleon during the Hundred Days, in addition to *Histoire parlementaire,* xl (1838), 97-380, see E. Gallo, *Les cent-jours,* Paris, 1924; A. Houssaye, *1815,* Paris, 1939; L. Madelin, *Fouché,* 2 vols., Paris, 1900-1901. The *Moniteur* of April 27, 1815, reported favorably on his translation, *Théorie de la constitution de la Grande-Bretagne,* from the English work of Henry Brooke, and devoted three columns to the critique that he made in it of the Charter of Louis XVIII. The memoirs of Méneval, Bourrienne, Roederer, and Madame de Récamier, which were published later, all have miscellaneous information which is to be used with caution. In the *Souvenirs du comte de Montgaillard,* ed. by Ch. de Lacroix, Corbeil, 1895, there are no references to Barère; nor are there any in A.N., AF[III] 771 ter, carton 44, d. 158, of Montgaillard's papers.

The nature of Barère's journalistic services for Napoleon's government is treated in R. Holtman, *Napoleonic Propaganda,* Baton Rouge, La., 1950; M. van Schoor, *La presse sous le Consulat et l'Empire,* Bruxelles, 1899; E. Hatin, *Histoire politique et littéraire de la preses,* already cited, vi; and the work of H. R. Yorke given in Chapter vii.

His dealings with Izquierdo, in A. Fugier, *Napoléon et l'Espagne, 1795-1808,* 2 vols., Paris, 1930.

The annotated copy of the English pamphlet, which Barère countered with *Réponse d'un republicain,* is in the possession of *Maître* Theil of Tarbes; his annotations of the *Tableau politique de l'Europe* on the copy of that work in A.D.H.P.; and his own evaluation of the great worth of the bulletins that he addressed to Napoleon from 1803 to 1807, in *Fonds Barère,* No. 11. Details concerning his property, in A.D.H.P., *Greffe du Tribunal civil . . . ,* 9 aôut, 1834, and *E 55 Familles, liasse Lassalle.* The reports on his health, in A.P.P., AA 327.

The letters come from several sources. From E. Welvert, *Lendemains révolutionnaires,* Paris, 1907, come the letter to the First Consul in 1800, the letter to L. Gallois, of May 10, 1837, and Napoleon's letter to Fouché of Sept. 9, 1804. The note to Lucien Bonaparte in the early spring of 1800, in A.N., $F^{1d}$ II, 33, and the letter to Gaudin, in P. Giraud, "Barère nécessiteux," in *Rev. des Curiosités révolutionnaires,* II (1910-1911), 33-34. From the *Fichier Charavay,* 336 r., 333 r., 335 r., 331 r., respectively, the following: the letters to Louis Bonaparte in 1804 and 1806, his manuscript notes of 1804 for the projected work on the political errors of the French, the letters to his publisher, Renouard, from 1806 to 1809. The letter of 1810 to the author of the *Napoléonide* in *Le Carnet historique et littéraire,* VIII (1900), 292-293. The letter to Louis XVIII, in 1814 in *Le Semeur* (Tarbes), June 12, 1928.

On the wretched Demerville affair, *Barère* III, 110-124, and Aulard's *Paris sous le Consulat,* I. The details are in A.N., $F^7$ 6678, Nos. 40, 42, 43; A.P.P., 270, Nos. 106-110, 201-208, and 267. The *Procès instruit par le tribunal criminel du département de la Seine . . . ,* Paris, an IX, gives the testimony of the trial of the conspirators. Secondary works: L. Madelin, ed., *Mémoires de Fouché,* Paris, 1945; Fescourt, *Histoire de la double conspiration de 1800,* Paris, 1819; P. M. Desmarest,

## Notes

*Témoignages historiques,* Paris, 1833, and G. Hue, *Un complot de police sous le Consulat,* Paris, 1910.

For the biographical dictionaries, the Yorke, given in Chapter VII; P. C. Lecomte, *Mémorial ou Journal impartial et anécdotique de la Révolution,* 2 vols., Paris, 1801-1803, I, especially 316-323; *Biographie moderne,* ed. by Coiffier de Moret and others (1st ed., 1800), 3rd ed., 3 vols., London, 1811, I, 70-78; article "Barère," in *Lives of the Revolutionists,* London, 1818; J. B. Robert, ed., *Vie politique de tous les députés de la Convention nationale,* Paris, 1814, pp. 17-19; article "Barère" in Dr. Robinet and others, eds., *Dictionnaire historique et biographique,* 2 vols., Paris, 1815. Among the historians, Vicomte de Toulongeon, *Histoire de la France depuis la révolution de 1789,* 7 vols., Paris, 1801-1810, III-V; C. F. de Beaulieu, *Essais historiques sur les causes et les effets de la Révolution en France,* 6 vols., Paris, 1801-1803, V and VI; A. F. Bertrand de Molleville, *Histoire de la Révolution en France pendant les dernières années de Louis XVI,* 13 vols., Paris, 1801, XI, 457; Ch. de Lacretelle, *Histoire de France pendant le dix-huitième siècle,* 14 vols., 1808-1826, X-XII; A. Fantin des Odouards, *Abrégé chronologique de la Révolution en France à l'usage des écoles publiques,* 2 vols., Paris, 1801-1802, II, 219-306, repeated the views he had expressed in his *Histoire philosophique* of 1796.

## Chapter XVIII

As before, *Barère,* I, 167-174, III, 229-262, 275-392. For the escape from Paris and the search from 1815 to 1816, A.N., F⁷ 6678, dossier 12; F⁷ 6710; F⁷ 9175, dossiers 38467 and 41137; F¹ᶜ III, Hautes-Pyrénées, No. 9; and in A.A.P., AA 327.

Published accounts of the years in exile: Welvert, given above; A. Baron, "Les exilés de Bruxelles," in *Revue de Paris,* Ière série, XIX (1830), 13-25; M. A. Baudot, *Notes historiques sur la Convention,* Paris, 1863, pp. 186, 209; H. Saint-Ferréol, *Les proscrits français en Belgique,* Brussels, 1870, I, 13, 14. A. Galante-

Garrone, *Filippo Buonarroti e i Convenzionali in esilio,* Milan, 1953, pp. 44, 46.

Unpublished data on the Belgian years: A.N., F⁷ 6678 d. 12; A.D.H.P., *Fonds Fontan,* for the letters from Jean-Pierre in 1821; Archives de la ville de Bruxelles, *Police des Etrangers, 1822;* and Algemeen Rijksarchief at The Hague, *Secretariat of State,* secret file. A. Galante-Garrone kindly provided me with photostats of the two letters that Barère wrote to the Tussaus, which came from the Vadier family papers.

The two declarations of February and May, 1828, relating to the payments that Barère was making to Marguerite Lefauconnier are in the private archives of *Maître* Theil of Tarbes. The *Fichier Charavay,* 332 r., 331 v., 324 r., 327 v., and 330 v. and 331 r., for excerpts from various letters between 1825 and 1830; the letter to Lafayette, for which I am indebted to Professor Gottschalk, is now in the chateau of the Lafayette family.

The quoted passage expressive of the despondency which overwhelmed him is in *Fonds Barère,* No. 46.

Many old memoirs were reprinted during the Bourbon Restoration: those of Vilate, Louvet, Riouffe, Williams, Genlis, and Meillan. Among those published for the first time, see *Mémoires de Dumouriez,* Paris, 1822, Bk. III, ch. iv; P. T. Durand-Maillane, *Mémoires sur la Convention nationale,* Paris, 1825, p. 379; *Mémoires de Barbaroux,* Paris, 1822 (references are to the 1936 edition), pp. 159, 187, 217, 232; A. C. Thibaudeau, *Mémoires sur la Convention et le Directoire,* 2 vols., Paris, 1824, I, 88. The biographical dictionaries: *Biographie moderne ou Galerie historique,* 3 vols., Paris, 1815, I, 66, 68; *Dictionnaire des Girouettes,* Paris, 1815, p. 33; *Dictionnaire des Braves et des non-Girouettes,* Paris, 1816, p. 20; L. G. Michaud and others, *Biographie des hommes vivants,* 5 vols., Paris, 1816-1819, I, 202-209; *Biographie nouvelle des contemporains,* ed. by A. V. Arnault and others, 20 vols., Paris, 1820-1825, II, 109-116. For histories and pseudo-histories: R. J. Durdent, *Histoire de la Convention,* 2 vols., Paris, 1817-1818, I, 24, 123, and II, 247-248; Vicomte Conny de la Faye, *La France sous le règne de la Convention,* Paris, 1820, pp. 65,

105, 305; F. A. Mignet, *Histoire de la Révolution française* . . . , Paris, 1824 (references are to the 2nd edition), Bruxelles, 1835, II, 57; L. A. Thiers, *Histoire de la Révolution française*, Paris, 1823-1827 (references are to the Bruxelles, 1834 edition), II, 257, 410, 411, 448, and IV, 12, 13, 55, 58; J. G. M. Roques de Montgaillard, *Histoire de France depuis 1789 à 1825*, 9 vols., Paris, 1826, IV, 281-285.

## Chapter XIX

On Barère's last years in Tarbes, *Barère*, I, 177-196 and II, 262-265.

The *Fonds Barère*, No. 48, for his apostrophe against his family in 1835, and No. 68 for "Le Tartare à Paris," which Dr. Labougle excerpted in *Revue des Hautes-Pyrénées*, XXXII (1937) and XXXIII (1938). Labougle also published Barère's farewells to Paris in *Bull. de la Soc. Acad. des Hautes-Pyrénées* (1947-1948, mimeographed).

His unflagging interest in literature, the arts, and history, in *Fonds Barère*, Nos. 5, 7, 9, 10, 22, 47, 58; his religiosity and hostility toward the aristocracy, in Nos. 35, 77, 81; in contemporary politics, Nos. 6, 12, 13, 40, 41, 53, 75; on the Revolution and the era of Napoleon, Nos. 5, 28, 40, 55, 56, 60, 61, 88. For his changing opinions of Robespierre and Napoleon, see also *Barère*, I, 59-64, 116-119, 149-161, and II, 211-236.

On the settlement of his financial affairs: the *Greffe du Tribunal civil* already given; the donation of December 31, 1834, to Marguerite Lefauconnier and his will of June 16, 1840, in the private archives of *Maître* Blanc; the donation to Henry Lefauconnier of February 1, 1837, in the archives of *Maître* Theil.

His final political activity in the *Adresse* of 1831 and the *Notice* of 1834, which are supplemented by the reports of the prefects in A.N., F$^{1b}$ *liasse* 1833-1838 and F$^{1c}$ III, Hautes-Pyrénées. The letters of 1839 and 1840 to Dintrans, respectively in *Ann. hist. de la Rév. fran.*, VI (1929), 291-293, and *Fichier Charavay*, 339 r.

*Notes*

There is disappointingly little, besides *Barère*, II, 288-296, concerning the financial aid that he received. For the pension as a former magistrate, B.H.V.P., dossier Barère de Vieuzac; and *Fichier Charavay*, 339 r., for the letter to Dintrans in 1840. On the pension that he had as a man of letters, A.N., F$^{1c}$ III, Hautes-Pyrénées (1833-1834); *Fichier Charavay*, 326 r. and 331 v. The pension drawn on the privy purse of Louis-Philippe, in *Fichier Charavay*, 327 v., which cites the letter to Baron Fain, and 339 r. and 331 r. for the letters to Dintrans. An article by A. Chabaud, "Barère et les fonds secrets de Louis-Philippe," in *Ann. hist. de la Rév. fran.*, XII (1935), 546-547, raises the question whether Barère did not repay the benevolent government by writing inspired articles and doing espionage.

The correspondence between Barère and H. Carnot and David d'Angers on the editing and publication of his memoirs, in *Intermédiaire des Chercheurs et des Curieux*, XXIII (1890), 307-308, for the March 7, 1838, letter to David; the rest of the epistolary exchange is in B.N. Mss., Nouvelles acquisitions françaises, 24158, folios 41-45, and *Fichier Charavay*, 324 r. The disappearance of Barère's bulletins to Napoleon, which he had prepared for publication, in L. Caddau, "Trois lettres," cited above under Paris archives.

For the other letters to which the text refers: B.H.V.P., file Barère de Vieuzac, for the two letters to the young Pelleport; *La Rév. fran.*, V (1883), 173-176, for the letter of 1834 to *Maître* Lebrun; *ibid.*, XXXVIII (1900), 426-427, for the one to Souberbielle in 1839; *Revue rétrospective*, IV (1886), 284-288, for the letter to L. Gallois in 1837. For the letters between Buonarroti and Tussau concerning Barère, A. Saitta, *Filippo Buonarroti*, 2 vols., Rome, 1951, II, 57, 58, and the work of A. Galante-Garrone already given, in the Note for Chapter XVIII.

The admiring opinions voiced by his last visitors, in Bourdette, p. 182.

The historical verdict during the last decade of Barère's life: E. Dumont's *Recollections of Mirabeau*, London, 1832, p. 199; M. Dumas, *Memoirs of his own Time*, London, 1839, ii, 29; *Encyclopédie des gens du monde*, par une Société des Savants, 22 vols., Paris, 1837-1844, ii, 78-79; article "Barère" in A. Rabbe and others, *Biographie universelle et portative des contemporains*, Paris, 1834. For the histories, see L. Gallois, *Histoire de la Convention nationale*, 8 vols., Paris, 1837-1848, especially i, 268, and ii, 106-108, 303-307; T. Carlyle, *The French Revolution*, 3 vols., London, 1837, iii (of the London, 1904 reprinting), 149; and P. B. J. Buchez and P. C. Roux, *Histoire parlementaire*, 40 vols., Paris, 1834-1838, cited under Published Sources.

## Epilogue: The Historical Verdict

From 1841 to 1870. The obituaries are in *Allocution prononcée par Me. Lebrun . . . sur la tombe de M. Bertrand Barère de Vieuzac . . .*, Tarbes, 1841; the *Annual Register*, London, 1841, Appendix, 178; *The Times* (London), Jan. 21, 1841, p. 5. Among the Paris papers, the voice of the republican opposition, *Le National*, was the only one to devote space to a long obituary, Jan. 17, 1841, pp. 3-4. Other dailies which recorded Barère's death with little or no comment: the royalist *La Quotidienne*, Jan. 17, 18, and 20, 1841; the influential right-center *La Presse*, edited by Emile Girardin, Jan. 17, 1841; the Bonapartist *Le Constitutionnel*, Jan. 16, 1841; the venerable and still important *La Gazette de France*, Jan. 18, 1841; and the once progressive, now staid, *Le Temps*, Jan. 17, 1841. Surprisingly, the widely read *Le Siècle*, which was the organ of the left constitutional opposition, carried no mention of his death. Efforts to sample the provincial press brought scant returns, for the files of representative newspapers of southwest France were not available, and in other newspapers there was no mention of Barère's death. The brief comment in the *Gazette de Languedoc* is from the issue of Jan. 6, 1842.

For reviews of Barère's *Mémoires, Le Temps* of June 2, 1842, made a sympathetic reference to Carnot's preliminary *Notice*, which was published separately before the *Mémoires* themselves. For the *Mémoires* proper, see *La Gazette de France, Supplément* to the issues of July 13 and 15, 1843; *La Presse, Supplément* to the issue of Nov. 18, 1843; and *Le National*, under the signature of "Old Nick," on Dec. 19, 1843, Jan. 5 and 13, 1844. The hostile notice in the *Revue des Deux Mondes* is by A. Ladet, 4e série, xxxi (Sept. 1, 1842), 828-842, and Macaulay's as given in the Preface, in *Edinburgh Review*, clx (April, 1844), 275-351.

Of the memoirs of Barère's contemporaries, that of P. C. F. Daunou (1848) and those of Pétion, Buzot, and Barbaroux, edited by C. A. Dauban (1866), repeated accusations made in earlier Girondin writings. J. C. Lacretelle, *Dix années d'épreuves*, Paris, 1842 (reprint of 1875, p. 10), was not less hostile than he had been in his *Histoire*, given in the Note to Chapters xvi and xvii. There were passing unflattering references in the memoirs of General Pépé, Paris, 1847, iii, 426-427; J. F. Mallet du Pan, 2 vols., Paris, 1851; and L. Véron, Paris, 1853, ii, 215-220, 243-244. Of those more friendly in tone, see *Mémoires sur Carnot par son fils*, Paris, 1861, i, 511, 527, and the *Notes* of M. A. Baudot, given under Chapter xviii.

In the biographical dictionaries, the articles on Barère in A. Maurin, ed., *Galerie historique de la Révolution française*, Paris, 1843, iii, 37-39; Dr. Hoefer [pseud.], ed., *Nouvelle Biographie générale*, Paris, 1859, iv, 490-496; and L. G. Michaud, ed., *Biographie universelle*, 2nd ed., Paris, 1854, iii, 87-94. The brief works of A. Cuvillier-Fleury, *Portraits politiques et révolutionnaires*, Paris, 1851, pp. 295-311, and E. Fleury, *Dupin (de l'Aisne)*, Laon, 1852, *passim*, drew upon the pamphlet literature of the Thermidorians.

The histories: A. Esquiros, *Histoire des Montagnards*, 2 vols., Paris, 1847, especially i, 113, 126, 127-128, and ii, 250-257, 335, 383, 461, 464. Also A. Lamartine, *Histoire des Girondins*, 8 vols., Paris, 1847, ii, 248-250; J. Michelet, *Histoire de la*

*Révolution française*, 5 vols., Paris, 1847-1853, especially ɪv, 482, v, 112-114, vɪ, 208-237; L. Blanc, *Histoire de la Révolution française*, 12 vols., Paris, 1847-1862, especially vɪɪɪ, 447, xɪ, 59, 129, 140, x, 161, 163, 192, 226, 322; M. de Barante, *Histoire de la Convention nationale*, 3 vols., Paris, 1851-1853, *passim*; E. Hamel, *Histoire de Robespierre*, 3 vols., Paris, 1865-1867, especially ɪɪɪ, 81, 119, 527, 556, 694; and his *Histoire de Saint-Just*, Paris, 1859, pp. 453, 517, 518, 557; H. von Sybel, *History of the French Revolution*, tr. from the German, 4 vols., London, 1867-1869, especially ɪɪ, 224, ɪɪɪ, 41, 73, 74, 276, ɪv, 195; L. Mortimer-Ternaux, *Histoire de la Terreur*, 8 vols., Paris, 1861-1881, especially ɪv, 275, 379, v, 265, vɪ, 214.

E. Despois, *Le vandalisme révolutionnaire*, Paris, 1868, for a defense of the literary, scientific, and artistic services of the Convention; and J. Claretie, *Les derniers Montagnards*, Paris, 1867, pp. 46-47, for Barère's loyalty to the ideals of the Revolution.

From 1870 to 1914. Old memoirs, sharply critical, were reprinted or appeared in new editions: those of Vilate and Méhée *fils*, in 1875 and 1878; of Louvet, in 2 vols., in 1899; of Brissot, in 2 vols., in 1910; of Madame Roland, 2 vols., in 1905, ɪɪ, 265; of Bourrienne in 1899, also in an English translation in 3 vols., London, 1885. An English translation of P. Barras' *Mémoires*, Paris, 1875, was published in 4 volumes, London, 1895, ɪɪɪ, 338-348; and the *Mémoires* of Napoleon's secretary, C. F. Méneval, appeared in 3 vols., Paris, 1893-1894, ɪɪ, 490-491. The hostess of Barère during the days of the Constituent Assembly was Madame de Chastenay, *Mémoires*, 2 vols., Paris, 1896, ɪ, 113; Barère's colleague during the Hundred Days was A. Jal, *Souvenirs d'un homme de lettres*, Paris, 1877, pp. 293-295; and the fellow Montagnard exiled to Belgium was P. R. Choudieu, *Mémoires et Notes*, Paris, 1897, pp. 236-237.

Encyclopedias and biographical dictionaries: the articles on Barère in P. Larousse, ed., *Grand Dictionnaire universel*, 17 vols., Paris, 1865-1890, II; the third edition of Michaud's *Biographie universelle*, Paris, 1870, III, 87-94, which repeated the article of the volume published in 1854; *Encyclopédie universelle*, Paris, 1912; *Encyclopaedia Britannica*, 9th ed., London, 1889, III, 373-374, and 11th edition, 1910-1911, III, 397-398; the article by Aulard in *La Grande Encyclopédie*, Paris, 1891, and the same author's references in *Les orateurs de la Législative et de la Convention*, 2 vols., Paris, 1885-1886, I, 513 ff. More friendly appreciations in H. M. Stephens in his collection already given, *The Principal Speeches of the Statesmen and the Orators of the French Revolution, 1789-1815*, 2 vols., N.Y., 1892, II, Introduction; and the reviews of the English translation of Barère's *Mémoires* in *The Spectator* (London), LXXIX (1897), 146-147; *The Saturday Review* (London), LXXXIV (1897), 54-55; *The Academy* (London), LII (1897), 105.

For the activities of the Committee in Tarbes and the names and speeches on that occasion of the local and regional dignitaries who gave it their support: *Inauguration du monument à la mémoire de Bertrand Barère de Vieuzac au cimetière St. Jean à Tarbes, 14 juin, 1896*, Tarbes, 1896. The late Dr. Fontan kindly gave me a copy of the subscription appeal sent out on April 15, 1894, in the name of the Committee. The conservative *La Liberté des Hautes-Pyrénées* published a series of articles, July 26, 1894, and June 14-19, 1896, satirizing both the Committee and the object of its solicitude. The republican press, *Le Démocrate* and *Le Réveil républicain des Hautes-Pyrénées*, n.d., as excerpted in the *Inauguration* above, seconded the efforts of the Committee.

Many articles by students of Aulard and Mathiez appeared in the specialized reviews on the Revolution; also the biographies of Lindet and Jeanbon Saint-André, given under Modern Authorities. A. Souviron judiciously reviewed the facts in *Bertrand Barère, 1755-1841*, Pithiviers, 1906; as did F. de Cardaillac in the critical and penetrating article in *Revue des Hautes-Pyrénées*, III (1908), 350-394. E. Welvert, *Lendemains révolutionnaires, les Régicides*, Paris, 1906, gave details on

Barère's post-revolutionary career in Belgium, and G. Pouchet, *Les sciences pendant la Révolution,* reprint of 1896, pp. 57 ff., continued the pioneering study of Despois given above.

The historians openly hostile include H. A. Taine, *La Révolution française,* Paris, 3 vols., 1878-1885, II, 429, 455, III, 63, 107, 248 ff.; A. Sorel, *L'Europe et la Révolution française,* Paris, 8 vols., 1885-1904, III, 184 ff., 238 ff., 264, 383, 471, 513; L. Madelin, *La Révolution française,* Paris, 1909 (references are to the English translation, London, 1916), pp. 340, 342, 356, 414, 452; F. A. Aulard, *Histoire politique de la Révolution française,* 1901 (see index of English translation, 4 vols., London, 1910); *Cambridge Modern History,* Cambridge, 1908, VIII, 249. For more favorable treatments, H. M. Stephens, *The French Revolution,* 2 vols., N.Y., 1886-1891, I, 38, 99, II, 4, 7, 157, 313-314; and J. Jaurès, *Histoire socialiste: la Convention,* 4 vols., Paris, 1901-1904, II, 916 ff., 1124, 1164-1167, 1173, 1176, 1204, 1360, 1443 ff., 1546 ff.

Neither P. Kropotkin, *La grande Révolution, 1789-1793,* 2nd ed., Paris, 1909, pp. 717, 725, nor Lord Acton, *Lectures on the French Revolution,* London, 1910, pp. 99, 117, 257, 273, 289, 295, 332, 335, assessed Barère's personality or role.

From 1918 to the present. The monographs and biographies referred to in the text are given in Modern Authorities. See also the study by C. J. H. Hayes, *The Historical Evolution of Modern Nationalism,* N.Y., 1931, ch. iii, for the important part played by Barère in spurring and reflecting revolutionary nationalism; and the article of L. Gershoy, "Barère, Champion of Nationalism in the French Revolution," in *Political Science Quarterly,* XLII (1927), 419-430. J. Marchand edited an abridged edition of Barère's *La liberté des mers* (Paris, 1942) during the German occupation, which purported to show that Anglophobia was an essential component of French nationalist sentiment. The biography of R. Launay, already given, was uncompromisingly hostile, while the brief article by A. Martin in the *Dictionnaire de biographie française,* v (1951) 442-445, contained nothing new. The unresolved strife in the Hautes-Pyrénées continued in several newspaper articles. For opinions sharply critical of Barère, see *Le Semeur des Hautes-Pyrénées* (Tarbes), issues of June 12-14, 1928; also the issues of February-June, 1937, for J. Duffo's evaluation of Barère's *Eloges*, given in Notes for Chapter II. The Tarbais who were more sympathetically inclined expressed their views in *La Dépêche de Toulouse*, June 10, 1928, and in *Le Républicain des Hautes-Pyrénées* (Tarbes) on June 9, 1928. The archivist of the departmental archives, G. Balencie, expressed his regret in this same newspaper on March 7, 1941, that the centenary of Barère's death was ignored by "his ungrateful *patrie*, his natal town [and] his forgetful fellow-citizens." See also L. Gershoy, "Barère, Anacreon of the Guillotine," in *South Atlantic Quarterly*, xxvi (1927), 266-279; and "Barère de Vieuzac, Bertrand," in *Encyclopaedia of the Social Sciences*, N.Y., 1931, ii, 459.

The three histories of the French Revolution by Americans which are friendly in tone are: L. Gottschalk, *The Era of the French Revolution*, Boston, 1929, pp. 251, 266; L. Gershoy, *The French Revolution and Napoleon*, N.Y., 1933, pp. 134, 273, 290; C. Brinton, *A Decade of Revolution (1789-1799)*, N.Y., 1934, p. 121. *The French Revolution* by C. D. Hazen, 2 vols., N.Y., 1932, ii, 633, 748, 788, is hostile in its interpretation. The treatment is neutral in the work by the English historian, A. Goodwin, *The French Revolution*, London, 1953, pp. 151, 152, 164, and extremely unfavorable in J. M. Thompson, *The French Revolution*, London, 1943, pp. 324, 351, 353-355, 358, 388, 421, 467, 510, 511-515. For the French historians, see Sagnac, Pariset, Lefebvre, and Mathiez, listed under Modern Authorities. R. Mousnier and E. Labrousse, *Le XVIIIe siècle . . . (1715-1815)*, Paris, 1953, is neutral in tone; and P. Gaxotte, *La Révolution française*, Paris, 1927 (English trans. of 1932), like Mathiez, is unfriendly.

*Index*

# Index

# Index

Voulland, Jean-Henri, 266

war, coming of, 117, 121-22; course of, 122, 124, 136f, 147f, 153, 170, 174, 187, 207
Washington, George, 57, 360
Waterloo, 339
Wellington, Duke of, 328, 340
West Indies, 88, 219
White Terror, 286f

William I of Holland, 349f, 356
Williams, Helen Maria, 165, 295, 430, 434

York, Duke of, 252
Yorke, H. R., 317, 326, 424, 431, 433
Young, Edward, 284
Ypres, 219

*459*

# DATE DUE

| | | | |
|---|---|---|---|
| | | | |
| | | | |
| | | | |
| | | | |
| | | | |
| | | | |
| | | | |
| | | | |
| | | | |
| | | | |
| | | | |
| | | | |
| | | | |
| | | | |
| | | | |
| | | | |
| | | | |
| 30 505 JOSTEN'S | | | |